— Enjoy — Steven Roby

BLACK
GOLD

THE LOST ARCHIVES OF JIMI HENDRIX

STEVEN ROBY

Foreword by Noel Redding

D1379368

Billboard Books

an imprint of Watson-Guptill Publications/New York

For Francine

A Love Supreme

Senior Acquisitions Editor: Bob Nirkind
Edited by Sarah Fass
Interior designed by Michelle Gengaro-Kokmen
Graphic production by Hector Campbell

Front cover photograph: Gered Mankowitz, Bowstirltd./Mankowitz.com/Star File

First published in 2002 by Billboard Books, an imprint of Watson-Guptill Publications,
a division of VNU Business Media, Inc., 770 Broadway, New York, NY 10003 www.watsonguptill.com

Library of Congress Cataloging-in-Publication Data

Roby, Steven.
    Black gold : the lost archives of Jimi Hendrix / by Steven Roby ;
foreword by Noel Redding.
        p. cm.
Includes bibliographical references (p.   ), discography (p.   ), and index.
    ISBN 0-8230-7854-X
  1. Hendrix, Jimi. 2. Rock musicians—United States—Biography. 3. Hendrix, Jimi—Archives. I. Title.
    ML410.H476 R63 2002
    787.87'166'092—dc21
                                                        2001005491

Manufactured in U.S.A.

2 3 4 5 6 7 8 9 / 09 08 07 06 05 04 03 02

Contents

Acknowledgments

No book involving research and interviews could happen without the support of many people, both friends and fans who came forward to support this project after hearing about it.

Noel Redding responded with an enthusiastic "Yes!" when I asked him if he would be interested in writing the foreword. Thanks, mate! Many long-term Hendrix archivists were extremely generous, granting access to their files and assistance with research. Kees de Lange graciously provided essential information and leads on Jimi's hard-to-trace pre-Experience years, and shared vital background information on obscure recordings.

Tony Brown allowed me to quote from his exclusive notes on the *Black Gold* tape, the 1970 Taj Mahal jam, and several other rare tapes; he also helped with the video/film entries in Part II. Just as I was finishing the manuscript, I was sad to hear that Tony had died of a heart attack. He was a good friend and one of the most detail-oriented Hendrix archivists I ever met.

Going far beyond the call of duty was Keith Bollinger. With superhuman strength, Keith hauled a large cabinet full of Hendrix files from Oregon to California and helped me with essential interviews with key people who had previously been overlooked. Keith Dion allowed me to rummage through his vast collection of books and helped with several important interviews. Producer Kevin Stein was enormously helpful in providing rare magazine articles, videos, and factual information. Professor Joel J. Brattin read the completed manuscript and offered many useful suggestions. And my editor, Bob Nirkind, who shared the same vision of this project from its beginning, also deserves my thanks. I'm eternally grateful to my second editor, Sarah Fass, for raising the bar a little higher. Her excellent skills made the manuscript shine.

I'd also like to extend my gratitude to the following individuals who gave me feedback and ideas: Phil Adams, Arano Alèn, Doug Bell, Robert Bowman, Alex Constantine, Bob Elliot, Jeff Evangelista, David Pearcy, Frazier Pennebaker, Vic Lewin, Kurt Max, Bob Priest, Leland Stein, Pekka Talvenmäki, Daniel Tehaney, and Ken Voss.

Special thanks to Dan Bessie, Maia Duerr, Bruce Madden, and Francine Szymanoski for reviewing the manuscript and providing helpful editorial advice, encouragement, and suggestions.

During the eight years that I published and edited the bimonthly international Jimi Hendrix fanzine *Straight Ahead*, many people from around the world offered their help and support, and some of the material in this book derives from their hard work. I would like to thank the entire staff of *Straight Ahead* and say that I miss working with all of you.

I'd also like to thank the following people for kindly granting interviews: Lou Adler, Rosa Lee Brooks, Arthur Brown, Eric Burdon, Randy California, Jim Capaldi, Michael Carabello, Ed Chalpin, "King George" Clemons, Don Covay, Billy Cox, Kathy Etchingham, Mike Finnigan, Freddie Mae Gautier, Richie Havens, Al Hendrix, Leon Hendrix, Abe Jacob, Melody Jones, John Kay, Carol Kaye, Arthur Lee, Curtis Mayfield, John McLaughlin, Melinda Merryweather, Billy Mitchell, Kirsten Nefer, Pat O'Day, Mike Quashie, Noel Redding, Carlos Santana, John Sinclair, Mike Sarne, Carol Shiroky, Alison Steele (the "Nightbird"), Juma Sultan, Dewey Terry, Jon Tiven, Chuck Wein, Steve Winwood, Lonnie Youngblood, and Gail Zappa.

Special thanks and more to my parents, Tom and Anita, who allowed me to blow my allowance on Hendrix albums, posters, and most importantly, concert tickets. See?—it paid off after all! Finally, thanks to Jimi Hendrix, the man who redefined the electric guitar as we know it—with hope that this book does justice to him and his work.

Noel Redding at home in Clonakilty, Ireland.
Deborah McNaughton

Foreword

Having had the honor of playing bass guitar (after being a guitarist) with the Jimi Hendrix Experience from September 1966 to June 1969, I was delighted when Steven Roby asked me to write a foreword to his book *Black Gold: The Lost Archives of Jimi Hendrix*. These are my personal observations of Jimi's desire to record, both on the road and in the studio.

Our first recordings in late '66 produced our first single, "Hey Joe." This session was produced by the late Chas Chandler (God bless him), the original bassist with the Animals. Chas "found" Jimi—then known as Jimmy James—in New York in 1966 and brought him to London, England, where the band was formed.

These first recording sessions were strange. Usually, after a club gig we'd go into different studios for a couple of hours to record. One of these earlier sessions produced the song "Red House." The lineup included drums, with Jimi on lead guitar and vocal. I played rhythm guitar, not bass. Most of these songs were rehearsed in the studio.

Going into 1967, we recorded *Are You Experienced* primarily at Olympic Studios (Barnes, London) with Chas producing. About this time, I first observed Jimi's interest in recording. He suggested ideas to Chas, as Mitch and I did.

After our first American tour in the summer of '67, we returned to Olympic Studios and recorded *Axis: Bold As Love* with Chas producing again. On the track "Bold As Love" we used a studio effect called phasing. As I recall, this meant setting up two four-track machines. (Things are much different now.) While they set it up, we were sent to the local pub for our pint of bitter. When we came back, the phasing sound was amazing! I'd first heard it on the Small Faces album *Ogden's Nut Gone Flake*. Both the Experience's first and second albums were recorded in a very short time.

In 1968, Jimi bought a small two- or four-track machine, which he took with him on the road. I never heard what he put on it—ideas for our next album, *Electric Ladyland*, perhaps. He later used the machine in his apartment in New York.

In the summer of '68 Chas, having started a family, left us as producer and manager. Jimi took over producing with Eddie Kramer helping. We were now recording at the Record Plant in New York. Without Chas around, Jimi would go to thirty or more takes, which I found silly. As Chas always said, "If you can't get it by the third take, take a break."

During this period, there were two days when I was at the studio and Jimi didn't show up. I did "Little Miss Strange"—my second song with the Experience. Mitch and I put down the track and vocals and Jimi overdubbed his guitar part. We also recorded in L.A. at TTG Studios in 1968. Some of these tracks later came out on albums after Jimi died. But on one album, the drums and bass were overdubbed by people who attempted to play what we originally recorded. I later met one of the people who overdubbed; he was so embarrassed![1]

I last saw Jimi at the opening of Electric Lady Studios in New York. We had a good chat, and he said he hoped to see me in London. Second week in September, I had a call from Gerry Stickells saying would I finish the European tour, as Bill Cox had become ill. I said, "Of course." Then on the eighteenth of September, 1970, I had a call at my hotel in New York saying, "A friend of yours is dead." I said, "Who's that?" They said, "Jimi Hendrix."

The guy was an amazingly talented and lovely bloke. The memory and message of Jimi's music and guitar playing thirty years after his passing on made an amazing impact on rock music; he influenced many, many musicians. Just before Christmas last year, I was in Holland for Fender as a judge on a guitarist thing. In the interval, a very young band got up. The *ten-year-old* guitarist played "Purple Haze"! I played with him at the end of the event.

Enjoy this book. Jimi's still playing in the sky. God bless him.

Noel Redding

1 Noel refers to *Crash Landing*.

Preface

Around the time of my fourteenth birthday, I asked my parents if I could go to a concert in Oakland that I'd heard announced on KSAN, the local "underground" FM radio station. It was the first concert I'd attended. I think I might have been encouraged to wear a tie, because back in 1969, it was a big event to go to a concert. We were living in San Francisco then, and my parents dropped me off. I remember being so excited that I made some kind of silly badge that said "I'm a Jimi Hendrix fan." I remember buying a program called *Electric Church* for three dollars, and sitting through opening acts Cat Mother and the All Night Newsboys and Chicago, whom I liked. All these huge amplifiers were lined up at the back of the stage.

Then *he* came on. After an electrifying set, Hendrix played a rare encore, "Voodoo Child (Slight Return)," with Jack Casady on bass.

I had already begun to collect records. My first two Hendrix records were British imports, and they differed from the American releases. "Foxy Lady" had been censored on my British copy, leaving out the line "Here I come...."

The following year, I begged, pleaded, and negotiated with my parents to let me see him again at the Berkeley Community Theatre. Berkeley's streets were deserted, except for the cops in full riot gear. There was a recording truck outside the theater with loudspeakers playing back the afternoon's rehearsals. The evening's concert was outstanding, and Hendrix seemed to be in a great mood.

Then a few months later, when my folks and I were in Hawaii, I got an advance on my allowance for a $5.50 nineteenth-row ticket, and I got to see Hendrix play at what turned out to be his last American concert. For the encore, "All Along the Watchtower," I rushed up toward the stage and was close enough to make eye contact. I could even see the inter-island airline tags on the amps from the band's recent flight after the Maui Rainbow Bridge concert. I took no pictures. Didn't bring a recorder. Could kick myself for not doing that! But over the last thirty years, I've amassed a collection of Hendrix tapes, interviews, videos, articles, and stories, and I've published *Straight Ahead* (1989–1996), a Jimi Hendrix fanzine, worked with the Hendrix family, hosted annual radio tributes, and still continue to uncover buried treasures related to Jimi Hendrix.

In his liner notes for *Morning Symphony Ideas*, a recent Hendrix release, archivist John McDermott writes that any attempt to unlock the mystery of Hendrix's inspiration is unlikely to succeed, since that inspiration was "harvested from a multitude of sources....Why even bother?" Far from being a bother, my expedition into the lost Hendrix archives has helped me to discover endless unmined riches.

In this book, I've attempted to explore Hendrix's multitude of musical inspirations for the first time, and to provide a complete picture of his copious creativity and unique ideas—many of which never had a chance to take flight. There is so much more to his story than the mistaken belief that he only performed for three or four years (as you'll discover, Hendrix was involved with a Top 40 hit in 1964) and left behind only four or five albums (there are hundreds of releases). For someone who was constantly on the road and endlessly jamming in the studio, he still found time to write ideas on any available scrap of paper. Hendrix generated an enormous wealth of lyrics and music, much of it incomplete at the time of his death. People's garages and attics have held some amazing written ideas, sketches, lyrics, and even tapes from Hendrix, stashed away for whatever reason. And a lot of material is still out there.

At various points in this book, I report conflicting accounts: Did Hendrix actually appear on a certain recording/tour/jam? I feel it's only fair, after this length of time, to present as many sides of each story as I can find. As much as possible, I've let Hendrix and those who knew him best have a voice. This will allow readers and listeners to form their own opinions or seek further information elsewhere.

Black Gold is organized into two parts. Hendrix's early influences, bands, and recorded works are covered in Part I. In Part II, with the help of several serious Hendrix archivists around the world, I've compiled a film and video reference guide. Both contain information about the availability of the recorded or filmed materials—whether they are lost, destroyed, missing, commercially available, or available only in the collectors' network.

More pieces of the "lost archives" are still being uncovered. With this book, I want to encourage those who are energized by Jimi's music to continue to explore the vast body of his lesser-known works. I hope to entice the curious and inspire the devotee.

Steven Roby
Spring 2002

The information in this book is continuously updated. E-mail me with questions or comments at letters@stevenroby.com.

INTRODUCTION: THE STORY SO FAR

Thirty-three years after its release, the 1967 Jimi Hendrix Experience single "Purple Haze" was inducted into the Class of 2000's Grammy Hall of Fame. At the end of 1999, both *Rolling Stone* and *Guitar World* magazines asked their readers to select the most important composers and musicians of the twentieth century. With thousands of amazing talents to consider, readers ranked Jimi Hendrix high in both polls. Interest in Hendrix isn't confined to the nostalgic reminiscences of baby boomers, either. While only a handful of Hendrix's established hits still receive radio play, his recordings still sell in the millions annually, and major rock, jazz, and blues artists continue to cite his influence.

Despite a relatively short musical career—from 1963 to 1970—Hendrix left behind a veritable mountain of music and writings. I have spent over thirty years sifting through the tapes available through the collectors' network, interviewing key eyewitnesses from that time, and tracking down documented items that have been completely lost, are currently missing, or are being hoarded.

When Jimi Hendrix died in 1970, his record label felt that there was little material "in the can" that could be considered for release. At the same time, a swarm of unauthorized (and sometimes fake) Hendrix recordings were poised to hit the market. To make matters worse, Hendrix's New York apartment had been ransacked; the culprits had stolen his guitars, clothing, private demo tapes, and handwritten notes for songs and future projects. If it wasn't for fans, worldwide archivists, and amateur detectives, the curtain might have been forever closed on the true story of Hendrix's unreleased works.

From September 24, 1966, the date Hendrix arrived in London, until his death on September 18, 1970, he made approximately 560 official appearances and logged hundreds of hours at various studios. Since his death, more than five hundred recorded titles have appeared that are devoted to him entirely or in part. Only the Beatles and Elvis Presley, whose careers lasted much longer, have generated more titles.

Hendrix's widely reported obsession with perfection in the studio caused his bass player, Noel Redding, to walk out in 1968. Chas Chandler, his producer/manager, interpreted this obsession as a lack of discipline in the studio. Around this time, Hendrix was noticed carrying two quality four-track tape recorders, which he often set up when he jammed. His compulsion for experimentation while jamming was notorious. In an article for *Guitar Player* (August 1997), Band of Gypsys drummer Buddy Miles characterized the 1969 Record Plant rehearsals as "eighteen-hour days for damn near three months."

Janie Hendrix, Hendrix's younger stepsister and now CEO of Experience Hendrix, claims to have listened to all his private recordings, and said, "It took us almost two months to listen to all that music."[1] In May 1994, Alan Douglas, former Hendrix record producer, testified that he had once listened continuously to the entire Hendrix library of studio recordings. Douglas confessed that it took him ten- to twelve-hour days, seven days a week, for a month, to complete the task. Afterwards, he said, he couldn't listen to anything else for a long while. Nothing else seemed worth listening to.[2]

Over the years since Hendrix's death, many of these tapes were stolen, held by studios for nonpayment of bills, or simply forgotten. Recently, it was discovered that Hendrix often gave away personally made demo recordings to lovers, fellow musicians, and close friends as mementos. Many of these people have finally come forward to share these recorded masterpieces. Some tapes have surfaced after someone discovered they had simply been misfiled. Others, however, may never see the light of day due to greed or carelessness.

In 1975, Hendrix's music returned to the pop charts and his recordings began selling to a wider audience. Part of the credit for this must go to Alan Douglas, who had just taken over as producer of Hendrix's records. Douglas began a media campaign based on newly discovered recordings. When hardcore Hendrix fans seriously scrutinized these "new" recordings, they discovered that the original band members' parts were often deleted and replaced by studio session players whose credits included backing disco queen Gloria Gaynor. This unpardonable travesty helped cause a growing army of fans to unite and seek out the original Jimi Hendrix recordings.

Bootleg records became one source for these fans to discover complete, unedited concert and studio recordings. However, these included little if any factual information; most bootlegs came in a plain white cover with a stamped-on title. Another source for new material became the network of collectors who distributed lists of rare tapes and memorabilia for trading. This barter system still exists, and with today's DATs and CD-Rs, the quality of these recordings has vastly improved.

Hendrix fans quickly learned that Jimi's unauthorized tapes were prized commodities, even though their legality was often in question. The number of underground Hendrix tapes increases annually because, as the late guitarist Michael Bloomfield once explained, "Jimi was a massive chronicler of his own jams."[3] Added to this wealth of musical material are audience recordings; Hendrix's fans in the '60s often brought their own portable recording equipment to his concerts. Many of these materials are widely available, but others are privately held, missing, or lost.

In the late 1980s and early 1990s, collectors and fans finally saw many of Hendrix's undocumented handwritten songs and essays surface. For a while, it seemed that every six months auction houses such as Sotheby's offered previously unheard recordings, poems, and other written works by Hendrix from the late 1960s. A large collection of his personal clothing, jewelry, and historic guitars from Monterey Pop and Woodstock followed. Thankfully, many of the most interesting items are now in collections like the Rock and Roll Hall of Fame in Cleveland, Ohio, and the Experience Music Project in Seattle, Washington, where they are available to scholars, and where at least some items are on public display.

Another victory for Hendrix devotees occurred in 1995, when Al Hendrix, Jimi's father, settled a two-year legal battle with his former lawyer to regain the rights to his son's music and image. Apparently, Mr. Hendrix nearly fell victim to a plan calling for a flat annual fee of fifty thousand dollars for his right to oversee future Jimi Hendrix projects. A new company called Experience Hendrix, run by Jimi's family members, was assembled and took on the difficult task of repairing the damage done over the past twenty-five years. To its credit, the company has restored the original Hendrix cover art to his recordings and improved the sound quality by finding original masters. It also continues to release collector-quality material on its private label, Dagger Records.

Over the course of my career as a collector and a reporter of Hendrix news, people have often suggested that I compile my wide range of interviews and archival recording information into book form. I've finally taken their suggestion. Tracking the lost Hendrix archives has been challenging, but the effort brings the achievements of one of the twentieth century's master musicians into sharper focus.

1 Will Fifield, "Are You Experienced...Yet?" *Costco Connection*, June 2000.

2 Alan Douglas Rubenstein, deposition given on 11 May 1994 in Los Angeles, California, for U.S. District Court, Western District, No. C93-537Z, page 203.

3 Michael Bloomfield, "Jimi Hendrix Remembered," *Guitar Heroes*, Spring 1992.

I was schooled by radio and records. My teachers were common sense and imagination.

JIMI HENDRIX, *DIE WELT*, JANUARY 15, 1969

CHAPTER ONE

BROOMSTICKS AND GUITAR PICKS: 1942-1961

When Jimi Hendrix was born in Seattle, Washington, on November 27, 1942, his father got word while in an Army stockade at Camp Rucker, Alabama. Private James Allen ("Al") Hendrix asked his commanding officer for an entitled furlough to go home. His request was denied. At that time, the Army didn't use airplanes to transport enlisted men for family matters, and with only a five-day furlough, Al wouldn't have had enough time to make the trip. He was warned not to go AWOL.

Back in Seattle, Al's teenaged wife, the former Lucille Jeter, was barely getting by. She moved from hotel room to boarding house with her son, whom she had named Johnny Allen. Al's Army pay wasn't making its way back home, so Lucille's main income came from her part-time waitress job. She had just turned eighteen and was probably too young for marriage, let alone the new responsibilities of motherhood. Until Al returned home from the service in 1945, Johnny Allen was usually looked after by his paternal grandmother, Nora Hendrix, neighbor Minnie Gautier, and occasionally by his mother, when she was sober.[1]

Lucille had a reputation for hard drinking and for frequenting Seattle's dancehalls, which were in full swing in the 1940s. In the book *Jackson Street After Hours*, Seattle's vibrant nightlife scene during the Second World War is described in great detail: "The district had gone plain wild....There were clubs with full casinos upstairs...and poker games that ran night and day. There wasn't a brand of liquor you couldn't buy....Even

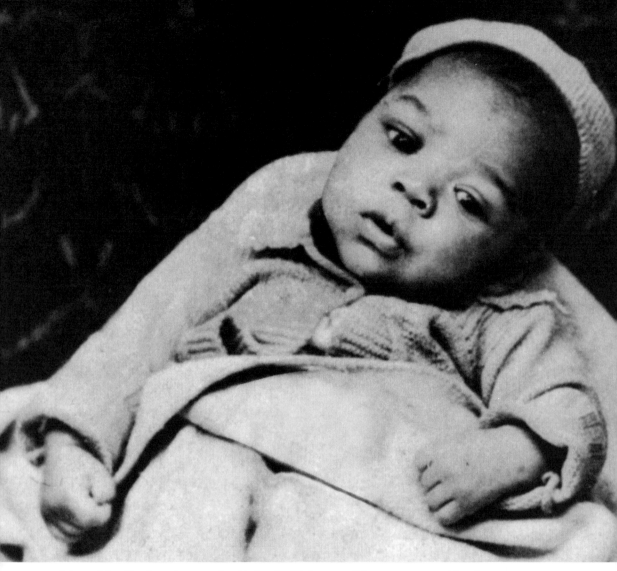

Johnny Allen Hendrix, eleven weeks old, Seattle, Washington, February 20, 1943. *Photofest*

heroin and cocaine were for sale. . . . Many of these spots were full-fledged cabarets, with a floor show, fancy décor, doormen, and waiters. Other were simply joints set up as an excuse to sell bootleg booze."[2]

Johnny Allen's maternal grandmother, Clarice Jeter, cleaned house for Minnie Gautier, a good friend and fellow church member. Minnie's daughter, Freddie Mae Gautier, was only twelve years old at the time, but she vividly recalls the unstable beginnings of the future Jimi Hendrix. "It must have been the first or second week in December [1942] when she came up on the porch with this bundle," she remembered. "At first, my mother thought it was something she was bringing over, but she came through the door and you could see these little feet sticking out. So, my mother said, 'Mrs. Jeter, whose baby is that you've got?' She replied, 'This is Lucille's baby.'" Freddie Mae Gautier said Lucille came home from the hospital and left the baby with her family. "So my mother took the baby and his feet were blue from the cold. The diapers had been soaked and not changed. They became solid with ice because we had some very cold winters then. . . . We had him most of the time until Al came back from the service . . . off and on for the first five years of his life."[3]

Before Al Hendrix left the military, he received a letter informing him that his son was being taken care of by the Champ family in Berkeley, California.[4] Al reported that Lucille "bounced around a lot,"[5] and he was surprised to learn of all the people who helped take care of the baby before he wound up with Mrs. Champ, a total stranger. When he was discharged, Al went to retrieve his son, whose name he changed to James Marshall in memory of his deceased brother. The new name was registered on September 11, 1946. Although Al began divorce proceedings while in the service, he reconciled with Lucille. Nonetheless, he believed her next son, born in 1948, was fathered by a Filipino man she was seeing at the time. Another son arrived the following year, from yet another father, and he too was given the Hendrix name.

Al and Lucille were finally divorced on December 17, 1951. Al was awarded custody of the three boys, James Marshall (called Jimmy), Leon Morris, and Joseph Allen, although the latter was given up for adoption. Finding work in the postwar economy was tough for Al, and he lost the house he was trying to buy.[6] He felt he had no choice but to send Jimmy and Leon to live with their Aunt Pat in Vancouver, British Columbia. In January 1958, Lucille was married again, to a longshoreman named Bill Mitchell. She had been in and out of hospitals with cirrhosis of the liver, and saw little of Jimmy and Leon. A month after her marriage, she was back in the King County Hospital, and died there.

Kathy Etchingham, Hendrix's lover and good friend from 1966 to 1970, related stories that Jimi told her about his difficult years growing up. "He had a loveless childhood, with no affection—just passed around from pillar to post," she said. "It seems to me he had an uncaring mother and a father that was rather possessive of him. Jimi couldn't wait to get away from home and it was the same for me. Who knows what he was feeling. It was just very strange. We both got away from home as soon as we possibly could. He had a hard time."[7]

"My mother and father used to fall out a lot and I always had to be ready to go tippy-toeing off to Canada," Hendrix recalled. "My dad was levelheaded and religious, but my mother used to like having a good time and dressing up. She used to drink a lot and didn't take care of herself. She died when I was about ten. But she was a groovy mother."[8]

Hendrix later wove his early turbulent times into the song "51st Anniversary." The memory of Lucille also occasionally filtered into Hendrix's poetry and songs, and his early loss may have led to his seeking solace in an all-consuming musical passion.

First Instruments

My first instrument was a harmonica which I got when I was about four, I suppose. Next, it was a violin. I always dug string instruments and pianos. Then I started digging guitars—it was the instrument that always seemed to

be around. Everybody's house you went into seemed to have one lying around.
Jimi Hendrix, *Melody Maker,* February 22, 1969

By the age of eight, Jimmy had picked up spoon-playing from his father. He then was given an old ukulele that had been thrown away, which had only one string. Listening to Al's collection of blues and R&B records, Jimmy became preoccupied with music and continued strumming on any household object—a cigar-box-and-rubber-band or the kitchen broom—while singing along to Elvis Presley's "Heartbreak Hotel" or "Love Me Tender."

Al Hendrix recalled, "I used to notice where we stayed at, I used to have him clean up the bedroom all the time while I was gone and when I came home I'd find a lot of broom straws at the foot of the bed. Afterwards, I used to say, 'Did you sweep the floor?' He said he did but I found out later he used to be sitting at the foot of the bed strumming the broom like he was playing the guitar."[9]

While Seattle didn't have a substantial black population at that time, there were local radio stations that played a mixed format of R&B and rock 'n' roll, with hits by artists such as Sam Cooke, Elvis Presley, Chuck Berry, and Little Richard. Leon Hendrix, Jimmy's half-brother, recalled that one day in 1957 during summer vacation, he and Jimmy met Little Richard. "One day there was this big Cadillac out in front of the house, Jimmy and I ran out and there was Little Richard himself sitting in the back seat. He had one of them doo-wop rags around his head and he stopped just to see us. His mother lived just around the corner and she knew how crazy about music we were, we all went to the same church then, Goodwill Baptist, 14th and Spring."[10]

In the summer of 1958, when Jimmy was fifteen, he bought a second-hand acoustic guitar from one of Al Hendrix's friends. "I learned to play on a guitar which belonged to one of my father's friends who came by to play cards," he remembered. "While the two men played, I would creep out onto the porch with the friend's guitar and see what I could get out of it. I didn't know that I would have to put the strings round the other way, because I was left-handed, but it just didn't feel right. I can remember thinking to myself, 'There's something wrong here.' One night my dad's friend was stoned and he sold me the guitar for five dollars."[11]

Al was happy that his son was doing something creative, staying out of trouble and off the streets. Jimmy practiced every day when he came home from school, playing along with his father's records by B.B. King and other blues legends. He told his father that someday he would be famous and Al wouldn't have to work anymore. Around the time Jimmy entered Washington Junior High School, Al bought his son his first electric guitar from Meyers Music, and got himself a saxophone. From that moment, the guitar became the most important thing in Jimmy's life. Some said later that he paid more attention to the guitar than he did to his girlfriends.

When I interviewed Al Hendrix in 1994, he talked about playing music with his son during those early years. "We were living in this beat-up old hotel on Terrace Avenue, in the Central area [of Seattle]. It was around the time when Jimmy got his first guitar. I used

James Hendrix, high school
senior yearbook, 1960.
*Garfield High School/Seattle
Public Library*

James Hendrix

to have this C Melody sax. We would sit around, and he'd be plunkin' away and I'd be blowin' on the sax. We'd try to pick out notes of our own. Anything that went on around there didn't seem to bother anybody. He didn't know how to play the guitar and I didn't know how to blow the sax, but we used to make a lot of noise."[12]

Because Al and the boys moved from place to place, Jimmy attended several different elementary schools and two junior highs before landing at Garfield High School, one of the roughest in Seattle. With his new guitar in hand, he found a circle of school friends who played various instruments. It's likely that the first band Jimmy joined was the Velvetones, and while he didn't stay with them for long, he got the chance to play in front of an audience, even if it was only on the lawn of Garfield High School.

Early Musical Influences

> *The first guitarist I was aware of was Muddy Waters. I heard one of his old records when I was a little boy and it scared me to death, because I heard all of those sounds. Wow, what was that all about? It was great.*
> Jimi Hendrix, *Rolling Stone*, March 9, 1968

One of Al Hendrix's landscaping clients worked in a music shop and offered him a deal on one of the first stereo turntables with detachable speakers. Al remembered that Jimmy was fascinated by it and would separate the speakers for a wider stereo effect, although there were few stereo records available at the time. In his book *My Son Jimi*, Al Hendrix wrote: "Jimmy would put my 45s on that turntable and play along on his guitar. He'd try to copy what he heard, and he'd make up stuff too. He lived on the blues around the house. I had a lot of records by B.B. King and Louis Jordan and some of the down-home guys like Muddy Waters."[13]

Another Chicago bluesman who influenced Jimmy during his early years was Chester Burnett, better known as Howlin' Wolf. In January 1951, Chess Records released Wolf's first single, "Moanin' at Midnight" b/w "How Many More Years." Rock author Robert Palmer described the blues classic: "'Midnight' began with Wolf alone, moaning in his unearthly moan. Willie Johnson's over-amplified guitar and Willie Steele's drums came crashing in together and then Wolf switched to harp, getting massive, brutish sound and pushing the rhythm hard. 'How Many More Years' featured Willie Johnson more prominently, and his thunderous power chords were surely the most *electric* guitar sound that had been heard on record. Wolf's rasping voice sounded strong enough to shear steel; this music was heavy metal, years before the term was coined."[14]

While young Jimmy was obviously inspired by Wolf's direct approach to the blues, as an adult he inspired Wolf. In 1967, Howlin' Wolf and his guitarist Hubert Sumlin were on tour in Europe and crossed paths with Hendrix at one of his concerts. Sumlin recounted the inspirational moment for the *House of Blues Radio Hour*: "I met this little ol' guy in England. He was over there to record his first album with the Experience. We were playing in Liverpool, and man...in walked this little ol' boy, well, I call him a little ol' boy because he wasn't as old as I was [laughs]. The crowd then opened up this gateway, a pathway for this Jimi Hendrix. I saw this guy come in with this hippie stuff. Wolf walked over to me and said, 'Who's that?' 'Hey man,' I said, 'I think that's Jimi Hendrix.' So Wolf passed him his guitar and he started playin' the guitar with his teeth, man. Wolf then said to me, 'Hey man, I'm fired.' And I said, 'No, you mean *I'm* fired and you're going to go ahead and hire Jimi Hendrix [laughs].' That's when I got down to the real nitty-gritty and I said I know I'm gonna have to play...I mean *really* gonna have to play."[15]

The Rocking Kings: 1959

> *In those days I just liked rock and roll, I guess. We used to have to play stuff by people like the Coasters. Anyway, you all had to do the same things before you could join a band—you all even had to do the same steps.*
> Jimi Hendrix, *Melody Maker*, February 22, 1969

One of Jimmy's high school friends was Anthony Atherton, whom I interviewed in 1994. He remembered that the Rocking Kings, formerly the Rocking Teens, "was formed by Hendrix's high school friend, Fred Rollins. Hendrix played bass on a six-string guitar. We played many social clubs and halls, like the Washington and Polish halls, The Shrine, Birdland, and the Boys' Club in the Central district. There was this disc jockey from KZAM by the name of Bob Summerise who used to come by and listen and sometimes tape us to later play on the air."[16] Summerise was the first local black deejay to play R&B on KBRQ in 1947.[17] On his regular two-hour *Cool Breeze* radio show, he played a mixture of rock 'n' roll by popular stars like Little Richard, Jerry Lee Lewis, Chuck Berry, Fats Domino, and Elvis Presley. Jimmy and his fellow band members searched for the records they'd heard on the radio (like Santo & Johnny's "Sleep Walk" and Eddie Cochran's "Summertime Blues"), to provide inspiration at their practice sessions.

Their manager, James Thomas, decided the Rocking Kings' lineup would include James Woodberry (piano and vocals—although sometimes Robert Green would play piano), Webb Lofton (saxophone), Walter Harris (saxophone), Ulysses Heath, Jr. (guitar), Lester Exkano (drums), and Jimmy Hendrix (playing bass on a six-string guitar). Their first gig was at the Washington National Guard Armory, near Kent, Washington, in 1959. They earned thirty-five cents apiece playing songs by the Coasters and other current groups. For a brief period, Jimmy's future with the band looked bleak. He didn't own an electric guitar or amplifier, and it was doubtful that his father would allow him to perform with the band in area nightclubs. But that would all change soon.

In the 1950s, Seattle's music scene was racially segregated. The doors of many clubs were closed to blacks. Two of the clubs the band could play were Spanish Castle and Birdland. Spanish Castle, just a few miles south of Seattle in Tacoma, was later immortalized in the song "Spanish Castle Magic" on Hendrix's second LP, *Axis: Bold As Love*. Birdland, originally located between 21st Avenue and Madison Street, was an exclusive black club that featured R&B performers. The Rocking Kings got their first musical break there, with a steady gig during Teen Dance Nights on Wednesdays, Thursdays, and Sundays until summer vacation started.

Pat O'Day, a deejay at Seattle's KJR radio around this time, recalled meeting Jimmy: "During the period between high school and the service, he would come out to the dances I would run...and Jimmy would always bring his amplifier along, in case somebody else's amplifier blew, which was frequently the case back in the early '60s. And because Jimmy wanted to gig, his deal was, we could use his amplifier if he got to play on stage. That was at a place called 'Spanish Castle,' which he eventually alluded to. That was the dream spot for him where all the hot bands played."[18]

Playing in a rock 'n' roll band was not always a dream come true—Jimmy's guitar was once stolen when he left it on the bandstand. Fortunately, his father replaced it with a guitar made by Danelectro. Jimmy painted it red and wrote the name of his high school sweetheart, Betty Jean, on the back. "It must have busted him [Al] for a long time," Hendrix later recalled. "I first had to prove that I could play a couple of songs on a guitar of a friend, but I still did get it."[19] Anthony Atherton recalled that Al's gift came with a price: "Jimmy had to work for that guitar by helping his dad out in the landscaping business. I know that for a fact because I used to go out there and dig some dirt, too! We'd be up at six A.M. getting busy before it got hot."[20]

The next stepping-stone for the Rocking Kings was a tournament sponsored by a

Catholic organization. They won the second-place trophy for All State Band of the Year, 1960. Next, they played for two thousand people at the annual outdoor picnic of AFL/CIO Union Local 242, where there was a great response to their rowdy blues set, which included Jimmy playing guitar behind his back. More opportunities came their way when the Rocking Kings were offered a tour of British Columbia and Alaska. However, their mighty Volkswagen never made it to the border due to engine trouble, so that evening the band took their equipment to Western Washington State College and negotiated a gig in exchange for a meal and cab fare home. After this incident, some band members got frustrated and moved on.

STATUS: *Unavailable. Several sources I interviewed in Seattle claimed that a certain individual, who wishes to remain anonymous, has a Rocking Kings audiotape recorded when Hendrix was in the band. Unfortunately, this person doesn't wish to sell, copy, or part with the tape.*

Birdland, Seattle, Washington, c. early 1960s. The club featured many top acts, such as T-Bone Walker and Ray Charles. MSCUA, *University of Washington Libraries, UW14489*

Thomas and the Tom Cats: 1960

During the summer of 1960, the Rocking Kings' manager, James Thomas, formed a new group called Thomas and the Tom Cats with Hendrix, Webb Lofton, and Lester Exkano from the Kings. They played Seattle's American Legion Hall for the "Cabaret Summer Style Dance." The advertisement for the show billed them as "a real swinging band." They also began playing at military installations—Paine Air Force Base (Everett, Washington), Larson Air Force Base (Moses Lake, Washington), and Pier 91 Naval Base (Seattle).

The gig at Larson Air Force Base, about two hundred miles from Seattle, paid thirty-five dollars plus transportation costs. On the way back, the car broke down and everyone was asked to chip in for repairs. Jimmy refused, claiming that he needed to bring all his money home; he'd walk home before paying. The band let him walk about five miles in the snow with his bright red Danelectro guitar and small amp in hand, but after the car was fixed, they picked him up. Jimmy grew tired of the transportation hassles and the distances traveled for low-paying gigs. He found it difficult to juggle going to school, working for his dad as a landscaper, and playing in the band.

At the time, Jimmy used a small amp with one twelve-inch speaker, so when the opportunity arose to play the Annual Seattle Seafair picnic and dance, he and James Thomas went to Meyers Music Store and rented a Fender amp with two fifteen-inch Lansing speakers. The band added Bill Rinnick and Richard Gayswood, alternating between saxophone and drums, and Leroy Toots on bass. The Tom Cats began playing the downtown Seattle nightclub Bors Brumo, and started wearing matching jackets, suits, and ties.

Al Hendrix was busy with his landscaping/gardening business and often called on his son and his friends to help. Jimmy hated doing manual work, so he often broke away and talked with one of Al's clients, Derneice "Melody" Jones. She was a music teacher, well versed in jazz piano, and loved to tell stories of her days in New York where she played at the Lafayette Theater with Fats Waller.[21] Al would find Jimmy and get him back to carry-ing stones or cement. "When Jimmy and I would talk, he would tell me about how he was going to learn how to play the guitar," Jones recalled, "and if it was the last thing he was going to do it would be to get his father out of this business. Jimmy would ask me about the bands in my record collection. He knew I was originally from New York and he was very curious about it. He was too young as a high school student to go in the places they'd call 'after-hours' so Jimmy would like me to tell him about the gangsters in New York and how they would shoot up the clubs. He had a way of playing the guitar that would almost talk to you. I wanted him to study music, but he didn't want to. He had those ideas in his mind of what he wanted to do and he was successful with them. I tried to explain to him about basic chord structure, but he'd rather take a shortcut and get there in a great big hurry. We would really go at it."[22]

Just weeks before his eighteenth birthday, Jimmy either dropped out or was kicked out of Garfield High. He later explained, "They said I used to be late all the time, but I was getting A's and B's. I had a girlfriend in art class and we used to hold hands all the time. The art teacher didn't dig that at all. She was very prejudiced. She said, 'Mr. Hendrix, I'll see you in the cloakroom in three seconds, please.' In the cloakroom she said, 'What do you mean talking to that white woman like that?' I said, 'What are you, jealous?' She started crying and I got thrown out."[23] This situation, combined with his family's constant moving and his preoccupation with music, probably provides a better explanation for Jimmy's departure from Garfield than his tardiness.

Unable to find another job, Jimmy went to work for his father for a few months, and thought about joining the Army. Two arrests by the local police hastened his decision.

STATUS: *Thomas and the Tom Cats recorded "Drive, Drive, Drive" b/w "One Day" (Nolta Records RB-22) after Jimmy left Seattle and joined the Army. The 45, released on November 16, 1961, is an up-tempo blues tune with lyrics. It does not feature Hendrix.*

According to The Virgin Encyclopedia of R&B and Soul (page 104), in 1961, record producer Phil Spector "worked his magic" with the vocal group the Ducanes by adding a guitar contribution from Hendrix to their first single, "I'm So Happy," which reached #109 on the Billboard singles chart in July 1961. However, Hendrix couldn't have performed on this doo-wop single — not only had he just joined the Army in May 1961, but the Ducanes were from New Jersey, and Hendrix was still in Seattle.

I volunteered to get it over with so that I could get my music together later on....I hated the Army immediately.

JIMI HENDRIX, *MELODY MAKER*, FEBRUARY 22, 1969

CHAPTER TWO

NO DIRECTION HOME: 1961-1963

Before he decided to join the Army, nineteen-year-old Jimmy was arrested on May 2 for taking a car without the owner's consent. Some say he was mixed up with the wrong crowd and was in the wrong place at the wrong time. However, three days later, he was arrested again for the same offense. Jimmy claimed that a friend came by his house with a sharp-looking car that he said belonged to his uncle, and they went for a ride. The Seattle police saw it differently. They again charged him with taking and riding in a stolen car, and sent him to the Rainier Vista 4-H Youth Center for seven days. Jimmy was released from the youth center on May 13, and never went back to complete his senior year in high school.

At his May 16 court appearance for the stolen vehicle charges, Jimmy said he had plans to join the Army. The Seattle court gave him a two-year suspended sentence, but the charges remained on his record. The next day, Jimmy enlisted in the Army for a three-year stint with the hope of becoming a paratrooper. This choice may have been influenced by his father's WWII service and stories about the paratroopers at Fort Benning.

Hendrix found that the only guitars in the Army were right-handed ones, and that Army life wasn't as glorious as the recruitment officer made it seem: "The Army's really a bad scene," he said. "They wouldn't let me have anything to do with music. They tell you what you are interested in, and you don't have any choice. The Army is more for people who like to be told what to do."[1]

In November, after he completed his basic training at Fort Ord, California, Hendrix went to Fort Campbell, Kentucky, to join the 101st Airborne Division. There he met Billy Cox who, like Hendrix, had a strong interest in music, and they became good friends. Cox had a strong musical background. His mother played classical piano, and he had an uncle who played saxophone with Duke Ellington's orchestra. Cox himself played trumpet, piano, and violin before picking up the bass guitar. He later played upright bass with his high school orchestra and was influenced by jazz bassists Ray Brown and Charles Mingus.

Cox first heard Hendrix playing a rented guitar in a practice room on the Army base. "I was coming from a theatre, and it was raining," he recalled. "We all ran and wound up on the doorstep of Service Club No. 1, waiting for it to stop raining. I heard this guy play-ing guitar with a sound I had never heard before. I went in and introduced myself, told him I played bass. I checked out a bass, and started jamming... three weeks later we were playing Service Clubs with a drummer from Toledo, Ohio called Gary Ferguson...."[2]

By January 1962, Hendrix had tired of playing the Army's guitars. He wrote home to his father, asking him to send his guitar. In the letter, he pleaded, "as soon as you can—I really need it now." Hendrix and Cox formed a band called the King Kasuals, with Gary Ferguson on drums. Hendrix met other musicians in the Army, including saxophonist Major Charles Washington, who started booking the band into the post's Service Clubs. "Two of the people that I had with me turned out to be Jimi Hendrix and Bill Cox," Washington remembered. "Jimi somehow would always manage to pawn his guitar before a gig, before a dance, and of course, the band had to go re-pawn it, repossess it. Nothing else could be used, of course, he had to have this specific guitar, and I think he played this particular angle against the band."[3]

Eventually the King Kasuals' music attracted club owners from nearby Clarksville, Tennessee, who visited the post and offered the band a gig at the Pink Poodle Club in town. "We never made any recordings..." recalled Cox, "most of the time we got fired from the gigs—we would play loud."[4] The King Kasuals had expanded, adding Harry Batchelor on vocals, Alphonso "Baby Boo" Young on guitar, Frank Scheffield on drums, and Tee Howard Williams on saxophone, with Hendrix on guitar and Cox on bass. Cox explained the addition of the new vocalist: "We were playing blues and R&B in that club. Jimi was too timid to sing and they laughed at me when I sang, so we had a singer named Harry Batchelor. We had two guitar players, bass, drums, and a saxophone."[5]

Hendrix completed parachute jump school, received his Screaming Eagle patch in February, and was promoted to Private First Class. "I made it in eight months and eight days!" he proudly told his father. Some of the imaginative guitar sound effects he later developed may have been influenced by this period of jumping out of planes. "Oh...the first jump is really out of sight.... At the beginning the plane is going roar, this roaring and shaking, and you can see the rivets is jumping around, talking about 'What am I doing here?'...a split-second thought went through me, like, you're crazy...knowing all the time, you say 'What the hell am I doing here?' And by that time, you're just there at the door, and all of a sudden you know, this flop, rush, and...you're just ohhhhhhh...falling-

```
HENDRIX'S MILITARY RECORD⁷

Hendrix James Marshall RA 19 693 532
Grade: PVT (E-2)(P)
Date of rank: 1 Oct 61
Department: ARMY-RA-ORDC
Height: 70"
Weight: 155
High School Level: General Educational Development Tests
Type of transfer: Discharged
Reason and authority: AR 635-209 SPN 46A
Effective Date: 2 Jul 62
Last duty assignment: HQ & Company A, 1st Maintenance Battalion,
  Support Group
Character of service: Under honorable conditions
Term of service (years): 3
Date of entry: 31 May 61
Net service this period: years 01, months 01, days 02
Home of record at time of entry: 2606 Yesler Way, Seattle, King
  County, Washington
Grade at time of entry: RCT (E-1)
Specialty number and title: 760.07 Supply Clerk Related
Civilian occupation: 1-38.01 Stock Clerk
Decorations: Parachutist Badge
Other service training courses: Basic Combat Training, Basic
  Airborne, Military Justice
Government life insurance in force: No
Blood group: "O"
SSAN: 534-42-4970
Lump sum payment made for 21 Days accrued leave. Para 9, AR 601-201
```

over-backwards feeling in your dreams. It's so personal because once you're out there, everything is so quiet, all you can hear is the breeze, 'shhhhhh,' you know, like that. You're there all by yourself, and you can talk very low, you can scream or anything, and I think how crazy I was for doing this thing, but I loved it anyway. And then you're supposed to look up, you know, and you see if your parachute is open, and if it's open, then you can say 'Thank the Lord.'"⁶

Shortly after making his twenty-sixth parachute jump, Hendrix broke his right ankle, which got him discharged from the Army in July. However, he continued to play the Pink

Poodle Club. While he had to put his onstage gyrations on hold, he sat on an amplifier with his cast outstretched until the ankle mended. In a May 24, 1967, Swedish radio interview, Hendrix summed up his Army experience: "I was in the Army for about thirteen months, and I got tired of that, it was really boring. So I pretended that I hurt my back, and I really did break my ankle, so I got out like that, you know. I started playing around all over the South."

STATUS: *Unavailable. In the September 1995 issue of* Guitar Player *magazine, Billy Cox recalled that he recorded some of the Army Service Club jams he did with Hendrix: "I've still got some tapes of those early days. We used to do some pretty fancy vocal duos."*

Post-Army Life

After his honorable discharge from the Army, Hendrix planned to return to Seattle. "My discharge came through, and one morning I found myself standing outside the gate of Fort Campbell on the Tennessee-Kentucky border with my little duffel bag and three or four hundred dollars in my pocket. I was going to go back to Seattle, which was a long way away…there was this girl [Betty Jean Morgan] there I was kinda hung up on."[8]

Hendrix headed to the nearby town of Clarksville, planning to leave the next day: "I went to this jazz joint and had a drink. I liked it and stayed. People tell me I get foolish, good-natured sometimes. Anyway, I guess I felt real benevolent that day. I must have been handing out bills to anyone who asked me! I came out with sixteen dollars left! And it takes more than that to get from Tennessee to Seattle! So, no going home, 'cos it's like two thousand miles….I thought first I'd call long-distance and ask my father to send me some money—he's a garden designer and does all right. But I could guess what he'd say if I told him I'd lost nearly four hundred dollars in just one day. Nope. That was out. All I can do, I thought, is get a guitar and try to find work here. Nashville was only twenty miles away— you know, big music scene. There had to be something doing there."[9]

Hendrix stayed in Clarksville for two months waiting for Billy Cox to be discharged. They rented a house together, and Cox co-signed for Hendrix's purchase of an Ibanez guitar at Collins Music Store. However, Hendrix had to return the guitar and wound up borrowing back a guitar he'd sold to an Army buddy at Fort Campbell.

"I moved to Clarksville where the group I was with worked for a set-up called W&W. Man, they paid us so little that we decided that the two W's stood for Wicked and Wrong,"[10] Hendrix said. He described how this music agency worked: "They used to come up on stage in the middle of a number while we were playing, and slip the money for the gig into our pockets. They knew we couldn't knock off to count it just then. By the time the number was over and I got a chance to look in the envelope it'd be maybe two dollars."[11]

"Later on, someone heard us in Clarksville and said there was a club in Nashville that could use a band," Cox recalled, explaining how they began to find work in nearby Nashville. "We went up, auditioned for the job, and immediately got hired full-time."[12]

The owner of the club, the Del Morocco, let them stay rent-free in the apartment upstairs.

Cox said that Hendrix's influences at the time included Chuck Berry and Albert King. Although he played many R&B standards, he wanted to branch out into new areas. "We played behind shake dancers and different groups that came to town," Cox added. "Jimi could play 'Misty' in the original key, 'Moonlight in Vermont,' 'Harlem Nocturne,' and stuff like that. He basically knew where he was going and how he was going about getting there. That other music bored him to a degree, and he wanted to be adventurous and reach for his own individuality in music. I made him a long cord so he could go offstage into the audience. The club wasn't that big, so he could even go out the front door and play on the sidewalk. A lot of people didn't know whether to clap or walk out, but they knew he was good."[13]

STATUS: *No recordings from this period have surfaced.*

The Hoss Allen Session

In November 1962, Hendrix was invited to his first known recording session. Billy Cox was hired for a session at King/Starday Records by William "Hoss" Allen (a.k.a. Hossman), the legendary disc jockey from Nashville's powerful radio station WLAC, and he brought Hendrix along.

"We used to cut down at King Records from about one in the morning until late at night," Hoss Allen remembered. "It was Billy Cox's session and he called me and said he had a guitar player he wanted me to hear. I told him I didn't really need him because I already had two guitar players, but bring him anyway. So Cox came down with Jimmy. He plugs in and I showed him the simple riff I wanted for the song. We started to record and I hear this wwwaaahhh! I thought someone had made a mistake. I called for take two and the same thing[:] wwwaaahhh! I had him plugged into the board so I just told the engineer to turn Jimmy's track off. He just played and played for about two hours and I didn't record a damn thing. How I wish I had that stuff now."[14]

At the time, Nashville was in the midst of a transformation from an unsophisticated country music capital to the internationally recognized center of a new recording industry. The R&B and blues scene, however, wasn't expanding. In his book *Just My Soul Responding*, Brian Ward explained the times and WLAC's pivotal role in promoting black music for a large white audience: "[WLAC in Nashville]...had switched to all-black programming in 1949 with 50,000 watts of 24-hour power and a Holy Trinity of rocking white deejays: Bill 'Hoss' Allen, 'Daddy' Gene Nobles and 'John R' Richbourg. 'WLAC was all we ever listened to. You could hear the station over the eastern half of the United States,' vouched singer James Brown."[15]

While Hendrix's first recording attempt was a letdown and a missed opportunity to garner interest from a key radio personality, he was still part of the new trend of black artists receiving more airplay on white radio. He may have just been ahead of his time, or in the wrong place at the wrong time. Regardless, he persevered, and his quest to find his own sound and the right set of musicians to play it with kept him going through these difficult early years.

Bobby Taylor and the Vancouvers

All I remember is, like, getting out of the Army and then trying to get something together, and then I was playing in different groups all around the, ah, States, you know, and in Canada. Playing behind people most of the time. . . .

Jimi Hendrix, CBC-TV interview, January 7, 1969

In the winter of 1962, Hendrix moved to Vancouver, British Columbia, to live with his grandmother Nora and her family. He joined the R&B band Bobby Taylor and the Vancouvers for a regular weekend gig at a nightclub called Dante's Inferno. This interracial sextet featured Bobby Taylor (vocals and keyboards), Wes Henderson, Robbie King, Ted Lewis, Eddie Patterson, and Tommy Chong (guitar)—later of the comedy duo Cheech and Chong.[16]

Chong and Taylor co-owned Dante's Inferno and the private after-hours club located upstairs, the Elegant Parlor. Both clubs attracted large crowds who came to do the new dance craze, the Twist. Hendrix performed in Vancouver at Dante's Inferno on the weekends, then traveled back to Seattle to play the Black and Tan Club during the week.

"I had a club in Vancouver called Dante's Inferno," Chong said. "Hendrix would come up from Seattle and visit the club, like a lot of brothers did, because we had the best-looking white women in town [laughs]. He was familiar with the band I was with at the time, Bobby Taylor & the Vancouvers. Jimi would come in and sit in with us from time to time. A few years later we had a hit on Motown called 'Does Your Mama Know About Me' [*Billboard* chart position #29, May 18, 1968], and we were playing over in England. . . . He showed up with an entourage that filled the club. His hair was out to here and looking like a peacock and he came up and said, 'Hey man, how are you doin'? You don't remember me, do ya?' I said, 'What do you mean?' He said, 'I used to jam with the band back in Vancouver.' I said, 'Wow and now you're Hendrix—Give me some money!' [laughs]. Jimi sat in that night and played bass with the band and we had a great time."[17]

STATUS: *Bobby Taylor and the Vancouvers' 1968 hit "Does Your Mama Know About Me" (Gordy 7069) does not feature Hendrix. No live performance tapes of Hendrix with Bobby Taylor and the Vancouvers have surfaced from either 1962 or 1968.*

Dante's Inferno's original building, located near the corner of Burrard and Davies in Vancouver, still houses a nightclub, which has had numerous incarnations over the years. In the late 1960s it was the Retinal Circus, featuring touring psychedelic ballroom bands like the Doors, Canned Heat, Country Joe and the Fish, and the Daily Flash. Currently it's a club called Celebrities.

I traveled all over the States, playing in different groups. I'd join and quit them so fast. I was playing in this Top 40 R&B soul hit-parade package, with patent-leather shoes and hairdos combed. When you're starving on the road, you'll do almost anything.

JIMI HENDRIX, *EYE*, JULY 1968

CHAPTER THREE

THE CHITLIN' CIRCUIT:

1963-1965

When Jimi Hendrix's name appears in rock history books, he is usually credited with setting his guitar on fire at the Monterey Pop Festival or playing an unorthodox, volcanic version of "The Star Spangled Banner" at Woodstock. Sadly, his deep roots in American black music are often ignored. Years before Monterey and Woodstock, Hendrix learned his craft and some show-stopping high jinks by playing behind top R&B headliners Curtis Mayfield, the Isley Brothers, Wilson Pickett, and a stream of other artists while touring across the South's TOBA (Theatre Owners' Booking Association) Circuit, also known as the "Chitlin' Circuit."

The Chitlin' Circuit was a series of black music clubs, bars, and theaters scattered over the southern half of the United States. Its name came from the many venues that offered chitlins, a soul food dish made from pig intestines (chitterlings) and kitchen scraps. In the 1960s, star-packed soul music tours often traveled by bus to play small towns that didn't even appear on maps. Although the would-be stars hoped for greater exposure while on the road, what they got was low pay and no luxuries. In the 1930s, TOBA circuit acts were mostly black vaudeville performers. These performers nicknamed TOBA "Tough on Black Asses" because they usually played in run-down dives or slept by the roadside since racism kept blacks out of most hotels. Thirty years later the circuit hadn't improved much. It was still essential for black performers to tour heavily to survive in the music business since the majority of artists played on the radio were white (acts like the Four Seasons, Lesley Gore, and Bobby Vinton).

As author Craig Werner wrote in his book *A Change Is Gonna Come*, "Black singers from the North who'd had trouble adjusting to crossover styles frequently found the Southern approach [to the music scene] liberating."[1] Where Motown's style was slick and refined, Southern soul had more raw energy and emotion. Black bands in the South played different music—funkier music with horns. Don Nix, a saxophone player with the R&B band the Mar-Keys ("Last Night") recalled: "All the black bands had horns. While everybody else was playing Elvis Presley songs with two guitars and a bass or whatever, we had a baritone, tenor, and a trumpet, and we played all rhythm and blues."[2]

Hendrix may have felt more comfortable with the Southern soul sound, which had a greater tolerance for improvisation among the backing musicians. This differed from the heavily arranged and perfectly orchestrated singles that Phil Spector was producing at the time.[3] While not everyone involved with Southern soul understood Hendrix's use of feedback and distortion, his distinctive style was better tolerated in this arena, where "mistakes" weren't always seen as a problem. However, he had to play harder and louder to be heard and noticed over a larger band with a tight horn section.

Singer Curtis Knight (born Mont Curtis McNear), who knew and occasionally performed with Hendrix between 1965 and 1967, described his first encounter with the guitarist in an Amsterdam radio interview in 1994: "When I met Jimi he was totally frustrated, because he had just come off of what we call a Chitlin' Circuit tour. Now what that is, is they have about six superstars like Ike & Tina Turner, Little Richard, James Brown, and others, and then they would have four or five musicians that backed up that whole package. They put them all in a Greyhound bus, and sent them on what we laughingly called the Chitlin' Circuit, which was down South. Now Jimi had to play very rigid, and he had to play only what was on their records, so you can imagine how someone with a talent of his magnitude, you can understand how frustrated he was to have to do that."

Hendrix recalled in a *Melody Maker* interview (February 22, 1969) how difficult it was to survive on tour during those years. "I learned how *not* to get an R&B band together. The trouble was too many leaders didn't seem to want to pay anybody. Guys would get fired in the middle of the highway because they were talking too loud on the bus or the leader owed them too much money." Hendrix later sang about many of his formative experiences on the road in the autobiographical song "Highway Chile."

In 1968, writer Michael Thomas of *Eye* magazine summed up the Chitlin' Circuit best when he wrote: "The soul circuit is tough. There are lots of great guitar players who never got past the end of the block. On the soul circuit there's no faking it. The soul circuit ends at the Apollo Theater in Harlem. Apollo audiences are the aficionados of black music. They're merciless and impatient. If they catch the least whiff of jive, they're not shy of showing the performer the door before he's finished his first song.... Jimi Hendrix came up from Atlanta [in 1964], played in the Wednesday-night amateur contest, and won first prize. And if the soul circuit ends at the Apollo, it begins there as well."[4]

Highway Chile: Early to Mid-'63

In the bars I used to play in, we'd get up on the platform where the fan was, in one of them nice hot greasy, funky clubs. We'd play there and it was really hot, and the fan is makin' love to you. And you really had to play, 'cause those people were really hard to please. It was one of the hardest audiences in the South . . . they hear it all the time. Everybody knows how to play guitar. You walk down the street and people are sitting on their porch playing more guitar. . . . That's where I learned to play, really, in Nashville.

Jimi Hendrix, *L.A. Free Press,* August 25, 1967

In early 1963, Hendrix left Vancouver, British Columbia, and headed south. By spring, he was back in the music scene in Biloxi, Mississippi, where he backed Slim Harpo, famous for "I'm a King Bee," and Chicago bluesman Tommy Tucker, whose big hit was "Hi-Heel Sneakers." In April, he returned to Nashville, Tennessee, and formed a short-lived group called the Imperials with his former Army buddy Billy Cox.

The King Kasuals at Nashville's Jolly Roger Club, May 1963. *Left to right:* Jimmy Hendrix (guitar), Billy Cox (bass), Harold Nesbit (drums), Leonard Moses (guitar), Buford Majors (saxophone), Harry Batchelor (vocals). *David Pearcy collection*

Later that year, Cox and Hendrix re-formed the King Kasuals, with Hendrix on lead guitar, Cox on bass, Harold Nesbit on drums, Leonard Moses on second guitar, Buford Majors on saxophone, and Harry Batchelor on vocals. Reportedly, Hendrix was too timid to sing with the band. In a letter to his father, Hendrix boasted that the King Kasuals was "one of the two best Rhythm and Blues bands in Nashville."[5] In addition to the band, Hendrix and Cox gained exposure by backing up singers Nappy Brown, Carla Thomas, and Ironing Board Sam in Nashville's music clubs.

Many R&B soul revues toured the South. In the spring, a show headed by singers Sam Cooke and Jackie Wilson caught the attention of Hendrix and Cox, who went to see them play at Nashville's Hippodrome. A flamboyant MC by the name of Gorgeous George (Theodopholos Odell George) hosted the show and warmed up the Chitlin' Circuit crowds before the main performers went on. Little Richard once referred to George as "a black guy who sported a blond wig and wore these fabulous clothes which he made himself."[6] Gorgeous George not only served as MC but was also a tour promoter, and his band backed up many of the stars on the bill. After the show, Cox and Hendrix approached George to find out if he had any openings. Although Cox wasn't impressed with his offer, Hendrix grabbed the chance and wound up on the road as a member of Gorgeous George's house band, the Odells.

Hendrix had some difficulties on the road with the tour, as Cox recalled in a *Guitar Player* interview in September 1987: "He got stranded in Atlanta, so he came back, and we wound up playing again. He did that about five times, because he was searching for his destiny. Somehow he knew destiny was calling him, but he didn't have a direction at the time." Although these tours as a sideman were not easy for Hendrix, performing with well-known artists such as Chuck Jackson ("Beg Me"), Jerry Butler ("I Stand Accused"), and Solomon Burke ("Everybody Needs Somebody to Love") was a great opportunity for exposure.

During the summer of '63, Hendrix joined Bob Fisher and the Barnevilles. The group included future Hendrix rhythm guitarist Larry Lee, Bob Fisher on trumpet and vocals, Willy Young on bass guitar, Sammy Higginbottom on saxophone, and Isaac McKay on drums. For a brief time, the Barnevilles performed live with the Marvelettes, who had previously scored Motown's very first #1 hit in 1961 with "Please Mr. Postman." The Barnevilles also secured a month-long tour in November with Curtis Mayfield and the Impressions. According to Billy Cox, Hendrix once accidentally blew up one of Mayfield's amplifiers while on the road. Fortunately for Hendrix, Mayfield and the Impressions were one of several headliners on a package tour and Mayfield never discovered the identity of the guilty party.

During this formative stage, Hendrix developed his own smooth, light-touch style of guitar playing, which was influenced by Mayfield, whose songs like "Gypsy Woman" and "People Get Ready" inspired Hendrix's arrangements of "Little Wing" and "Have You Ever Been (to Electric Ladyland)." In an interview with *Straight Ahead* just before his death, Mayfield fondly recalled Hendrix: "He was way before his time with music. I personally adored and respected him for his honest tributes. It's funny, but many of us blacks didn't know Jimi Hendrix, yet he worked with so many artists we knew like the Isley Brothers...going way back."[7]

STATUS: *Unfortunately, no recordings have surfaced from any of the groups Hendrix performed with during early to mid-1963.*

Lonnie Youngblood

We had a band in Nashville, Tennessee, and I got tired of playing [with] that 'cause they didn't want to move anywhere. They just wanted to stay there. So I started traveling and went to New York....

Jimi Hendrix, Swedish radio interview, May 28, 1967

In late 1963, Hendrix was playing at the Baron in Nashville, Tennessee, with Larry Lee, a fellow guitarist. A tour promoter there encouraged Hendrix to go to New York, where he said he could earn top money. Lee recalled: "He [Hendrix] said New York is just a big country town and we can take this town, man. Jimi had no responsibility, he was just footloose and fancy-free. I knew it couldn't be that easy in New York, it scared me."[8]

In the winter of 1963, Hendrix met saxophone player Lonnie (Thomas) Youngblood in New York City. Youngblood went on to sign a record deal with Fairmont Records, a subsidiary of Philadelphia's Cameo-Parkway label, and formed his own band called Lonnie Youngblood and the Bloodbrothers. He hired Hendrix, an unknown guitar player, bought him a prized Fender amplifier, and they entered a small New York studio to do some recording. Their sessions yielded two Fairmont singles: "Go Go Shoes" b/w "Go Go Place" (F-1002) and "Soul Food (That's a What I Like)" b/w "Goodbye, Bessie Mae" (F-1022), both of which were released in 1963.[9] "(My Girl) She's a Fox" (with Richard and Robert Poindexter[10] on vocals), another track from the session, was not issued at the time. With the exception of "(My Girl) She's a Fox," which sounds like a precursor of Hendrix's "Little Wing," the songs are undistinguished, upbeat R&B tunes. As a session player for Youngblood, Hendrix was paid around twenty-five dollars per session.

Hendrix left Youngblood in 1964 on good terms, and went on to work with the Isley Brothers, who already had several hit recordings, and Don Covay, who was up-and-coming. Youngblood continued playing his sax for many R&B acts. He later inspired and supported some of the biggest names in R&B, such as Sam and Dave, Baby Washington, Buster Brown, Ben E. King, Chuck Jackson, Joe Tex, Jackie Wilson, and Chuck Berry. Youngblood earned the nickname "The Prince of Harlem" by working every one of the thirty-five clubs in Harlem.

For a brief time in 1965, Youngblood was a member of R&B singer Curtis Knight's band, the Love Lights. On a recently discovered live recording, Knight is heard saying: "For the past forty minutes, you've been listening to the music of the Love Lights, featuring Handsome Harry [Henderson] on lead guitar and good-looking Tito [surname unknown] on the drums and the fabulous Jimmy James [Hendrix]. Long tall Handsome Ace [possibly Horace Hall] on the bass. Yours truly, Curtis Knight here. We're gonna take a short break, we'll be right back." Youngblood can be heard playing sax on the band's cover of James Brown's "I Got You (I Feel Good)." The Love Lights played New York's Cheetah Club and Philadelphia's Uptown Theater, and the R&B club circuit in between, but not much is known about the band.

During this time, a second Youngblood-Hendrix recording session took place. This session at New York City's Abtone Studios produced three takes each of "Wipe the Sweat" and "Under the Table." For the past thirty years it was also assumed that the R&B tracks "Sweet Thang" and "Groove Maker" featured Youngblood as the main artist. However, Hendrix also recorded with several other upcoming performers at this time, and Billy LaMont and Jimmy Norman,[11] respectively, were the main performers on these two tracks, although they've never been properly credited.

In 1969, after Hendrix had become one of rock music's highest-paid performers, he visited Youngblood at Small's Paradise, a famous black-owned nightclub in Harlem, for an impromptu reunion. The two jammed on stage and, in Youngblood's words, "tore the joint completely out."[12] A photograph of the jam graced the cover of the 1971 LP *Two Great Experiences Together* (Maple, LPM 6004), but the music on the LP contained the 1963 Youngblood-Hendrix sessions. In addition to the jam in 1969 at Small's Paradise, Youngblood says that he and Hendrix spent three days at New York's Record Plant, never leaving the studio, and recording enough material for "at least two albums."[13]

After Hendrix died, many records were released worldwide, exploiting his fame. Among these recordings were several of the 1963 Youngblood-Hendrix sessions, which sold over two million copies posthumously.[14] "The [record] companies wanted to say they had a little more activity by Hendrix, so they found some Hendrix wannabes and put them on the tracks," Youngblood explained. "And what they really did was they messed the tracks up with the overdubs."[15] In 1986, Audio Fidelity Enterprises was sued for distributing and marketing eight different "patently fraudulent" albums that allegedly featured Hendrix but actually did not. Lonnie Youngblood had no part in any of the releases and at one time tried to sue the various parties involved. In a 1987 interview with CBS Television, Youngblood said this about the rip-off recordings: "You're not buying Hendrix...that's not Hendrix singing...that's not Hendrix playing."[16]

STATUS: Jimi Hendrix: The Early Years *(U.K., 1994, Charly Records CDCD 1189) is the best release on CD for authentic Youngblood-Hendrix recordings. In addition to the two Fairmont singles, Hendrix can also be heard playing guitar on "Under the Table (Parts I, II, & III)," "Wipe the Sweat (Parts I, II, & III)," "(My Girl) She's a Fox" (a.k.a. "Fox"), "Groove Maker," and "Sweet Thang." Hendrix sings the lead vocal on "Wipe the Sweat (Part III)."*

In addition to the fake recordings previously mentioned, the original Youngblood-Hendrix sessions have also been altered. With the exception of Jimi Hendrix: The Early Years, *many releases contain a stereo remix, a mono remix, or other audio enhancements. For example, the original release of "Soul Food (That's a What I Like)" clocked in at two minutes and forty-eight seconds. However, when this track was released on the CD* Cherokee *(1993, DNR 001), it was stretched to an unimaginable six minutes and thirteen seconds and included an overdubbed clapping track to suggest it was a live recording.*

"Sweet Thang" b/w "Please Don't Leave" was released on the 20th Century Fox label (45-6707) in 1966 and listed Billy LaMont as the main artist. At the time, LaMont was a very popular R&B singer in Newark, New Jersey, who was responsible for Youngblood's first recording contract. Youngblood has confirmed that Hendrix plays guitar on this version of "Sweet Thang."[17] *It is uncertain whether Hendrix plays on "Please Don't Leave," since the producing and writing credits are different from those on the A-side.*

No recordings of the 1969 impromptu jam at Small's Paradise in Harlem or the three-day jam session at New York's Record Plant studios have surfaced. The onstage photograph with Youngblood and Hendrix that appeared on Two Great Experiences Together *remains the only documentation of their 1969 reunion. The Love Lights' live recording is available in the collectors' network.*

Faye Pridgeon and Harlem

How did sadness enter my life, fate asks . . . I reply without a word or sound. . . . One slip of the tongue . . . I slip deeper into everlasting sorrow. Broken hearted am I. My pride attempts to comfort me, but love dampens my eyes to where I can't see. Love . . . Hurt love takes over and cries out — 'This pain I cannot bear. I beg mercy in [the] name of forgiveness.'

Jimi Hendrix, from a letter to Faye dated September 1, 1965,
printed in *Gallery,* September 1982

The period Hendrix spent in Harlem in early 1964, when he was first trying to conquer this "big country town," remained a mystery until Fayne ("Faye") Pridgeon appeared in the 1973 Warner Bros. documentary on Hendrix (*A Film About Jimi Hendrix*) and wrote a magazine article in 1982 ("I Remember Jimi," *Gallery*). Pridgeon was the mysterious foxy lady in tight skirts and high heels whom fans saw with Hendrix, but knew nothing about. She remembered Hendrix as "the skinny kid . . . I'd met way back when. [He] chain-smoked, ate badly, and never dressed adequately for the weather, but had a *warmth*, that none of the other fast-rapping dudes had."[18] Even though he had many other girlfriends through the years, Hendrix continued to visit Pridgeon whenever he was in New York City.

Hendrix first met Pridgeon in early 1964 while looking for a gig at Harlem's Palm Café, a popular nightclub on 125th Street. With his processed hair and shiny black pants, he approached Pridgeon and found out she was the ex-girlfriend of R&B singer Sam Cooke. Cooke frequented the Palm Café because of Ralph Cooper's nightly live radio broadcast from the club on WOV, called *The Ralph Cooper Radio Show*. In his book *Amateur Night at the Apollo*, Cooper recalled: "I broke a great many rhythm and blues and early rock artists from my live broadcast booth at the Palm Café. . . ."[19] They would stop by to chat on the air and occasionally sing a number. Since Cooke was playing at the Apollo Theater, Hendrix asked Pridgeon if she could get him into the show. She pulled a few strings and got him backstage to meet Cooke.

Pridgeon and Hendrix's romantic relationship developed quickly. She wrote of their first encounter: "I met him in the afternoon, and here it was dark and we were in bed. After that first night, I never left, he never left."[20] They often went to her mother's house for home-cooked soul food, a treat Hendrix missed when he was on the road. Pridgeon's mother also had a great blues-record collection—Ruth Brown, Muddy Waters, Junior Parker— all his favorites, and Hendrix often pulled out his guitar and played along to the records.

Life together wasn't easy for Hendrix and Pridgeon. Money was tight; they lived on sardines, crackers, and an occasional meal from her mother. Pridgeon described their situation in the Warner Bros. film: "We'd get our door plugged by the hotel. We'd get thrown out. We'd pawn the guitar. We'd come back. We'd borrow guitars from people to, you know, to play, do a gig. We'd eat good for a minute, you know. It was just that, you know, on and off all the time. And we were starving to death, you know."

After being thrown out of the Siefer Hotel, they moved in with twin brothers Arthur and Albert Allen in Harlem. But the living arrangement was awkward, as one of the Allen brothers explained in the Warner Bros. documentary: "The first time I met Jimi he was like shacking over, him and Faye. There was just something about Jimi that I dug. It was his guitar playing, I guess it was, plus he used to keep a lot of blues records around. He had thousands of them. . . . Faye was his girlfriend at this time. And she walked on out and swished, because she was bad herself, in her own right."

Hendrix had to prove himself in Harlem, and Pridgeon explained how difficult it was for him to get gigs: "We used to go to Palm's [sic] Café and places like Small's Paradise, the Spotlight—places around 125th Street, in the Harlem scene, you know. . .he'd tell them he wanted to sit in, right? And these old fuddy-duddy, rough-dried ain't-never-beens, you know, they ain't gonna give him a break, so like they just act like they don't even know that he's there. Finally they would let him come in, you know, and play. And then they get up and really just mess up so bad behind him it was incredible, you know. And he'd be looking all disgusted on the stage, and he'd keep looking back at 'em, and then the other guys come and tell him he'd got to turn it down, you know, and take him through all kind of changes."[21]

One ray of hope for Hendrix during this time was winning first prize in an amateur contest at the Apollo. Ralph Cooper began the regular Wednesday-night amateur competition in an effort to save the Apollo Theater from closing during the 1930s. In the '60s, new talent such as Ronnie Spector, Wilson Pickett, and Hendrix were all winners on Amateur Night. Billy Mitchell, tour director at the Apollo Theater, told me that he was thirteen years old when he saw Hendrix perform at Amateur Night at the Apollo. Mitchell said that Hendrix played a standard R&B hit with the Apollo Theater house band led by Reuben Phillips. "The audience loved him," Mitchell recalled, "and really got into his groove."[22] Hendrix was awarded first prize, which entitled him to return the following week, perform again (possibly two songs), and receive his prize of twenty-five dollars. He later acknowledged this honor in a radio interview.[23]

STATUS: *In 1996, Sotheby's auctioned two reel-to-reel tapes of previously unknown Hendrix material from 1968. According to the auction catalog, on the first reel — entitled "The Faye Tape" — Hendrix sings for nearly half an hour about his first reefer experience and gives a rather erotic homage to Pridgeon with the lyrics: "Have mercy, little girl, you makin' me so hard and wet."*

In Cooper's book Amateur Night at the Apollo, *he discussed his live radio show in the early 1960s, The Ralph Cooper Radio Show. Cooper wrote that his shows were taped.[24] It is possible that Hendrix's performances with bands at the Palm Café were broadcast, recorded, and preserved, but no tapes of Cooper's airchecks are known to exist.*

The Isley Brothers

> One of the Isley Brothers heard me playing in a club and said he had a job open. Sleeping outside between them tall tenements was hell — rats running across your chest, cockroaches stealing your last candy bar, so I figured, 'Yeah, I'll gig.' They used to make me do my thing, because it made them more bucks or something. Most groups I was with, they didn't let me do my own thing.
>
> Jimi Hendrix, *New Musical Express*, January 14, 1967

Hendrix began his tenure as the lead guitarist with the Isley Brothers in March 1964, while keeping his options open for work with other R&B acts. Tony Rice, a former associate of soul singer Joe Tex, recommended Hendrix to Kelly Isley. After seeing him play, younger brother Ernie Isley recalled, "Kelly was then questioned by his brothers about this hopeful addition to the band: 'Is he better than that guy with James Brown?' 'Yeah.' 'Is he better than that guy we saw in Cleveland at two o'clock in the morning?' 'Yeah.' Kelly then asked him if he would like to play guitar in the Isley Brothers band, and Jimi responded with a great big, 'Yeah man, I'd love to,' mostly because he was unemployed. After Jimi tuned up and started playing for about 45 seconds, Kelly said, 'Okay, you've got the job.'"[25] Hendrix then became one of the I.B. Specials, the group's touring band. The I.B. Specials were Gene Friday (organ), Al Lucas (bass), Bobby Gregg (drums), Marve Masey (saxophone), Douglas MacArthur (horns), and Jimmy Hendrix (guitar).

The Isley Brothers — Rudolph, Ronnie, and O'Kelly — have had four decades of Top 10 R&B records.[26] Starting in Cincinnati in the late 1950s, the three brothers began as a gospel group and recorded a few doo-wop singles. They won Amateur Night at the Apollo, and hit it big with the call-and-response rewrite of "Shout" in 1959. They followed with "Twist and Shout," a sock-hop and house-party staple from 1962.

In the liner notes to the Isley Brothers album *In the Beginning*, Ronnie Isley wrote: "Tony

The Isley Brothers with Jimmy Hendrix at the
Hejazz Grotto, New Haven, Connecticut, 1964.
Sal Manzi, courtesy www.rarerockphotos.com

[Rice] said the kid was the best, and that he played a right-handed guitar with his left hand. He tells me the guy's name is Jimmy Hendrix. Tony said Jimmy had sat in with the Palm's [sic] Café band one night and had killed everybody, so we made a date to meet him and hear him."

Shortly after passing the audition, Hendrix recorded "Testify (Parts 1 & 2)" with the Isley Brothers at New York's Atlantic studios.[27] During this time, Hendrix lived with the Isley Brothers for a while. Ernie Isley recalled for *Rolling Stone*'s February 6, 1992, issue just what it was like to have him in the house: "He would play in the hallway of our house while we were in the dining room. With his back to us, no amplifier, the sound and the feeling emanating from him was quite something."

The Isleys and Hendrix began a brief tour either at the end of March or in early April, covering Montreal, Canada, Bermuda, and Hendrix's hometown, Seattle, before returning to New York. While in Seattle, Hendrix had his guitar stolen, missed the tour bus, and was stranded. Once Hendrix returned to New York and reunited with the Isley Brothers, Kelly Isley replaced his stolen guitar with a new Fender Duo-Sonic, complete with an Epiphone "Tremtone" Vibrato.

Ernie Isley was too young to tour but remembers that his older brother Kelly talked about Hendrix impressing the British pop band the Animals. The two bands shared the same bill on one occasion. Animals members Eric Burdon and Chas Chandler, who both later became musically involved with Hendrix, got their first look at this remarkable young guitar player at this time. In *Experience Hendrix* (Summer 2000), Ernie Isley recalled: "In the middle of a show, Kelly might say, 'Come on out here, Jimi [*sic*] and show them how it's done. Ladies and gentleman, Jimi Hendrix.' And he'd do something like play the guitar behind his back....The Animals were going out of their minds."

Two more recording sessions took place on August 5 and September 23 before the Isley Brothers and Hendrix set off on a thirty-five-day tour that began September 28. Hendrix wrote home to his father, "We've been to all the cities in the Midwest, East & South." Sometime around mid-October or early November, Hendrix quit the Isley Brothers when he reached the familiar surroundings of Nashville, Tennessee. He seemed fed up with the routine: "I had to conform...the so-called grooming bit, you know, mohair suits, how I hate mohair suits! I was playing with the Isley Brothers and we had white mohair suits, patent leather shoes and patent leather hairdos. We weren't allowed to go on stage looking casual. If our shoelaces were two different types, we'd get fined five dollars. It got very boring, you know, 'cause you get very tired playing behind other people all the time, you know. I quit them [the Isley Brothers] in Nashville...."[28]

STATUS: *The original 1964 Isley Brothers singles that included Hendrix were:*
- *"Testify (Part 1)" b/w "Testify (Part 2)" (T-Neck 45-501), recorded on March 21, 1964, released in June 1964*
- *"Move Over and Let Me Dance" b/w "Have You Ever Been Disappointed" (Atlantic 45-2303), recorded on August 5, 1964, released in September 1964*
- *"The Last Girl" b/w "Looking for a Love" (Atlantic 45-2263), featuring singer Dionne Warwick, recorded on September 23, 1964, released in November 1964*

Shortly after Hendrix's death, the Isley Brothers released In the Beginning *(1971, T-Neck TNS 3007). It was intentionally remixed so that Hendrix's guitar was more prominent. The album never made it to CD. The recording contained nine songs, eight featuring Hendrix:*
- *"Have You Ever Been Disappointed (Parts 1 & 2)"*
- *"Move Over and Let Me Dance (Parts 1 & 2)"*
- *"Testify (Parts 1 & 2)"*
- *"The Last Girl"*
- *"Looking for a Love"*

In 1990, The Isley Brothers Story, Vol. 1 Rockin' Soul: 1959-68 *(1991, Rhino R2 70908) was released. It featured these songs with Hendrix: "Testify (Parts 1 & 2)," "The Last Girl," and "Move Over and Let Me Dance." Three Hendrix–Isley Brothers tracks that originally appeared on the* In the Beginning *LP are absent from the CD format — "Have You Ever Been Disappointed (Parts 1 & 2)" and "Looking for a Love," all recorded at Atlantic Studios, New York. In the liner notes to the Rhino release, Adam White wrote: "These were the dog days of their career, with no hits and only "The Last Girl" (an uncharacteristic, neo-Bacharach*

31

ballad) to sustain them. Unappreciated in its country of origin, this single became a cult classic in England...." Despite the Isley Brothers' heavy tour schedule, no live recordings that include Hendrix have surfaced.

*In 1991, United Artists released The Isley Brothers: The Complete UA Sessions (CDP-7-95203-2). According to the liner notes, eight songs from the January 14, 1964, recording session, probably with Hendrix, are included on this release; the three marked with asterisks were previously unreleased: "My Little Girl," "Open Her Eyes," "Love Is a Wonderful Thing,"²⁹ *"Footprints in the Snow," "Who's That Lady," *"The Basement," *"Conch," and "My Little Girl (version 2)."*

If, in fact, Hendrix does perform on these tracks, his guitar work is not as strong as on In the Beginning. Archivist Phil Adams believes Hendrix appears on "My Little Girl," since the intro and especially the bridge have a Hendrix-like feel to them. On the second version, the guitar is more to the front of the mix and drives the band. "Love Is a Wonderful Thing" has a rhythm and recurring lead guitar lick that is similar to Hendrix's later style on "Testify." In "Who's That Lady," the bridge has the Curtis Mayfield influence heard on Hendrix's other early recordings, and on the track "The Basement," the 7#9 chord — which guitarists refer to as "the Hendrix chord" — is used. This chord appears in many Hendrix songs, including "Foxy Lady" and "Purple Haze."

Don Covay and the Goodtimers

But who can rest in New York? I got a job with another band.
Jimi Hendrix, *New Musical Express*, January 14, 1967

By 1964, Hendrix had a reputation around New York City for being a flamboyant guitar player. He was known as the guy wearing chains who would do flip-flops and "eat" his guitar. He earned a living playing as a session guitarist.

In my research for this book, I discovered evidence that Hendrix played on Don Covay's 1964 hit "Mercy, Mercy" b/w "Can't Stay Away" (Rosemart 45-801). I first tried to reach Covay in 1994, but he had just suffered a stroke and was recuperating. I then tried to find George Clemons, who sang background vocals on "Mercy, Mercy." Clemons, a.k.a. King George, started singing in Harlem clubs during the mid-1960s and met Covay while performing at the Apollo Theater. In my interview with Clemons, I asked him how Covay happened to select Hendrix for the track. He explained: "Curtis Knight, Jimmy, and I all used to live in the same apartment building—around 81st Street. Jimmy used to come into my house to sleep, as his guitar was always in the pawnshop. Don Covay came around shopping for a record deal. He used to come down to the Harlem clubs looking for somebody to use...on the songs he was looking to sell to Atlantic [Records]. He'd say, 'I got this tune I want you to help me out with...come on down to the studio....Can you sing this part? Can you play this part?' Before the song came out, Jimmy was going around to some of the small clubs and played it on an experimental basis."³⁰

Don Covay, c. 1990s. © *Lynn Goldsmith*

The liner notes for *The Definitive Don Covay* (Razor & Tie RE 2053) state that Don Covay and the Goodtimers recorded the classic "Mercy, Mercy" at A-1 Studios in New York on May 18, 1964. Other than Ronald Miller on bass, the musicians are listed as "unknown." Hendrix's studio involvement may not have been documented because he might have been paid under the table for his session work, as was the custom at the time.

Hendrix told *Rolling Stone* in a 1968 interview that he showed R&B guitarist Steve Cropper how to play "Mercy, Mercy." Hendrix's reference to this song suggested that he played the original part on the record, and then showed this part to Cropper. This evidence pointed toward Hendrix's involvement with the record, but I still wanted to hear directly from Covay to confirm this.

The English magazine *Juke Blues* published a story on Don Covay around the time I began writing this book. The article said that Covay's health had improved and he had given them a brief interview. After making some phone calls and writing a few e-mails, I finally spoke with Covay directly. He was extremely friendly and confirmed that Hendrix had played guitar on "Mercy, Mercy."[31] We also spoke about his obscure LP called *Funky Yo-Yo*, which also featured Hendrix on guitar. It turns out that this album comprises demo tapes that Covay had forgotten in his closet. Covay particularly remembered that Hendrix was involved in the track "Three Time Loser" from that album.

"Mercy, Mercy," Covay's first major hit, was released on September 5, 1964, and climbed to #35 on *Billboard* magazine's pop chart. At age twenty-one, Jimmy Hendrix was a contributor to this Top 40 single. In his short career, "All Along the Watchtower" was Hendrix's only American Top 40 hit with his own band.

Hendrix continued to play "Mercy, Mercy" as a member of Curtis Knight and the Squires in 1965. The Jimi Hendrix Experience also played it; with only a few original songs under their belt, Hendrix, Noel Redding, and Mitch Mitchell often performed cover songs in the band's early stages. There is evidence that they played it on January 14, 1967, at the Beachcombers Club and again on February 2 at the Flamingo Club while touring England.

STATUS: *The 1964 album Mercy! (Atlantic S104) by Don Covay and the Goodtimers featured "Mercy, Mercy" and four other tracks with Hendrix: "I'll Be Satisfied," "Can't Stay Away," "Take This Hurt off Me," and "Please Don't Let Me Know." In addition to Covay, Hendrix, Miller, and Clemons playing on these tracks, it is possible that Bernard Purdie (drums), Horace Ott (piano/organ), and Bob Bushnell (rhythm guitar/bass) also contributed. "Mercy, Mercy" was released on The Definitive Don Covay (Razor & Tie RE 2053) in 1994.*

Don Covay's obscure album Funky Yo-Yo (released in 1977, Versatile 1123) features these tracks: "Yo-Yo (Part 1)," "I Don't Think I Can Make It," "Three Time Loser," "An Ugly Woman," "Yo-Yo (Part 2)," "Love Is Sweeter on the Other Side," "You Can't Get Something for Nothing," and "Your Love Has Got to Me." Covay asserts that Hendrix is on "Three Time Loser"; he may also be on "Love Is Sweeter on the Other Side." The beginning notes of "Three Time Loser" sound similar to Hendrix's later composition "Red House."

Steve Cropper

Steve Cropper turned me on millions of years ago and I turned him on millions of years ago too, but because of different songs. Like we went into the studio and we started teaching each other. I found him in this soul food restaurant eating all of this stuff, right across from the [Stax Records] studio in Memphis. I was playing in this Top 40 R&B Soul Hit Parade package....

Jimi Hendrix, Rolling Stone, March 9, 1968

After quitting the Isley Brothers in 1964, Hendrix joined another R&B tour package in November that featured B.B. King, Jackie Wilson, and Sam Cooke. Hendrix didn't accompany Cooke or Wilson, but played behind Gorgeous George, who opened the show with a few songs and then took over as MC. When the tour arrived in Memphis, Tennessee, Hendrix grabbed the opportunity to meet R&B guitarist Steve Cropper, of Booker T. and the M.G.s, at the famous Stax Records recording studio.

Hendrix told *Rolling Stone* about their encounter: "So anyway, I got into the studio and said, 'Hey man, dig, I heard you're all right, that anyone can come down here if they've got a song.' So we went into the studio, we did a song, and after that, it was just with the guitar and he was messing around with engineering. It's just a demo acetate. I don't know where it is at now. After we did that we messed around the studio for four or five hours doing different little things, it was very strange. He turned me on to a lot of things. He showed me how he played certain songs and I showed him how I played 'Mercy, Mercy.'"

In recent years, Steve Cropper has come forward to explain his side of the story of how he met Hendrix. In the liner notes to *Drivin' South*, Cropper recalled: "Jimi came into Stax one day, and somebody said 'There's this guy out the front wants to see you.' Well that used to happen once or twice a day on a regular basis, and they'd be told 'Well, Steve's real busy, but if he has time he'll try to see you.'... So I finally came out about 5 o'clock, one of the girls was still there and she said 'Did you see that guy who wanted to talk to you today?' And I said 'No, why, he's still hanging around?' and she said 'Yeah...I think he came in from outta town—he's not a local guy' and I felt real bad, y'know, that somebody had sat there all day long....I went over and introduced myself, and he said 'yeah I play a little guitar, up in New York, a few places' and I said 'Uh, great, what have you played on?' and he named a few things, then came up with a Don Covay record ["Mercy Mercy"]. I said, 'You played on that!!—'cause that was one of my favorite records—that lick that's in there, that funky little intro lick.'

"So we ate and I said 'Why don't you come over to the studio?' He didn't have a guitar, and, of course, he was left-handed, but he took one of mine and turned it upside down, and tried to show me this lick—upside down!—which I never did quite get, but anyway....We hung out for a bit, though we never did make any recordings or anything, like it says in those books....Later we ran into each other a few times on the road. Next time I saw him, I was playing Monterey with Otis, and he was JIMI HENDRIX!"[32]

According to session bassist Roland Robinson, Hendrix returned to the Stax recording studio a short time after he and Cropper met, but Cropper wasn't there. Hendrix set up his guitar and amp anyway and played with some of the guys in the studio. After they witnessed his wild style, "they laughed and walked out of the studio."[33] Hendrix packed up his stuff and soon joined the Little Richard tour.

STATUS: *Unknown. Cropper says that he and Hendrix never recorded anything together, yet Hendrix claimed they did. If a Hendrix-Cropper demo acetate was recorded, it has not surfaced.*

Little Richard

> *I was in Kansas City, Missouri, and I didn't have any money so, you know, this group came up and brought me back to Atlanta, Georgia, where I met Little Richard and I started playing with him for a while.*
> Jimi Hendrix, Stockholm radio interview, May 28, 1967

As a youth, Hendrix went backstage to meet Little Richard at one of his Seattle concerts. Years later, Hendrix had the opportunity to join Little Richard's band, the Upsetters. According to Little Richard, Hendrix's father was contacted for approval before Jimmy joined the tour. He claims Al Hendrix responded, "Jimi just idolizes Richard. He would eat ten yards of shit to join his band."[34] Under the name Maurice James, Hendrix performed and recorded with Little Richard from January through July 1965, minus an interlude playing with Ike and Tina Turner and an ambitious young R&B singer, Rosa Lee Brooks.

Despite several unnecessary comebacks, it is safe to say Little Richard (Richard Penniman), rock's greatest prima donna, hit his peak in the mid-1950s. His outrageous sexuality, flashy costumes, and his '50s rock 'n' roll hits "Tutti Frutti," "Long Tall Sally," and "Lucille" were his trademarks. In mid-tour in the late '50s, Little Richard suddenly quit rock 'n' roll to turn his attention toward religion, eventually becoming an ordained minister in 1961. The following year he even joined a religious musical tour with Sam Cooke. Religion was enough for Penniman until the early '60s and the "British Invasion." With both the Rolling Stones and the Beatles adopting Little Richard's screaming and head-shaking theatrics and citing him as an influence, Little Richard heard the call. Nonetheless, with his last hit six years behind him, his was a difficult journey back to the music scene.

In 1965, the Little Richard band toured the southern states and made a brief stop in Nashville, Tennessee. While there, Hendrix performed with the Upsetters, without Little Richard, with two singers known as Buddy and Stacey (formerly of the King Curtis band) on a musical variety TV show called *Night Train*. The band played "Shotgun," a new up-tempo song by saxophone player Jr. Walker that was making its way up the charts. In a rare videotape of the show, Hendrix can be seen in the background playing the guitar by fanning and elbowing it, moving in time with the other players. This is the earliest known footage of Hendrix performing—a perfect example of his attempt to break out of the "just another sideman" mold.

Little Richard wasn't especially pleased with Hendrix's theatrics, as he disclosed in an interview with *Rolling Stone* (December 15, 1994): "Jimi Hendrix…was my guitar player, and you know, we didn't know he could play with his mouth. One night I heard this screamin' and hollerin', and they were screamin' and hollerin' for him! I thought they were screamin' for me. But he was back there playin' the guitar with his mouth. He didn't do it again, 'cause we made sure the lights didn't come on that area no more. We fixed that!"

When Hendrix was on the road with Little Richard, he called his friend Billy Cox about joining Little Richard's band, but Cox was busy with the Kasuals and declined. As Cox recalls, Hendrix wouldn't take no for answer: "I looked up one Sunday and this bus pulled up in front of my house. Out came Little Richard and Jimi to try to get me on the road, but I had other obligations, so I couldn't go."[35]

When the Little Richard tour rolled into Los Angeles, Hendrix decided to call it quits. In a letter to his father dated February 19, 1965, Hendrix wrote that he was staying at Hollywood's Wilcox Hotel. Blues guitarist Albert Collins, who briefly filled Hendrix's spot in the Upsetters, says that Hendrix went on to play with the Drifters during this time. Hendrix also recorded with Rosa Lee Brooks and played a few shows with the Ike & Tina Turner Revue, including San Francisco's Fillmore Auditorium. Although Hendrix often said in interviews that he toured with Ike and Tina, Tina Turner said that he was never part of their backup band. "If Jimi Hendrix had ever been on our stage, believe me I'd remember him."[36]

Sometime in early April, Hendrix made the difficult decision to rejoin Little Richard. Before leaving Los Angeles, Hendrix recorded "I Don't Know What You Got, but It's Got Me (Parts 1 & 2)" (Vee Jay 65-8657) with Don Covay on organ. The single peaked at #12 on the R&B charts on November 27, 1965—Hendrix's twenty-third birthday—but barely made it to *Billboard*'s Top 100, reaching #92. There are rumors that Hendrix recorded with Little Richard for the Modern Record label in Los Angeles, but nothing has ever surfaced to substantiate this.

As the tour bus left Los Angeles for Atlanta, Hendrix said his goodbyes to Rosa Lee Brooks. After leaving Atlanta, Little Richard and the Upsetters headed for New York, where Hendrix either was fired or quit. Little Richard's brother and tour manager, Robert Penniman, said Hendrix was always flirting with the girls and was late for the bus, so he was told that his services were no longer needed. Hendrix's version, revealed in an article in the *New York Times* (February 25, 1968), differed dramatically: "Once with Little Richard, me and another guy got fancy shirts 'cause we were tired of wearing the uniform. Richard called a meeting. 'I am Little Richard, I am Little Richard,' he said, 'the King, the King of Rock and Rhythm. I am the only one allowed to be pretty. Take off those shirts.' Man, it was like that. Bad pay, lousy living, and getting burned."

In May 1970, Little Richard enjoyed another successful return to the stage, performing for a new audience. He followed Janis Joplin's set at the Atlantic City Pop Festival, and had plans for a television special with a guest list that included all of the people he inspired. He told *Rolling Stone*: "I'm going to do it from Caesar's Palace [Las Vegas]. They're gonna have me talkin' to the Beatles, playin' with Elvis…Tom Jones…a thing with me and Jimi Hendrix playing."[37] It would have made an entertaining evening, but Hendrix never performed with Little Richard after 1965.

STATUS: *Shortly after Hendrix died in 1970, piles of Little Richard–Jimi Hendrix LPs were released. Many of the record jackets depicted superimposed shots of Hendrix with Little Richard, implying that the record inside was a "newly discovered" or "lost" recording from their time together. Neither was the case. Many of the recordings featured an unknown guitar player using a wah-wah pedal – a technology that was not available until mid-1967.*

Hendrix did appear with Little Richard on "I Don't Know What You Got…" (the final single Vee Jay records released before the label folded) and "Dancin' All Around the World." Both can be found on Little Richard: 20 Greatest Hits (Deluxe DCD-7797 USA).

A live recording with Little Richard and Hendrix surfaced in 1996. A Boston disc jockey owns a tape of a concert that took place in 1964 at Revere Beach, near Boston, Massachusetts. The concert was broadcast on WTBS 88.1, MIT (Massachusetts Institute of Technology) Radio. The tracks listed on the tape are: "I Saw Her Standing There," "Lucille," "Send Me Some Lovin'," Medley: "Rip It Up/Tutti Frutti/Jenny, Jenny," "Shake a Hand," and "Whole Lotta Shakin'." The tape was recorded on a Scotch 190 reel-to-reel at 7.5ips.

Also recorded on the same reel was a performance with Maxine Brown and Don ("Sugarcane" Harris) & Dewey (Terry), with Hendrix playing guitar in the backup band. I asked Dewey Terry about this show. "Jimi would let the guitar feed back," Terry said, "and that would piss Richard off because it would cover up his vocals, especially during 'Lucille' and 'Tutti Frutti.'"[38] Unfortunately, the section of the tape with Maxine Brown and Don & Dewey suffers from numerous abrupt tape stops.

Little Richard has claimed that Hendrix was also involved in a live recording at the Domino Club in Atlanta, Georgia, in December 1965. These recordings appeared on the LPs The Incredible Little Richard Sings His Greatest Hits – Live! (Modern 1000) and The Wild & Frantic Little Richard (Modern 1030). In reality, these do not feature Hendrix, who had joined Curtis Knight and the Squires and was in New York at the time. Another rumor that needs to be cleared up concerns the version of "Lawdy Miss Clawdy" that appears on the Lifelines: The Jimi Hendrix Story box set (Reprise 26435-2). Despite what the liner notes state, this Little Richard track does not feature Jimi Hendrix playing guitar.

Rosa Lee Brooks and Arthur Lee

I worked with him [Little Richard] all over the U.S., finally landing in Los Angeles and playing more gigs with Ike and Tina Turner.

Jimi Hendrix, *New Musical Express*, January 14, 1967

Rosa Lee Brooks, publicity photo, c. 1965. *Bauer Studios*

Discovered by fans in the early 1970s, the single "My Diary" (Revis 1013) was once thought to be the earliest known Jimi Hendrix recording. The opening Curtis Mayfield–like guitar riff is undeniably Hendrix. However, not much was known about the singer, Rosa Lee Brooks, or the recording session, until I spoke with her in May 1992 and she explained some of the details behind this obscure single.[39] "My Diary" never charted, although it received some minor airplay in the Los Angeles area.

For thirty years, Brooks remained silent about her relationship with Hendrix, never revealing her story for any magazine or biography. After reading *Straight Ahead*, she came forward and granted me an interview. Brooks's best recollection was that they met at the Wilcox Hotel's California Club in Los Angeles. They were there as non-performers, enjoying the New Year's Eve festivities of 1964, watching the Ike & Tina Turner Revue, and they became *very* well acquainted. (Other sources claim that Hendrix did not arrive in Los Angeles until mid-February, when he was touring with the Ike & Tina Turner Revue.) Brooks said that after they spent the night together, Hendrix awoke and began composing the tune that later became "My Diary." "He played that great opening," says Brooks, "and then sang the first verse, 'I know that I will never love again, I know that I will be my only friend.'" Brooks says that she wrote the rest of the lyrics, and several weeks later the single was recorded.

On the way to the studio, which was actually just a converted garage behind producer Billy Revis's home, Brooks picked up Arthur Lee (born Arthur Taylor Porter) to help with background vocals. Lee made his claim to fame with the rock group Love in the mid-1960s. The band had a string of hits including "My Little Red Book" and "Seven & Seven Is." This was also the first time, according to Brooks, that Hendrix and Lee met. (The two would record together again in 1970.) Also at the session was "Big Francis" (surname unknown) on drums and Alvin (surname unknown) on bass. Both of these musicians were recruited from Major Lance's band, which had the 1963 hit "Monkey Time." The horn section for "My Diary" included session players provided by Billy Revis, and according to Brooks, the female background singers were the Pointer Sisters.

Brooks's information filled in several gaps; however, one item didn't jibe. On the original label of the 45, Arthur Lee is credited as composer, and he emphatically states to this day that he was the *only* composer for "My Diary." The line in "My Diary," "Even our birthday is on the *same* old day," further supports his claim. "The reason I wrote the song was that my girlfriend's mother had found her diary. That's what the song is about. I had to break up with my girlfriend because of this whole deal. We were born on the same day. I was born on the seventh and so was she. Love later had a hit with 'Seven & Seven Is.' That's the same chick. I was hung up on her! Her name was Anita."[40] Brooks's claim that she was the composer is not confirmed by the song's lyrics. She was born on October 16, 1943, and Hendrix was born on November 27, 1942.

In an interview I conducted in 1993, Arthur Lee recalled meeting Hendrix, who was then calling himself Maurice James: "The first time I met Jimi Hendrix was at Revis Records on Western Avenue in Los Angeles. I only played keyboards at the time, but I told Jimi I wanted a Curtis Mayfield feel to the song, like "Gypsy Woman" [a 1961 hit by the Impressions]. Billy Revis said he knew a guitar player that could play like Curtis Mayfield, and that's what I wanted because I didn't play guitar at the time. Jimi was working with Little Richard at the time."

After cutting "My Diary," producer Billy Revis said he wanted a B-side to complete the single. Brooks says Alvin (the bass player) showed everyone at the session a new dance called the U-T, in which one forms the letters U and T with the arms. The song "Utee" was quickly penned, borrowing a melody line from the January 1965 Dobie Gray hit, "The 'In' Crowd," and the B-side was complete. Proud of the results, Brooks recalled, "Just listen to the solo, with its high-frequency rock sound...he [Hendrix] was the Father of Rock!"[41]

Brooks said she never saw Hendrix again after he rejoined the Little Richard tour sometime in April, heading for Atlanta. His last contact with her was a postcard sent from New York, asking for sixty dollars to get his guitar out of a pawnshop.[42]

STATUS: *The limited-release single is long out of print. An even rarer acetate was also pressed on the Gold Star label. The location of the original master tape is unknown.*

"My Diary" has been featured in several syndicated radio documentaries. The first several notes of the song are definitely Hendrix's guitar style for this period: smooth and sweet. It's unfortunate that some oldies revival label hasn't released this song in a collection.

Curtis Knight and the Squires

I quit Little Richard over a money misunderstanding and to rest. He didn't pay us for five and a half weeks, and you can't live on promises when you're on the road.

Jimi Hendrix, *New Musical Express*, January 14, 1967

After quitting Little Richard's band, Hendrix found himself back in New York and hungry. In postcards sent home to his father, he wrote that he was out of work in August. In October 1965, Hendrix took a non-touring job with a club band called the Squires, headed by Curtis Knight. The grueling days and nights of the Chitlin' Circuit were finally over.

Curtis Knight hailed from Fort Scott, Kansas, but moved to Los Angeles, California, in the 1950s. He began his musical career as an aspiring soul singer, which led to a role in the low-budget movie *Pop Girl*. In Knight's words, "It wasn't exactly nominated for any Academy Awards."[43] Since he was earning very little money and trying to survive on a diet of black-eyed peas, Knight got fed up and took the next Greyhound bus out of L.A. to try his luck in New York.

In his 1974 Hendrix biography, *Jimi*, Knight talked about reconnecting with Hendrix when he was one step away from being evicted from the run-down Hotel America. Hendrix had pawned his guitar for money to buy food, and Knight helped him with his back rent and gave him a right-handed sunburst Fender Duo-Sonic guitar. Knight recalled: "I rushed out to my car and got the guitars and amp ... I knocked on the door and went in. There, lounging on his double bed, was a very beautiful chick of about nineteen ... Fayne Pridgeon ... Jimi plugged in the guitar and the amp, and it seemed almost like one single movement and as though he were reunited with a long-lost love. I told him that the guitar he was playing was my gift to him and that if he wanted he could be my lead guitarist from that moment on."[44]

Over the next eight months, Hendrix played a variety of small clubs in New York and New Jersey with Curtis Knight and the Squires. Their varied set list included classic blues songs like B.B. King's "Sweet Little Angel," Jimmy Reed's "Bright Lights, Big City," and an outstanding version of Bo Diddley's "I'm a Man," with Hendrix on lead vocal. A live recording made on December 26, 1965, further demonstrates the freedom Hendrix was given in the Squires to cut loose on a solo. During a one-chord jam titled "Drivin' South," Knight shouts to Hendrix, "Eat that guitar! Eat it—eat it!" as ear-piercing notes are played to an appreciative crowd. "Drivin' South" is actually a cover of an Albert Collins tune—"Thaw Out," from his 1962 album, *Kool Albert Collins*.

During this time, Hendrix also toured for ten days with the band Joey Dee and the Starlighters, of "Peppermint Twist" fame. The Starlighters' lineup included drummer Jimmy Mayes, singer Tommy Davis, Charles Neville (of the Neville Brothers) on saxophone, and Hendrix on guitar. Hendrix talked about this tour in an interview with *New Musical Express* (January 14, 1967): "I got a job with another band. I had all of these ideas and sounds in my brain, and playing this 'other people's music' all the time was hurting me. I jumped from the frying pan into the fire when I joined up with Joey Dee & the Starlighters. I played Cleveland . . . with Joey Dee at the Arena in some rhythm and blues show that had Chubby Checker in it. Nobody talked to me. I was just another Negro artist. After sucking on a peppermint twist salary I had to quit and began playing with a juke-box band. . . ."

One of the people who knew Hendrix best at this time was his new girlfriend, Carol Shiroky. While Hendrix was in the Squires, Shiroky was Knight's girlfriend. "Jimmy and I started making eyes at each other through a whole performance at the Lighthouse club and Curtis noticed it. . . . Next thing Curtis walked out and Jimmy came over and sat down at the table. . . . Three days later I moved in with Jimmy. He used to come home really pissed off about four nights out of six, for whatever reason—angry at Curtis, fighting with the band, fighting with the material. We had a conversation shortly after this about staying in the band with Curtis. I told him he didn't need Curtis. Curtis needed him! He said, 'Because it's Curtis's guitar.' I said, 'Excuse me? That's the only thing that's keeping you with Curtis?' He said, 'Yes.' So two days later we went to Manny's [Music] and I bought him his first Strat."[45]

Across the street from Hendrix's hotel was a nightclub called the African Room, where Trinidadian singer and dancer Mike Quashie performed on a regular basis. Quashie brought the Limbo—which later became a dance hit for Chubby Checker—to America in the early 1960s. Carol Shiroky introduced Hendrix to Quashie; they became close friends and kept in touch through the years. Recalling the New York nightlife scene with Hendrix, Quashie told me, "It was a wild life . . . Joey Dee at the Peppermint Lounge . . . James Brown coming in . . . Jayne Mansfield shaking her behind."[46]

Hendrix played his final gig with Curtis Knight and the Squires on May 20, 1966, at the Cheetah Club in New York City. Before leaving the band, he signed an agreement with Ed Chalpin, a New York record producer. Chalpin had been working as an independent producer since 1961, creating foreign cover versions of American and British hits for his company, PPX Enterprises. The agreement Chalpin drew up required Hendrix to record for him exclusively for three years (October 15, 1965, through October 15, 1968). In return, Hendrix received one dollar in cash and the rights to one percent of the "retail-selling price of all records sold for his production efforts, and minimum scale for arrangements he produces." Hendrix recorded over sixty songs for Chalpin and PPX while he was with the Squires—twenty-six studio and thirty-five live recordings.

After the Experience's phenomenal success, Chalpin took the opportunity to market his two-year-old recordings of Hendrix with Curtis Knight. Hendrix's new record company, Warner Bros., initiated a lawsuit to halt the release of these records. On March 7, 1968, Hendrix gave his deposition regarding his recollection of the Knight recording sessions and the contract he signed with Chalpin in October 1965. The proceedings took place in the U.S. District Court and lasted three and a half hours, producing a 170-page document. In an article for *UniVibes* magazine, Joel J. Brattin noted that the Hendrix questions and answers were taped, and later transcribed by a notary public, but the deposition tapes are missing. The New York court ruled that however unfair, the 1965 agreement between Hendrix and Chalpin's PPX Enterprises was not illegal.[47] In an interview with *Rolling Stone* (March 9, 1968), Hendrix spoke about the recordings: "When I played it [the record], I discovered that it had been recorded from a jam session I did in New York. We had only been practicing in the studio. I had no idea it was being recorded. On one side of the disc is 'Hush Now'...I only play the guitar, the singer's voice has been superimposed. On the other, 'Flashing,' all I do is a couple of notes. Man, I was shocked when I heard it. Curtis Knight's album was [taken] from bits of tape they used from a jam session, bits of tape, tiny little confetti bits of tapes."

STATUS: *In Hendrix's lifetime, four Knight-Hendrix singles and two LPs were released. The LP Get That Feeling, released in December 1967, reached #75 on the Billboard charts and remained there for twelve weeks. The other LP, Flashing, released in 1968, did not chart at all. After Hendrix's death, a large number of the released recordings were based on the studio or live tapes made during his eight months with Curtis Knight and the Squires. Of the sixty-one different songs released, many were edited, remixed, or intentionally altered to create a "new" song.*

In 1996, producer Ed Chalpin rereleased his Curtis Knight–Jimi Hendrix recordings yet again, as The Authentic PPX Studio Recordings, a six-volume CD set (sold separately), pressed in Germany. The covers are more authentic-looking than their predecessors from the '70s, with better photographs and more information. The Authentic PPX Studio Recordings (CBH Records) include: Volume One: Get That Feeling (SPV-085-44222); Volume Two: Flashing (SPV-085-44212); Volume Three: Ballad of Jimi (SPV-085-44682); Volume Four: Live at George's Club (SPV-085-44692); Volume Five: Something on Your Mind (SPV-085-44892); and Volume Six: On the Killing Floor (SPV-085-44902.)

Hendrix archivist Doug Bell has painstakingly scrutinized all (yes, all) of the Knight-Hendrix recordings and releases. He reports that The Authentic PPX Studio Recordings are "tremendously compressed, and there is a lot of metallic harshness. Also many of the mixes have overdubs, or are edited or incomplete."[48] Bell also pointed out that there is an audio-tape making the rounds in the collectors' network with ninety minutes of live Curtis Knight and the Squires with Hendrix, which is a mixture of mono, simulated stereo, and true stereo cuts. Although it is nearly free of overdubs and edits, it seems to have some fake crowd noise added.

In addition to the PPX recordings, Hendrix also appeared with the Squires on an instrumental called "No Such Animal (Parts 1 & 2)," recorded in 1965. The single was released on Audio Fidelity Records (AF 167) only a few months after Hendrix's death. This upbeat tune with Hendrix's high-energy solo may well be the guitar showpiece from this period.

After Hendrix left, Knight continued working but was known solely for his Hendrix association. In 1974, Knight wrote his own Hendrix biography, Jimi, and then moved to London. Knight wrote another book on Hendrix in the mid-1990s—Starchild, published by Abelard Productions. This second book was even more self-serving than Jimi. Knight wrote that he and Hendrix were stuck in a car during a snowstorm in upstate New York one winter night in 1965. They feared that they would freeze to death, and Knight claims a cone-shaped craft landed and an alien freed their vehicle from the snow. According to Knight, only he and Hendrix saw the UFO. Curtis Knight died of prostate cancer on December 29, 1999, in Amsterdam, the Netherlands.

Jayne Mansfield

> *Edward, you can't use my name.*
> Hendrix to producer Ed Chalpin during a studio session, July 1967

Toward the end of 1965, record producer Ed Chalpin brought in his new session guitarist, Jimmy Hendrix, to play backup on a single for Jayne Mansfield. When her acting career started to fade, Mansfield turned to singing pop singles, with less than spectacular results.

During the peak of Marilyn Monroe's career, it seemed that every Hollywood studio wanted to find its own Marilyn. Twentieth Century Fox quickly signed Jayne Mansfield and featured her in a string of B movies, stereotyped as the "sexy dumb blonde." In reality, Mansfield had a high I.Q. of 163. Her films never amounted to much, but her shapely figure drew attention around the world.

When I interviewed Chalpin about the Mansfield-Hendrix single, he was surprised that anyone knew of Hendrix's involvement. "How did you get that information? It doesn't have Hendrix's name on it, does it? I didn't give them permission to use his name," said Chalpin.[49] I told him that my magazine had been the first to report it and that recent biographies had since listed it.

Chalpin eventually revealed that Hendrix played bass and then added a guitar track to Mansfield's vocals. The session took place at New York City's Dimensional Studios (a.k.a. Studio 76 Inc.) where Chalpin recorded many of the Curtis Knight–Hendrix tracks. "As the Clouds Drift By" (London HL 80065) featured Mansfield on lead vocal, with a string section, piano, over-echoed drums, and female background singers. Chalpin told me that Hendrix played on both "As the Clouds Drift By" and the B-side, "Suey." However, Hendrix can be heard more prominently on the latter. "Suey" was probably written in all of ten minutes. With silly lyrics breathlessly delivered by Mansfield, like "It makes my knees freeze" and "It makes my liver quiver," this bump-and-grind tune was no doubt a

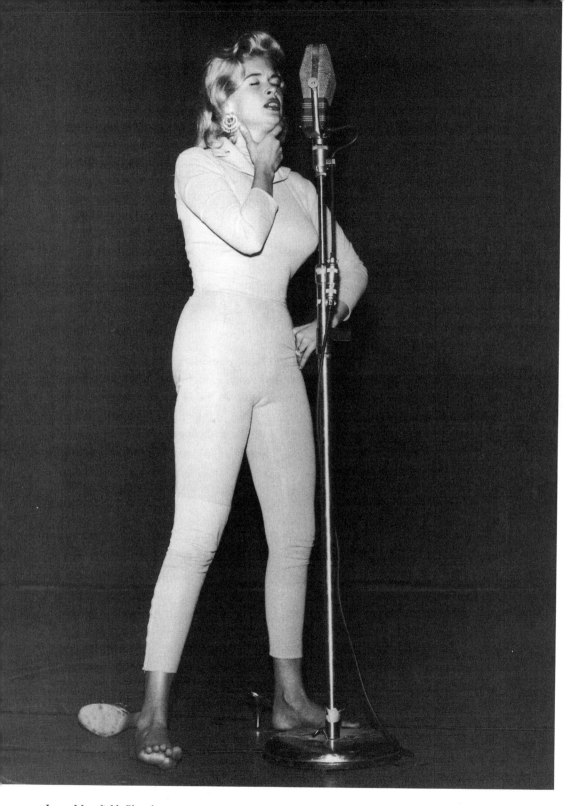

Jayne Mansfield. *Photofest*

quick filler for the flip side. Chalpin added that Hendrix was in the studio while Mansfield sang; it is interesting to imagine the two exchanging glances. In addition to Hendrix's walking bass line and guitar work on "Suey," this song has a drummer, an organist, and two trumpets.

Chalpin told me one of the other session players for the Mansfield recording was the late Philadelphia deejay, Douglas "Jocko" Henderson, who was sometimes referred to as "the black Dick Clark." Henderson did a morning show on New York's WLIB and then an evening show on Philadelphia's legendary WDAS. Henderson also staged R&B revues at Loews State Theater and the Apollo in Harlem.

On April 14, 1967, Mansfield attended a Jimi Hendrix Experience show in Bolton, England. She was in town for a performance two days later at the same theater.[50] On June 29, 1967, while on her way to fill in for the stage version of "Gentlemen Prefer Blondes," Mansfield died in a car accident. The single "As the Clouds Drift By" b/w "Suey" was released a few weeks later, on July 21.

STATUS: *This Mansfield single may be the most bizarre recording with which Hendrix was involved. In 1994, the Legend label officially released Jayne Mansfield: Too Hot to Handle (CD 6008). This CD contained the obscure recordings "As the Clouds Drift By" and "Suey," along with Mansfield's other attempted vocal works. The nifty package included a 3-D pop-up of Mansfield, a picture disc, and a twenty-four-page booklet. However, there is no mention of Hendrix in the liner notes.*

I used to have these dreams then. It sounds a bit silly, but it's the honest-to-God's truth. I used to dream in Technicolor that 1966 was the year that something would happen to me. So eventually it's come true, 1966 is my year in Technicolor.

JIMI HENDRIX, *OPEN CITY*, AUGUST 24, 1967

CHAPTER FOUR

MY OWN SCENE, MY OWN MUSIC: 1966

endrix's premonition of good fortune for 1966 came true, but not without a few bumps along the way. In a postcard sent home to his father on January 13, he expressed his grief with life in the big city: "Everything's so-so here in this big raggedy city of New York. Everything's happening bad here…tell Ben and Ernie I play the blues like they NEVER heard."[1] But shortly after he wrote this postcard, his luck began to change.

In 1966, Hendrix found the opportunity to develop his own style and break free from playing behind R&B headliners. "I always wanted more than that," he later told the *New York Times*. "I was just passing time till then. I wanted my own scene, my own music, not playing the same riffs."[2]

After a few gigs and sessions with legendary R&B saxophonist King Curtis, Hendrix eventually got to Greenwich Village, where he wrote hundreds of songs and played what he called "my rock-blues-funky-freak sound."[3] The people and musicians in the Village were more friendly and accepting of him than Harlem audiences had been. He no longer felt like an outcast and didn't have to beg his way onto a bandstand. He dropped the high-conked pompadour image and settled on an unkempt mane of bushy hair.

Hendrix arrived on the Greenwich Village scene at a time of neighborhood conflict. Local residents wanted to get rid of the congestion and loitering in the area that was caused by young people who enjoyed the music and carefree lifestyle. A letter from an angry youth to the *Village Voice* summed up the situation: "You didn't like the way we dressed. You didn't like the way we looked. You didn't like our guitars. You didn't like our long hair, but my dear pretentious hypocritical prejudiced zombies, it was really our zest and love of life that you do not like. We are not evil, it is you who are evil. Well, you might get rid of MacDougal Street, but you will never get rid of us. You are the past, we are the future."[4]

After several months of determined performing in the Village, Hendrix and his howling guitar and charismatic stage presence began to ignite the local music scene. Had it not been for a few fortunate events, he couldn't have continued on very much longer. "We were making something near $3 a night," Hendrix later recalled. "You know we were starving...I don't think I could have stood another year playing behind people."[5] What he lacked was a manager to help expose him to a bigger audience, but that would soon change. "I was living off sympathy until my English friend appeared from nowhere," he later added, "and persuaded Chas Chandler to come down where I was gigging and give an ear."[6] Hendrix's Technicolor dream was about to become reality.

King Curtis and the All Stars

On January 21, 1966, Hendrix took a break from playing with Curtis Knight and the Squires to do recordings in New York for legendary R&B sax player King Curtis (Curtis Ousley). The session produced the single "Help Me (Get the Feeling) (Parts 1 & 2)" (Atco 45-6402). He then joined King Curtis's band, the All Stars, and toured Texas, Oklahoma, and Louisiana in much better conditions than the Chitlin' Circuit.

Cornell Dupree, a rhythm guitar player for King Curtis, said that Curtis had hired Hendrix for his wild guitar playing because he wanted to update his band's sound: "At that time Jimi could do some Albert King, but in a different definition....He wasn't playing the acid thing, it was more R&B, greased...I mean funky!"[7]

It's hard to find any recorded evidence of Hendrix playing those greasy and funky sounds with King Curtis, since many of Curtis's titles are now out of print. "Help Me (Get the Feeling)" credits Ray Sharpe with the King Curtis Orchestra as the artist, and King Curtis, Ray Sharpe, and Cornell Dupree as composers. Session details for "Help Me" show the guitarist as Cornell Dupree; however, vocalist Ray Sharpe claimed that Hendrix played on the session. It is possible that Sharpe confused this date with an unreleased session recorded on November 29, 1965—the first time King Curtis recorded "Help Me." No personnel details are known for that session.

Hendrix joined King Curtis's band on January 13, 1966, and by the end of January, they were on the road playing in Houston, Dallas, and Ft. Worth, Texas. Since the January 21 "Help Me" session is believed to have had Sharpe's vocals dubbed over a rhythm track, it is also possible that his vocals were dubbed in Texas. Hendrix's guitar part may have been overdubbed there, too. In addition to Hendrix on lead guitar and Ray Sharpe on vocals, the other musicians on the session were King Curtis (tenor sax), Melvin Lastie (trumpet), Willie Bridges (baritone sax), Cornell Dupree (rhythm guitar), Chuck Rainey (bass), and Ray Lucas (drums).

Van Morrison deserves credit for the melody of "Help Me," since it so closely resembles his composition "Gloria" (originally released in 1965 by Them). The horn part loosely borrows from another song of that era as well, "Watermelon Man," a Top 10 hit for Mongo Santamaria in 1963, and a song King Curtis had previously covered.

In February 1966, King Curtis and the All Stars, now with Hendrix in tow, toured Oklahoma, Louisiana, and California. At the end of April, the band entered Atlantic's recording studios in New York City. The personnel shown on the musicians' union session sheets for April 28 were Ray Sharpe (vocal), King Curtis (tenor sax), Jimmy Hendrix (guitar), Cornell Dupree (guitar), Chuck Rainey (bass), and Bernard Purdie (drums). The session produced "Linda Lou," "I Can't Take It," and "Baby How About You." These unreleased missing tracks may have been destroyed in a 1978 Atco/Atlantic warehouse fire. It is possible, however, that some of them were mastered for a future release and sent to another location. Typically, unissued material that was never mastered was destroyed, but there are a few exceptions to the rule:

- Anything that had been sent abroad for release was saved. Apparently, there were some unissued Guitar Slim sides, for example, that survived because tapes were sent to Japan at the time.[8]

- There is also a theory that anything recorded in studios other than Atlantic would probably exist as a rough studio tape, *if* it could be located.

- Some producers, such as Leiber and Stoller, made multiple versions of recordings and kept the alternates.[9]

- A second Atlantic warehouse stored much of the unissued material. However, only persons with access to the Atlantic vaults can verify whether there are any unissued items there.

There may be more King Curtis–Hendrix tracks elsewhere in other vinyl graveyards. In 1968, a Swedish reporter asked Hendrix about a King Curtis record released in Sweden with Hendrix's name on the jacket. He responded, "On that record I'm just one of the several guitar players in the studio. On many of the tracks, I don't play one single note.... It's King Curtis's record all the way through."[10] The LP Hendrix was probably referring to is *The Loving Feeling* (released April 1966, Atco 33-189). However, none of the six tracks that identified the session guitar players listed Hendrix, or even anyone in King Curtis's own band. King Curtis archivist Ray Simonds described the record as lacking a familiar sound: "There's hardly any evidence of guitarists at all. It's a very middle-of-the-road thing."[11] If this were the album in question, it wouldn't be the first (or the last) time Hendrix's name was used to sell a record on which he did not play.

May turned out to be a roller-coaster ride for Hendrix. At the beginning of the month, Atlantic Records held a party in New York City for all of their recording artists. Hendrix attended, played with King Curtis, and sat in with R&B singers Wilson Pickett and Percy Sledge. Shortly thereafter, King Curtis fired Hendrix.

According to singer Bobby Womack, Hendrix violated Curtis's strict dress code for his band members on stage, a pattern that began during his days with Little Richard. "King Curtis would say, 'I would make him wear a tie and he didn't want to wear no tie,'" Womack recalled. "He would leave the sleeves of his shirt all loose. I would say, 'Man, put these cufflinks in and wear it neat.' He'd say, 'I like it like this.' He'd turn his git-tar down but he would still overshadow a person like King Curtis. When he would play with his teeth, they'd give him an ovation because they thought he was crazy, but the artist at the front would think he was tryin' to take the show."[12] Hendrix was probably fed up with playing the same old tired R&B riffs and decided to play it his own way.

It has also been alleged that Hendrix conceived a daughter during May. Tamika Laurice James was supposedly the result of a short-term live-in relationship with sixteen-year-old Diana Carpenter.[13]

STATUS: *Despite information published elsewhere, no reliable documentation (such as session sheets from the musicians' union) has ever surfaced to confirm that Hendrix played on "Blast Off" (Atlantic 2468), another King Curtis single. "Blast Off" was recorded on May 31, 1966, and offers no recognizable clues that Hendrix is featured. The flip side, "Pata Pata," was recorded on October 20, 1967, and also had no Hendrix involvement. "Help Me (Get the Feeling) (Parts 1 & 2)," the only confirmed King Curtis–Hendrix single, is no longer in print but continues to make the rounds in the collectors' circle.*

A King Curtis album titled Live at Small's Paradise *(originally released on Atco 33-198) was recorded on July 22, 1966, about a month after Hendrix left the band. Although there was no Hendrix involvement with this record, the release gives a good example of the music he was most likely playing live as one of King Curtis's All Stars. The tracks on* Live At Small's Paradise *include: "Tough Talk," "Philly Dog," "Preach," "Blowin' in the Wind," "Peter Gunn/Get Along Cindy," "Pots and Pans," "The Shadow of Your Smile," "Road Runner," "Something on Your Mind," and "Soul Theme."*

Jimi James and the Blue Flames

I just got tired, man, I just couldn't stand it anymore. So I just went down to the Village and got my own little group together named The Rain Flowers. We had two names, The Rain Flowers and The Blue Flames, any one of those names is all right, you know.

Jimi Hendrix, Swedish radio interview, May 28, 1967

After being fired by King Curtis, Hendrix rejoined the Squires for a two-week run (May

12–25) at New York's Cheetah Club (Broadway at 53rd Street). The Cheetah, which had just opened, featured three floors of dancing, underground movies, and a boutique that sold the daring new topless swimsuit. The *New York Times* called the Cheetah "A nice noisy home-away-from-home where one can frug without appearing to conform."[14] Hendrix abruptly quit the Squires but returned to the Cheetah as guitarist for the R&B group Carl Holmes and the Commanders for a brief gig (May 27–June 3) he got through the New York musicians' union.

Now on his own, without a band or a steady engagement, Hendrix found a comfortable environment in New York's Greenwich Village to explore his creative musical ideas. Bob Kulick, a fellow Village guitar player in 1966, described the bohemian musical scene back then: "At that time, Greenwich Village was New York's equivalent of San Francisco's Haight-Ashbury. At night and on weekends the streets were packed. You could walk around and see tremendous talents like the Lovin' Spoonful, Richie Havens, Mike Bloomfield, and Paul Butterfield. Hendrix was obviously drawn to the Village because of the scene and because he was accepted."[15]

Hendrix took the advice of folksinger Richie Havens, who had suggested that he leave Harlem and, as he put it, "Get your behind to the Village now!"[16] Havens says he was completely amazed when he first saw Hendrix perform at the Cheetah with Carl Holmes and the Commanders. He couldn't quite figure out how Hendrix was playing the guitar with his teeth, so he actually got on the floor and tried looking up under the stage for a better view. After the show, Havens pulled him aside and told him to go to the Café Wha?, a tiny Greenwich Village coffeehouse at 117 MacDougal Street with a club in the basement, and ask for the owner, Manny Roth (David Lee Roth's uncle). Havens coached Hendrix: "You can do this, you can do your own thing . . . you don't need to be backing up other people."[17]

Hendrix visited many Greenwich Village coffeehouses and clubs before forming his own group. Some bands remember seeing him with pad and paper taking notes, which led them to ask what he was doing.[18] He disarmed them by carrying on a friendly conversation about music that would lead to a jam. He grew his hair long and bushy, started listening to Bob Dylan, and began hanging out with the poets and former beatniks in the neighborhood. He eventually found a loft on Hudson Street with roommates Buzzy Linhart, Roger McGuinn, and David Crosby—fellow performers seeking new musical directions.

At the MacDougal Street café called the Cock n' Bull, Hendrix discovered Tim Rose's rendition of "Hey Joe" on the jukebox. Rose, like Hendrix, was a struggling Greenwich Village singer and guitarist. He recorded "Hey Joe (You Shot Your Woman Down)" (Columbia 4-43648) in April 1966, but his version never entered the national charts. Many groups from this era, like the Leaves, covered the song at a fast tempo, but Rose played it slowly and began with a distinctive blues-based guitar lick.[19] Hendrix was so inspired by Rose's slow version that he began including "Hey Joe" in the set list of his new group, Jimi James and the Blue Flames.

Hendrix called his new band the Blue Flames for two reasons: it had worked for blues

An ad for the Cheetah Club announcing Curtis Night [*sic*], May 12, 1966.
Originally appeared in the Village Voice. © *Village Voice Media*

singer Junior Parker, and it conveniently rhymed with James. Every now and then Hendrix switched the group's name to the Rain Flowers, probably just for fun. This was also the period when he changed the spelling of his first name. Carol Shiroky, his girlfriend at the time, recalled that the Café Wha? had a blackboard in front, where Hendrix insisted on spelling his first name "Jimi," not "Jimmy." She further asserted that Chas Chandler, Hendrix's soon-to-be manager, may have been responsible for giving him his last name back, but "Jimi was the one responsible for spelling his [first] name that way. That was something very personal with him," she said, "for whatever reason, I don't know."[20]

Hundreds of Hendrix's handwritten songs were left behind in the various seedy hotels that he was thrown out of when he couldn't pay rent in 1966. They have nearly all long since disappeared. One that survived was a poem Hendrix wrote and gave to Carol Shiroky in 1966. During my interview with her, Shiroky told me Hendrix wrote it in disgust over working with Curtis Knight and playing repetitive material. She said he got up from bed in the middle of the night and wrote the poem, threw it at her, told her to read it, and then went back to bed. The name of the poem was "My friends of fashion turned out to be my enemies of thought."

Jimi James and the Blue Flames played the Café Wha? for a little over three months. Here, Hendrix debuted his version of "Wild Thing" on June 26, Shiroky's birthday. "He came home one night asking me if I'd heard that song [the Troggs' #1 single] on the radio. He came flying out of the bathroom, butt-ass naked . . . picked up his guitar and started playing it."[21]

The Blue Flames included Randy Wolfe (rhythm guitar), Randy Palmer (bass), and Danny Casey (drums). Since there were two band members named Randy, Hendrix called Wolfe (who formed the rock group Spirit in 1967) "Randy California" to distinguish him from the Texas-born Palmer, whom he called "Randy Texas." Randy California remembered: "I didn't even know his name was Hendrix. I always thought it was Jimi James! I think Jimi kind of protected me from some of the stuff back then because I was so young. I remember the music, being tired at 12:30 at night, and having to take the subway back home."[22]

Hendrix had initially met the fifteen-year-old Wolfe at Manny's Music. "He [Hendrix] was in the back of the store playing a Strat," Wolfe recalled. "Our eyes caught each other and I asked him if I could show him things I learned on the guitar. He then gave me the Strat and I played him slide guitar. He really liked it and invited me to come down that night, which I believe was his first night of this gig at the Café Wha? I don't think he played anything solo before then. Some type of real spiritual affinity or connection happened between us. It was like we knew each other."[23]

When Hendrix wanted to practice at the Café Wha? in the afternoon, he occasionally jammed with "Frankie Drums" (as Frank Von Elmo was nicknamed then), a fifteen-year-old drummer who played hooky from school. "Our jams would last about ten to fifteen minutes," Von Elmo recalled. "He was very much into the blues. It sounded like B.B. King on acid. He would throw out tunes and I would fill in the beats. The sessions that I did with Jimi were recorded, but he kept the recordings. Jimi would tape everything."[24]

On one occasion, bass player Randy Palmer got sick and Jeff Baxter (later of Steely Dan and the Doobie Brothers) filled in. Baxter recalled the circumstances: "I played on and off for a while with Jimi James and the Blue Flames. I was working at Manny's music shop, and I made a guitar trade with Hendrix. I traded him a white Stratocaster for a Duo-Sonic. I said, 'Here is the guitar for you. I'll string it left-handed, you'll love it,' and from then on he started playing the Strat. He was working at the Café Wha? and he said, 'Why don't you come down some night?' And then one time his bass player got sick and I went down and sat in playing bass....I played with him for about two months. That whole R&B guitar style that we take for granted now grew out of what Jimi was doing. It's been integrated into most guitarists' work, but in many cases they don't even realize how much of it originated with Jimi."[25]

Jimi James and the Blue Flames mostly played cover songs of mid-'60s hits in a funky bar band style. Hendrix played songs that he would carry over into the Experience: "Hey Joe," "Like a Rolling Stone," "Wild Thing," and "Mr. Bad Luck" (a.k.a. "Look Over Yonder"). He also paid tribute to his R&B roots with "In the Midnight Hour," "Shotgun," and "Mercy, Mercy." Hendrix's Village friend Paul Caruso fondly remembers them playing the Beatles' song "Rain" with the bass player singing the backward part at the end. Other eyewitnesses assert that Hendrix and the Blue Flames performed embryonic versions of "Third Stone from the Sun" and "Foxy Lady."[26]

On one occasion, Hendrix had the opportunity to meet his musical idol, Bob Dylan. Greenwich Village in 1960 became a regular hangout for folk musicians, but by 1966, the mood had changed. Dylan's hair was now shoulder-length and some of his lyrics were drug-oriented. His single "Rainy Day Women #12 & 35" was being banned by radio stations because of its double-entendre chorus, "Everybody must get stoned." Hendrix later remembered that their meeting at the Kettle of Fish, another club on MacDougal Street, was more hysterical than historical: "I saw him [Dylan] one time, but both of us were stoned out of our minds. I remember it vaguely....We were both stoned there, and we just hung around laughing. Yeah, we just laughed."[27]

After only a month in the Village, Hendrix began to be noticed. Richie Havens introduced him to record producer Giorgio Gomelsky, whose prior production credits included the British acts the Yardbirds, the Kinks, and Brian Auger. Gomelsky had just arrived from England and brought with him renowned session guitarist Jimmy Page, who later joined the Yardbirds and went on to form Led Zeppelin. Although nothing ever came of this meeting, the buzz was just beginning among producers and managers about the new raw talent in their midst.

The Rolling Stones arrived in New York on July 2 during their fifth North American tour. After their concert in Forest Hills, Queens, guitarist Keith Richards, his girlfriend Linda Keith, and the rest of the Stones went to the famous discotheque Ondine's, where Hendrix was performing with the Blue Flames. Some reports say that Hendrix was more polished at Ondine's than at his performances later in July at the Café Wha?[28] Although Linda Keith wasn't very impressed with the band, she gravitated toward the guitarist who played solos behind his head. While Richards was away on tour, Linda had a brief relationship with Hendrix, who stayed with her for about a week at the Rockefeller Center Hilton.

During this time, Hendrix wasn't paying attention and someone walked off with the white Stratocaster that Carol Shiroky had purchased for him several weeks earlier. In an effort to help him, Linda borrowed Keith Richards's new white Stratocaster for Hendrix's upcoming audition with two well-known record producers. According to Shiroky, when Richards discovered his guitar was missing he wasn't very happy: "Keith Richards came down to the Café Wha? with a gun wanting to blow Jimi's head off! He had Keith Richards gunning for him, but they managed to talk it out."[29] Shiroky also recalled that Linda introduced Hendrix to LSD at this time. "I remember I had to go look for him. He said, 'I met these English people, and this English chick...and, oh by the way, she gave me this drug called acid, and at one point I looked into the mirror and thought I was Marilyn Monroe.'"[30]

While Hendrix finally had his own band together, it was hard for him to make decent money. Randy California later recalled that the Blue Flames played five sets a night, six nights a week at "pass the hat" clubs, where they only brought in "seven or eight bucks a night"[31] shared among all the band members. This arrangement was common at the time, since certain Village coffeehouses avoided the legal hurdles to obtaining a cabaret license by simply not paying their bands and letting them work for tips.

John Hammond, Jr. (son of Columbia Records talent scout and producer, John Hammond, Sr.), was playing blues down the street at the Café au Go Go (152 Bleecker Street). Hammond, Jr., came in one August night to watch Jimi James and the Blue Flames at the Café Wha? He was so taken by the set that he asked Hendrix to back up his band. Hendrix gratefully accepted the offer. While this brought him a little more money, he had to run between the two clubs to earn it. Luckily, Hammond did only two sets per night. In the middle of a set, Hammond would stop and introduce Hendrix and let him play two songs. Hammond arranged a two-week booking at the Café au Go Go where "everybody who's who came to hear us: Bob Dylan, the Beatles [who played Shea Stadium in August], and the Animals all came in."[32]

Jeremy and the Satyrs were an early jazz-rock fusion group enjoying an extended run at the Café au Go Go when Hendrix sat in with them. Mike Mainieri, the Satyrs' vibist, recalled, "It was like being around Miles [Davis]. You knew you were in the presence of greatness, someone doing something really original. No one had to tell you, you knew. Those days sitting-in was common, you went to hear music and you never knew who might turn up. We just played the blues, but Jimi played the shit out of them. And yes, he influenced young jazz musicians. I wanted that volume and I wanted to bend those notes like he did. So, I got an echoplex and worked out a way to do it on vibes. Those were exciting times."[33]

The Café au Go Go also had a Sunday evening "Blues Bag" jam session until 4:00 A.M. featuring new blues artists like Paul Butterfield, Elvin Bishop, and Michael Bloomfield. Hendrix would come to watch and occasionally sit in. "Hendrix knew who I was, and that day, in front of my eyes, going off, missiles were flying—I can't tell you the sounds he was getting out of his instrument," Bloomfield remembered. "He was getting every sound I was to ever hear him get right there in the room with a Stratocaster, a Fender Twin Reverb amp, a Maestro Fuzz Tone, and that was all. He was doing it mainly through extreme volume. How he did this, I wish I understood."[34]

Folksinger Ellen McIlwaine (whose stage name was Judy Roderick at that time) was playing guitar and piano at the Café au Go Go when Hendrix came in and asked her if he could accompany her. McIlwaine described the scene: "There were about five acts. And I

An ad for one of Hendrix's final shows at the Café au Go Go with
John Hammond, Jr., September 13, 1966. He was billed as the "Blue Flame."
Originally appeared in the Village Voice. © *Village Voice Media*

made a dollar fifty a night [laughs]. One night...John Hammond came to play...the
backup band was Jimi Hendrix and his band. We sort of got to know each other, hanging
around backstage and stuff, and after that week finished Jimi came back in and said, 'Can I
come back and play with you?' I fell on the floor and then I picked myself up. And I said,
'Sure!' So he did and mostly I played piano and he played guitar, and he sat down. I'd never
seen him do this before or since. And it was probably a strange experience for him to play
with a woman. In folk, there were a lot of women, but not in rock 'n' roll. He sat down and
he didn't try to steal the show, and he didn't do all his gyrating or anything. And he played
very gently and very sensitive, and it really was an experience. Anybody that got hold of
him sensed that he'd be very famous. He was shy and very withdrawn, he didn't speak a lot,
and music was everything to him."[35]

Several previously published books on Hendrix have placed Bryan "Chas" Chandler's
initial discovery of Hendrix on July 5, 1966. After further research, I discovered that they
met on August 3, when Chandler was in New York during the Animals' final U.S. tour, performing at the Rheingold Central Park Music Festival.[36] Chandler, then playing bass with
the Animals, recalled: "The night before we were to play in Central Park, someone played
me Tim Rose's version of 'Hey Joe.'...Later that evening...Linda Keith...told me she was
going out with this guy in the Village that I had to see. So, I made arrangements to meet

her the next afternoon. I went down to the Village again and saw Jimi James and the Blue Flames at the Café Wha?"[37] Guitarist Bob Kulick continues the story: "One afternoon Jimi played at the Café Wha? and Chas Chandler was there. Chas sat in the back, and I remember him being so impressed with Hendrix that he knocked a milkshake all over himself."[38]

Chandler set up a series of meetings with Hendrix at a bar across the street, and discussed what it would be like if he went to England to perform. After one meeting, Hendrix asked Randy California if he'd like to join him, but California was too young to take that bold step. Chandler's courting continued and he was astonished that Hendrix's talents had gone unnoticed. "I just sat there and thought to myself, 'There's got to be a catch here somewhere, somebody must have signed him up years ago.' I just couldn't believe that this guy was just standing around and nobody was doing anything for him."[39] Chandler did discover that Hendrix was still under some minor contracts, which he was able to buy out, but Hendrix neglected to mention the Chalpin PPX contract, which would cause frustrations in years to come.

The real clincher in Chandler's proposal was the offer for Hendrix to meet the legendary British guitarist Eric Clapton. In a 1992 radio interview, Chandler explained: "He had a lot of doubts about coming to England. His actual words to me at the time were, 'What's the point in me coming to England as a guitar player? You've got Eric Clapton and Jeff Beck over there. You don't need one more guitar player.' And then he turned around and said, 'If you can guarantee that you'll introduce me to Clapton, I'll come to London.'"[40] Shortly after this discussion, Chandler made the necessary arrangements for Hendrix to travel overseas.

STATUS: *Unknown. Randy California was reported to have a tape of Jimi James and the Blue Flames performing live. California died on January 2, 1997, drowning off the coast of Molokai, Hawaii. Before his death, California was working on an album, subsequently released as* California Blues *(Crew 2204), on which he performed a version of "Mr. Bad Luck" (a.k.a. "Look Over Yonder"), which he said he cowrote with Hendrix during the Café Wha? period. No other club recordings have surfaced.*

The Jimi Hendrix Experience

They didn't want to let me in.

Jimi Hendrix, *Rave,* February 1967

On Friday, September 23, Hendrix sat in first class on a flight from John F. Kennedy International Airport, New York, to London's Heathrow Airport. His new manager, Chas Chandler, and Terry McVay, the Animals' road manager, accompanied him. Hendrix traveled light, packing only his guitar, a bag with hair rollers, and a jar of Valderma cream for his blemished complexion.

When the plane landed, Hendrix and his management had a six-hour argument with immigration officials. Chandler convinced them to allow Hendrix into the U.K. because he was the composer of several songs and had come to Britain, among other reasons, to collect his royalties. Hendrix told *Rave* magazine in February 1967, "They carried on like I was going to make all this money in England and take it back to the States." When the issues were resolved, Hendrix and Chandler checked into the Hyde Park Towers. A few hours later, Hendrix got his first taste of jamming in England at the Scotch of St. James Club.

In 1966, Kathy Etchingham was an attractive twenty-year-old hairdresser by day, and at night she was a deejay at the trendy Cromwellian Club in London, a hangout for the likes of John Lennon, Keith Moon, and Eric Clapton. Etchingham lived upstairs from pianist George "Zoot" Money and his wife Ronni. Shortly after Chandler and Hendrix arrived in England, Ronni told Etchingham that Chandler had brought back a wild-looking guy from America and everyone was invited down to the Scotch of St. James Club to see him play guitar. Etchingham described the atmosphere when Hendrix made his first public perform-ance in England: "The whole club was absolutely still, like something special was going on. I fought my way through the crowds and we stood there and watched."[41] Chas Chandler then pulled his new discovery off the stage because British immigration had assigned Hendrix a seven-day non-work permit with restrictions—if he were caught working, with or without pay, he would be sent back home.[42]

Chandler introduced Hendrix to Etchingham, who recalled, "Jimi leaned over towards me and said, 'I want to tell you something.' He then kissed my ear, and said, 'I think you're beautiful.' When we arrived back at the hotel, Jimi looked at me and said, 'Should we go to my room?' and I said 'Yes, all right then.' So I went off to his room...I stayed...that was it."[43] Hendrix and Etchingham became lovers and stayed lifelong friends.

Drummer Jim Capaldi (Traffic) had a group in 1966 called Deep Feeling. Capaldi remembers what must have been another one of Hendrix's early jams in England: "When Chas first brought Jimi to England, the first proper gig that he brought him to was ours. We didn't have a set...he [Hendrix] just came up and said, 'Blues in E.' He just had a guitar and plugged in the same equipment. We were all impressed. Dave Meredith, our bass player, said that they [Chandler and Hendrix] really liked us and wanted us to audition."[44]

A few days later, Chandler began assembling Hendrix's new band. One of the first recruits was Noel Redding, who originally auditioned for a guitarist slot in the New Animals. Eric Burdon was in charge of the auditions and remembered, "Chas [Chandler] knew I was putting a new band together and that I was looking for a guitar player. Noel Redding had come to audition. I was giving him the 'don't call us, we'll call you' routine, when I noticed Jimi standing in the back of the room. As Noel was leaving, Jimi grabbed a hold of him and asked, 'Do you want to play bass?' We did get a chance to jam before they all left."[45] After signing Redding, Chandler spent the following week auditioning drummers.

One week after arriving in England, Hendrix not only met Eric Clapton, but also played on stage with the hard-rock power trio Cream. Several accounts have stated that he first approached Clapton about jamming, but Cream bassist Jack Bruce insists that he met Hendrix first, in a pub just a few hours before Cream's show at Polytechnic College in London. "This

The Jimi Hendrix Experience, 1966. *Left to right:* Noel Redding, Jimi Hendrix, Mitch Mitchell.
Pictorial/Star File

person came up to me and said, 'Oh hello, I'm Jimi Hendrix. I'd like to sit in with the band.' And I said, 'Well, people don't usually do that! But you know, you're welcome, but you'll have to ask the other guys.' Which he did, and he sat in and he blew us all away. I've got a [Cream] tape of the next day.... Eric was trying to play [like] Jimi, and failing miserably."[46]

Cream's drummer, Ginger Baker, initially had a negative reaction to Hendrix's performance with the band: "Jimi met Jack and Eric without me being around. So I arrived at the gig and Jack came up to me and said, 'Hey man, Jimi Hendrix is here and he wants to sit in with us.' I said, 'Who the fuck's Jimi Hendrix?' Jack said, 'He's this great American guitar player,' and I said, 'Yeah, but we got a guitar player...Eric's a guitar player.' Nobody ever sat in with us before or afterwards. It took some convincing. So, Jimi appeared on stage and was playing quite good...then he started his showmanship bullshit. Our music was good enough, and we didn't have to get into all sorts of gyrations and pretend to fuck the guitar. At this point he lost me...it left me totally cold."[47]

Hendrix's first song with Cream was Howlin' Wolf's blues classic "Killin' Floor." He also played one other song that has never been identified. Clapton has said that Hendrix immediately stole the show, partly due to his magnificent talent and partly due to the fact that Ginger Baker and Jack Bruce had never heard Howlin' Wolf's song before. In 1998, Clapton told *Mojo* magazine: "It was phenomenal, but then again you can do that if you walk on stage like that, because they [Cream] have already given you the power of inviting you on. Especially since I'd never met him or seen him before. How could you possibly compete with that? I was unprepared, man."[48]

Sitting in the audience for Cream's concert was another famous English guitarist, Jeff Beck, from the Yardbirds, Clapton's former band. Beck described the experience: "Along comes Jimi, who sits in and upsets the whole apple cart—playing with his teeth...doing almost circus tricks with the guitar. Even if it was crap—which it wasn't—it got to the press. People wanted that. They were starved for theater and outrage. None of us realized that someone would come along and whip the carpet out from under us in quite such a radical way."[49] Unfortunately, no photos or recordings have ever surfaced to document this historic musical event.

After seeing Hendrix's victorious challenge to Clapton's guitar throne, Chandler's next concern was to locate a drummer for the band. John "Mitch" Mitchell, heavily influenced by jazz drummer Elvin Jones, made the final cut. He recalled the circumstances of the rehearsals: "Chas called me up and said, 'If you're interested you should come and play with this guy who is the best thing you've ever seen on two legs that plays guitar.' It was apparent that he was a good guitarist, but at that stage, I was more knocked out that he could cover so many styles as well. I think we did 'Have Mercy Babe' [Covay's "Mercy, Mercy"] first."[50] After the first rehearsal, Chandler called Mitchell the next day and told him if he would like to join the band, there were a week's worth of gigs lined up in France with Johnny Hallyday (the French Elvis Presley).

Hendrix, Redding, and Mitchell, as the Jimi Hendrix Experience, signed a seven-year contract on October 11 with co-managers Chandler and Michael Jeffery. Two days later, a concert in Evreux, France, marked the first public appearance of the Jimi Hendrix Experience. *L'Eure Éclair*, a French newspaper, reported, "Johnny Hallyday's latest discovery was a singer and guitar player with bushy hair, a bad mixture of James Brown and Chuck Berry, who pulled a wry face onstage for a quarter of an hour and also played the guitar with his teeth. He ended the first half of the concert that was followed by a long pause."[51] No recordings from this debut show are known to exist, but a concert played five days later (October 18, 1966) at the Olympia in Paris was recorded and broadcast on French radio. Two songs from this show, "Killin' Floor" and "Hey Joe," are featured on *The Jimi Hendrix Experience*, a box set released in 2000. The third and final song in the set, "Wild Thing," has never been released.

After returning from France, Chandler prepared the Experience to record a debut single, "Hey Joe," on October 23. The arrangement was simple and resembled Tim Rose's version in many respects: text, key, tempo, opening blues-guitar riff, and choral backing. However, Hendrix's arrangement "transforms the original bass into a guitar plus bass melodic riff that resembles those of Motown's James Jamerson."[52] To embellish the basic recording, Chandler brought in a popular female vocal trio, the Breakaways (Jean Hawker, Margot Newman, and Vicki Brown). Touted by *Melody Maker* as "three working mums who earn lots of loot," the Breakaways worked with popular performers like Dusty Springfield, Lulu, and Cilla Black.[53]

One of the many interesting outtakes to surface in recent years was an early demo version of "Hey Joe" with Hendrix adding his lead vocal track. As he starts to sing the first line, he is caught off guard by his nervous voice coming in clearly through the headphones, and he says, "Oh, Goddamn!" He tells Chandler in the booth, "Hey, make the voice a little lower and the band a little louder." Hendrix was always insecure about his vocal talents, but thought if Dylan could swing it, surely so could he.

With the A-side completed, Chandler need to fill the flip side. Originally, Hendrix talked about doing a cover of "Land of 1000 Dances," a 1966 hit for Wilson Pickett, but Chandler explained the advantages of writing his own material and the resulting publishing royalties. Hendrix was inspired to pen "Stone Free" on October 24 after a jam with Deep Feeling at the Knuckles Club in London. "'Stone Free' was written, totally arranged in one night," Chandler later recalled. "We sat together, and I encouraged him just to express himself, write about how he felt, about the women around, everything, and that's what he did. We'd work on arrangements closely together on those kinds of songs, but there'd still be things he came up with that amazed me."[54] Hendrix based "Stone Free" on his own experiences as a struggling musician on the road. Even his previous R&B influences shine through this song as the bass line comes close to Rufus Thomas's "Philly Dog." "Hey Joe" b/w "Stone Free" (Polydor 56139) was released in England on December 16, and peaked at #6 on the British charts.

A major shift came about in the British recording industry during 1966. British companies like Phillips and Pye, which started their own distribution networks, splintered EMI and Decca's long-term domination of the hit parade. By midyear, the major record labels began dealing with independent producers, who started gaining recognition with their hits on the charts. Kit Lambert and Chris Stamp, managers of the Who, planned to launch their new independent label, Track, during 1967. Lambert and Stamp originally wanted to issue "Hey Joe" on Track in time for the 1966 holiday season, but instead they struck a deal with Polydor to release the single on December 16, 1966, since Track was not yet ready for business. "Hey Joe" charted during the first few weeks of January 1967 and stayed in the Top 30 for eight weeks alongside established artists like the Supremes, Wilson Pickett, Elvis Presley, and Herman's Hermits.

Singer Arthur Brown and his group, The Crazy World of Arthur Brown, had been together for a short while in the latter part of 1966 and shared the Track Records label with Hendrix. Brown recalled Hendrix's first single and how it was promoted: "'Hey Joe' was the first big single that had the effect of being very musically adventurous. Lambert and Stamp were really good image manipulators . . . they gave him a hard image in spite of the fact that he was dressed pretty weird. I don't know that the public initially recognized him for his guitar playing so much, although there were a cadre of people who'd been into Clapton and the blues scene that drew on that. I think that the mass populace had the overall image of the wild man."[55]

Another factor contributing to the success of "Hey Joe" was England's offshore pirate radio stations. These illegal stations began as a free enterprise reaction to the state-run British Broadcasting Corporation (BBC). Since the BBC prohibited advertising, the pirate stations saw a niche and were financially supported by sponsors and advertising revenue. The offshore stations helped promote many new acts, including the Jimi Hendrix Experience.

In exchange for guaranteed airplay by the pirate radio stations, Michael Jeffery reportedly signed away a portion of Hendrix's publishing royalties for "Stone Free." Radio London and Radio Caroline had approximately twenty-two million listeners per week around the time that Hendrix's first single was released on December 16.[56]

On December 1, 1966, Hendrix signed an exclusive four-year recording, management, and publishing contract with Yameta Company Limited, a Bahamian corporation originally developed as a tax shelter for the Animals. The agreement allowed Michael Jeffery to deduct an astounding forty percent from Hendrix's earnings and the British attorney who set up the tax shelter took an additional ten percent. Mitchell and Redding were considered employees of Yameta, but only had a verbal agreement for a percentage of concert receipts. The manipulation of the Experience had started, and other questionable contract arrangements were just around the corner.[57]

Chandler often had Hendrix, with or without Mitchell and Redding, cut demos at the end of a scheduled recording session. He'd then take the reel-to-reel copy home, where he and Hendrix perfected the song and prepared it for a future session. A demo for "Third Stone from the Sun," for example, was cut in December and then revisited in the studio the following month. The result was a combination of two sessions: one at De Lane Lea studios (January 11) and the final segment at Olympic Sound Studios (April 4 and 10), where it was also mixed.

STATUS: *Several unauthorized raw session tapes of the Experience's first visits to the studio have filtered out to the public. Unedited versions of "51st Anniversary" and "Can You See Me," recorded on November 2, 1966, have also surfaced, as well as four takes of "Hey Joe" and an instrumental version of the R&B song "I Can't Turn You Loose," with horns and organ, recorded on November 24, 1966. These have appeared on the bootlegs* **Olympic Gold: Volumes 1 and 2,** *among other titles.*

Written Work in Progress

"Ain't No Telling" was part of the first batch of songs Hendrix penned when he arrived in England; it appears on Hyde Park Towers stationery. This early concept for the song contains Hendrix's three-step program for those having relationship problems: "1. Don't answer the phone, 'cause it might be your baby. 2. Don't act the fool when she arrives. 3. After breakfast, look at your watch and say, 'It's time to pack.'"[58] Hendrix wrote his set list for the January 14, 1967, gig at the Beachcombers Club in Nottingham on the front side of the stationery. He returned to the idea for the song almost nine months later when it was recorded at Olympic Sound Studios on October 26, 1967.

In the song "Are You Experienced," Hendrix refers to "trumpets and violins/I can hear in the distance...." The idea first came about from a short poem he wrote in late 1966 or early 1967 titled "Trumpets and Violins, Violins." This beautiful poem is filled with colorful images like "wine colored tears," "the purple sands," and "the sunset whisper of trumpets and violins." The poem was never recorded, but was auctioned off by Sotheby's for $1,760 in 1990.

Star Club, Hamburg, Germany, March 1967. *Günter Zint/K&K/Star File*

Everywhere I go they tell me about one group who got up like us and the fella tried to play the guitar with his teeth and his teeth fell out all over the stage. That's what you get for not brushing your teeth I tell 'em! You can't be too careful.

JIMI HENDRIX, *NEW MUSICAL EXPRESS*, MAY 13, 1967

CHAPTER FIVE

THE EXPERIENCE BEGINS: 1967

With a few gigs and recording sessions now under its belt, the Jimi Hendrix Experience was ready to take on the new challenges that 1967 had to offer. Hendrix's apprenticeship on the Chitlin' Circuit and Chas Chandler's cleverly crafted "wildman" press image paid off with the English audiences. Sure there was Elvis, but they'd never seen a guitar player who took so many moves to the extreme. He played the guitar with his teeth, stroked the neck suggestively, bashed it against the speakers, and at times played it with one hand while pointing to some pretty girl in the back row with the other hand. Mitch Mitchell recalled, "It was pretty freaky for people to see this bizarre black man playing with his teeth with two skinny English boys. For us it was fun. We knew, between the three of us in the band, that the band was cooking."[1]

Journalist Keith Altham wrote, "Hendrix is a one-man guitar explosion with a stage act which leaves those who think pop has gone pretty with their mouths hanging open. What this man does to a guitar could get him arrested for assault."[2] While Altham appreciated Hendrix's showmanship, other critics found the performance too provocative and vulgar. To their charges Hendrix defensively responded, "I don't consider it anything like that. It's a spontaneous action on my part and a fluid thing. It's not an act, but a state of being at the time I'm doing it. My music, my instrument, my sound, my body are all one in action with my mind. What people get from what I do is their scene. It's in the eye of the beholder."[3]

Hendrix's "state of being" onstage heightened the band's profile in the increasingly competitive rock performance scene. Some British bands incorporated open aggression into their acts. Their image and unapologetic destructiveness were natural publicity fodder. The Who often set off exploding smoke bombs and bashed amps, while the Move would destroy cars, axe television sets, and have two women strip in time to the music. Singer Arthur Brown's audiences saw his metal helmet set on fire during the finale of his show.

In order to grab some headlines and not be outdone by these other bands, Hendrix also dabbled in pyrotechnics. On a suggestion or a dare, he set his guitar aflame while performing "Fire" during a show at the Finsbury Park Astoria in England. Mitch Mitchell explained the circumstances: "We thought we've got nothing to lose....What have we got, lighter fluid? Why not? The guitar was an old guitar anyway, you know the stage manager is going to have a heart attack...what have we got to lose?"[4] Chas Chandler continued the story: "We soaked it in petrol and deliberately set light to it. The organizers were running around in circles trying to find the culprit and examine the guitar that had mysteriously disappeared. I distinctly remember [theater agent] Tito Burns waving a fist at me shouting, 'You can't get away with things like this, Chas—if we find that guitar, I'll have you prosecuted.' Of course, we all maintained it was an accident and Jimi even wore a bandage to make it look good."[5] The audience was stunned.

It might be hard to imagine, but there was also a fair amount of Beatlemania-type hysteria associated with the Jimi Hendrix Experience in the band's early days. *Melody Maker* reported in April, "The Experience was mobbed as they went into the Odeon [Blackpool, England]. Jimi lost a lot of hair to girls with scissors, and drummer Mitch Mitchell received leg injuries."[6] Hendrix told Keith Altham in May 1967, "We'd step outside the stage door where the teeny boppers were and think 'Oh they won't bother us' and get torn apart!"[7] Noel Redding wrote in his book *Are You Experienced?*, "We got torn apart coming out of the hall, losing clothes, glasses, hair. Girls in the audience would scream our names louder than we could play our songs."[8] The teenage mass hysteria, while annoying sometimes, only helped to boost record sales.

The Jimi Hendrix Experience kept four singles and two albums in the British charts for three-quarters of 1967. In June, the group had three records chart at the same time: "Purple Haze," "The Wind Cries Mary," and the debut album, *Are You Experienced*. The Experience's British success was recognized by *Variety*, which noted, "Jimi Hendrix has been churning out repeated clicks [successful hits]."

"Purple Haze"

On December 26, 1966, Hendrix wrote the lyrics to "Purple Haze" in his dressing room at the Upper Cut Club in England. The basic track was recorded on January 11 at De Lane Lea studios. Overdubs were done on February 3 and 7 at Olympic Sound Studios. The song became the second Experience single—"Purple Haze" b/w "51st Anniversary" (Track 604001)—and a concert staple for Hendrix, played from 1967 through 1970.

Although both the press and many fans interpreted the song to be about a psychedelic experience, Hendrix later revealed it was about a dream he had that was similar to a story about a purple death ray that he had read in a science fiction magazine. The magazine, it turned out, was *Fantasy and Science Fiction,* and it had run a condensed version of Phillip José Farmer's 1957 novel *Night of Light: Day of Dreams,* which had recently been released in paperback for the first time.[9] Hendrix later told reporter Tom Lopez (a.k.a. Meatball Fulton) how frustrated he was with the shortened version of "Purple Haze" that was released to the public: "The song had about a thousand words.... It just gets me so mad 'cause that isn't even 'Purple Haze.'...You should have heard it, man. I had written it out. It was about going through...through this land. This mythical...because I like to write a lot of mythical songs...like the history of the wars on Neptune."[10]

When reviewing the latest pop singles for *Melody Maker* in 1967, Paul McCartney had this to say about "Purple Haze": "Jimi freaks out and sounds all the better for it. I thought it would be one of the things people might keep down, but it's breaking through all over. You can't stop it. I really don't know if it's as commercial as 'Hey Joe' or 'Stone Free.' I bet it is though. Probably will be. Fingers Hendrix. An absolute ace on the guitar. This is yet another incredible record from the Twinkle Teeth Hendrix!"[11]

In an article entitled "Scene's Wildest Raver," the *New Musical Express* (January 28, 1967) asked Hendrix how he wrote songs: "I dream a lot and I put my dreams down as songs. I wrote one called 'First Look Around the Corner' and another called 'The Purple Haze,' which was about a dream I had that I was walking under the sea." This article jumped the gun a little when it reported: "Most of the tracks for Jimi Hendrix's first LP have now been completed. As yet untitled, it is planned for an early April release by Polydor. The album includes six self-penned numbers, 'Can You See Me,' '51st Anniversary,' 'Third Stone from the Sun,' 'Here He Comes,' 'Foxy Lady,' and 'Purple Haze.'" The article made a few minor mistakes in its list—"51st Anniversary," "Here He Comes," and "Purple Haze" were not on the Track LP—but with "Hey Joe" at #8 in the charts and Hendrix breaking attendance records (1,400 at London's Marquee Club), who cared?

STATUS: *"Purple Haze" was released on March 17 in the U.K. and June 19 in the United States. When it was released in America, Warner/Reprise took the precaution of writing "deliberate distortion, do not correct" on the original tape box. The single was more successful in the U.K., reaching #3; in the States, it only climbed to #65. "Purple Haze" was left off the original British version of* Are You Experienced. *However, when the LP was released in America, it was the album's opening track.*

In 1990, Sotheby's auctioned Hendrix's original handwritten nine-page draft for "Purple Haze — Jesus Saves" (his original title). The lyrics were valued at $8,000–$12,000, but were purchased for $17,600 by the Rock and Roll Hall of Fame.[12]

A unique alternate version of "Purple Haze" with a different ending can be found on The Jimi Hendrix Experience *(MCA 088 112 320-2). Some unofficial releases have included an alternate mix of "Purple Haze" that spotlights Hendrix's eerie whispers and moans, which get lost in the commercial mix.*

Along with "Purple Haze" and "51st Anniversary," "First Look Around the Corner," "Here He Comes," and a demo of "The Wind Cries Mary" were also recorded at De Lane Lea studios on January 11. "First Look Around the Corner" has never been officially released, nor is it available in the collectors' network. Two versions of "Here He Comes," better known as "Lover Man," have been released officially, but neither is from the January 1967 sessions. The 1997 Hendrix CD South Saturn Delta (MCAD-11684) features a version recorded on October 29, 1968, at TTG Studios. The version found on the Jimi Hendrix Experience box set was recorded on April 4, 1967.

The "Fluffy Turkeys" Session

In January, Hendrix attended a recording session for the new progressive rock band Soft Machine, which shared the same management. The group consisted of Robert Wyatt (drums/vocals), Michael Ratledge (keyboards), Daevid Allen (guitar/vocals), and Kevin Ayers (bass/vocals). In Michael King's book on Robert Wyatt, *Wrong Movements*, he reported that a recording session took place for a song called "Fluffy Turkeys," composed by the session's producer, Kim Fowley. Although some details are unclear, there is speculation that the "Fluffy Turkeys" session lineup included Jimi Hendrix (guitar/bass/vocal) and Robert Wyatt (drums/vocal).

King cleared up an old rumor when he wrote that Hendrix did not play on "Feelin', Reelin', Squeelin'," the B-side to the Soft Machine single "Love Makes Sweet Music" (Polydor 56151, produced by Chas Chandler), as once thought. Daevid Allen explained: "Jimi Hendrix and us were both signed to the same management so we found ourselves following each other in and out of various studios throughout various stages of recording and mixing. Yeah, Jimi did some things with us, although nothing was ever used. We tried out different things together."[13]

STATUS: *Unknown. The "Fluffy Turkeys" demo has never surfaced commercially or in the collectors' network. You can hear Hendrix's early influence on guitarist Daevid Allen, however, on an early Soft Machine track called "I Should Have Known"; the guitar tone is almost identical to Hendrix's on "51st Anniversary." None of the Soft Machine–Hendrix recordings that Allen mentioned have ever surfaced.*

The First Major Package Tour

In early February, the British press announced that the Jimi Hendrix Experience was a confirmed act for the Walker Brothers–Engelbert Humperdinck–Cat Stevens tour scheduled to begin on March 31. The Walker Brothers, a pop trio from Los Angeles and the tour's headliner, were more popular in England than in the U.S. At the time, Humperdinck (born

Hendrix backstage with Gary Leeds of the Walker Brothers and Cat Stevens (lower right), spring 1967. This photo was taken at the start of the Experience's first U.K. tour.
Pictorial/Star File

Arnold George Dorsey) was enjoying success with his Top 10 hit ballad "Release Me (and Let Me Love Again)." Cat Stevens offered his brand of folk music on a first single titled "I Love My Dog." How the Experience was supposed to fit in was anybody's guess.

Drummer Mitch Mitchell explained what it was like going on the road with this unusual bill: "In England, we used to have these very strange tours that would go around to the cinemas . . . it was the nearest thing to vaudeville. It was like the end of an era. Five acts, all thrown together on a coach, for say three weeks, and you'd go up and down England, two shows a night. It was the pits in some ways, but there's nothing that has taken its place. In some ways it was pretty fun. A few people on the coach were complaining about us being a bit loud. It was a very young audience. Mums and dads didn't mind their kids going to see these shows because they knew it was all very safe."[14]

Bassist Noel Redding, who had previously worked with Humperdinck doing demos, was asked to play with him again on this tour. "The Experience would typically open the show and Humperdinck would follow," Redding explained. "On the first night of the tour, his guitar player quit. Since I played guitar for him before, I was the only one who could fill in. So after I used to do the spot with the Experience, playing bass, I used to rip around to the other side and there would be a chair there with a guitar and a can of beer. I would play guitar for Humperdinck off stage. I was looking through the hole, watching the cues from Humperdinck and the bass player, while sitting in this chair off stage."[15]

It was not uncommon for musical acts that played harder rock sounds to appear with pop groups, either on tour or in British clubs. Arthur Brown described the English club scene in 1967: "You had the Flamingo Club, which had a circuit that was bringing in black soul [music]. And then you had the Marquee Club, which was starting its circuit...[and] Alexis Korner's Rhythm and Blues, where the Rolling Stones had started. The general scene was an underground beginning of the sort of bluesy stuff, which had been developed for quite awhile with Clapton and such."[16]

In the February 4 issue, *Melody Maker* printed the full schedule for the Jimi Hendrix Experience's English club dates, and Chas Chandler was quoted as saying: "Everything has happened as we hoped and believed it would. We are deciding now whether to release a new single or an album first." In *Melody Maker*'s Pop 50, Hendrix had pushed aside the Rolling Stones' "Let's Spend the Night Together," taking over the #4 slot with "Hey Joe."

The Stones and the Beatles seemed to welcome Hendrix more than fear him. Mick Jagger and other musicians often dropped into London clubs to hear his brilliant guitar playing. Stones bassist Bill Wyman recalled that when the Experience played the Bag o' Nails club on January 11, "The audience read like a *Who's Who* of rock. Paul McCartney, Ringo Starr; Pete Townshend and John Entwistle of the Who; Brian Epstein [the Beatles' manager]; Alan Clark and Bobby Elliott of the Hollies; Eric Clapton, the Small Faces, the Animals, Donovan, Georgie Fame, Denny Laine, and Lulu all marveled at the inspired guitar work of a guy who had been discovered in the States."[17]

STATUS: *There is said to be a sixty-minute tape of the Experience's February 1 gig at the New Cellar Club, but it has yet to debut in the collectors' network. However, there are raw studio takes of "Purple Haze," "La Poupée Qui Fait Non,"[18] and "Fire" from the February 7 session at Olympic Sound Studios. There are four takes of "Red House" and five takes of "I Don't Live Today" from the February 23 session at Olympic Sound Studios in circulation in the collectors' network. An incomplete recording of the February 25 concert at the Corn Exchange, Chelmsford, Essex, England, has recently surfaced. The seven-minute tape features "Like a Rolling Stone" and "Stone Free."*

The Experience's Earliest Known Club Recording

Hendrix, with his flamboyant dress and wild, untamed hair, fit in well with Britain's emerging psychedelic scene. There was plenty of good music at such underground clubs as the UFO (pronounced "you-foe") in London, where Pink Floyd and Soft Machine were the house bands. However, when the Experience played a series of shows at workingmen's clubs in northern England, the scene was much different. Kathy Etchingham explained: "One or two of the clubs were all beer and sawdust...always thick with smoke and the men would sit yelling at each other over the tables with their sleeves rolled up. No one here realized that they were in the presence of the greatest rock talent of Jimi's generation, nor would they have cared if they had."[19]

The Experience's February 2 performance at London's Flamingo Club was unofficially recorded by someone in the audience, allegedly a well-known British guitarist. The forty-six-minute tape captured "Killin' Floor," "Mercy, Mercy," "Can You See Me," "Like a Rolling Stone," "Rock Me Baby," "Catfish Blues," "Stone Free," "Hey Joe," and a version of "Wild Thing" that also included parts of the Beatles' "Day Tripper." This is the earliest known audience recording of the Experience's British club tour. The set list displays some carryovers from Hendrix's R&B days as well as his time spent in Greenwich Village.

On the tape, "Killin' Floor" opens the set, but the recording starts in the middle of the song, so there are no stage introductions. Hendrix then introduces the second song as "Have Mercy," "a Top 40 R&B rock 'n' roll record." The song is played much faster than the version he did with Don Covay back in 1964. "Can You See Me" follows next, with Mitchell displaying some of his best drumming in keeping up with the song's many breaks. The small Flamingo Club audience claps politely after the song comes to an abrupt ending. Hendrix then takes a few moments to retune his guitar and slows the pace down for "Like a Rolling Stone." A master at blending diverse musical elements, he segues Dylan's popular folk tune into B.B. King's "Rock Me Baby," with the crowd roaring in approval.

The highlight on this tape is "Catfish Blues." It must have been a delight to be able to watch Hendrix cut loose in a small club like this. He moves the solo from a Muddy Waters style into John Lee Hooker and then closes with a few bars from the blues classic "Spoonful."

Just when it sounds like they might let up, the Experience fires back with fierce renditions of "Stone Free" and "Hey Joe." Hendrix finally announces that he's going to play the "English anthem," saying, "Don't get upset, 'cause these two cats [Mitchell and Redding] are English." After a few brief moments of feedback, "Wild Thing" kicks in. While not as exhilarating as the version he'd later play at the Monterey Pop Festival, it is still a respectable delivery. We hear the club's MC futilely trying to speak above the fading explosion from Hendrix's amp in an attempt to get another round of applause for the Experience. Finally, as the MC dedicates the already-cued record "Baby Please Don't Go" to Hendrix, the tape ends.

STATUS: *This tape continues to make the rounds in the collectors' network and has been bootlegged several times.*

The *Are You Experienced* Sessions

The first session for the *Are You Experienced* LP began on October 23, 1966, in London. Sixteen sessions later, on April 4, 1967, the project concluded. The album was recorded at three different London studios—CBS Recording Studios, De Lane Lea Music Ltd., and Olympic Sound Studios. Chandler made the decision to do the bulk of recording at

Olympic because it was the newest and most advanced studio in Europe. Although Olympic offered only four-track recording (American studios had eight-track), its studios were acoustically alive.

In between playing numerous club dates, the Experience managed to find time to record. "The Wind Cries Mary" was recorded on February 7, and is a disguised tribute to Kathy Etchingham, whose middle name is Mary. After she and Hendrix had an argument about her cooking, Etchingham walked out, and Hendrix penned this heartfelt ballad. This recording session reportedly lasted six hours. Other than "The Wind Cries Mary" and vocal overdubs for "Purple Haze," there are no further details of what songs may have been recorded.

The following day, the Experience recorded several takes of "Remember" at Olympic Sound Studios. "Remember" is an R&B tune in true Otis Redding style, and it was probably the most oddly placed Hendrix song on the album—amidst the other psychedelic pop songs. When *Are You Experienced* was released in the United States, this track, along with "Can You See Me" and "Red House," was not included.

The February 20 session at De Lane Lea studios produced "I Don't Live Today," a song Hendrix often dedicated to the American Indian at live performances. With its weird and freaky fade-ins and fade-outs, the song quickly became a staple on FM radio in 1967. The band returned to Olympic Sound Studios on the twenty-sixth and recorded an untitled twelve-bar jam with horns, as well as a track titled "Gypsy Blood." Neither of these tracks was considered for the LP, and they remain unreleased.

On March 29 the Experience recorded three takes of "Manic Depression" and six takes of "Remember" at De Lane Lea studios. Another song recorded at the session, called "Teddy Bears Live Forever," was never released. At the time, Hendrix was seeing a woman who was nicknamed Bil.[20] In one of his letters to her, Hendrix wrote, "Teddy Bears Never Die." When Bil asked him what he meant, Hendrix told her he had just recorded a song about teddy bears.

On April 3, the Experience recorded the LP's title track, "Are You Experienced," along with "May This Be Love" and "Highway Chile," at Olympic Sound Studios. "Are You Experienced," a true psychedelic symphony, features a blend of backward- and forward-recorded guitars and drums that transports the listener to another world. "May This Be Love" continues in the same vein, but in a dreamier mode. "Highway Chile," as previously mentioned, was a Hendrix composition reflecting on his restless time on the Chitlin' Circuit. This track did not officially surface in the U.S. until the *Smash Hits* album was released in 1969.

Are You Experienced predates the use of Hendrix's familiar trademark, the wah-wah pedal, but many special effects were used on the record to create what some called hallucinatory art in music. Author Michael Hicks described psychedelic rock music like Hendrix's as "reverberant, unstable in harmony, juxtapositional in form . . . the music's parameters go through devices that create molten shapes in timbre. Psychedelic music . . . depersonalizes the listener with its excessive length, repetition, volume and spatial depth."[21]

Many of these psychedelic special effects can be heard on some of the album's "freak-out tunes," as Hendrix called them. The title track and "Third Stone from the Sun" used studio techniques like reversing the direction of the guitar-track tape or slowing down a vocal track for an effect resembling the imagined voice of an alien spaceship commander. Many artists like Hendrix began experimenting with their own versions of psychedelic audio effects, following in the footsteps of Beatles songs like "Rain," "I'm Only Sleeping," and "Tomorrow Never Knows."

Although *Are You Experienced* became a great commercial success and was part of the soundtrack to 1967's so-called "Summer of Love," fellow rock guitarist Eric Clapton was jealous that Hendrix achieved success in a very short time: "I was angry. Because he'd [Hendrix] come here to England and we'd gone to America and made *Disraeli Gears* and came back to deliver it. And no one wanted to know. You'd go to a club and they'd say, 'Have you heard Jimi's album?'—Yeah, it's fine, great. I mean what the fuck's going on here? No, I was furious."[22]

STATUS: Are You Experienced (Track 612 001) was released in the U.K. on May 12, 1967. The tracks included were: Side A: "Foxy Lady," "Manic Depression," "Red House," "Can You See Me," "Love or Confusion," "I Don't Live Today." Side B: "May This Be Love," "Fire," "Third Stone from the Sun," "Remember," "Are You Experienced."

The album was released in America on September 1, 1967 (Reprise RS6261). Side A: "Purple Haze," "Manic Depression," "Hey Joe," "Love or Confusion," "May This Be Love," "I Don't Live Today." Side B: "The Wind Cries Mary," "Fire," "Third Stone from the Sun," "Foxy Lady," "Are You Experienced."

Are You Experienced spent over one hundred weeks on the Billboard Top 200 Albums Chart, seventy-seven of those in the Top 40. Not only was it a great album, but it was affordable and easy to find. Forbes magazine noted at the time: "With the proliferation of shopping centers and supermarkets the whole system of marketing the records changed. Drugstores, discount stores, and every store with high traffic became a potential outlet. The passion for music, combined with the fact that youngsters today have a good deal of money to spend, created a totally anticipated demand for LPs even though LPs cost about five times as much as singles. Originally designed for classical records, LPs now bring in more than 75% of the revenues of popular records. All the factors combined to burst the record industry wide open...the five leading record companies, Columbia, Warner Bros/7 Arts [Hendrix's label], RCA, Capitol, and Metro-Goldwyn-Mayer, controlled about 55% of the market."[23] Are You Experienced and Sgt. Pepper's Lonely Hearts Club Band were partially responsible for 1967's record-setting $67-million income for the British recording industry.

Monterey to Monkees

Paul McCartney was influential in placing Hendrix on the bill at the Monterey Pop Festival in June 1967. When McCartney visited San Francisco in April, the festival's advisory board convinced him to join Paul Simon (Simon and Garfunkel), "Papa" John Phillips (the Mamas and the Papas), and others in selecting bands to play the three-night, two-day pop-rock blowout. McCartney recommended that the Jimi Hendrix Experience be included in the festival, and John Phillips immediately called Chas Chandler in London to book the date.

McCartney's interest in Hendrix dated back to the American guitarist's arrival in England in 1966. He caught Hendrix's first gig in London and began to follow him around like a devoted fan. McCartney told *Guitar Player* magazine, "People used to ring me up and say that Jimi's playing Blaises [club] tonight, or at the Bag o' Nails, and I was there."[24] Of course Hendrix was a fan of the Beatles, too. When *Sgt. Pepper's Lonely Hearts Club Band* was released in England on Friday, June 4 (two weeks before the Monterey Pop Festival), Hendrix took time to learn the title track and played it at the Experience's gig at the Saville Theatre on Sunday, June 6. The Beatles were in attendance (Brian Epstein also ran the Saville) and were blown away by Hendrix's blazing, psychedelic guitar rendition of their tune. When it came time for Hendrix to be noticed in America, it didn't hurt to have the Beatles in his corner.

The International Pop Music Festival held at the Monterey County Fairgrounds was hailed as "the most outstanding assemblage of popular music groups ever brought together in one place."[25] One hundred and twenty-eight musicians from the United States and several foreign countries took part. The festival received international press coverage from *Life*, the *Times* (London), and publications from Paris and Berlin. ABC-TV was also on hand videotaping the event for a fall special. The Beatles, who did not attend, sent their own small film crew over so that they would be able to see what they had missed. The seven-thousand-seat stadium was sold out each night.

Eric Burdon and the New Animals replaced the Beach Boys, who dropped out of the lineup. Burdon recalled what it was like hanging out with Hendrix prior to his performance: "The brightest moment for me was watching JH [Jimi Hendrix] paint his guitars for that night. It was by sheer luck that I went by the motel where he was staying. You see, they didn't have any telephones in the rooms, just one in the motel lobby. I had rented a motorcycle and swung by there to check it out. In the courtyard, I saw him out there with a bucket of paint, a paintbrush, and two of his axes, including the one he was going to sacrifice that night. I thought 'this is like some Navajo chief, burning sage, getting ready to commit himself to the forces.' It wasn't until later that I discovered that there was a lot of Indian blood in Jimi's family. This whole scene I was witness to was an indication to me that there was much more to this man than I could fathom out in just one night."[26] Burdon was so inspired by all the events at the festival that he later wrote a hit song called "Monterey" that beautifully captured some of its essence.

"Sure Woodstock was THE EVENT," Burdon recalled, "and history looks at it as the peak, but Monterey was the crown jewel of concerts. Monterey was Jimi's return back to the States. In Jimi's head, it was his first hometown gig. He was at his best showmanship. I remember going out to the front few rows near the press box where I had my seat. These kids next to me were asking, 'Who's going to follow The Who?' The pressure was mounting and it was very exciting. As soon as I heard it was going to be Jimi, I rushed to my seat to see the show. These kids then asked, 'Who is this Jimi Hendrix?' And I replied, 'You'll find out.' Part way through Jimi's set, I looked over and noticed their big smiling faces giving me the thumbs up."[27]

After Monterey, the Experience played Bill Graham's Fillmore West and picked up a few more dates in California and New York before things got bizarre—the band went on tour with the Dick Clark Caravan as the opening act for the Monkees.

Not everyone liked the Experience's music or their stage show. On July 5, New York radio station WMCA's program director, Joe Bogart, took his twelve-year-old daughter to see the Jimi Hendrix Experience at the Rheingold Festival in New York's Central Park. Hendrix played a blistering set, as evidenced by Linda McCartney's photos of him playing with his teeth, between his legs, and behind his head.

After the show, Bogart publicly announced that he "would never program a Hendrix record on his station."[28] WMCA, once cited as "the nation's leading influence on record sales,"[29] had hired Bogart because of his background and his claim that he knew what Young America needed to hear. His timing could not have been worse for WMCA listeners. "Purple Haze" (Reprise 0597), the second American single for the Experience, was released only two weeks before Bogart's ruling. Besides Hendrix, Bogart also banned *The Who Sell Out* and passed on Traffic's music, saying that they were not a popular group. His bans were ineffective and out of touch with the new music marketplace. To eliminate the "rotting corpse stinking up the airwaves,"[30]—the repetitious sound heard on Top 40 AM radio in the late 1960s—long psychedelic album tracks were now being played in static-free stereo on hip FM stations.

Rock 'n' roll FM stations started programming designated album cuts as record companies began promoting and selling the album as an individual unit, as the single had been in the 1950s and early 1960s. FM stations also played new albums long before their release. Eric Clapton brought a tape of Cream's *Disraeli Gears* to San Francisco's "underground" FM radio station KMPX two months before its release as an LP.

KMPX may also have been the first station in America to play "Purple Haze." Bob McClay, a former disc jockey there, says he received an unreleased acetate pressing of this record from a friend in England before it was released there on Track Records. The only information McClay was given about the record was that it had been recorded by an American guitarist with two English musicians, collectively known as the Jimi Hendrix Experience. Hendrix's second album, *Axis: Bold As Love*, was also played at KMPX weeks before it came out. All this freedom and wild new music on the airwaves upset the mainstream AM stations.

In 1967, Gordon B. McLendon, who owned a chain of radio stations, spearheaded a campaign to clean up the lyrics of pop music. He enlisted the help of the American Mothers Committee and told them in a speech: "We've had all we can stand of the record industry's glorifying marijuana, LSD, and sexual activity. The newest Beatle record, out next week, has a line about '40,000 purple hearts in one arm [*sic*].' Is that what you want your children to listen to?"[31]

Given the growing uproar over the impropriety of rock lyrics, it is surprising that Hendrix's manager, Michael Jeffery, considered sending him on tour with the Monkees, a group that cashed in on their squeaky-clean image for an innocent teen audience.

The Monkees were America's answer to the Beatles—four wacky young guys from Hollywood, rather than Liverpool. Two American producers, Bob Rafelson and Bert Schneider, developed a popular TV series after observing the success of the Beatles' film *A Hard Day's Night*. In 1965 they placed an ad in the Hollywood trade papers looking for "four insane boys, age 17–21," and after auditioning 437 candidates, they selected Michael "Mickey" Dolenz, Peter Tork (Thorkelson), David Jones, and Robert Michael Nesmith, passing up guitarist Stephen Stills and future mass murderer Charles Manson. Instead of using local radio to promote their sugar-pop records, the Monkees used their weekly television show. This new method of reaching America's record buyers was so successful that the Monkees actually knocked the Beatles off the top of the charts.

Monkees singer Mickey Dolenz first saw Hendrix in 1966 playing with blues singer John Hammond, Jr., in Greenwich Village. The following year, when Dolenz and Peter Tork attended the Monterey Pop Festival and watched Hendrix playing, Dolenz suggested to his management that they add Hendrix to the Monkees tour as an opening act. Dolenz recalled, "The Monkees was very theatrical in my eyes and so was the Jimi Hendrix Experience. It would make a perfect match. Jimi must have thought so too, because a few weeks later he agreed to be our opening act for an upcoming summer tour. Jimi would amble out onto the stage, fire up the amps and break into 'Purple Haze,' and the kids would instantly drown him out with, 'We want Daavvy!' God it was embarrassing."[32]

Noel Redding also describes some of the negative aspects of playing with the Monkees: "We had done Monterey, L.A., New York, and suddenly someone said . . . 'You're on tour with the Monkees.' So, we were picked up and driven to this plane that said 'The Monkees' on it, given a Monkees badge, and then were taken to this posh hotel in Miami. All the Monkees were there. We met them and gave them peanuts. We then started doing gigs with them. Lyn Randell from Australia opened the show and then we'd go on, dying deaths at all times. The Monkees' band would go on first, play a few songs, and then the Monkees would go on, while the band played for them. When they arrived on stage, it was like screamsville. Someone then said we were obscene and we couldn't do this tour anymore. We weren't obscene . . . we used to barf all the time. Suddenly we were off the tour and back into playing these underground clubs. We did that for a couple months and went back to England."[33]

When the Experience was "yanked" from the Monkees tour after only five gigs, an explanation was needed to satisfy the curious teen magazines. Certainly, they couldn't mention that Hendrix gave the finger to the audience at Forest Hills Stadium before storming offstage, so Chas Chandler, music critic Lillian Roxon, and Michael Jeffery concocted a press release saying that the Daughters of the American Revolution (DAR) were so upset with Hendrix's outrageous stage antics that he had to go.[34] Hendrix jokingly told the press,

"Some parents who brought their kids complained that our act was vulgar. We decided it was just the wrong audience. I think they're replacing me with Mickey Mouse!"[35] The final Experience show in Forest Hills, on July 16, was reported to have had a hostile audience, with most of the objections coming from the parents.[36]

"I was very sorry to see him go," Dolenz remembered. "Before he did, we did have some great times; running around the New York City psychedelic scene like kids in a candy store, tripping at the Electric Circus and jamming until all hours of the night in the hotel room with Peter [Tork] and his buddy Stephen Stills."[37]

STATUS: *Unfortunately, no recordings have ever surfaced from this tour with the Monkees. By mutual agreement, the Jimi Hendrix Experience quit the tour and started to get its own bookings.*

The *Axis: Bold As Love* Sessions

The axis of the earth, if it changes, it changes the whole face of the earth, like every few thousand years. And it's like love in a human being, if he really falls in love, deep enough, it'll change him. It might change his whole life so both of them can really go together.

Jimi Hendrix, Swedish radio interview, January 8, 1968

The *Axis: Bold As Love* sessions, recorded at Olympic Sound Studios in England, began on May 4 and ended on October 31. The album was released in England on December 1, 1967 (Track 613003), and in America (Reprise RS 6281) the following month.

The critics loved *Axis: Bold As Love* for its wonderful blend of R&B, hard rock, and Mose Allison–influenced jazz. *Rolling Stone's* review called Hendrix "one of rock's greatest guitar players," and cited the LP as "the finest Voodoo album that any rock group has produced to date."[38] The lyrics touched home, too, as Hendrix's half-brother Leon recalled: "'Castles Made of Sand'... it's about my family. The Indian war chief is about me. The first verse is about Mom and Dad fighting and the third verse is about my mom and her dying."[39] With the release of this LP, the world seemed to stop spinning on its axis for many fans, and only revolved on the turntable.

Axis: Bold As Love was the first Hendrix album to explore new electronic devices built for the guitar by Roger Mayer. Recording engineers Eddie Kramer, George Chkiantz, and Andy Johns played a key part in the distinctive sounds on this LP. Kramer was born in South Africa, and in the mid-1960s went to work for Pye Studios in England, where he learned to work with American studio equipment and hone his on-location recording skills. From there, he went to work for Regent Studios and then Olympic, where he worked with the Beatles and the Rolling Stones, among many other bands. It was there he met and began working with Hendrix.

Kramer explained how he got the Hendrix sound on tape: "I would fill the four basic

The Jimi Hendrix Experience, publicity photo, 1967. *Günter Zint/K&K/Star File*

tracks with stereo drums on two of the channels, the bass on the third, and Jimi's rhythm guitar on the fourth. From there, Chandler and I would mix this down to two tracks on another four-track recorder, giving us two more tracks to put on whatever we wanted, which usually included Jimi's lead guitar and vocals as well as backing vocals and some additional percussion."[40]

Kramer experimented with Hendrix's sound, especially during the recording of "If Six Was Nine." "Olympic Studios often recorded classical sessions, so they built special platforms to hold all the members," he recalled. "We had pulled one of the platforms forward and put Mitch's drums on it. We also put a mic above and below the platform in order to record a foot-stomping track. Jimi was the 'stomping leader.' Graham Nash and Gary Leeds of the Walker Brothers had stopped by and were recruited to walk. I compressed the foot stomps so much that you can hear the compression kick in and out. To add even more to the song, at the end of the tune Jimi played a recorder that he had purchased for two shillings from a street vendor."[41]

In 1959, recording engineer Larry Levine had inadvertently discovered a sound effect that was further developed for psychedelic audio enhancement in the mid-1960s. By super-imposing two identical dubs of the same material played at minutely different speeds, Levine created a composite sound that seemed to "whoosh" like the air blowing from a jet airplane. This sound, referred to as "phasing," dominated the 1959 recording by Miss Toni Fisher called "The Big Hurt" (Signet 275),[42] and was later found on the 1967 single "Itchycoo Park" (Immediate 501) by the Small Faces.

When Hendrix asked Kramer to produce an underwater sound he had heard in his dreams, this proved a bit of a challenge. "I had been experimenting with phasing and its possible uses for Hendrix," Kramer remembered, "and when I played the results for him he yelled, 'That's it! That's the sound I've been hearing in my dreams.'"[43] Phasing can be heard on the song "Bold As Love" near the end, when Mitchell starts a drum roll, seconds before Hendrix's guitar kicks in.

The phasing effect excited Hendrix, who shared his feelings about it with the press only weeks after Axis had been released: "[Phasing] makes it sound like planes going through your membranes and chromosomes. A cat got that together accidentally and he turned us on to it. That's the sound we wanted, it was a special sound, and we didn't want to use tapes of airplanes, we wanted to have the music itself warped."[44]

After four days of mixing and perfecting the thirteen Axis: Bold As Love tracks, the project ended on October 31. Hendrix and Chandler were living together and Hendrix took one of the completed final master tapes back to their apartment before any safety copy was made. One night, on his way to a party, eager to play Axis for his friends, Hendrix grabbed the master that contained side one of the album. But on the way back home, he left it in a taxicab. Eddie Kramer explained: "During the mixing of the Axis album, we ran into a problem because Jimi had lost the master tapes of all the mixes we had done. We had to come back in and re-create everything. There was one song, 'If Six Was Nine,' that I could never get close to in terms of its quality and the vibe I achieved on a rough mix, which was included in the first batch of mixes. We were scratching our heads because we couldn't get that sound back again. Chas then said, 'Does anybody have a take of that track ["If Six Was Nine"]?' Noel popped up and said he had a copy at home. Chas then sent him home to get it. He came back with this tiny three-inch tape with the reel falling off that I had to iron out all the wrinkles. It was at 7 1/2 ips˙ and it was a nightmare. The tape was then transferred to 15 ips and that's the version you hear on the record."[45]

STATUS: *On May 4 at Olympic Sound Studios, Hendrix revived "Mr. Bad Luck,"a song he had played in 1966 during his Greenwich Village days with the Blue Flames. It was once considered for Axis: Bold As Love, but during the production stage, the track was deleted from the lineup. It officially debuted on the 1988 radio special, Jimi Hendrix – Live and Unreleased and then on disc on Lifelines: The Jimi Hendrix Story. Al Hendrix apparently had this tape stashed away in storage until producer Bruce Gary asked him for it.*

A still unreleased tune called "The Dragon of Carlisle" was recorded on May 5. Mitchell also stated in the May 6 issue of Disc magazine that his song "The Mind Octopus" would be included on the next album (Axis: Bold As Love). According to Noel Redding, however, this song was never recorded.

The mono version of Axis: Bold As Love (on both the Track and the Reprise labels) sounds radically different from the more common stereo release. Since mono records were being phased out in the late 1960s, only a limited number of copies were pressed. A mono version of Axis in excellent condition can command as much as five hundred dollars.

In February 2000, engineer Eddie Kramer began enhancing the original Axis mono mix for a new release on Classic Records. Kramer explained the difference between the original mono mix and the stereo mix: "'EXP' lost much of its galactic power as the circular effects created for the stereo master were effectively canceled in mono. Other songs such as 'Spanish Castle Magic' and 'Ain't No Telling' placed Jimi's vocal more forward in the mix. Perhaps the most unique track was 'Little Wing.' Jimi's guitar and vocals were much drier while the drum reverb was much more present. It was experimentation . . . the entire [mono] album was all mixed in one day!"[46]

The Lost Live EP

The May 13 issue of the *New Musical Express* reported: "Plans for the first live EP by the Jimi Hendrix Experience were announced by the group's manager Chas Chandler this week. The record is tentatively set for release by Track in mid-June, and will feature four stage numbers associated with Hendrix including Bob Dylan's 'Like A Rolling Stone' and Chip Taylor's 'Wild Thing.' Six more tracks were recorded last weekend by the trio, which currently has two entries figuring in the *New Musical Express* Chart. Its latest waxings include a composition by bass guitarist Noel Redding, 'She's So Fine,' which is being considered as a possible single."

STATUS: *At the time, it was popular for bands in Britain to release EPs (extended plays) to keep current with listeners and fans. It's more than likely that Chandler had the May 7 Saville Theatre concert recorded for an EP. The set list included "Foxy Lady," "Can You See Me," "Hey Joe," "Stone Free," "Like a Rolling Stone," "Purple Haze," "The Wind Cries Mary," and "Wild Thing." This concert recording remains unreleased.*

The In Sound, United States Army Public Service LPs (USA-IS 67 and USA-IS 51)

As the Vietnam War continued, the U.S. Army developed a promotional campaign to try to make it seem like a groovy idea for young men to enlist. In the first spot, Chicago's Top 40 morning deejay, Harry Harrison, who had a slick but friendly all-American voice and personality, simulated a "call-in-your-request" radio show in which a caller (usually someone in the military) would request a song (which was already pre-cued). Harrison would then promote the song, noting how quickly it was moving up the charts, and eventually play it. As the tune faded out, Harrison would announce that the featured artist was going to join him in the studio.

In Hendrix's case, he was given thirty seconds of airtime to talk about his entire musical career before being told they were out of time. Harrison then came in and did his pitch for the Army, reminding his audience, "It's your future, your decision, choose Army!" Recorded in mid-1967, the record was slated for broadcast during the week of October 30, 1967. The song used was "Purple Haze." In addition to the Experience, Harrison also had Cream and other rock groups as guests.

A second interview segment with the Experience was broadcast on February 5, 1968, but probably recorded in June 1967. Harrison interviewed Noel Redding this time, and Hendrix is heard laughing in the background. After another call-in request, Harrison segued into "Foxy Lady" from the newly released *Are You Experienced.* As before, a plug for the U.S. Army was slyly placed in this public service spot.

STATUS: *Unreleased commercially, an audiotape of this promotional record with both selections is in circulation in the collectors' network.*

Rare Recorded Jams

In 1997, guitarist John Mayall reported that Hendrix had appeared on one of his records: "To hear him [Hendrix] live was an exciting event. He sat in with us two or three times. One track, 'The Lesson,' a very slow blues taped down at the Speakeasy [in early 1967], later came out on our *Diary of a Band* record. And it was so unlike what you'd expect of Hendrix, so quiet and subtle. Unless you were told it was him, you'd never ever know. Mick Taylor handed the guitar to Jimi who plays this solo, which is the most low-key thing he could have possibly played. He wasn't listed on the record for contractual reasons."[47]

STATUS: *Diary of a Band was released on two separate LPs in February 1968 — Volume One (Decca SKL 4918) and Volume Two (Decca SKL 4919). "The Lesson" is a very short up-tempo tune recorded at Kings College, and is quite different from Mayall's recollection. There is, however, a similar song called "My Own Fault," recorded on November 2, 1967, at the Speakeasy. According to the liner notes, this track more than likely features Mick Taylor, not Hendrix, given the playing style and confusing circumstances over the date, song title, and club location. Diary of a Band was released on CD in 1994 (844 029-2 and 844 030-2).*

The Bo Hansson and Janne Karlsson Jam

Hendrix's jam with the Swedish jazz-rock duo Hansson & Karlsson was recorded in Stockholm, Sweden, on September 11, 1967. After a concert at the Gröna Lund, Hendrix went to see this house band at a small club in Stockholm. Anders Lind, a deejay at the club, believes that a Swedish A&R representative from Polydor introduced Hendrix to Hansson & Karlsson. Lind recorded Hansson & Karlsson on a regular basis, using two microphones and a Revox tape recorder. On this occasion, he taped two to three hours of them jamming with Hendrix, but as he described it, "Well, it's just jamming really. None of Jimi's songs and mostly all H&K material...more jazzy kind of music."[48] Hansson & Karlsson later opened for Hendrix on January 7, 1968, when he performed in Copenhagen. A few weeks later, at Olympic Sound Studios, Hendrix began developing his arrangement of their song "Tax Free," which he continued to play live during most of 1969.

STATUS: *Unreleased. Anders Lind, now a partner in the Swedish independent label Silence Records, claims to have possession of the tapes of Hendrix playing with Hansson & Karlsson. He says he still gets phone calls and letters from fans who want to hear these recordings.*

Great Jams, No Tapes

The following jams, had they been captured on tape, would have contained some of the most outstanding musical sets in rock history. Unfortunately, as the eyewitnesses recalled, no one was around with a tape recorder.

MONTEREY POP JAMS

In John Rocco's book *Dead Reckonings*, he talks about a multi-group jam that took place before the Monterey festival officially started: "Pigpen (Ron McKernan), Hendrix, Jerry Garcia...they're all into it [jamming]. And as soon as the other musicians hear about it they're going, 'Yes...count us in too.' We get everything ready, and then Jorma Kaukonen and Jack Casady from Jefferson Airplane, Garcia and Hendrix come out on stage...cranking through 'Walking The Dog'...and 'Good Morning Little Schoolgirl.'"[49]

Roger Daltrey of the Who noted: "The unfortunate thing about Monterey that isn't on film...just before we went on, Hendrix, the Who, Brian Jones, Mama Cass, Janis Joplin was there, and everyone was having the most incredible jam in the dressing room that was under the stage. I've never heard Hendrix play as good as that. No one recorded it or has it on film."[50]

Mickey Dolenz of the Monkees stated that after the Monterey Pop Festival concluded, he spent the rest of the night listening to Hendrix and other musicians jamming in one of the empty livestock barns at the fairgrounds.[51] The late John Cipollina, guitarist for Quicksilver Messenger Service, corroborated Dolenz's recollection: "I remember we got in a good jam afterwards, me, Jorma [Kaukonen of Jefferson Airplane] and Hendrix and I think Jack Casady [of Jefferson Airplane], and I think Bob Weir [of the Grateful Dead] was there, too, and it went on for four hours before they kicked us out of the place. The sun was coming up. It was like, 'Come on, hippies. Don't you have a Volkswagen bus to live in or something?'"[52]

SAM AND DAVE

Guitarist John Kay, who formed the hard-rock band Steppenwolf in 1967, recalled a performance that took place about a week after the Experience played the Monterey Pop Festival. On June 26, the Experience played the Whisky A Go-Go in Los Angeles, and as Kay recalls: "The Sam & Dave Revue was playing.... After their first set, during intermission, the dance floor was raised to serve as a makeshift stage. So the club owner gets on the microphone and says, 'And now, ladies and gentleman, a special treat... direct from his triumph at the Monterey Pop Festival, the Jimi Hendrix Experience!' He then walked out on stage doing 'Hey Joe.' I was diggin' it!"[53] Elmer Valentine, owner of the Whisky, had this to say about the Hendrix jam: "We tried to book him after Monterey, but his price was too high. But one day he announced he was coming to jam with Sam and Dave and we had one of the biggest houses yet."[54]

STEPHEN STILLS

Guitarist Stephen Stills has spoken about a lengthy jam that took place within this time frame at his house in Malibu, California, with Hendrix and his band: "I had a house out at the beach and we started to play at about 3 o'clock in the morning. I then heard a knock on the door and it's the local cop, wondering who is in there. I showed him my lease. He said, 'We didn't get any complaints, but we heard the noise and we didn't know that anybody was living here.' He then asked, 'Would you mind if we just sit across the street and monitor our calls so we can listen to you?'"[55] Noel Redding recalled that the Experience's performances at the Whisky A Go-Go on July 2 were off because the band was too tired, no doubt from the extended jam at Stills's house.

JOHN HAMMOND, JR., AND ERIC CLAPTON

John Hammond, Jr., recalled a jam with Hendrix that took place at the end of July: "When he [Hendrix] came back to the U.S. on his triumphant return he was put on the tour with The Monkees, opening the show. He was really bummed out about that. I saw him in New York when he had just blown that tour, and he was really totally depressed by it. He came into The Gaslight and jammed with me there. I had a little band together at the time, and we talked about old times. The next night, he and Eric Clapton came in and jammed with me."[56]

Written Work in Progress

In 1967, Hendrix penned several ideas that were never brought to fruition. These include: "A Cry from One Soul to Its Mate," "Eyes and Imagination," "Please Help Me," and "The World Eats" (a poem cowritten with Nancy Rainer).

We're working on a really different presentation to what we're doing...we're using films and stereo speakers in the back of the auditorium, all over the place. It will be so natural, in a rehearsed way.

JIMI HENDRIX, *EYE*, JULY 1968

CHAPTER SIX

MUSIC IN 3-D: 1968

The year 1968 was very successful for Hendrix and the Experience. The band's first three LPs all rode high in the charts. *Rolling Stone* bestowed the title Performer of the Year on Hendrix for creativity, electricity, and "balls beyond the call of duty."[1] Fellow guitarist Frank Zappa praised Hendrix's performances and described them for *Life* magazine's readers: "The flailing, wailing freakout of the Hendrix Experience whips flesh as well as soul. The sound of his music is extremely symbolic: orgasmic grunts, tortured squeals, lascivious moans, electric disasters and innumerable other audial curiosities are delivered to the sense mechanisms of the audience at an extremely high decibel level. In a live performance environment, it is impossible to merely listen to what Hendrix does...it eats you alive."[2]

The Experience was still playful in 1968 and often pulled pranks to break up the monotony of touring. Seattle deejay Pat O'Day recalled: "It happened in Seattle at the Olympic Hotel on the 12th floor. This was Jimi's idea, and it turned out very comical. Since the hotel had a very nice restaurant on the top floor, the type where conservatives would dine, Jimi suggested that they (groupies included!) take off all their clothes and go out into the hallway and stand in front of the elevators. I think Mitch and Noel—and you know they only weighed about 125 pounds soaking wet with their great big bushy hair—along with the groupies, went out and stood in a row, right across the hall, in front of the elevators, and pressed that floor's button! The elevators were filled with people going to the

Hendrix's captivating smile, 1968. *Dagmar/Star File*

roof that night. When the doors would open, people would look out and see these naked bodies, right? All of them with big bushy hair—one black guy and five or six white people. The elevator would then come back down, from the roof, with the same people who had to look again to make sure they'd really seen it!"[3]

Despite rumors that the band would break up, as Cream and many others did that year, members of the Experience ventured outside the group, performing with other musicians and bringing back fresh ideas. Redding developed a new side group called Fat Mattress, and Mitchell jammed with John Lennon and Keith Richards during the taping of the television special *Rock and Roll Circus* (which never aired). Hendrix, meanwhile, delved into his own musical experiments and side projects.

One less productive experiment involved a taxi driver who dropped Hendrix at the studio. Along the way, Hendrix casually invited the driver down to jam sometime. The driver turned up half an hour later ready to jam and completed a six-hour session with Hendrix. The session had to be scrapped—Hendrix apparently did not have the heart to ask him to leave.

In addition to jamming in the studio, Hendrix appeared around New York, playing with everybody. Hendrix's concert sound technician, Abe Jacob, recalled: "Jimi played at a couple of clubs around New York where they did recordings from the club sound-board...The Scene, Generation, and Ungano's."[4] Hendrix was notorious for jumping onstage during an encore to jam with other performers.

Some of these previously lost recordings have recently turned up on bootlegs. One example is the jam on April 15 at the Generation Club in New York, when Hendrix jammed with blues legend B.B. King (guitar and vocals), Elvin Bishop (guitar and vocals), Paul Butterfield (harmonica), Al Kooper (organ), Buzzy Feiten (bass), Don Martin (guitar), and Phillip Wilson (drums). "We had kind of a jam get-together...with Al Kooper of Blood, Sweat & Tears and Jimi Hendrix," B.B. King recalls. "I remember Jimi recording what we played that night. He was supposed to give us a tape....When I die, if I can find Jimi, he's going to give me my tape, because that was a memorable occasion."[5]

At times, the jams aren't as good as one would expect considering the talented lineup. As the tape begins King gives a rambling introduction that lasts about twenty minutes. There are some great solos, but they are sometimes hindered by the abundance of musicians on stage at the same time, all waiting to take a solo. One hundred and twenty minutes of this jam exist in excellent stereo soundboard quality.

The *McGough and McGear* Sessions

In 1963, as the Beatles were gaining recognition, Paul McCartney's younger brother Mike was trying to do the same. Mike McCartney, who changed his last name to McGear to avoid cashing in on his older brother Paul's fame, teamed up with Roger McGough and John Gorman to form the band Scaffold. As a side project in 1968, Mike and Roger collaborated on an LP they titled *McGough and McGear*. Paul McCartney performed, produced, and helped gather an all-star cast of musicians for the album, including Hendrix, Mitch Mitchell, Graham Nash, Dave Mason, Spencer Davis, and John Mayall.

The session with Hendrix took place on January 20 at De Lane Lea studios in London, England. According to Mike (McCartney) McGear, "Hendrix turned up at the recording studios, on his own, carrying a small guitar case. After a half-dozen takes, it was decided that the first take was the best. Unfortunately, a careless tape operator had erased every take but the last."[6] Hendrix appeared on two of the LP's tracks, "So Much" and "Ex-Art Student."

Hendrix also joined Graham Nash, John Mayall, Jane Asher (Paul's girlfriend at the time), and Dave Mason for a track that did not make the album, "Oh to Be a Child" (a.k.a. "Toy Symphony"). The merry bunch of big kids banged on toy instruments and noisily stomped up and down the corridors for this unusual recording. To avoid legal complications, the Parlophone label prohibited the guest performers' names being listed on the LP. As a result, sales of *McGough and McGear* lagged.

STATUS: *Out of print. McGough and McGear (Parlophone PCS 7047) was originally released in October 1968 and is very difficult to find. When the album was released on CD in 1989 (EMI CDP 7 98177 2), it was disclosed that the sessions had been paid for by the Beatles' newly formed company Apple, making it the first "Apple" record, even though it wasn't on the Apple label. The McGough and McGear CD is now a rare collector's item sought by both Beatles and Hendrix fans. The track "Oh to Be a Child" turned up on the 1992 CD The Scaffold: The Best of the EMI Years (EMI CDP 7 985022).*

The Hendrix Hotel Suite Recordings

For a brief period in 1968, Hendrix held a hotel suite at the Warwick Hotel on West 54th Street in New York. There, on March 18, he recorded some private versions of "All Along the Watchtower" and "Bright Lights, Big City" using his portable tape recorder. He let the tape run as his Greenwich Village friend Paul Caruso and drummer Jimmy Mayes engaged in some friendly name-calling. An impromptu jam of Jimmy Reed's "Bright Lights, Big City" (which Hendrix jokingly called "Bright Lights, Big Titties") concludes this hotel suite recording.

On April 8, Hendrix moved to the Drake Hotel (on East 56th Street) while Mitchell and Redding left for London. Away from the pressures of a recording studio, Hendrix found solitude and freedom. He worked out many ideas for songs that he had scribbled on any available scrap of paper. A tape made in his Drake Hotel suite includes demo recordings for *Electric Ladyland*—"Long Hot Summer Night," "1983...(A Merman I Should Turn to Be)," "Moon Turn the Tides...Gently, Gently Away," "Voodoo Chile," and "Gypsy Eyes"—as well as for three songs in progress—"Angel," "Cherokee Mist," and "Hear My Train a Comin'").

While at the Drake Hotel, Hendrix invited New York reporter Albert Goldman to his suite to preview some of the early mixes for the *Electric Ladyland* album. Goldman recalled the meeting in great detail: "Settling me in a deep chair, he filled my glass, offered me a giant joint, and began to spin the tapes from which his next LP would be cut. In the tight little world of the earphones, I heard thunderous sounds like salvos of howitzers. Hendrix leaned over and purred: 'It's the gods making love.' The tunes that followed spanned a wide spectrum of pop music. I recall shouting, talking blues, backed with a heavy, raunchy beat: a long exotically instrumented jam session, reminiscent of Roland Kirk...psychedelic melodies that sing of sensuous surrender. All these songs I recall as one does the other pictures in a gallery that houses a masterpiece."[7]

STATUS: *The March 18 tape is in circulation among collectors and runs five minutes. Another Warwick suite tape features Hendrix playing "Hear My Train a Comin'" and "Room Full of Mirrors" with Paul Caruso on harmonica.*

The Drake Hotel tape runs thirty-six minutes. Hendrix recorded this stereo masterpiece on his portable equipment. In 1996, a graphic novel titled **Voodoo Child: The Illustrated Legend of Jimi Hendrix,** *published by Penguin, was sold packaged with a CD of these rare demo recordings.[8]*

In 1996, Sotheby's auction house offered a tape of never-before-heard demos from Electric Ladyland *that included the previously unknown track "The Devil's Return." This tape, recorded in 1968, remains unreleased and uncirculated.*

Record Plant, May 1, 1968.
Linda McCartney/Star File

The Lost ABC-TV Documentary

"It's like 'Voodoo Child.' Somebody was filming us as we were doing that.... It was like, 'Okay, boys, look like you're recording.' It was in the studio and they were recording it.... So it was one-two-three and then we went into 'Voodoo Child.'"

Hendrix reflecting on the filming by ABC-TV of "Voodoo Child (Slight Return)" in the studio, *Rolling Stone*, March 19, 1970

On May 3, ABC-TV began sixteen days of filming a documentary titled *Jimi Hendrix Experience*. Michael Jeffery conceived the project and then hired a film crew from the network. According to several sources, Hendrix was filmed in concert, in the recording studio, and in his hotel room watching television.

The first log sheet, dated May 3, 1968, notes that a cameraman named Roy shot the first 2,500 feet of film. It lists the following activities:

- Shot of a girl [Nancy Reiner, Jeffery's girlfriend] sketching Jimi as he plays guitar and sings, preparation for a recording.

- Managers and recording engineers listening outside of recording room.

- Hendrix performing; Drummer; Back-up guitarist (bass).

- Hendrix reading paper with friend.

- Inside recording studio with Eddie Kramer, Interview with Kramer—He says, "Jimi's music is here to stay. Jimi is easy to work with, imaginative and quick. Jimi appeals to 12–16 year-old teeny-boppers and the 20-up older age group as well."

- Interviews with Michael Jeffery and Chas Chandler—discussing Jimi's talent.

- Hendrix playing guitar in the recording studio [Record Plant].

- More of Hendrix recording; Hendrix in sound room with Kramer; Hendrix writing lyrics.

- More of Hendrix and back-up musicians playing to the recording.

One of the highlights of this documentary is the inclusion of "Voodoo Child (Slight Return)" from the May 3 Record Plant sessions. The complete original session tapes, released on bootleg several years ago, revealed that Hendrix, Redding, and Mitchell ran through eight takes of "Voodoo Child (Slight Return)." Take eight, the ultimate guitar extravaganza, was selected as the master and appeared on the double LP *Electric Ladyland*.

According to the next log sheet, dated May 18, 1968, a cameraman named Stanford shot 1,600 feet of film in Miami, Florida. The segments are listed as follows:

+ Jimi Hendrix in outlandish clothes leaving hotel.

+ Members of his group joining him in limousine.

+ Shots of girls drinking beer during the ride in the car.

+ Hendrix and his friends getting into a helicopter flight; Helicopter flight.

+ Shots of the concert advertising poster.

+ Hendrix in a restaurant, surrounded by young people.

+ Girls at pool; Jimi followed by a crowd of young people.

+ Shots of them arriving at the stadium.

+ Daylight performance; Young people watching; More of Hendrix and his band.

The Jimi Hendrix Experience was originally booked to perform on both Saturday and Sunday at the Miami Pop Festival, but torrential rains washed out the second day's events. Engineer Eddie Kramer was flown to Miami to record the group's performance at the festival. Recordings were made on Saturday, but the second day's cancellation forced the promoters into bankruptcy, and both the audiotape and film footage were seized. To date, only a single quarter-inch audiotape and one two-minute video clip of the Experience at Miami Pop have surfaced in the collectors' network.[9] This ABC-TV clip includes Hendrix walking to the stage with his guitar, eating a sandwich in his dressing room, and performing "Foxy Lady" on stage. If further film footage does exist, it could be some of the best, since there is very little film documentation for 1968, the Experience's best year.

The final log listing, also from Miami, is dated May 19, 1968. Stanford was once again the cameraman and his log for this footage listed the following:

- Interview with rock guitar singer, Jimi Hendrix discusses his work, friend of Hendrix group listens to interview.

- Hendrix talks about getting started; plays Blues, Rock and Free Form music.

- Hendrix introduces Frank, friend and back-up member of the group; they discuss audience reactions.

- When he's [Hendrix] not playing music, he likes football. He says he's working on new type of music which will give pop more respect. Discusses the moods and ideas.

There is also a listing in the documents for "EDITED FILM." This section may have contained sections from Hendrix's performances at two May 10 concerts at the Fillmore East—historic shows that Sly and the Family Stone opened for the Experience.[10] The documents describe "Jimi in a light show" with "lights flashing on stage" and the "audience in the foreground." An audience recording from one of the shows captured the Experience playing an electrifying interpretation of Dylan's "Can You Please Crawl out Your Window?" and the longest known version of "Red House"—seventeen minutes. If footage of this concert still exists, it may well be stunning.

STATUS: *All of the listings in the ABC archives pertaining to this Hendrix documentary are marked "LOST ABC 9/73." Some speculate that an employee walked off with the historic footage, but its whereabouts remain a mystery.*[11]

The *Electric Ladyland* Sessions

Electric Ladyland, the Experience's third LP, is one of the most original rock albums of the twentieth century, capturing Hendrix during the experimental peak of his brief career. It has been recognized many times by various print and media polls for its radical recording techniques, and for Hendrix's exceptional playing and immaculate timing. Jas Obrecht, author and associate editor of *Guitar Player* magazine, said, "The real importance of *Electric Ladyland* is that it's the only complete view we have of Hendrix's conception of a record start to finish. Plus it's the first time that I'm aware of a person using a studio as yet another instrument in the band: the swirling movements of sound, the layers, the way things were overdubbed and panned right-to-left—things like that made it the complete 'head song' experience in a way no other album was before that."[12]

Only three weeks after the release of *Axis: Bold As Love*, the Jimi Hendrix Experience began work on *Electric Ladyland* at Olympic Studios in England. On December 20, work began on "Crosstown Traffic," which borrowed a few chords from "Spanish Castle Magic." Traffic's Dave Mason helped on background vocals and Hendrix played a comb and a tissue-paper kazoo. The following day, work continued on "Crosstown Traffic" and on an early version of "Have You Ever Been (to Electric Ladyland)," with Hendrix later adding the bass part. Some of the songs originally recorded on four-track in England were transferred to the short-lived one-inch twelve-track machine at the Record Plant.

On January 21, Noel Redding walked out during a session for "All Along the Watchtower," frustrated with Hendrix's decision to do endless takes. As a result, Redding appears on only five of *Electric Ladyland*'s sixteen tracks. Despite Redding's departure, Hendrix remained focused and inspired. He brought in outside musicians, including Brian Jones from the Rolling Stones, who played piano and percussion. According to engineer Eddie Kramer, Jones was too stoned and his efforts on the piano were not used. Dave Mason was brought in and played twelve-string guitar. A mix of "All Along the Watchtower" without any of the elaborate studio effects that were added later can be heard on *South Saturn Delta*.

On March 13, the recording sessions relocated to New York's Record Plant, which

CNE Coliseum Arena, Toronto, Canada, February 24, 1968. Toronto Star

opened in late 1967 with the help of Chris Stone, the national sales manager for Revlon cosmetics. Stone and Revlon mogul Charles Revson invested $300,000 to get the studio up and running. "I used to come over to the [Record Plant] studio on my lunch hour to do the paper work," Stone recalled. "[Engineer] Gary [Kellgren], having worked all night, would often be out cold on the couch, with Jimi still in the studio glaring through the haze of speakers. They would sometimes go three and four days without stopping. Out of those sessions came *Electric Ladyland*, the Record Plant's first record. Other people have taken credit for the record, but about ninety percent of it was done in Studio A in New York with Gary and Jimi."[13]

Chas Chandler quit the sessions for *Electric Ladyland* on May 8. His decision to leave put Hendrix in charge of production with assistance from engineer Eddie Kramer. Eric Burdon later observed: "I think that when he and Chas parted ways, it was the end of the magic spell. Chas can be a complete bastard to people, and that's why he was a manager. Of course, he was the right kind of bastard for Jimi because he wouldn't take any of his shit. So, their two egos broke down, flowed together, and came up with the apex of Hendrix's career, the three wonderful albums. A producer does a lot of the work a musician doesn't want to do. That's where these guys come in and either enhance the product or totally fuck it up. So, in Jimi's case, when the producer left, he was bungling around from one idea to the next. Since Jimi didn't write music, the body of his work had to be captured on magnetic tape."[14]

Hendrix wrote "Rainy Day, Dream Away," another track on *Electric Ladyland*, in the middle of a heavy storm in Miami, Florida. Thirty-five minutes of the session still exist on tape, beginning with a long funk jam and followed by ten takes, six of which are under two minutes; three of the longer outtakes are really exciting. The tenth take was the one selected for the LP. Mike Finnigan, who played organ in true Jimmy Smith style on "Rainy Day, Dream Away/Still Raining, Still Dreaming," recalled: "We just jammed a little bit and started rolling tape. It was not something that was talked out or discussed. A couple of ideas happened while we were just jamming around, like the ending. It's kinda raggedy on the record, but that's just right off the top of our heads, we were just looking at each other. The only instruction we had from Jimi was, 'I want to play a shuffle, and we're going to play just one change.' 'Rainy Day' was a real laid back session. Larry Faucette played congas and Freddie Smith was the tenor [sax] player."[15]

Hendrix had some initial ideas for *Electric Ladyland*'s cover shot. One included popular fashion model Vera von Lehndorff (a.k.a. Veruschka): "First I wanted to get this beautiful woman, about six-foot seven, Veruschka, she's so sexy...we want to get her and have her leading us across this desert, and we have like these chains on us, but we couldn't find a desert 'cause we was working and we couldn't get a hold of her 'cause she was in Rome. But we have this one photo of us sitting on Alice in Wonderland, a bronze statue of it in Central Park, and we got some kids and all."[16]

Linda Eastman (later McCartney) photographed Hendrix, Mitchell, and Redding in New York's Central Park, sitting on a statue surrounded by both black and white children.

In a memo sent to Warner Bros., Hendrix clearly expressed his desire that Eastman's Central Park shot be used for the cover: "Please use the color pictures with us and the kids on the statue for front or back cover—outside cover.... Any other drastic change from these directions would not be appropriate according to the music and our group's present stage. We have enough personal problems without having to worry about this simple yet effective layout."[17] Instead, Warner Bros. opted for a solarized head shot for the front cover and a stiffly posed group shot for the back.

If this disregard for Hendrix's wishes wasn't frustrating enough, when *Electric Ladyland* was released in the U.K., its cover featured twenty-one nude women covering their genitals with Hendrix LP sleeves, posters, and photos. Several top record retailers refused to display the album and sold it only in brown wrappers. When the British press tracked down Hendrix for comment, he pleaded ignorance: "I don't know anything about it. I don't decide which pictures will be used on my records. In the States, this album had photographs of Noel, Mitch and me on the cover."[18]

In 1993, when the Hendrix catalog moved from Reprise to MCA, Hendrix's original cover concept for *Electric Ladyland* was again ignored. Producer Alan Douglas decided to remove all the original Hendrix cover art and replace it with covers that he felt would appeal to a new generation of Hendrix fans.[19] Four years later, when the Hendrix family took control of the catalog, they restored the original covers. Nonetheless, they missed yet another opportunity to finally carry out Jimi's original wishes for Eastman's cover photo.

After months of remixes, overdubs, and alternate takes, *Electric Ladyland* was completed on August 27. In a letter sent to Warner Bros. with the finished tapes, Hendrix wrote: "We would like to make an apology for taking so very long to send this but we have been working very hard indeed, doing shows and recording. I did the production.... I really took the bulk of it through from beginning to end on my own, so that I can't deny that it represents exactly what I was feeling at the time of production."[20]

When the *Electric Ladyland* tapes were mastered, many of Hendrix's brilliant audio ideas were lost. Until 1969, Reprise (a division of Warner Bros.) used Columbia Records' mastering facility, ignoring Hendrix's instructions, which were clearly written on the tape box: "SPECIAL PHASE EFFECTS ON TAPE: DO NOT CHANGE." After the album was released, Hendrix expressed his dismay with the final result. "When it came time for them to press it, quite naturally they screwed it up, because they didn't know what we wanted. There's 3-D sound being used on there that you can't even appreciate because they didn't know how to cut it properly. They thought it was out of phase."[21]

Electric Ladyland's first single, "All Along the Watchtower" b/w "Burning of the Midnight Lamp" (Reprise 0767), was released in America on September 21. The single reached #20 on *Billboard*'s charts and is Hendrix's only Top 40 credit with his own band. Hendrix's superb arrangement of this Bob Dylan tune inspired many critics and musicians. In the November 23, 1968, issue of the *New Musical Express*, Tony Palmer wrote: "Listen to the single...the sound is by Hendrix, orgasmic, sputtering, aching, as if the entire fabric of the world is being torn apart. It is an assault...which must be like the roaring one hears moments before being disintegrated by an exploding hydrogen bomb." Guitarist Carlos Santana has admitted that it's his favorite Hendrix song: "That song affects me the same way every time I hear it...because of the marriage of supreme lyrics and supreme playing. 'All Along the Watchtower' is one of the songs that if they were to play it on the radio, three times in one day, it would be a hit again."[22]

During 1968, Hendrix's version of "All Along the Watchtower," with its opening line "There must be some kinda way outta here..." seemed to become part of the soundtrack to the Vietnam War. Since Armed Forces radio was tightly controlled, GIs set up pirate radio stations in the fields and broadcast to troops fighting in rainforests and rice paddies. Vietnam veteran Michael Kelly recalls, "I just spun the dials...lo and behold there's Midnight Jack broadcasting: 'Midnight Jack, man, I'm deep in the jungle.' 'Oh, bad news, my man,' he says. 'What can I play for you man?' He's gone for about 30 seconds and I imagine he's putting a reel-to-reel tape on, y'know, and here comes Jimi Hendrix...."[23]

Electric Ladyland was released in the United States on October 16 and in the U.K. nine days later. It's hard to imagine today that an album such as this, filled with lush audio delights like stereo panning and 3-D sound effects, would even have been considered for release in boring mono. While no one has ever turned up an actual copy, Track Records planned to release the album in mono, and assigned it the catalog number Track 612 008/009.[24]

Although *Billboard* magazine mistakenly titled the album *Electric Landlady* for its first chart entry at #179, the following week *Electric Ladyland* went to #98 and then shot up to #9. As the Experience played to sold-out auditoriums across America, the LP quickly reached #1 in the U.S., overtaking Janis Joplin's *Cheap Thrills*. *Electric Ladyland* proved to be Hendrix's greatest commercial success.

STATUS: *The following tracks are all outtakes from the Electric Ladyland sessions.*

- ◆ *"Dream" b/w "Dance" (EMI—unreleased acetate mono single). "Dream" is the A-side to the acetate single that was pressed in early 1968 and intended for Redding's private collection. The Experience went into Olympic Sound Studios on December 21 and finished it in a week. "Dream" was written by Redding and features him on lead vocals. "Dance" (a.k.a. "Touch You") is another Redding demo that was never further developed. Hendrix later pinched the melody to use in his song "Ezy Ryder." Either track would have made an interesting B-side to the "Up from the Skies" single (Reprise 0665; released on February 26, 1968), but "One Rainy Wish" was used instead. Both tracks remain unreleased, but have appeared numerous times on bootleg recordings.*

- ◆ *"Little One." Listed on the session tapes as "Mushy Name," this song features Hendrix, Mitchell, and Dave Mason of Traffic on sitar and slide guitar. Mitch Mitchell recalled: "I've seen something listed from that period at Olympic called 'Mushy Name.' God knows what that was, could be one of mine that has never surfaced, including a vocal, which hopefully will never see the light of day."[25] The track is not as bad as Mitch imagines. Take one (3:32), recorded in January '68 at Olympic*

Studios, is the more restrained of the two. Take two (3:57) features Dave Mason playing a wonderful slide guitar against the psychedelic backdrop of a sitar, with Hendrix's rhythm guitar and Mitchell's slick drums. Both tracks are unreleased, but have surfaced many times on bootleg recordings.

♦ *"Tax Free." This was written by Sweden's Bo Hansson and Janne Karlsson. Hendrix heard their instrumental while touring Sweden in 1967 and decided to record it. On January 26, the Experience recorded five basic takes, the fifth being the most successful. When production switched over to the Record Plant in New York, Hendrix finished the track on May 1, adding several imaginative overdubs. The Experience added "Tax Free" to their set list during early 1968 and continued to play it live in early 1969. The studio track first appeared on the War Heroes LP (Reprise MS 2103) in 1972 and then on South Saturn Delta in 1997.*

♦ *"My Friend." Like its 1967 predecessor "Takin' Care of No Business," this song takes place in an imaginary barroom. Without Mitchell or Redding, Hendrix on bass was joined in the studio (on March 13) by the Fugs' guitarist, Ken Pine, on twelve-string guitar; Joey Dee and the Starlighters' drummer, Jimmy Mayes; and Paul Caruso (a personal friend) on harmonica. Stephen Stills also contributed a brief piano introduction. "My Friend" has appeared on two posthumous Hendrix albums, first in 1971 on The Cry of Love (Reprise MS 2034) and in 1997 on First Rays of the New Rising Sun (MCAD-11599).*

♦ *"Somewhere." Although it was recorded at New York's Sound Center studios in March 1968, this song was not selected for use on Electric Ladyland. In 1971, Mitch Mitchell revisited the track and overdubbed a new drum piece at Electric Lady Studios. "Somewhere" was officially released in 1975 on the Crash Landing LP (Reprise MS 2204), but session players replaced all of the original bass and drum tracks, except for Hendrix's vocal and guitar tracks. In 2000, the 1968 version of "Somewhere" (without the overdubs) was included in the Jimi Hendrix Experience box set. It is still unknown who originally played bass on this track.*

♦ *"Three Little Bears/South Saturn Delta." This extended jam was recorded on May 2 at the Record Plant. The first half was released in 1972 on the War Heroes LP (Reprise MS 2049). The U.S. version had parts of Hendrix's frustrated comments censored ("Oh, fuck me" and "Stop that shit, stop it"). In 1999, Experience Hendrix released the Jimi Hendrix: Merry Christmas and Happy New Year EP (622-001-039) which contained "Three Little Bears." The complete extended jam is only available on bootleg recordings.*

♦ *"South Saturn Delta." On June 14, at the Record Plant, an experimental recording session featured Hendrix with a small horn section. This session used Eddie Kramer and arranger Larry Fallon. The horn parts were added to Hendrix's unfinished composition originally recorded on May 2, 1968. Fallon remembers: "He [Hendrix] wanted to experiment with something, and then we were going to do a whole album in that particular kind of concept. Of course the record companies came in and* said that the album wouldn't be commercial enough."²⁶ *This track was released on* South Saturn Delta *in 1997.*

♦ *"Little Girl." One complete take of this song, which was written by Noel Redding, was recorded on May 17 at the Record Plant; however, Hendrix did not take part in this recording.*

♦ *"Cherokee Mist." This track was recorded on May 2 at the Record Plant. Hendrix recorded it twice during the* Axis: Bold As Love *sessions, but perfected it on this date without Redding present. This beautiful homage to his Native American ancestry was finally released in 1990 on* Lifelines: The Jimi Hendrix Story *(Reprise 9 26435-2); this version is now out of print.*

♦ *"Room Full of Mirrors." A short 1:25 demo of this song with Paul Caruso on harmonica was recorded on August 12, 1968. It was officially released in 2000 on the* Jimi Hendrix Experience *box set. Hendrix developed the song later in 1969.*

♦ *"How Can I Live." Redding and Mitchell recorded this in August while Hendrix was working on the final mix for* Electric Ladyland. *It remains unreleased.*

The TTG Studios Sessions

Following Hendrix's successful *Ladyland* sessions, the Experience spent almost ten days at TTG studios in Los Angeles during the later part of October (18, 20–25, 27, and 29) to record tracks for their fourth studio album. After playing six shows in three nights, October 10–12, at San Francisco's Winterland Arena, the band went to Los Angeles for a few well-deserved days off and moved into a $1,000-per-week rented house in Benedict Canyon that had once been occupied by the Beatles.

TTG, which stood for "Two Terrible Guys," was the brainchild of Tom Hidley and Ami Hadani, who previously worked for A&R studios in New York. Hidley and Hadani started TTG in 1965 and attracted rock stars like Hendrix, the Monkees, and Eric Burdon, who all wanted to use the studio's innovative technology—the world's first sixteen-track, two-inch recorder. This equipment doubled the capacity of the eight-track recorder, which was state-of-the-art in 1968, by increasing the tape width and modifying the motors on the machine. This became one of the greatest marketing ploys in recording studio history; since TTG was the only studio with the sixteen-track, two-inch recorder, musicians who started a session at the studio, like Hendrix, were forced to finish there.²⁷

The next time Hendrix returned to New York's Record Plant, he raved to Gary Kellgren and Chris Stone about TTG's wonderful sixteen-track facilities. "Hendrix came into the Record Plant just jumping up and down because he'd been to L.A. and was taken by Eric Burdon to this studio in L.A.," Chris Stone recalled. "He had no idea where it was, but he said they had something that made his guitar sound good."²⁸ Kellgren and Stone were so impressed with Hidley's design breakthrough that they opened a Los Angeles branch of the Record Plant and hired Hidley as director of technical operations.

Eric Burdon recalls this special time with Hendrix: "We hung out and listened to some new unmixed material. He could have been anywhere doing anything; he was the toast of the town, and yet there we were, sitting up on a hill, smoking joints, listening to music, feeling like we was on top of the world…which I guess we were."[29] While Hendrix and the Experience worked on their next album, Burdon was in another studio at TTG recording his *Love Is* LP (MGM 2619002) with the New Animals.

The first TTG session started on Friday, October 18, with two new Hendrix songs, "Messenger" and "Izabella." Neither yielded a master take. On Saturday the band took another day off and Hendrix attended Cream's farewell concert at the Los Angeles Forum. After the show, Hendrix gave a wild party at the Benedict Canyon house that lasted until five in the morning, and, as a result, he wound up smashing his Corvette Stingray and nearly went over a three-hundred-foot cliff. Photographs taken in the studio around this time show Hendrix with a bandage over his eyebrow.

Sessions resumed at TTG on Sunday, October 20, and lasted through Friday, October 25. Over this six-day period, several tracks were recorded that were later released posthumously, either officially or on bootlegs. "Look Over Yonder," a remake of "Mr. Bad Luck," a tune from Hendrix's Café Wha? days in New York, later appeared on the *Rainbow Bridge* soundtrack and, in 1997, on *South Saturn Delta*.

The breathtaking "New Rising Sun Overture," with an unaccompanied Hendrix on guitar and drums, was recorded October 23. The track was abandoned until 1974, when engineer John Jansen decided to combine segments of this song with three other Hendrix recordings. The experiment yielded "Captain Coconut," enhanced by new overdubs and eventually released in 1975 on *Crash Landing*. In 1994, producer Bruce Gary rediscovered the unedited "New Rising Sun Overture" while compiling the *Jimi Hendrix: Blues* CD. In its original form, "New Rising Sun Overture" runs nine minutes, but it was edited down to 3:21 when released on 1995's *Voodoo Soup* (MCAD-11236), now out of print.

At some point during the TTG sessions, Hendrix jammed with Cream's bassist, Jack Bruce. They met through a tailor named Genie Franklin whom they both employed in L.A. She invited Bruce to play at a recording session with Hendrix. Bruce recalled, "I went there, but it was so chaotic. I didn't stay very long. There were loads of people there…too many to even know who they were…that's the only thing I ever recorded with him; you can't really tell who's who because people were swapping instruments. It was not a good thing."[30] While there is a bootleg CD of this session, no official release ever occurred.

With the daily influx of musicians at Hendrix's TTG sessions, the decibel levels were sometimes more than the studio could handle. "We had leakage everywhere," Tom Hidley recalls, "and we're talking five or six musicians on a floor of a studio that would hold 80 musicians. And the sound pressure was so loud I could even hear it through the windows. We came to a very fast realization that the acoustics that were satisfactory for the days of acoustic recording weren't going to cut it for these loud bands."[31]

On October 25, Hendrix played bass for Soft Machine's drummer Robert Wyatt on a tune called "Slow Walkin' Talk." Wyatt recorded the demo at TTG for a possible solo project, and later recalled the circumstances behind the collaboration with Hendrix:

"The Experience had this place up in L.A. . . . and they had a place that was much bigger than they needed, so they gave me a room there. And there was a studio [TTG] out there that they had permanently booked, so I went in to try out some solo stuff on a keyboard they had. The one thing I couldn't play was bass so Hendrix came in and offered to play bass himself. I'd never have dreamt of asking him. As far as I remember it was a single take. And it's a really weird bass line the way it leaps out at you, and varies with each verse. He was very scared of being boring, Hendrix, which, of course, he never was."[32] Wyatt later added lyrics to the song and rerecorded it as "Soup Song." The original demo version with Hendrix on bass was officially released in 1994 on Wyatt's own compilation, *Flotsam Jetsam* (Rough Trade R3112).

Hendrix began expanding the three-piece sound of the Experience by bringing in drummer Buddy Miles and organist Lee Michaels. Miles and Michaels joined the group for a passionate rendition of "Red House" on October 29. It had become obvious to everyone around him that Hendrix wanted to take his music in a new direction. On the same day as this TTG session, Hendrix spoke with reporter Alan Welsh for *Melody Maker*, stating that the Experience would be breaking up soon: "Mitch and Noel want to get their own thing going . . . so very soon, probably in the new year, we'll be breaking the group [up,] apart from selected dates."[33]

UPI reporter Sharon Lawrence was invited to one of the TTG sessions and later recalled the chaos and excitement there: "I dropped by TTG Studios to watch him at work. It was quite a scene. A stream of girls dressed in their best Mod finery trooped in, eyeing each other, touching up their hair and their make-up every five minutes in the crowded control booth, like a bunch of sparrows all intent on capturing the same worm. The session didn't go well. Jimi was nervous about his singing, literally hiding in the tiny vocal booth, making agonized attempts to sound strong and assured, redoing the vocals over and over."

"Finally," Lawrence said, "the party dolls were urged to disappear. Noel and Mitch also left while Jimi stayed to listen to the playback. He was dejected by what he heard, obviously annoyed with himself. He put on his jacket and prepared to leave. Abruptly, he took it off again and purposefully strode into the main recording room. He picked up his guitar and started into one of his classic blues numbers—'There's a red house over yonder . . .' He played and sang with so much feeling that the engineer could barely speak: 'Man, that was magnificent.'"[34]

Another TTG studio gem that has not been officially released is a track called "Calling All Devil's Children." Two versions of this song have surfaced from the twenty-seven takes, the second version longer, with comic vocal overdubs by Hendrix and guests in the studio. Hendrix pretends to be a preacher or a politician rapping to America's youth, warning them about the evils of money. As the song continues, the plot shifts to a "hippie party," and Hendrix and gang wrap it up shouting "It's a bust!" and "Flush the toilet!" (to get rid of contraband).

In addition to "Calling All Devil's Children," several other tracks that were recorded remain unreleased. Mitch Mitchell recalls, "A lot of strange things came out of that period at TTG Studios, in L.A.—like a session with [British keyboard player and band leader] Graham Bond—most of which have never been released. Jimi and I had a play with Carole Kaye, the bass player who did a lot of sessions for Motown, after they moved to L.A. She was brilliant, scared the shit out of me."[35]

Following the Experience's recording sessions, TTG studio engineer Angel Balestier transferred the sixteen-track session tapes to the twelve-track format so that they would be compatible with the Record Plant's machines. Then Michael Jeffery evaluated all the TTG sessions and picked the best tracks to complete the Experience's fourth studio album, which was quite a task, since Hendrix gave explicit orders to Balestier at the beginning to keep tape rolling and never let it run out during the sessions.

STATUS: *When the tapes were all reviewed, the following tracks were deemed to be of album quality: "Calling All Devil's Children," "Electric Church," "Messenger" (take 15), "Look Over Yonder" (take 17), "The New Rising Sun Overture" (take 2), "Peace in Mississippi" (take 15), "Izabella" (take 18), "Jam #1" with Lee Michaels and Buddy Miles, "Jam # 2" with Lee Michaels, "Jam #4," and "Jam Session" (take 6). Most of the tracks listed here have been scattered over various posthumous official and bootleg releases, however, and a few remain "officially" unreleased.*

Eire Apparent's *Sunrise* Sessions

> *Right now I'm producing the Eire Apparent, which is a hard rock Irish group. They do more of a tinge of folk in it, but like Irish folk.*
> Jimi Hendrix, *Hullabaloo*, February 1969

After the Experience finished recording at TTG, sessions began for Eire Apparent's debut album titled *Sunrise* (Buddah Records BDS 5031). With production credits under his belt for his efforts with Buddy Miles, Hendrix was asked to produce Eire Apparent's album with assistance from engineer Eddie Kramer.

Eire Apparent formed in early 1967 when Northern Irish guitarist Henry McCullough teamed up with Belfast musicians Eric Stewart (bass), Ernie Graham (rhythm guitar, vocals), and David Lutton (drums) to form a psychedelic band originally called the People. When they moved to London in late 1967, Chas Chandler signed them for a deal with Track Records. To promote their first single, "Follow Me" (Track 604019), Chandler sent them on tour in 1968 with Hendrix, Soft Machine, and the New Animals. In Canada, McCullough was sent back to Ireland for visa problems, and guitarist Michael "Mick" Cox took his place.

Hendrix produced all songs on *Sunrise* except "Got to Get Away" and "1026." In addition to production credits, he also added his solos and special guitar effects to the music, such as the laughing sounds found on "The Clown." Also featured on the LP were Noel Redding and Robert Wyatt.

During the sessions for *Sunrise*, Eddie Kramer and Hendrix had a difference of opinion.

Kramer was used to being in charge at the mixing board and felt threatened when Hendrix started calling the shots. "With the Eire Apparent sessions he wanted to take control of the whole process, and I was annoyed at that," Kramer recalls. "I think he was trying to expand his horizons, but he was trying to take over my gig. We had a parting of the ways because of this project. I didn't even finish it."[36]

Production for *Sunrise* then moved to London's Polydor Studios and Polydor Records engineer Carlos Olms was brought in to help finish the record. Olms noted that Hendrix worked from eleven o'clock at night until nine in the morning to get the exact sound he wanted on tape. Hendrix completed work on *Sunrise* during the first week of January 1969.

The album's first single, "Rock 'n' Roll Band" b/w "Yes I Need Someone" (Buddah 201039) was released in the U.K. on March 3, 1969. In America, "Rock 'n' Roll Band" was coupled with "Let Me Stay" (Buddah 2011-117). The English LP was released two months later and included the songs "The Clown," "Let Me Stay," "Magic Carpet," "Mr. Guy Fawkes," "Someone Is Sure to (Want You)," "Morning Glory," "Captive in the Sun," "Got to Get Away," "1026," "Yes I Need Someone," and "Rock 'n' Roll Band."

The same week that *Sunrise* was released, *Melody Maker* published an interview with Hendrix. In the article, he expressed the joy he got from producing, but mentioned his dissatisfaction with the results: "I enjoy doing that [producing] as long as I like what they are playing. I liked doing the Eire Apparent record, but it was never really finished according to my standards."[37]

STATUS: *Sunrise* **is out of print. Both Repertoire Records (Germany, 1991) and One Way Records (USA, 1993) released the original LP on CD and included the single "Rock 'n' Roll Band," which was not on the original American LP.** *Sunrise* **was recorded at the Record Plant (New York, August 1968), TTG (Los Angeles, October 1968), and Polydor (London, January 1969). The engineers were Eddie Kramer, Gary Kellgren, Tony Bongiovi, Jack Hunt, and Carlos Olms.**

Cat Mother and the All Night Newsboys

On November 1, the Experience began a short tour, playing mostly on the weekends through the first of December. Joining them as a supporting act was a New York band called Cat Mother and the All Night Newsboys. Cat Mother, also managed by Michael Jeffery, included Bob Smith (keyboards, vocals), Michael Equine (percussion, vocals), Charlie Chin (guitar, banjo), Larry Packer (lead guitar, violin, mandolin), and Roy Michaels (rhythm guitar, bass, vocals). Founding member Michaels had begun his career as a member of the Au Go Go singers with Stephen Stills and Richie Furay. Sometime during the scheduled tour dates, Hendrix agreed to produce Cat Mother's album *The Street Giveth . . . and the Street Taketh Away* (Polydor 24-4001).

Hendrix entered the Record Plant studios on November 6 to begin production. He did not play guitar, but offered suggestions from the control room. According to John

Hallenstadion, Zurich, Switzerland, May 31, 1968. *Barrie Wentzell/Star File*

McDermott's book *Sessions*, the complete multitrack tapes recorded for this album have disappeared and are "mysteriously absent" from both the Polygram and Hendrix tape libraries. All that remain are two reels of "tepid jamming with Hendrix accompanied by an unknown guitarist."[38]

STATUS: The Street Giveth . . . and the Street Taketh Away, *now out of print, was released in May 1969, while Cat Mother was still a supporting act on the Experience's tour. The album generated a successful single that reached #21 on Billboard's Top 100, "Good Old Rock 'n Roll," which was a medley of 1950s rock hits ("Sweet Little Sixteen," "Long Tall Sally," "Chantilly Lace," "Whole Lot of Shakin' Going On," "Blue Suede Shoes," and "Party Doll"). After Hendrix helped kick-start Cat Mother's career, the band went on to record another album for Polydor and two for United Artists.*

Hendrix's Movie Manuscript

Hendrix revealed his fascination with becoming a movie actor in 1967 when he told a reporter for the underground newspaper *Open City,* "When I was a little boy I wanted to be a cowboy or a movie star. Quite naturally they didn't have many colored cowboys around, so I decided on the movie role."[39] As the concept for a movie emerged, plans for the Experience to star in a fantasy film were first made public in October 1968. The *New*

Musical Express announced that production for a movie would start the following year, but little detail was provided in the article other than that the film project would be an extension of a light show with musical content. The public was unaware that in 1968 Hendrix had privately written a thirty-three-page movie manuscript titled *Moondust*.

When Hendrix returned to England in March 1969, he again mentioned the subject of an Experience film to the British press. "I've written music and a screenplay for a film," he told *Melody Maker,* "and they are getting it together." But with the dismal failure of the Beatles' 1967 film *Magical Mystery Tour* and the growing turmoil within the Experience, the Hendrix film project was canceled.

Hendrix's original *Moondust* manuscript was auctioned in 1992 for $16,500. The Sotheby's auction catalog gave prospective buyers a thorough description of the manuscript's contents. On page one, Hendrix listed the characters for the movie: The Powerful Sound King, his two friends, the supernatural innocent girl, the supernatural witch, the visual god, party people, and the good guy. Obviously, Hendrix would have played "The Powerful Sound King." Mitchell and Redding, mentioned on page three, would have played his "two friends." The Sotheby's catalog notes asserted that the *Moondust* characters were based on the individuals found in a 1966 issue of Marvel Comics' *Spiderman* entitled "The Birth of a Super Hero." According to Sotheby's, Hendrix often carried this particular issue around with him.

Until this manuscript surfaced in 1992, no one realized that Hendrix had a talent for scriptwriting. Throughout the thirty-three handwritten pages, Hendrix detailed his ideas for camera angles, lighting, and dialogue. The Sotheby's catalog described one of the imaginative scenes: "As the music continues on, people are becoming hypnotized by the sounds. At this point, a girl gets so completely wrapped up in what's happening that she tears the shirt off a stranger at the next table, and without a word spoken, they fall to the floor, making love. This happens three or four times with different couples."[40]

STATUS: *In 1993, author Bill Nitopi compiled and edited a large collection of Hendrix's handwritten works for a book titled* **Cherokee Mist: The Lost Writings of Jimi Hendrix** *(HarperCollins, 1993). This book, now out of print, reprinted twenty-six pages of the* **Moondust** *manuscript.*

Written Work in Progress

Hendrix worked on the following songs, essays, and other written ideas in 1968. Many of these turned up in auctions in the 1990s.

"As I Looked into My Crystal Ball," "Calling All the Devil's Children," "Catch That Bug," "Cryin' Blue Rain," "Grey Village of North Grey Isle," "Heaven and Angels," "Hello Night Bird," "Hospital Snore," "Kiss the Sunshine: Kiss the Sunshine," "My Friend," "One Kiss of Your Eyes," "Poor Miss Clara Crenshaw," "Return Little Bird," "Roman Empire USA,"

"Thank You God," "That's What Happens When You Get—Just a Little Too Stoned," "True Love—Blue Love," "You Wait."

Rare Recordings

◆ One of the afternoon sound check rehearsals was recorded during the Experience's three-day stint at the Winterland Arena in San Francisco (February 2–4).

STATUS: *"Can You Please Crawl out Your Window" was recorded from the soundboard and is in circulation through the collectors' network.*

◆ One of the strangest stories about the acquisition of a rare Hendrix tape concerns a soft-drink vendor at the Winterland Arena in San Francisco. When the arena closed in the late 1970s, he was given a thank-you gift—an original reel from the soundboard made by Bill Graham's sound crew at Winterland. The forty-six-minute tape, recorded at one of the February 1968 shows, features "Killin' Floor," "Red House," "Catfish Blues," "Dear Mr. Fantasy," and "Purple Haze."

STATUS: *This tape was sold to Experience Hendrix in 1998 and remains unreleased.*

◆ The March 15 show at Clark University in Worcester, Massachusetts, was recorded and filmed by Tony Palmer for the BBC documentary *All My Loving*. Only a short clip of "Wild Thing" made it into the documentary.

STATUS: *Experience Hendrix recently purchased the rest of the footage. To date, all that has been released on the Dagger label is* **Live at Clark University,** *a seventy-minute CD of music and interviews with the Experience from that show.*

◆ A soundboard recording was made for the Experience's show on July 6 at the Woburn Music Festival in Woburn Abbey, England. Caesar Glebbeek, editor of the Hendrix fanzine *UniVibes*, now owns this tape. Over the years, *UniVibes* has offered its subscribers three CDs of rare Hendrix recordings. Alan Douglas allowed the fanzine to release the CDs based on the agreement that all profits would be donated to charity. Shortly after Experience Hendrix took control in 1995, *UniVibes* approached them with a similar offer for a fourth CD featuring the Woburn Abbey Experience concert, but was turned down.

STATUS: *Glebbeek informed his subscribers in his December 1999 issue that he would release the complete Woburn Abbey Hendrix soundboard on July 6, 2018, since "one does not need any clearance for recordings over 50 years old." The fifty-minute soundboard recording features "Sgt. Pepper's Lonely Hearts Club Band," "Fire," "Tax Free," "Red House," "Foxy Lady," "Voodoo Child (Slight Return)," and "Purple Haze."*

◆ The Jimi Hendrix Experience played New York's prestigious Philharmonic Hall on November 28. Originally, the band was to perform at Carnegie Hall, but the booking was refused on the grounds that Hendrix's audiences got out of hand and would destroy auditorium fixtures. This refusal gave rise to one of the Experience's most unusual concert billings. Promoter Ron Delsner persuaded Philharmonic Hall to host the show under the condition that classical overtones be added to the evening's performance. The two shows that night, billed as "An Electronic Thanksgiving," were opened by baroque harpsichordist Fernando Valenti and the New York Brass Quintet, and at one point, Mitch Mitchell made an early stage call to play percussion with them. The Jimi Hendrix Experience was the first rock act ever to perform at Philharmonic Hall.

The Experience's performances at the Philharmonic received outstanding reviews. Robert Shelton of the *New York Times* wrote: "It all begins to make sense if we view the superstar, Mr. Hendrix, as a great classical virtuoso. He breaks strings, as did Paganini. He postures, as did Liszt. He deals in thundering climaxes, as did Beethoven. He explores the range of colors and effects of his guitar-turned-orchestra, as did Stravinsky with other instruments."[41] Ed Ochs's review for *Billboard* magazine declared, "Hendrix punished two guitars till they cried out in great gulps of psychedelic agony and flashed his classical-type virtuosity for a savage bunch of teeny-boppers."[40]

STATUS: *Three different audience recordings were made of the Experience's first show at Philharmonic Hall but, surprisingly, no recordings of the second show have surfaced. The longest tape runs seventy-five minutes and is of fair-to-good audio quality. The second and third recordings are shorter, fifty-five and twenty-five minutes respectively, and have very good audio quality. One of the earliest Hendrix bootlegs issued on vinyl was* **Live at Philharmonic Hall.**

Great Jams, No Tapes

The following is a list of jams in which Hendrix participated during 1968 for which no recordings are known to exist.

ALBERT KING AND JANIS JOPLIN

In 1999, a live CD called *Albert King with Stevie Ray Vaughan: In Session* (Stax SCD-7601-2) was released. At the start of the track titled "Blues at Sunrise," King raps about a previously unknown jam that took place in San Francisco while the Experience played both Fillmore West and Winterland on February 1–4, two shows per night. King recalled the jam as vividly as if it had taken place yesterday: "This is that thing I recorded with Jimi Hendrix and Janis Joplin at the Fillmore West . . . 'Blues at Sunrise.'" After a solo he tells Vaughan, "See, you got to play the Jimi Hendrix thing, 'cause he was on this too. Later on in the song Jimi said, 'Let's play some blues,' I said, 'Okay, but not without the queen,' though, that's Janis. She came out with a little glass, she always had a little glass, God rest

An Electronic Thanksgiving, Philharmonic Hall, New York, November 28, 1968. *Dagmar/Star File*

her soul. She said, 'What's happening?' I said, 'We're going to play some blues, and we want you to start it off, honey.' She said, 'Cool!' and Jimi hit two or three more licks." Although the late Albert King mentioned that the jam was recorded, no tape has ever surfaced.

GARFIELD HIGH JAM

During the beginning of the Experience's second tour of America, Hendrix returned to his hometown, Seattle. The mayor of Seattle was ready to give Hendrix the key to the city, but since it was a national holiday (Lincoln's Birthday) and City Hall was closed, the event was canceled. To make up for the oversight, Garfield High School agreed to give Hendrix an honorary diploma.

On February 13, Hendrix visited Garfield High School accompanied by local deejay Pat O'Day, who organized the event. In an interview in *Straight Ahead*, O'Day recalled: "Jimi actually got kicked out of high school. And here he returns to Seattle as a big, big star. And HE wanted to go back to his high school, and make things right. However, the funny thing was his high school was all black—about 85% black, so the students at the high school were totally unaware of Jimi Hendrix. It wasn't their type of music."

O'Day made arrangements with the principal, Frank Fidler. "I told him all about Jimi," O'Day said, "and Frank thought that it would be a great motivational tool for the students to see one of their own who had made it big internationally, in the white world and the music world. Nevertheless, we didn't know what to do. Jimi didn't know what he wanted to do either. He didn't think he should set up his equipment and play. Besides, his equipment was already shipped out from the concert the night before.

"We set up a combination pep assembly for a basketball game and for Jimi's personal appearance. I said to him that morning, 'Here's what we'd better do. Let's get up and I will introduce you, say a few words about what has happened to you, and then let's let the students ask some questions. And that would be a good way to fill the time.' The cheer-leaders got up and did some cheers for twenty-five minutes, getting ready for the game. And then it was Jimi's turn. I was there to introduce Jimi.

"Jimi came to the microphone and said, 'I've been here and there, and everywhere, and it's all working,' and at that point, he stopped talking and stood there. I went up and took the microphone and said, 'Jimi, you have a lot of people that are fascinated by your incredi-ble fame, and some people here would like to ask you some questions, find out how you did it, find out what your feelings are.' There was a long pause, and Jimi was uncomfortable—I was uncomfortable, too. But it was Jimi's idea! He insisted on it! Finally one student raised his hand and asked, 'How long have you been gone?' Jimi replied, 'Oh, about 2000 years.' Then another student asked, 'How do you write a song?' And Jimi said, 'Right now, I'm going to say goodbye to you, and go out the door, and get into my limousine, and go to the airport. And when I go out the door, the assembly will be over, and the bell will ring. And as I get into the limousine and hear that bell ringing, I will probably write a song. Thank you very much.' And with that, Jimi raised his hand and gave a little wave."[43]

In a conflicting story, Hendrix told the press that he *did* perform at Garfield High School. Perhaps Hendrix had his guitar and plugged into one of the school band's amps: "I went to Garfield High School, my old school where they kicked me out when I was just 16. I did a concert for the kids there. Just me. I played with the school band in the gymnasium. Only thing wrong was that it was eight in the morning. They cancelled first class to listen to me."[44] If this event actually happened, and had been taped, it would make for a most amusing recording.

JONI MITCHELL

Singer-songwriter Joni Mitchell met Hendrix at the Capitol Theatre in Ottawa, Canada, on March 19. "After his set, he came down, and he brought a big reel-to-reel tape recorder," Mitchell recalled. "He introduced himself very shyly and said, 'Would you mind if I taped your show?' I said, 'Not at all.' And later that evening, we went back, we were staying at the same hotel. He and his drummer Mitch [Mitchell], the three of us were talking. It was so innocent. But management, all they saw was three hippies. We were outcasts anyway. A black hippie! Two men and a woman in the same room. So, they kept telling us to play lower. It was a very creative, special night. We were playing like children."[45]

BUDDY GUY

One of the legendary blues artists that Hendrix often cited as a big influence was Buddy

Guy. "I got to know Hendrix very well," Guy says. "The first night I met him [April 5] the audience was saying 'Hendrix!' and I was saying, 'Who's that?' We got to know each other by him asking me if he could tape what I was playing. And I said I don't care who tapes what I am playing. We got to sit down and know one another. We got to jam some. Every time I got to New York and play he would say, 'Could I sit in and jam?,' and I said, 'Yeah.'"[46]

TED NUGENT

Amboy Dukes guitarist Ted Nugent jammed with Hendrix in New York during the middle of April: "We did a couple of dressing room things where he played this kind of [inspirational] stuff....If you had seen what he accomplished in one night in New York when I played with him, it would have changed your life. It changed mine. The way he played, the notes he chose, the borders he broke down, and the ground that he created—it was absolutely earth-shattering."[47] When the Amboy Dukes recorded their version of "Baby Please Don't Go," Nugent managed to toss in a quick riff from "Third Stone from the Sun," a tip of the hat to Hendrix.

FRANK ZAPPA, ARTHUR BROWN, AND JOHN LEE HOOKER

Since the second day of the Miami Pop Festival (May 19) was canceled due to intense rainstorms, some of the musicians took refuge at the Castaways Hotel. In the evening, Hendrix, Redding, Frank Zappa, Zappa's drummer Jimmy Carl Black, John Lee Hooker, and Arthur Brown all jammed at the Wreck Bar inside the hotel. Michael Jeffery's secretary, Trixie Sullivan, recalled the jam session as "absolutely incredible."[48]

THE JEFF BECK GROUP

British guitarist Jeff Beck, who replaced Eric Clapton in the Yardbirds, formed a new band, simply called the Jeff Beck Group, in 1968. The hard-rock unit included Rod Stewart on vocals, Nicky Hopkins on piano, Mickey Waller on drums, and Ron Wood on bass. Beck remembered a two-week gig at the Scene, a club in New York City, that year, and his jam with Hendrix afterwards: "We went out one night, after we'd finished up at The Scene. We'd already played two hours of raving rock and roll, with him [Hendrix] coming up for the encore. Then we went to the New York Brasserie to have something to eat...at four a.m. he said, 'Let's go back to the hotel.' I thought, Thank God; he'll fall asleep and I'll go off home. But instead, he'd start playing music and we'd go out somewhere else at five o'clock. This kind of thing was just an everyday occurrence with him. I'd be history two days afterwards, and he'd still be at it."[49]

In addition to Hendrix's jam with the Jeff Beck Group at the Scene, he also sat in with them at the Daytop Music Festival on June 16 on Staten Island, New York. Hendrix later invited bassist Ron Wood over to his place and gave him some early B.B. King records. "I spent the whole day sitting in his room," Wood recalls. "He was playing me all these ideas and all of these tapes he'd made. And for some reason [I forgot]. I guess I was so caught up in it at the time."[50]

Café au Go Go,
New York City,
April 17, 1968.
Amalie R. Rothschild/Star File

JOE TEX

Mitch Mitchell recalled an occasion during the summer of 1968 when Hendrix asked him to play some R&B at New York's Town Hall, failing to mention that it was a Black Power benefit: "I was sleeping in the hotel room, and Jimi came by, guitar case in hand. It was about one o'clock in the morning, and he said, 'I want you to come with me right now...there's a play.' So I said, 'Okay, fine,' and we jumped in the car and went downtown to this mammoth hall. As we walked through the door, I could see that this was a giant black hootenanny, and Joe Tex and his band were onstage. Quite frankly, I was the only white person in the place . . . getting up to play with Jimi, Joe Tex and a big 17-piece band, no rehearsal, no nothing! We were taking all kind of chances musically."[51] In his book, *Jimi Hendrix: Inside the Experience*, Mitchell added, "I did the best I could, and it was OK. I wouldn't have missed it for the world."[52]

ALVIN LEE AND LARRY CORYELL

Alvin Lee of Ten Years After recalled the night (possibly in June) guitarist Larry Coryell and Hendrix sat in with his group: "It was just one number and in the end they had to turn the power off to stop us. In the small clubs, it's all jam things. You learn a hell of a lot more."[53] Coryell picks up the story from here: "The only jamming I ever did with him onstage was at The Scene. I don't have any tapes of myself jamming with Hendrix . . . we never played guitar to guitar. He almost always played bass."[54]

STEPPENWOLF

John Kay of Steppenwolf recalled a jam that took place in midsummer. "It must have been the second or third night we were playing," he remembered, "and Jimi walked in with Buddy Miles, whom we had known before because Buddy was still with the Electric Flag at the time. I don't think it was Rick Derringer . . . it must have been someone else from the McCoys, a tall lanky keyboard player whose name escapes me at the time, and they all wanted to jam. So, we said fine! It was this kind of a mix and match thing . . . our guitar player stayed up for a little bit . . . everybody sat in on a rotating manner. At one point, we just got off the stage and dug the whole thing. Later that night, Teddy was ready to shut the club down and we all left; Jimi was sitting in a Corvette outside. He asked me to come over and we chatted briefly . . . and said something about 'Thanks for letting us play.'"[55]

Organist Mike Finnigan, the "tall lanky keyboard player" mentioned by Kay, also recalled this unrecorded jam: "We went down to The Scene and Steppenwolf was playing there and Buddy Miles and Jimi and I sat in. Jimi blew up an amp immediately. He fucking blew this amp up before we even played, just turned it on, and hit a couple of things and smoke came out! They had some spare gear there, thank God. I thought, 'Oh this is a nice sound check, here we sit in and fuck up your stuff.' We just played a few jams, two or three tunes, and we had a good time."[56]

GRAHAM BOND, BUDDY MILES, AND ERIC BURDON

Ann Moses, editor of the teen magazine *Tiger Beat*, wrote about a superstar jam that took place on September 18: "Buddy Miles, former drummer for the Electric Flag, opened this week at The Whiskee-a-go-go [sic] with his newly formed group—Buddy Miles Express. . . . For the last number of the night, the group on the Whiskee stage consisted of Jimi Hendrix (lead guitar), Graham Bond (organ), Buddy Miles (rhythm guitar), Noel Redding (bass), Mitch Mitchell (drums) and Eric Burdon (vocals)."

Most people would like to retire and just disappear from the scene, which I'd LOVE to do, but then there's still things I'd like to say. I wish it wasn't so important to me, I wish I could just turn my mind off, you know, and forget about the scene.

JIMI HENDRIX, *INTERNATIONAL TIMES*, MARCH 28, 1969

CHAPTER SEVEN

THE END OF THE BEGINNING: 1969

In early 1970, *Rolling Stone* asserted "Jimi Hendrix made no music in 1969," and mockingly awarded him the "No News Is Big News Award."[1] The magazine's judgment was based solely on the fact that Hendrix's only musical release that year was a best-of compilation called *Smash Hits* (Reprise MS 20250). Its staff overlooked the amount and range of music he played that year, exploring jazz and other non-pop musical avenues. There was plenty of big news for Hendrix in 1969.

The performance year began on January 4, when the Jimi Hendrix Experience appeared on the British TV variety show *Happening for Lulu*. The show was hosted by Lulu, the Scottish pop singer who became famous for her hit "To Sir, with Love," the theme song to the 1967 Sidney Poitier movie of the same name. In 1968, her show debuted on the BBC and its producer, Stanley Dorfman, described it as "45 minutes of live, unscripted, anything-can-happen television."[2] An unscripted event during the Experience's perform-ance prompted Terry Quinn to write in his TV column for the *New Musical Express*: "I have the feeling that it might be some time before Jimi Hendrix works on BBC-TV again!... viewers might remember that Jimi performed THREE numbers... Jimi was only supposed to do TWO numbers and he threw in the third at the last moment as a tribute to Cream. Having declared his 'Hey Joe' rendition, for which he couldn't remember the words, as 'rubbish'! This was a complete surprise to Lulu, not to mention her producer who

The Experience at the BBC-TV studios, Shepherd's Bush, London, England, January 4, 1969. This photo was taken moments before the live broadcast of *Happening for Lulu*. *Barrie Wentzell/Star File*

had to do some frantic on-the-run changes in the final minutes of the programme! You can believe me that the startled look on Lulu's face as she said 'Thank you very much Jimi' was for real."[3] Hendrix's unannounced stunt resulted in the BBC's *Six O'Clock News* being delayed.

The Last European Tour

On January 8, the Experience began what would be the trio's final European tour, performing twenty-four concerts in sixteen days in Sweden, Denmark, Austria, and West Germany. Their first concert was in Gothenburg, Sweden.

Noel Redding has said that Hendrix was "sullen" and "removed" during this final Experience tour of Europe. He stated: "On the whole, I can't understand how anyone who saw us could have liked the group... we were very tired and very bored, and it showed. We were playing the same songs for so long it became sloppy. No wonder Chas wasn't interested when Jimi asked him in Gothenburg [on January 8] to become our manager [again]."[4] Some of the concert tapes do seem to reflect the band's high stress level as their final days neared. As further evidence of his lack of interest, Hendrix told the audience in Stockholm, Sweden

Salvation, Greenwich Village, New York City, September 10, 1969. *Jay Good/Star File*

(January 9, first show) to be patient because the group hadn't practiced in a while, and then he muttered slightly off-mic, "You wouldn't know the difference anyway."

But the Experience's creative fires still burned. Despite Redding's observations, the band received some wonderful concert reviews on this tour. Wolfgang Vogel wrote of the January 17 concert in Frankfurt, Germany: "Hendrix is the master. Musically he reaches far beyond the listening habits of his audience.... He doesn't abide by scales... never does he stick to the given time signature during his chorus... this is utopian music. We can hear music which will one day enter the history of music as a revolution like bop or free jazz."[5] The January 19 concert in Stuttgart also received high praise: "He only has to touch the strings lightly, and the instrument starts to talk and whine and moan and scream up to 100 decibels, dangerously tearing your eardrums. He drags the neck of the guitar sensually across the microphone stand, sending streams of ecstasy through the bodies of the teens... his tonal orgasms resist any attempt to be categorized."[6]

When the Experience played the Sportpalast in Berlin on the twenty-third, a political riot erupted. "We never found out anymore of what it was about but we were told it was going to happen," Noel Redding recalled. "I walked on stage and the first thing I saw, virtually, was someone being beaten up in the audience. The police had to surround the stage in the end. We were forced to stop. I just couldn't believe the stupidity of it."[7] A local reporter further described the frightening situation at the Berlin venue: "Thousands of youngsters besieged the aisles, occupied seats that they had not paid for, and threw firecrackers. The tired flank of grandfatherly looking ushers had long left the battlefield of ongoing failure."[8]

STATUS: *Thirteen recordings were made from this tour. They are: Gothenburg, Sweden (January 8, second show); Stockholm, Sweden (January 9, both shows professionally recorded); Copenhagen, Denmark (January 10, both shows); Hamburg, Germany (January 11, first show); Münster, Germany (January 14); Nuremberg, Germany (January 16); Frankfurt, Germany (January 17, second show); Stuttgart, Germany (January 19, first show); Vienna, Austria (January 22, both shows); and Berlin, Germany (January 23).*

Although audience members made the majority of extant recordings, the sound quality runs from good to excellent. The January 10 Copenhagen concert is the most noteworthy and features some of the best-recorded versions of "Tax Free," "I Don't Live Today," and "Purple Haze." The Frankfurt, Stuttgart, and Vienna concert tapes also have extraordinary moments. The Frankfurt show in particular has some of the most inspirational versions of "Red House" and "Little Wing" that collectors have heard so far.

The *Electric Church* Sessions

At the end of January, Hendrix flew from London to New York for a business meeting to discuss building Electric Lady Studios. He also intended to establish a publishing company to be called Bella Godiva Music. During his New York stay, Hendrix began producing the second Buddy Miles Express album, *Electric Church* (Mercury SR-61222), at Mercury Sound Studios.

In a note dated February 5, Hendrix advised his management that he was serious about being recognized as a record producer: "Please make clear to Mercury that in due time the Buddy Miles Express' new LP will be one of the biggest for Mercury and we are working very hard on it and it would seem to be honestly fair for my name alone to appear as producer....I know a name on an LP jacket sounds like a small tut, but one of my ambitions is to be a good producer."[9] Hendrix's busy tour schedule over the next few months interfered with his role as producer and he produced only four of the album's songs: "Miss Lady," "'69 Freedom Special," "Destructive Love," and "My Chant."

STATUS: *Archivist John McDermott pointed out in his book* Jimi Hendrix: Sessions *that nearly all the multitrack master tapes from the* Electric Church *sessions have been lost, stolen, or destroyed, leaving only the quarter-inch album master. One session tape has surfaced, most likely from the March 15 session, for "Destructive Love," which features Hendrix playing guitar with the Buddy Miles Express. On the tape, Hendrix can be heard asking from the control booth if there is an amp in the studio that he could plug into. It* *seems that he wanted to help out because the band was dragging. With Hendrix on guitar and adding vocals, the band and the track became much more focused. Often referred to as the "Blue Window Jam" or "Crying Blue Rain," this unreleased track continues to make the rounds of the collectors' network. Electric Church was released in June 1969 on LP and has never been released on CD.*

Larry Young (Khalid Yasin)

Sometime in the early spring of 1969, organist Larry Young met Hendrix and they jammed at the Record Plant. Their collaborations yielded some incredible music. "It's Too Bad" and "World Traveler" are Hendrix compositions with lyrics, blending Young's abstract funkiness with Hendrix's R&B rhythms. "Young/Hendrix," a wild and moving instrumental jam, featured the two artists trading solos, then merging again in tight unison. One other short instrumental jam was recorded, but it abruptly ended when everyone could tell it was going nowhere.

Like Hendrix, Young began playing with local R&B groups in his teens and later with professional musicians. Inspired by the music of John Coltrane, with whom he later developed a strong friendship, Young was also fascinated by Coltrane's interest in Islam. Young also worked under the Sunni Muslim name Khalid Yasin. Some of his well-known recorded works include *Unity* (1965, Blue Note CDP 7 784221 2) and Miles Davis's *Bitches Brew* (1969, Columbia C2K 65774). Fellow jazz organist Brother Jack McDuff dubbed Young "the Coltrane of the organ."[10] In 1969, Young was a founding member of drummer Tony Williams's band Lifetime, which also included guitarist John McLaughlin.

STATUS: *Most of Young's jams with Hendrix are now out of print. In 1980, Reprise released the album* **Nine to the Universe** *(HS 2299), which featured the track "Young/Hendrix." The album's liner notes incorrectly state that the session took place on May 14, 1969 — Hendrix was recording with Johnny Winter and Stephen Stills on this date.* **Nine to the Universe** *was never officially released on CD.*

A version of "It's Too Bad" has been available in the collectors' network, and the Jimi Hendrix Experience box set (MCA 088 112 320-2) featured an alternate and longer mix of that song. Some Hendrix collectors dispute the February 11, 1969, recording date listed on the box set's liner notes because the music sounds similar to the recordings made on March 25, 1969, at the Hendrix–John McLaughlin session. If these collectors are correct, this may not even be Khalid Yasin on organ. John McLaughlin stated in the February 1975 issue of **Circus** *magazine that Duane Hitchings of the Buddy Miles Express was playing organ when he arrived at the studio.*

The Royal Albert Hall Concerts

After touring Germany, Hendrix returned to England with Mitchell and Redding for an engagement at London's esteemed Royal Albert Hall. Since this was the Experience's first English concert in over six months, tickets for the show on February 18 sold out within three hours. Michael Jeffery quickly arranged for a second show on February 24, which sold out as well.

While there is an audience tape of the concert on February 18, rumors continue that a soundboard tape may have also been made. In an interview with *Straight Ahead*, Abe Jacob, the Experience's live sound engineer, was asked if this concert and others may have been professionally recorded. He replied, "Well, I did some of those. Where those tapes are today, I have no idea. They were just mono reel-to-reel of the mixing board. I did do a mono 1/4" reel of Royal Albert Hall, I remember. That was the format back then in England."[11]

Former Traffic drummer Jim Capaldi joined Hendrix and others on stage for a jam at the Royal Albert Hall on the twenty-fourth. Capaldi sensed the end was near for the Experience: "I had a strong feeling about Jimi when we played that show at the Albert Hall. It was like the end of it really. He just stood there on the stage playing blues and it was like, totally gone, a separation. It's all over. The Experience was over... all the great stuff from that period was over. I don't know what he would have done next, but the first phase, that was it."[12]

STATUS: *All that has surfaced of the February 18, 1969, Royal Albert Hall show is a ninety-minute audience recording with very good audio quality. The tape includes: "Tax Free," "Fire," "Hear My Train a Comin'," "Foxy Lady," "Red House," "Sunshine of Your Love," "Spanish Castle Magic/Message to Love," "The Star Spangled Banner," "Purple Haze," and "Voodoo Child (Slight Return)."*

An unreleased soundboard tape of the afternoon rehearsals at the Royal Albert Hall on February 24 has surfaced. This thirty-minute tape starts with the band playing "Hey Joe" and includes five takes of "Hound Dog" and two takes of "Voodoo Child (Slight Return)." It concludes with a powerful version of "Hear My Train a Comin'." The entire evening's concert was professionally recorded and filmed as well, but the horrid sound quality on highly edited official recordings from this show have haunted record stores since the early 1970s.

A 102-minute soundboard tape from the February 24 Royal Albert Hall show, which is available on bootleg, includes: "Lover Man," "Stone Free," "Hear My Train A Comin'," "I Don't Live Today," "Red House," "Foxy Lady," "Sunshine of Your Love," "Bleeding Heart," "Fire," "Little Wing," "Voodoo Child (Slight Return)," "Room Full of Mirrors," "Purple Haze," and "Wild Thing." Although Abe Jacob only remembered making a mono tape, this is an excellent stereo recording.

Jamming with Rahsaan

"I really would like to meet Roland Kirk and I'd like him to play with us ... I really think we're doing the same things. We have different moods and I think some of the moods are on the same level that Roland Kirk is doing."

Jimi Hendrix, *Melody Maker*, June 1967

Writer Bill Milkowski described how Hendrix's musical interests were evolving in 1969: "He was listening to more jazz, enjoying the sound of [John] Coltrane, [Ornette] Coleman, McCoy Tyner, and Rahsaan Roland Kirk—who was like an idol to him. Jimi's own musical ideas were probably closer to Kirk's than to the modal concepts of Coltrane or Miles. Since Hendrix was able to play three guitar parts simultaneously, he must have felt an immediate affinity for Kirk, who could play three wind instruments at once. And Kirk's amazing mastery of circular breathing techniques allowed him to blow unusually long, sustained lines, which matched Jimi's own legato guitar lines. Kirk and Jimi communicated on a mutual plane, recognizing that the blues was at the heart of their respective styles."[13]

Roland Kirk, accidentally blinded as a child, dreamed of playing two saxophones at once. He worked in various R&B bands in his early teens and was considered a professional musician by age fifteen. Kirk followed his dream and developed a unique fingering style that allowed him to play several harmonies with three instruments simultaneously. Although the tenor saxophone was his main instrument, Kirk reportedly mastered more than forty different instruments, including the manzello, stritch, flute, nose flute, and clarinet. His original style and commitment to music made him a major jazz figure.

In an interview with reporter Jay Ruby at the Copter Club in Manhattan on January 31, 1968, Hendrix revealed that he had jammed with Kirk, but didn't specify when it took place: "I had a jam with him [Roland Kirk] at Ronnie Scott's in England, in London, and it was great. I was so scared! I really got off. He was really great . . . the cat, he gets all those sounds and so forth. I might just hit one note and it might be interfering . . . but we got along great. He told me I should have turned it up or something."[14]

This 1967 jam probably took place when Roland Kirk played his two-week gig at Ronnie Scott's between October 30 and November 11. Although the exact date is unknown, Hendrix's schedule included recording with the Experience at Olympic Sound Studios on October 30 and 31, a show in Lancashire on November 8, an appearance in Holland on November 10, and another show in Brighton on November 11. Therefore, it's probable that this jam occurred during the first week of November.

In addition to the 1967 jam, Hendrix also jammed with Kirk at Ronnie Scott's on March 8, 1969, and back at his London apartment on Brook Street the following day. A recent book by John Kruth, *Bright Moments: The Life and Legacy of Rahsaan Roland Kirk*, goes into great detail about the famed 1969 Kirk-Hendrix jam, and discusses an alleged tape of the jam. Kruth quotes bassist Vernon Martin, who recalled the players who took part at the jam at Ronnie Scott's: "Jimmy Hopps was on drums, Ron Burton played piano, and I was on bass. I can't recall but I think there was somebody blowin' trumpet. Playin' with Jimi was a very high gospel mixing of elements of rhythm and country/blues guitar with tremendous energy."[15]

Hendrix archivist Keith Dion, also a big Kirk fan, researched the alleged Kirk-Hendrix tape after reading Kruth's lengthy account of trying to get it from a man in Los Angeles. After Dion heard the tape, he recognized it was not the genuine Kirk-Hendrix jam, but the poorly recorded Tinker Street Cinema jam from August 10, 1969. While the Tinker Street Cinema jam sounds avant-garde, this lineup of musicians produced something that must be a far cry from the genuine Kirk-Hendrix jam.

Although Hendrix never wrote a will, he did say that he would rather have a jam session than a funeral, and two of the musicians that he wanted at that jam were Roland Kirk and Miles Davis. As Hendrix told *Melody Maker* (March 8, 1969): "For that, it's almost worth dying, just for the funeral."

STATUS: *As of this writing, no recordings of the Kirk-Hendrix jams have surfaced and there is no proof that any recordings were made.*

The Olympic and Record Plant Sessions

After the Royal Albert Hall concerts, Hendrix spent some time with his girlfriend Kathy Etchingham, taking her to Experience recording sessions at London's Olympic Sound Studios and watching bands at clubs like the Speakeasy. The couple had recently set up residence in a flat that turned out to be next door to the former home of composer George Frederick Handel.

On March 13, Hendrix flew to New York to record with Buddy Miles. Etchingham joined him the week after, and noted that the atmosphere in New York differed from the casual atmosphere in London. "When I caught up with him he was staying in New York at the Pierre Hotel," Etchingham recalled. "It was at this time I encountered a rather peculiar looking man who displayed a gun and a bag with packets of cocaine. Between the drugs and the hangers-on, it was getting too much to take, so I up and came back to England. It was just more comfortable here."[16]

On March 18, Hendrix entered New York's Record Plant studios for a solo recording of "The Star Spangled Banner." Recording studios in America were then upgrading their equipment to handle more tracks and produce a fuller sound. Although Hendrix had been recording in the twelve-track format, he was one of the first to use the Record Plant's new sixteen-track recording system. Engineer Tony Bongiovi remembered how frustrating it was to work with Hendrix at this time: "I used to get up there for a 7:00 session at night and Hendrix would show up at like six in the morning. He'd go to the Steve Paul Scene [club] all night."[17] After Hendrix recorded the basic track for "The Star Spangled Banner," he overdubbed many rhythm and solo guitar tracks. Bongiovi recorded some tracks at half speed so that when the song was played at normal speed, the guitar overdubs would sound like they were at double speed.

As the first day of the North American tour approached, the Jimi Hendrix Experience practiced in the studio. "We warmed up for this tour with photo sessions and recording sessions at New York's Record Plant, scheduled from midnight to eight in the morning," Noel Redding recalled. "Compared to the low output of the *Electric Ladyland* sessions, even getting one track done in eight hours seemed a major advance."[18]

STATUS: *Tracks from the Olympic Sound Studios sessions (February 14–16) have surfaced on numerous bootlegs over the years. Some of these tracks include: "Midnight Lightning" (guitar and vocals only), "Cryin' Blue Rain," "Room Full of Mirrors," "It's Too Bad" (a.k.a. "Shame, Shame, Shame"), "Sunshine of Your Love," and "Lover Man."*

Hendrix's astonishing studio solo version of "The Star Spangled Banner," recorded at the Record Plant on March 18, remained out of print for twenty-five years until its compact-disc debut on the Jimi Hendrix Experience box set in 2000. "Gypsy Boy," also recorded on this date, surfaced on the 1975 LP Midnight Lightning; however, studio session players replaced the original backing tracks by Billy Cox and Buddy Miles.

Sessions at the Record Plant on April 7 and 9 produced "Stone Free" and "Lullaby for the Summer" (an embryonic version of "Ezy Ryder"). One of the successful takes of "Stone Free" was issued posthumously on The Jimi Hendrix Experience. "Ships Passing in the Night" was recorded on April 14 and featured Hendrix backed by unknown piano and trumpet players. On April 17, Hendrix recorded "Keep on Groovin'" with girlfriend Devon Wilson on vocals, Paul Caruso on harmonica, and an unidentified percussionist. Twenty-five minutes of this jam have made the rounds in the collectors' network.

The Last North American Tour

The last North American tour for the Jimi Hendrix Experience began on April 11 in Raleigh, North Carolina, and ended on June 29 in Denver, Colorado. According to one eyewitness, Hendrix opened the April 11 concert with the following remark: "Hi, we're the Jimi Hendrix Experience . . . remember when we opened for the Monkees two years ago and you walked out to get peanuts?"[19] Later on in the show, another fan recalled that Hendrix shot something out of his guitar neck that resembled shaving cream. This "ejaculating guitar" trick was never repeated.[20]

On April 18, the Experience performed two shows in Memphis, Tennessee. An audience recording made at the Ellis Auditorium Amphitheater captured the concert to which Hendrix invited his former Army friend Billy Cox. After shows in Houston and Dallas (April 19–20), Hendrix invited Cox to fly to New York and meet with him on the twenty-first. The meeting resulted in a three-day marathon recording session at Record Plant studios on April 21, 22, and 24. Redding and Mitchell were absent since they returned to Los Angeles on the twenty-first. Although the drummer for these sessions has never been identified, the trio covered a lot of material, including "Room Full of Mirrors," "Bleeding Heart," "Crash Landing," and four reels of "Mannish Boy."

The next stop on the Experience's tour was the Forum in Los Angeles, California. A professional recording was made for a proposed live album, which was to include another show a few weeks later at the San Diego Sports Arena. Shortly thereafter, engineer Eddie Kramer and Hendrix began to mix the concert tapes at a studio in L.A. At the same time, without Hendrix or Kramer's knowledge, Reprise brought another engineer to a separate studio to prepare an album of the Experience's performance at the 1967 Monterey Pop Festival.

Both of these projects were abandoned and the recordings were stored in the Warner Bros. tape library. *Smash Hits* (Reprise MS 2025) was instead quickly issued by Reprise in July 1969. Reprise also revived the live Monterey Pop album in 1970 and released *Historic Performances Recorded at the Monterey International Pop Festival* (MS 2029) just a few days after Hendrix's death.[21]

The "lost" 1969 live album, with selected tracks from the Royal Albert Hall, the L.A. Forum, and the San Diego Arena, was never released. In 1990, twenty-one years later, Reprise released *Lifelines: The Jimi Hendrix Story* (Reprise 9 26435-2), a four-CD box set that included a 1988 Hendrix radio special (without commercials) and the 1969 L.A. Forum concert. Many fans were upset that they had to shell out fifty dollars to get a previously unreleased live album—they couldn't have cared less about the three-disc radio show. The whereabouts of the afternoon sound check rehearsal at the L.A. Forum, which was also recorded, are unknown.

The day after the concert at the L.A. Forum, the Experience played the Oakland Coliseum. Halfway through the set, Redding jokingly announced to the crowd that Mother's Day was approaching, and "if any ladies out there would like to become a mother... come see us after the show." Seconds later, several women were seen leaving their seats, possibly volunteering for the cause.[22]

Unbeknownst to the crowd, Jefferson Airplane members Grace Slick, Paul Kantner, and Jack Casady were watching the show from backstage. As the Experience ended their set to a standing ovation, they returned quickly for an encore, and Casady joined them. Despite being mistakenly introduced by Hendrix as Jack Bruce, Casady plugged in on bass, while Redding switched over to rhythm guitar. An audience member recorded the entire eighty-five minute set, including the encore of "Voodoo Child (Slight Return)," but stashed away the reels of tape for twenty-eight years. In 1997, the tapes were sold to Experience Hendrix, which has since marketed them as a double CD on Dagger Records called *Live at the Oakland Coliseum* (DBRD2 11743).

The Experience tour headed east to New York, then south to Tuscaloosa, Alabama, where they played Memorial Coliseum on May 7. In his book, *Are You Experienced*, Noel Redding described this Southeast section of the tour as horrifying: "We were replaying the [1967] Monkees tour—same halls, same crowds... the audiences were creepy and there were no chicks afterwards."[23]

Pat O'Day, then with Concerts West as a concert promoter, also remembered another creepy situation during this time: "Jimi walked into the auditorium, and the police were a little antsy anyway about the whole thing because they couldn't understand a black act with a white audience. Jimi walks in the door with his tight leathers on, and his bushy hair, with his arm around this little blonde. And I tell you that the police lieutenant there came very close to losing control of his men. They wanted to take Jimi apart right there! One of the deputies told me, 'The man has no right comin' in here, into our city building, with a white lady like that. I can't take it, and I'm not gonna stand for it! I don't know what I'm gonna do, but I'm gonna do something.' It was tense, very tense!"[24]

The Los Angeles Forum, Inglewood, California, April 26, 1969. *Tom Nyerges/Star File*

On Friday the ninth, the band arrived in Charlotte, North Carolina, and performed at the Charlotte Coliseum. Although the show received a fantastic review in the mainstream press, the local underground paper, the *Inquisition,* reported that there were problems with Charlotte law enforcement officers, especially a plainclothesman patrolling the aisles looking for people who might be recording the concert: "He [a plainclothesman] approached our seats and asked if the movie camera which I was holding was a tape recorder. Unconvinced it was not a tape recorder, he took it and examined it, then decided that I was right after all, that it was indeed a movie camera. After returning it, he began hassling my friend."[25] Perhaps as a result of this increased concert security, neither audio nor film footage of this show has surfaced.

Ray Brak of the *Charleston Gazette* interviewed Mitchell and Hendrix the following day. Hendrix told Brak that the group was bored and wanted to delve into side projects. "Hendrix is interested in television," Brak wrote. "He also wants to get a book together and do an album on his own 'that could include everything from acoustical guitar to the Mormon Tabernacle Choir.'" Hendrix discussed a final album for the Experience and some plans for the future: "'We're not sure what the title will be, but I think we'll call it *The End of the Beginning.* . . . I have a song on abortion and a song on Vietnam. . . . Music is stronger than politics. I feel sorry for the minorities, but I don't feel a part of one. . . . I want to do a concert at Carnegie Hall with Miles Davis and Roland Kirk. We're trying to get that together right now. We just can't go on playing concerts like this. After this tour is over and our album is ready, I'm going to take a long vacation—maybe in Morocco or Sweden or way in the Southern California hills."[26]

The Experience played a concert at the Fairgrounds Coliseum in Indianapolis, Indiana, on May 11, before taking a four-day break from touring. Hendrix, however, used the "time off" to record with his friends Johnny Winter and Stephen Stills.

STATUS: *Between April 11 and May 11, the Jimi Hendrix Experience played fourteen concerts, seven of which were recorded. These seven recordings include: Philadelphia, Pennsylvania (April 12); Memphis, Tennessee (April 18, second show); Dallas, Texas (April 20); Los Angeles, California (April 26, stereo soundboard recording by Abe Jacob for Wally Heider Recording); Oakland, California (April 27); Toronto, Ontario, Canada (May 3); and Indianapolis, Indiana (May 11).*

Jamming with Johnny Winter

During a midweek break from the Experience's tour schedule in May 1969, Hendrix went to the Record Plant studio with his friends Stephen Stills and Johnny Winter after jamming at The Scene. Stills, who had recently left Buffalo Springfield, had just announced the completion of a new album with David Crosby and Graham Nash (*Crosby, Stills & Nash*), and Winter had just signed a five-year contract with Columbia Records.

Winter explained the circumstances behind this amazing Record Plant jam: "What we would often do after the club closed is go over to a studio where he [Hendrix] had recording time booked regularly, and play around with things, maybe for several hours and then some other day listen to the tapes to pick out the good parts for ideas to work into songs."[27] During this extended guitar workout, Hendrix was fascinated with Winter's old bottleneck blues techniques. "I mean, you just couldn't show that man anything new," Winter recalled. "It was just a case of Jimi watching how I used the bottle-neck when playing. All I was doing was more or less demonstrating the basic technique to him."[28] The master tape box indicates that this session started at 7:45 A.M. and ended at 10:00 A.M.

In his book *Jimi Hendrix: Sessions*, author John McDermott identified the date of this recording at the Record Plant as May 7. However, on that date Hendrix was playing an Experience concert at the Memorial Coliseum in Tuscaloosa, Alabama. More than likely, the session with Johnny Winter, Stephen Stills (on bass and guitar), and Dallas Taylor (on drums) took place on May 15. McDermott says that the tapes from this session feature up-tempo jams, titled "Jam #1" and "Jam #2," that are based on the melody line to Hendrix's "Earth Blues." Winter and Stills apparently both tried unsuccessfully to follow Hendrix's directions before attempting another new song called "Ships Passing in the Night."

The only track released from this session is "The Things I Used to Do," originally recorded by Guitar Slim (Eddie Jones). In an interview with *UniVibes* magazine, Johnny Winter revealed that there was more to this session than just this release: "There are four cassettes, a whole lot of things he [Hendrix] did in different ways and some stuff that hadn't been released before. It's a kind of interesting bunch of tapes and 'The Things I Used to Do' was on that. It was okay for an impromptu kind of jam."[29]

STATUS: *"The Things I Used to Do" was first used in a 1975 radio broadcast sponsored by Crawdaddy magazine. Since there were limited "radio-station only" copies pressed, it became a highly prized — and high-priced — collector's item. In 1988, a six-hour syndicated radio special called* Jimi Hendrix: Live and Unreleased *featured this Winter-Hendrix-Stills jam. When this radio special (without commercials) was released to the public in 1990 as* Lifelines: The Jimi Hendrix Story, *it included "The Things I Used to Do." It is now out of print.*

After Hendrix died, a live bootleg album from a 1968 jam at the Scene incorrectly stated that Winter played with Hendrix and Jim Morrison. Winter did not perform on this Scene club jam, and according to Winter, he never even met Morrison.[30]

Playing the Festivals

> *Our music is part of blues. I call it Electric Church Music. It's a very hard and harsh and primitive sound, not necessarily good or bad or stoned. You get the feeling you're going to get something out of it if you let your mind flow with it. It should be played outside . . . that's where an Electric Church is supposed to belong. There should be no barriers to this type of thing.*
>
> Jimi Hendrix, *San Jose Mercury News,* May 26, 1969

As the tour resumed on May 16 in Baltimore, Maryland, the Experience played a few more indoor arenas before performing at open-air festivals. Abe Jacob, the Experience's concert sound engineer, described what it was like on the road from a technical viewpoint: "We had all of the band's equipment, all of the sound equipment, very few lighting instruments, posters, and other merchandising fit in one truck. Concerts today are in anywhere from five to twenty trucks. It was a basic and very simple setup soundwise. It's unbelievable what we were able to do. But it was his performance—it was what he extracted from his amplifiers, with Noel and Mitch doing the rhythm together. Even though everyone thought of him as being exceptionally loud and fierce, he was a master of dynamics. He knew exactly how to control volume so the vocal line came through, which made the sound [mixing] easy. The sound was mixed from the audience. There was no monitor mix. We had two small vocal monitors. After the first tour, we put four amplified loudspeakers behind Mitch, which gave him a little better feeling on stage. He would always say his drums were not loud enough, at least to his ears."[31]

On May 25, the Experience left San Diego and flew north to San Jose to headline the second annual Northern California Folk Rock Festival. Approximately 80,000 youths attended the event, which was held over the course of three days (May 23–May 25) at the Santa Clara Fairgrounds. Hendrix was the biggest name amongst the roster of top recording groups listed on the bill.

KSJO, the local San Jose FM rock station, broadcast doubts that Hendrix would appear as advertised. The station said that previous promoters had claimed that big-name stars would appear at an event, but the stars had not appeared, and the station faced charges of fraudulent advertising by the Federal Communications Commission. As a result, the festival's promoters immediately filed suit against KSJO for $2.2 million in damages for the "slanderous" announcements. After two days of hearings in Superior Court, KSJO agreed to stop any further "non-appearance" announcements until a performance fee was paid to Hendrix's management. On Friday, May 23, Michael Jeffery was paid $15,000— the remainder of the previously agreed performance fee. The *San Jose Mercury News*'s headline read: "Yes, There Is a Jimi Hendrix—Judge Agrees He'll Be Here."

The *Mercury News* noted in its concert review that "Hendrix did strange magical things to his followers. A blonde beauty shed her mini-blouse and bare-breasted to the throbbing vibrations. A blank-faced deputy sheriff extracted a round from his cartridge and loaded the round into his stage-facing ear [to block the sound]. Thousands stood, arms flung skyward, both hands flagging the 'V' peace symbol. One fan pressed his forehead on the stage, just inches from the flying feet of Hendrix, to sponge up the sound of the supersonic vibes."[32]

One person who was highly influenced by Hendrix's performance at this festival was Carlos Santana: "I was really fortunate to catch the show at the Santa Clara County Fairgrounds. I recently found a cassette of it. Somebody actually recorded it that day. When I listen to it, I'm still blown away. I remember when the P.A. died and all you could hear was Jimi Hendrix's guitar. You could hear all these waves of spirits crying through his guitar. So, when the P.A. came on again we were like catapulted into the Milky Way. When the P.A. was off, it sounded like he was inside a little nucleus, or a proton, you know those little things you study when you were in high school. When it came back on, we were like ... Oh my God! How can he do this? It was scary because I had a little bit of experience watching people like B.B. [King], Peter Green, and Jeff Beck, but I had never heard anybody express electric music the way he did that day. Most performances that he did, he would always find a time or a space where he would just go out! Away from the song, away from the arrangement, away from the norm of what people wanted to hear—the 'Purple Haze'—he would just go out. It was incredible to be assaulted with all these screaming winds. He would really control that instrument like a jazz player or a blues player would. It was like controlling a demon and making it sing."[33]

After a few tour dates in Hawaii, the group returned to California. On June 20, Hendrix and the Experience appeared at the Newport '69 Pop Festival at Devonshire Downs, north of Hollywood. The three-day event had an excellent lineup of artists and bands, but seventy-five people were arrested, and the violent crowd caused extensive property damage. The *Los Angeles Free Press* labeled the festival a "sham," and wrote: "It wasn't Pop, although it might have been, had people been able to hear some of the really good music that did come down, but a totally inadequate sound system, plus the steady drone of a police helicopter, managed to obliterate any of the music that filtered back more than 100 feet from the stage ... an estimated 30,000 people waited for seven hours to experience Jimi Hendrix. By the time he did appear, at twelve midnight, the vibrations from the audience were hardly conducive to a good performance."[34]

As Hendrix started the opening notes to "Hear My Train a Comin'," you could hear the strain in his voice as he said "Fuck off, will you shut up?!" The music stopped and Hendrix told the unruly crowd, "We hope we're not playing to a bunch of animals, so please don't act like some. Just lay back, OK?" Tension mounted in the audience and on stage. Out of desperation, Hendrix said, "Y'all just choke yourselves. Fuck off!" and he resumed the song with altered lyrics: "It's too bad you don't love me no more, people, too bad you all have to act like a clown."[35]

The set performed by the Experience lasted about sixty-five minutes—about fifteen minutes less than most shows—yet they were paid $100,000, over a third of the entire talent budget for the festival's thirty-three acts. When the other bands on the bill heard this, they grew resentful toward Hendrix.

To make up for what the local press called "a very unenthusiastic performance," Hendrix returned on Sunday to jam with Eric Burdon, Buddy Miles, and other musicians. Hendrix's performances at Newport Pop were never officially authorized to be recorded. When Michael Jeffery heard about the tapes, he obtained the quarter-inch soundboard tape reels made at the festival and moved them to the Hendrix tape library.[36]

STATUS: *Between May 16 and June 29, eight recordings were made: Baltimore, Maryland (May 16); Providence, Rhode Island (May 17); New York, New York (May 18); San Diego,*

California (May 24, stereo soundboard recording by Abe Jacob for Wally Heider); Northern California Folk Rock Festival, Santa Clara, California (May 25); Newport '69 Pop Festival, Northridge, California (June 20, soundboard recording from reels 5 and 6); Newport '69 Pop Festival, Northridge, California (June 22, with Buddy Miles on drums and vocals, Eric Burdon on vocals, Tracy Nelson on background vocals, Bob Arthur on bass, Cornelius 'Snooky' Flowers on sax, Tom Webb on sax, Lee Oskar on harmonica, and others; soundboard recording from reels 14, 15, and 16); and Denver Pop Festival, Denver, Colorado (June 29).

A New Beginning

A couple of years ago all I wanted was to be heard. Now I am trying to figure out the wisest way to be heard.

Jimi Hendrix, *Los Angeles Times*, September 7, 1969

On June 7, Hendrix temporarily moved into a penthouse suite at the Beverly Rodeo Hotel, a small, semi-posh hotel where a rock star could go incognito. There he began composing and rehearsing with Billy Cox, who moved in a little later. Some of Hendrix and Cox's efforts were recorded, including a new song titled "Izabella." This open slot on the tour schedule turned into a two-week working vacation.

In a June 17 interview for *Rolling Stone*, Hendrix dropped the bombshell that he would be expanding the group and adding Billy Cox as the new bass player. Hendrix also mentioned that he and Cox would like to merge with the Buddy Miles Express, and "get three soul sisters, regardless of whether they're Italian or Irish or whatever, so long as they got feeling. We have this family thing we're trying to get together, and then the money will come."[37] While there had been tension in the Experience for some time, Hendrix apparently never directly informed Redding or Mitchell that the band would be splitting up. Redding says he first got word at the Denver concert that he was going to be replaced—but not from Hendrix, from a reporter. "I went up to Jimi that night, said goodbye, and caught the next plane back to London," Redding told *Rolling Stone*. "I don't think Jimi believed I'd do it. Later on, he phoned and asked me to come back; I said, 'Stuff it.'"[38]

Hendrix gave an insightful interview to researcher Nancy Carter during this period. Carter, a student at the University of Southern California, wanted to ask Hendrix imaginative and philosophical questions for her Master's thesis. She was granted an interview because she was a good friend of Eric Burdon and Noel Redding.

It was not an easy interview; Carter had sixty percent hearing loss in both ears and only thirty minutes to complete the interview. She could read lips, but recalled "Jimi mumbled too much to make any sense." Carter added: "In my interview you will hear me cut him off a lot of times as I was trying to guess what he is saying. Jimi really gave his answers a lot of thought."[39] No one told Hendrix in advance that Carter had a hearing impairment and he openly discussed controversial topics such as the education system, abortion, antiballistic missiles, and bridging the generation gap through better communication. "I came in the evening with my little tape recorder to the Beverly Rodeo Hotel," Carter recalled. "When I knocked on the door, Jimi came out wearing nothing but this red kimono. He was really very nervous. I knew he was virtually self-educated and he knew I was a schoolteacher and an educator. Even though I couldn't hear everything he was saying, I knew he wanted to get his message across. I was impressed by his answers also."[40]

Around this time, Hendrix also met independent film producer Chuck Wein, who had produced a number of films for Andy Warhol. Wein, like Hendrix, had previously lived at the seedy Hotel America in New York, and he knew Devon Wilson, Hendrix's on-again off-again girlfriend. He and Hendrix shared common interests in UFOs and reincarnation, and Wein offered to give Hendrix a tarot-card reading. While Wein placed the cards, Hendrix shared his idea about stacking up a huge number of amps and playing in the Grand Canyon. They fantasized about beaming sounds over thousands of square miles and wondered what effect it might have on people's consciousness.

To aid Hendrix in his search for "higher cosmic consciousness," Wein gave him books like *The Tibetan Book of the Dead*, *The Secret Places of the Lion: Ancient Influences on Earth's Destiny*, *Spacemen in the Ancient East*, and *Secrets of the Andes*. "It was no hard sell to somebody who was ahead of the game," Wein said, "and already having many out of body experiences. He believed in healing with music and color, and that's when I gave him the books. He wanted all the material he could find on UFOs, death, and reincarnation."[41]

One night out on the town, Hendrix and Wein stopped at Help, a popular all-night health food restaurant in L.A. that was frequented by many a stoned-out rock-and-roller. There Wein introduced Hendrix to his friend Emilie Touraine. "She had a 200-page notebook filled with every song Jimi had ever written, including molecular structure diagrams and color codes," Wein recalls. "We went over to her house and she started to take out these records. She would say, 'Now I'm going to play you pure yellow.' Of course we had all dropped acid. Then she played Wagner and the whole room went yellow. The same thing happened when she put on Pink Floyd."[42]

Touraine subscribed to the theory that every note has a color, and all colors have different healing abilities, similar to Tibetan and other belief systems of healing with tones and colors. This music/color concept had intrigued Hendrix for some time. Songs like "One Rainy Wish" and "Bold As Love" were filled with themes of colors and emotions. In 1967, Hendrix told *Disc and Music Echo*: "I want to get color into music. I'd like to play a note and have it come out a color."[43] All of these new ideas fascinated Hendrix, and eventually Wein, Touraine, and Hendrix worked together on a movie project, based in part on esoteric beliefs, called *Rainbow Bridge*.

STATUS: *Nancy Carter's interview with Hendrix on June 15 can be found on* **Hendrix Speaks** *(Rhino R2-70771). There is also a collectors' tape with ten minutes of Hendrix and Cox practicing together in their suite at the Beverly Rodeo Hotel. They covered three takes of "Izabella" and an instrumental jam that has been given the name "Distortion Blues."*

The Lost Episode of *The Tonight Show*

Jimi Hendrix's first major appearance on American television was July 7 on the *Dick Cavett Show* (ABC-TV). Three days later, he appeared as a guest on *The Tonight Show* (NBC-TV).

Judging from the sole existing evidence of a homemade audiotape, Hendrix's appearance on *The Tonight Show* must have been quite an event. In a serious moment, the guest host, comedian Flip Wilson, asked Hendrix to explain why many people felt his performances were a spiritual experience. "If they dig the sounds . . . it's like church actually," Hendrix replied. Wilson then invited Hendrix to "whip a light sermon" on the viewers. After introducing Billy Cox as his new bass player, Hendrix was joined by *The Tonight Show*'s drummer, Ed Shaughnessy, and they attempted to play a new song called "Lover Man," but halfway through the tune, Hendrix's amp cut out. Wilson ad-libbed and stalled for a few minutes, and introduced Hendrix again. This time the temporary trio made it through the song just fine.

Rolling Stone had its own spin on the show: "First he [Hendrix] goggled his way through a rap with guest host Flip Wilson, who tried to hip-talk himself onto Hendrix's level while patting a huge watermelon on his desk. Then just as Jimi was getting into a good number on his axe, his amp blew, and he sauntered off stage, leaving a hapless session drummer (with pasted on side-burns) and bass player in an impromptu jam that never had a chance of jelling."[44]

STATUS: *Lost or destroyed. While videotapes of Hendrix's 1969 performances on the* Dick Cavett Show *have surfaced, the* Tonight Show *episode with Hendrix is missing or was destroyed. Some have speculated that Carson Productions Group may have erased episodes that didn't feature Johnny Carson as the host. Others point to a fire at the NBC studios that destroyed many valuable tapes. Collectors hope to find a film copy that may have been sent overseas for Armed Forces Television. All that exists is the homemade audio recording taken from the original broadcast.*

The Formation of Gypsy Sun and Rainbows

Shortly after the Experience gave their final concert in Denver, Colorado, Mitch Mitchell and Noel Redding returned to England and Hendrix began to look for a new drummer. A private audition took place in early July at New York's Café Au Go Go club with bassist Willie Weeks and drummer Bill Lordan.

"Jimi was looking for members to be in his new Gypsy Sun and Rainbows band," Bill Lordan recalls. "We jammed three days in a row; Willie Weeks was on bass, and I was on drums. There was more than a day of an audition because he liked us and asked us to come back the next day and wanted to hear us again . . . Jimi ran us through the full gamut of his roots when we auditioned. He would play up-tempo R&B to slow blues. He was trying to see if we could keep up with him. He would start the song and not tell us anything, then just say, 'Follow this,' or 'What would you play to this?' Jimi really liked my playing and he thought Willie was a fine bass player too. He needed somebody and had tried different people."[45] Unfortunately, Weeks and Lordan were a package deal, and Hendrix had to pass on the duo since he had already promised Billy Cox the bass position.

Hendrix and Cox had parted ways in 1963, but Cox had kept up his musical chops by touring with Wilson Pickett, Gene Chandler, and Buddy Miles. In 1966, he was hired by Nashville deejay William "Hossman" Allen for a TV show called *The !!!! Beat.* Cox performed as a member of the Beat Boys, the show's house band, along with blues guitarist Clarence "Gatemouth" Brown. At the time, *The !!!! Beat* was the only nationally televised music show devoted exclusively to R&B, and it featured legendary performers such as Otis Redding, Carla Thomas, Percy Sledge, Little Milton, and Freddy King.

"A lot of people had problems with myself playing bass with Jimi," recalls Billy Cox. "I don't know why or what the problem was. In fact, before I got on the road with him they auditioned about five or six bass players. Very good ones in my estimation, but I wound up playing the music because I could play it better and I enjoyed it! I came from the same school, the same time period, and Jimi and I grew musically together. When he asked me to play with him, I said 'You have your choice of getting one of the best bass players in the world.' He said, 'That's why I picked you.' This was the greatest compliment I ever received from any human being on this planet."[46]

Around this time, Hendrix's management signed a lease on an eight-bedroom Georgian-style stone house, complete with horses, at the end of secluded Taver Hollow Road near Shokan, in upstate New York. Albert Grossman, manager for Janis Joplin and Bob Dylan, owned the house. The intention was to provide Hendrix with a peaceful retreat where he could explore new musical ideas with his eclectic circle of musician friends—Juma Sultan, a former progressive jazz percussionist/bassist/flautist; Larry Lee, a Memphis blues guitarist whom Hendrix knew from his days in Nashville; Billy Cox on bass; Jerry Velez, a second percussionist and acquaintance from the Scene club; and former Experience drummer Mitch Mitchell.

Hendrix's friends—now fellow bandmates—Billy Cox and Larry Lee showed up first. Hendrix returned from a vacation in Morocco and moved in on August 7 to begin rehearsals for their performance at Woodstock. One new song titled "Woodstock Jam" was recorded on the seventh, but was mistakenly taped over.[47] The group jammed on other new songs at a local auditorium, the Tinker Street Cinema, in nearby Woodstock on August 10.

Percussionist Juma Sultan was living in Woodstock, New York, when he encountered Hendrix in 1969. They had met previously in 1966 when both lived in Greenwich Village, but had never played together. In 1969, Sultan had a group called the Aboriginal Music Society. Saxophonist David Sanborn and harmonica player Paul Butterfield stopped by to jam, as did others. Unique music would often emerge.

Gypsy Sun and Rainbows remained together from August through October 1969. Sultan recalled how it started: "There's a place in Woodstock called the Village Green. It's right in the center of town, on Tinker Street. I was sitting out there one day with my drums

Auditions at the Café au Go Go, New York, July 1969. *Left to right:* Willie Weeks, Bill Lordan, and Hendrix. *Rob Lewis Collection*

when Mike Jeffery and Jimi came by. He had just got into town and he invited me to come by and jam. So, that night I went over to the house and just he and I played the entire evening. Gypsy Sun and Rainbows was his own individual thing; guys get together, play, and then they'd go their own way, all the time exchanging ideas. What Jimi wanted to do was not be so taxed all the time. He figured here I am, we have a house, and maybe they will let me rest a bit. What he was thinking about when he pulled all of us together was that each of us had our own individuality. Billy [Cox], Gerardo [Jerry Velez—brother of singer Martha Velez], Larry [Lee] and Mitch [Mitchell]—we could make some albums, jam, do some concerts, put some space in between and then come back together."[48]

During the rehearsals, it was uncertain if Mitchell would be returning to play drums, and auditions were held for other drummers. Sultan explained that there may have been other tensions as well: "When he [Hendrix] was pulling this band together, he really didn't want to use Mitch...[who] didn't come in until a week or two before the [Woodstock] festival.... He didn't practice.... Finally, when he came up, they [Hendrix's management] started bringing up the road guys like Eric Barrett. Before that, the roadies didn't like it because there were too many blacks around. They had a phobia."[49]

On August 10, a little more than a week before the gigantic Woodstock Music and Art Fair, Hendrix, Sultan, and Velez performed at the tiny Tinker Street Cinema to a crowd of fifty people. "It was a Saturday night midnight concert which I organized," Sultan recalled. "We had Jimi, I was playing bass, Earl Cross on trumpet, Ali Kaboi on drums and two of Santana's percussionists. There were about sixteen guys there. It was filmed in 16mm and recorded on two-track. There is currently an audience tape floating around that was recorded on cassette."[50]

The Tinker Street Cinema jam, as it is known among collectors, was advertised, but Hendrix's name was not used. The Aboriginal Music Society opened the show. The tape that Sultan referred to includes his songs "The Dance" and "Sundance," followed by a high-energy fusion jam that includes "Earth Blues" and "The Star Spangled Banner." The entire concert lasted longer than what was captured on the forty-minute audience tape.

Although the group sounded a little rough around the edges, this large ensemble may have been the type of band Hendrix wanted. "Jimi expressed to me that he was tired of playing in the same keys and that he wanted to play with horns," Sultan explains. "[Many] of his riffs were horn riffs, so when I invited him to play at Tinker Street he didn't want to play the standard tunes. That's also how the material for Woodstock came together."[51]

Mitch Mitchell finally showed up at the Shokan house, and wasn't too happy with what he found. "Apparently, they'd been working there for about ten days when I got there, but you'd never have known," Mitchell recalled. "It was probably the only band I've been involved with that simply did not improve over that length of time."[52]

STATUS: *A professional multitrack tape machine that engineer Eddie Kramer had installed at the house captured a majority of the jams. Some of the first recorded evidence of this new band was made on August 8, with Hendrix (vocals and guitar), Larry Lee (rhythm guitar), Billy Cox (bass), and Jerry Velez and Juma Sultan (both on percussion). This tape lasts twenty-eight minutes and includes an early version of "Machine Gun," "Message to Love," and a medley of "Mannish Boy/Izabella/Room Full of Mirrors." The tape concludes with a song called "Ain't Got Nobody" with Lee on lead guitar, Cox on bass, and either Velez, Sultan, or Hendrix on drums. A recording made the following day includes two of Sultan's original songs, "The Dance" and "Sundance."*

The forty-minute audience recording of the August 10 concert at Tinker Street Cinema features "The Dance," "Sundance," "Earth Blues," and "The Star Spangled Banner." The next known recording was made on Wednesday, August 11, and features "Izabella," "Message to Love," "Beginnings," "If Six Was Nine," "Why I Sing the Blues," and various instrumental free-form jams. A recording on the fourteenth captured "Lover Man," "Hear My Train a Comin'/Machine Gun," and "Spanish Castle Magic."

Unfortunately, no tapes have surfaced of Lordan and Weeks' audition with Hendrix.

The Complete Woodstock Set

Dig, we'd like to get something straight. We got tired of the Experience...it was blowin' our minds. So, we decided to change the whole thing around, and call it Gypsy Sun and Rainbows. For short, it's nothin' but a Band of Gypsys.

Hendrix's introduction at the Woodstock festival, August 18, 1969

On August 15, about 450,000 young people had hiked out to Max Yasgur's six-hundred-acre dairy farm, about fifty miles from Woodstock in upstate New York, for "three days of peace & music." The Woodstock Music and Art Fair offered its patrons a full day and evening's worth of top rock, folk, and soul music talent in exchange for a seven-dollar-per-day ticket. However, after thousands more showed up than anticipated, the organizers declared it a free festival.

On July 19, Hendrix signed an agreement for $18,000 to close the festival, but was later paid a total of $32,000 and an additional $12,000 from Wadleigh Productions for the film rights to his set. Michael Jeffery insisted that Hendrix headline the festival and play the final set on Sunday, August 17, but a torrential downpour and technical difficulties put the program behind schedule. Gypsy Sun and Rainbows did not go on until eight o'clock on Monday morning.

Over the three-day festival, there were two births and three deaths. Apart from an onstage argument between Who guitarist Pete Townshend and Yippie leader Abbie Hoffman, there were no real fights. The real hassle, however, was figuring out how to squeeze in Hendrix and his band on the final night.

When Gypsy Sun and Rainbows arrived at the festival at about 8:00 P.M. on Sunday they were told about the delay in getting groups onstage and asked to wait it out. At one point during all the confusion, Hendrix got ill, possibly from bad drinking water backstage, and had to be taken to the medical tent.[53] Within a few hours, he felt better and was able to enjoy sets by Crosby, Stills, Nash & Young and the Paul Butterfield Blues Band.

As the festival shut down for the night, Hendrix and his band spent the evening in a cottage. "It was about three muddy fields away," Mitch Mitchell recalls. "We squelched over there and spent the night literally freezing. Our enthusiasm dried up even more when it became apparent we were to get on-stage not Sunday as planned but in the very early hours of Monday morning."[54] At 6:00 A.M., the 1950s revival band Sha Na Na hit the stage, and Gypsy Sun and Rainbows followed their set.

The complete 140-minute Gypsy Sun and Rainbows set at Woodstock featured "Message to Universe," "Hear My Train a Comin'," "Spanish Castle Magic," "Red House," "Master Mind," "Lover Man," "Foxy Lady," "Beginnings" (a.k.a. "Jam Back at the House"), "Izabella," "Gypsy Woman/Aware of Love," "Fire," "Voodoo Child (Slight Return)/Stepping Stone/The Star Spangled Banner/Purple Haze/Villanova Junction," and the encore, "Hey Joe."

According to Juma Sultan, Hendrix's manager wanted to control what Hendrix played at that time and got upset when he started becoming independent. "Jimi was thinking for himself," Sultan explains. "Before, management would say, 'You gotta be here,' and he'd say, 'Okay,' and then he started questioning them and they didn't like that. Anybody that helped him to be a self-thinker they would try to wipe out. They tried to offer me a separate contract not to play with Jimi and I turned them down. Management tried to step in at Woodstock. Jimi wanted to do a piece with just conga and acoustic guitar, and they wouldn't allow him to do it! He had a tune we rehearsed and he really wanted to bring this out, but they nixed it. It was too folkie. They had already had an acoustic act, Richie Havens. That gives you an idea of the degree of control they had over him artistically."[55]

Sultan feels that Hendrix's image is still controlled, even posthumously. "If you've ever seen the film outtakes of the 'Star Spangled Banner,' you'd see we were really kickin' it with him, but when you hear the album, you hear nothing," Sultan says. "They couldn't hear the sound that Jimi wanted, these embellishments. This was due to management being in there and the engineer in total control. It was too extreme, too free. In terms of the music, the public has never really heard the true sound."[56]

Billy Cox agrees that the public may have not experienced the true spirit of the Gypsy Sun and Rainbows performance: "At the time we were playing, there were over 200,000 people there. It was unfortunate that in the movie they showed Jimi playing toward the end of the festival with scenes of them cleaning up etc., but that was not so, it was edited in the film. When we got on stage, we had a full-fledged crowd. They were very energetic and the energy that they were sending up, we were sending back to them. Jimi was at his height and at his peak."[57]

When Hendrix was asked a few days later about his feelings about the Woodstock festival, he responded, "It was a success for the simple fact that there was one of the largest gatherings of people . . . in a musical sense. It could have been arranged a little more tighter, but it was a complete success compared to all the other festivals that everybody tried to knock here and there. I hope we have more of 'em, you know, it'd be nice."[58] Inspired by the positive vibes that lingered, Hendrix wrote an inspirational poem titled "500,000 Halos" a short time after the festival. (The poem was auctioned in the early 1990s.)

After Woodstock, Gypsy Sun and Rainbows performed two more concerts: the United Block Association benefit in Harlem on September 5, and their final show at the Salvation club in New York City on September 10. The group also made several studio recordings from August 28 through September 9 at the Hit Factory in New York.

STATUS: *There has never been an official release of Hendrix's complete performance at the Woodstock festival (only bootleg recordings made from edited soundboard tapes). The jagged trail of official Hendrix Woodstock releases began in June 1970. Cotillion/Atlantic Records released* Woodstock *(Cotillion SD 3500), a three-record set, with most of the final side devoted to Hendrix's medley of "The Star Spangled Banner/Purple Haze/Instrumental Solo." The choice of songs was good, but they had been poorly mixed and highly edited.*

United Block Association Benefit, Harlem, New York City, September 5, 1969.
Star File

Riding high on this successful release, Cotillion came out with **Woodstock II (Cotillion 2400)** ten months later. This double LP (dedicated to the memory of James Marshall Hendrix) gave Hendrix an entire side, but the album suffered from audio problems similar to those of its predecessor.

For the next twenty-three years, Hendrix fans traded tapes and purchased expensive bootleg recordings to hear more of what really went down during the legendary Woodstock set. In 1994, just in time for the twenty-fifth anniversary of Woodstock, producer Alan Douglas released **Jimi Hendrix: Woodstock (MCAD-11063)**. It was by far the best-sounding effort, but Hendrix's original set was chopped up and rearranged to fit on a single CD. Douglas was criticized for this, but he felt it was his only choice to make a commercial success.

In 1999, MCA and Experience Hendrix attempted to correct the mistakes of the past and released a double CD titled **Jimi Hendrix: Live at Woodstock (MCAD2-11987)**. This thirtieth-anniversary release has a running time of 96:41, longer than the previous CD but *still leaving out some set material. Experience Hendrix producers deleted the beautiful Curtis Mayfield–Jerry Butler medley, "Gypsy Woman/Aware of Love," and guitarist Larry Lee's original "Master Mind." The only explanation was found in David Fricke's liner notes: "Some things are meant to be preserved on bootlegs." Besides song deletions, the double CD omitted several solos and Hendrix's comical comments to the crowd. The liner notes also incorrectly state that the performance took place on August 19 instead of on the eighteenth.*

The Mike Ephron Jams

Hendrix stayed in Shokan for a while after the Woodstock festival. During the third week in September, he and Sultan jammed there with keyboardist Mike Ephron. Around this time, *Rolling Stone* sent reporter Sheila Weller to the upstate New York retreat to find out what new music he was creating. After listening to a tape from a previous night's jam, Weller was enthusiastic: "A beautiful fusion of disparate elements, disjunct and unified at alternating seconds. Now chaotic, now coming together. 'Cosmic music,' they call it. Ego-free music. Not the sort of stuff the wax lords make bucks off. Not the kind of sound guaranteed to extend the popularity of a rock superstar."[59]

In an interview, Sultan told me how this informal jam session came about: "I knew Mike [Ephron] from New York City, but not so much musically. One night he happened to show up at the house for a jam. We recorded that on two-track. I was recording everything we did. The tapes were only intended for archival purposes."[60]

These avant-garde 1969 recordings were used on the very first Jimi Hendrix bootleg, *This Flyer*, which appeared in a number of record stores in April 1970 and featured Hendrix on guitar, Ephron on clavichord, and Sultan on percussion and flute. Some four thousand copies were pressed and distributed in the U.S. and the U.K. Upon hearing that someone was capitalizing on one of his jam sessions, Hendrix expressed his dismay to the British press: "I haven't had many records out in a while. Those pirate tapes . . . some cat went to a private practice session with a tiny tape recorder and made a pirate LP. The quality must be terrible."[61]

Following Hendrix's death, several more bootlegs appeared that were culled from other segments of these 1969 "rented house" tapes with Sultan and Ephron. One series was imaginatively titled *Jimi Hendrix at His Best, Volumes 1–3* (Saga 6313, 6314, 6315), and the liner notes purposely (and erroneously) stated that the material was recorded in 1964 to avoid legal complications from Ed Chalpin or Michael Jeffery. Sultan claims that Ephron was responsible for these releases: "Mike showed up at my house. I was out of the country at the time . . . he convinced my wife to turn over the tapes . . . he took the tapes and went off to Jamaica, did a mix and pressed some records."[62]

STATUS: *Since the original albums with Hendrix, Ephron, and Sultan are now out of print, the only way to hear these recordings is on tapes found in the collectors' network. If listeners are patient enough to sift through the hours of "cosmic music" in the Mike Ephron jams,*

they will find some true Hendrix gems like "Earth Blues," "Flying (Here I Go)," and "Gypsy Boy (New Rising Sun)," all in an embryonic stage. Of lesser value, but still interesting, are "Monday Morning Blues" and "Key to the Highway." Perhaps only those with a dedicated and brave heart will endure the nine untitled instrumental Ephron-dominated jams.

The Alan Douglas Sessions

During 1969, Hendrix grew discontented with business problems, an endless tour schedule, and the limitations of a three-piece rock band. He moved away from the tight structure of pop and settled into the more improvisational areas of blues and jazz. One of the influential people Hendrix met who seemed to share his vision and imagination was producer Alan Douglas (Rubenstein). In 1969, the Douglas International Corporation (DIC) had established its market niche with albums by Muddy Waters, Richie Havens, Malcolm X, and the book *The Essential Lenny Bruce,* which sold 400,000 copies. Also that year, Douglas had set up an office in London, which was supervised by producers Chris Stamp and Danny Halperin, who handled Hendrix's European label, Track Records.

Hendrix's girlfriend at the time, Devon Wilson, introduced him to Douglas, and Hendrix asked Douglas to come by the studio and assist him in October. Douglas was more knowledgeable about music than Hendrix's manager Michael Jeffery, and their relationship strengthened. In 1992, Douglas recalled the time he met Hendrix. "I'd recorded Muddy Waters and people he admired," he recalled, "so we talked about that. We were both recording at the Record Plant, and one day he came to my house at one in the morning and asked if I would come down to the studio with him. I immediately saw what was happening. It was chaos. Nobody was supervising; he was basically jamming. I stayed in the studio with him for four months trying to help him produce himself. That was the best way to work with him. He was very sophisticated; he knew what he wanted. But his main problem was that he wanted too many things at one time. It was a pain for him to have to work with a manager you couldn't talk to and an engineer who thought he was a producer."[63]

Hendrix used the privacy of the Record Plant to record and experiment almost every night, away from business demands and the pop scene, while his own dream studio was under construction. One of the people working at the Record Plant was teenager Tommy Erdelyi, later known as Tommy Ramone of the Ramones, who watched Hendrix recording all-night sessions with Douglas on songs like "Izabella." "They kept doing that over and over again," Erdelyi recalls. "Then he [Hendrix] would go home and listen to 'Izabella,' and go, 'Well, I don't like any of this.' He would do many takes of a guitar solo, but the thing was, each one was better than the last. He didn't seem to be satisfied...he would work all night on them, and these tracks of guitar solos would pile up."[64]

At the same time, Hendrix was also interested in working with Douglas on a book based on Hendrix's poetry, essays, and all the scraps of paper crammed with his thoughts and ideas. Douglas has said that there was talk of developing these ideas into a film: "He wrote a very interesting film script. He wanted to do all sorts of new things like an incredible blues album where he didn't have to worry about a rhythm section, Gil Evans conducting the band, so all Jimi would have to do was get up in front and blow."[65]

One of the first Douglas productions involving Hendrix took place on September 30, 1969, at the Record Plant sessions for LSD guru Timothy Leary. Douglas assembled Stephen Stills on guitar, Buddy Miles on drums, John Sebastian on guitar, and Hendrix on bass to record an instrumental track based on Joni Mitchell's newly penned song "Woodstock." He then overdubbed selections from Leary's press conferences and titled the track "Live and Let Live." In an effort to sell more copies of the album, which was titled *You Can Be Anyone This Time Around* (Douglas 1), a sticker was placed on the shrink wrap indicating that Hendrix and others played on the recording. The album was to be part of Leary's 1970 campaign for governor of California, but when the LP was released in April, Leary was in jail for drug possession. Reprise later reprimanded Hendrix for this unauthorized appearance.

As their friendship grew, Douglas continued to expose Hendrix to other musical influences, like the ghetto rap of the Last Poets and the hypnotic horn of Miles Davis. Hendrix was receptive to these new sounds during this period, as Eric Burdon explains: "He just wanted to play—*all the time*—he just wanted to jam . . . keep the flow going. By that time Jimi had burned so many axes and made so many psychedelic sacrifices that the audience's chant became 'Burn the guitar! Burn the guitar!' And at this time, Jimi was trying to reach Miles Davis and become the jazz icon that he should have been. In fact, he would have created a new jazz that we all need and a kind that's missing today."[66]

STATUS: *In 1992, the Rykodisc label released the long out-of-print LP* You Can Be Anyone This Time Around *on CD (RCD 10249). It came complete with a reproduction of the Timothy Leary campaign poster, and included the track with Hendrix, "Live and Let Live." The CD is now out of print. Over the years, many tapes of Hendrix's recording sessions with Alan Douglas producing have filtered out to the collectors' network.*

Miles Davis and Gil Evans

Maybe Miles will turn up for this one . . . maybe . . . maybe not.
Jimi Hendrix, *Uncut 2000*, September 16, 1970

Rock music and jazz were just getting acquainted in the late 1960s. In 1968, Miles Davis admitted to listening to Sly and the Family Stone, James Brown, and Jimi Hendrix after his wife played some of their records for him. Initially, Davis was not very keen on Hendrix's early recordings with the Experience. He once referred to it as "hillbilly music" because of Mitch Mitchell and Noel Redding, "the two English guys in his band."[67] But as Davis said in the December 13, 1969, issue of *Rolling Stone*, "Jimi Hendrix can take two white guys and make them play their asses off . . . white guys can only play a certain tempo."

When Davis began to infuse jazz with elements of rock, it caused a disturbance among his regular audience and prompted one jazz critic to write, "It was like finding a raised lavatory seat in a nunnery." The rock community, on the other hand, seemed more accepting of jazz influences. As Davis continued exploring this new territory, he released *In a Silent Way* (Columbia CK 40580), recorded on February 18, 1969, which involved several players who would soon cross Hendrix's path—Herbie Hancock on electric piano, Chick Corea on electric piano, Wayne Shorter on tenor sax, Dave Holland on bass, Joe Zawinul on electric piano and organ, John McLaughlin on guitar, and Tony Williams on drums. If this recording had taken place later, it might have involved Hendrix, and I believe we would have witnessed a radically new artistic sound and direction from Hendrix.

The rock press praised Davis's album. *Rolling Stone* critic Lester Bangs described the track "It's About That Time" as "A terse restrained space jam...allowing more of Miles' fierce blues ethos to burn through...this is the one that might be connected to Miles' interest in Hendrix and Sly [Stone]."[68] Frank Glenn, in his liner notes for the album, further explained Davis's new direction, "[Davis] has incorporated the best of jazz, so-called contemporary rock sounds and rhythms...and the technique of the 20th century composer using polyrhythms (many rhythms at once) and polytonalities (different chords played together). The form is free, and from this freedom a masterful outgrowth of composition has emerged."

During my many years of collecting rare Hendrix tapes, one of my greatest hopes was to find a recording of Miles Davis and Jimi Hendrix. Both Davis and Hendrix collectors have often asked me if such a tape exists. Although no official studio recording session occurred, the two great musicians did play together on one occasion. Davis met Hendrix in 1969 through Alan Douglas, whom he mistakenly identified as Hendrix's manager: "I first met Jimi when his manager called up and wanted me to introduce him to the way I was playing and putting my music together. Jimi liked what I had done on *Kind of Blue* [1959, Columbia CL 1355] and some other stuff and wanted to add more jazz elements to what he was doing. He liked the way Coltrane played with all those sheets of sound, and he played the guitar in a similar way. Plus, he said he had heard the guitar voicing that I used in the way I played the trumpet. So we started getting together...and talking about music. I found out that he didn't read music. There are a lot of great musicians who don't read music—black and white—that I've known and respected and played with. So I didn't think less of Jimi because of that. Jimi was just a great, natural musician—self-taught....Once he heard it he really had it down. We would be talking, and I would be telling him technical shit like, 'Jimi, you know, when you play the diminished chord....' I would see this lost look come into his face and I would say, 'Okay, okay, I forgot.' I would just play it for him on the piano or on the horn, and he would get it faster than a motherfucker. He had a natural ear for hearing music."[69] Davis later noticed that Hendrix started incorporating some of the things he learned from their encounter on the 1970 *Band of Gypsys* album. Hendrix's control of the tremolo arm and feedback during "Machine Gun," for example, combine elements of jazz and rock.[70]

When Carlos Santana was interviewed by *Straight Ahead,* he recalled the events that led to Hendrix and Davis getting together: "I think he [Hendrix] had such a ferocious appetite to explore new music. There was a healthy, wholesome rivalry happening between Jimi Hendrix and Miles Davis. They used to call each other. I know this because their women would call and tell me about it [laughs]. In those times, we used to call those ladies 'monitors' because they would monitor and tell you everything. Miles called Jimi and told him that he was going to put together an incredible band. So, Miles put together [John] McLaughlin, [and] Billy Cobham, on [A *Tribute To*] *Jack Johnson*. When Jimi heard about this, he was shook up because this stuff was serious. This made Jimi want to explore the possibilities of working with Gil Evans and Roland Kirk. It wasn't jazz in the straightjacket sense of jazz changes, but in a free spirit, in a free expression kind of thing that was happening in the sixties. Miles . . . [was] helpful in helping Jimi Hendrix and a lot of people develop a vaster point of view than just playing some loud blues."[71]

Michael Carabello, who played percussion with Santana and jammed with Hendrix at a 1969 Record Plant session, had this to add about Hendrix's interest in Davis: "At this time there was a different little clique of musicians hanging out with Jimi other than all the guys from Europe. Jimi was experimenting musically at this time and the throw down was going to be Miles Davis, Jimi, Buddy Miles, and probably me and Chepito [Areas, second percussionist with Santana], and who knows who on keyboards. Can you imagine the possibilities with Hendrix and Miles together? New York back then was a melting pot of musicians. Not just Miles, but Chick Corea and Herbie Hancock. You would go to a club and see these guys playing and it would be no big deal. This is probably why Jimi loved New York."[72]

Carabello also mentioned the possibility that a lost Davis-Hendrix tape might still be out there. "When people went into the studio back in those days, you didn't actually have a tune to record," he said. "You went in, they turned the tape machine on, and you could mess around. That's why Alan [Douglas] had Jimi in the studio so much at that time. . . . I imagine Miles [Davis] is on a track somewhere, even if it was done at home. It wasn't unlikely for somebody to go over to somebody's house or apartment and lay it down just on cassette."[73]

After the initial meeting between Hendrix and Davis, Alan Douglas booked a session at the Hit Factory studios in New York. Douglas's concept was to have Hendrix and Davis play three original tunes and use drummer Tony Williams at Davis's request. Douglas's arrangement between CBS [Davis's label] and Warner Bros. [Hendrix's label] stated that the final product would be released on Reprise. About a half hour before the session was to start, Douglas received a call from Davis's manager, who said that before Miles went into the studio, he would need a $50,000 advance. Shortly after, Tony Williams called and demanded $50,000 as well. Frustrated by their demands, Douglas canceled the session.

After the Isle of Wight concert (August 30, 1970), a second Davis-Hendrix meeting was scheduled in London to discuss a future recording session. Unfortunately, it was also canceled because Hendrix went on tour in Sweden while Davis toured in France. Two weeks later, Hendrix remained optimistic that something would come together. He told reporter Roy Carr: "I'm still supposed to be making an album with Miles. When that will happen I don't know, or who else will be there . . . who'll play on it. Probably Tony Williams. Should be a gas when it eventually happens. Like Miles, I want to invent a new kind of music, a new kind of jazz. He's already done it. Maybe it's not jazz; maybe it's... It doesn't sound like the music I've already recorded... I'll be doing something very different. It was supposed to happen several months ago, but money got in the way, money always gets in the way.... But that's just Miles."[74] Hendrix was referring to Miles's insistence on a high studio fee.

Another session that never got off the ground was with the late jazz composer and arranger Gil Evans. Evans had previously recorded three albums with Davis and was negotiating a record deal with Hendrix, much like the Miles Davis collaboration. "Miles met Jimi in the late '60s, and I'm sure he turned Gil on to Jimi's music," saxophonist Howard Johnson recalled. "Then Jimi got in touch with Gil. When the Isle of Wight Festival was going on, I ran into Gil on the street. He was really excited, and told me we were going to start working on an album with Hendrix as soon as Jimi got back to the States."[75] Gil Evans picked up the story from there: "He was coming into town [New York] that following Monday [September 21]. Alan Douglas arranged for us to meet—he'd given him the [Miles Davis–Gil Evans] *Sketches of Spain* album. And the idea was for him to make a guitar record—not to sing. Because Alan felt, as I felt too, he wasn't appreciated, even by himself."[76] In later years, Alan Douglas said he had Gil Evans writing some big band arrangements for Hendrix and wanted to formulate a "heavyweight jazz-rock fusion kind of thing."[77]

STATUS: *There are no known Davis-Hendrix recordings. A tape that circulated among Hendrix collectors was thought to be the historic Davis-Hendrix jam. At first, the unreleased track called "Ships Passing in the Night," with the Davis trademark muted trumpet, raised a few eyebrows. However, it was found to be a demo that Hendrix worked on with some undocumented session players, recorded April 14, 1969, at the Record Plant in New York. It did not involve Miles Davis.*

Although the Gil Evans–Jimi Hendrix collaboration never happened, Evans paid tribute to Hendrix at Carnegie Hall in 1974 with a concert of Hendrix's music. The album The Gil Evans Orchestra Plays the Music of Jimi Hendrix *(CPL1-0667) followed this event.*

The John McLaughlin Jams

I think real music is coming together. It's going to get like the jazz scene.... These cats are trying to produce real music ... to hell with the imaginary thing. Jamming—it's kind of like making love to one another musically. Like painting a picture together.

Jimi Hendrix, *Melody Maker,* **March 15, 1969**

In 1969, guitarist John McLaughlin, who had just signed with Alan Douglas, began working at the Record Plant on the album *Devotion* (Douglas 3). Joining McLaughlin on the album were Buddy Miles on drums and Larry Young on keyboards. While this album was being recorded in the Record Plant's lower level, Hendrix worked in the studio upstairs.

On one fortunate occasion, the two guitarists met. A few days after his arrival in the

U.S., McLaughlin recorded with Miles Davis for his 1969 album *In a Silent Way*. He later jammed with Hendrix at New York's Record Plant, where Hendrix was playing with Buddy Miles, bassist Roland Robinson, and guitarist Jim McCarty (of the Buddy Miles Express). At the request of Mitch Mitchell, McLaughlin went to the Record Plant with the intention of jamming with Hendrix, not recording.

In 1996, I interviewed John McLaughlin and asked him how the jam with Hendrix took place: "It was through Mitch Mitchell. Mitch and I go back to working with Georgie Fame in the early sixties. In 1969, I was playing with Tony Williams. Mitch was a big fan of his and he would come to see us play at the Vanguard. One night Mitch invited us to the Record Plant. I came down with Larry Young and Dave Holland [Miles Davis's bassist, 1968–70]. Basically, we played, but it was difficult because at the time I was using a hollow-body acoustic…like a country guitar. The volume on it was so low and Buddy Miles was playing drums so loud. Dave Holland was there and Jimi played electric. It wasn't really a playing session…it was just hanging out…having a good time. I've only heard a little bit of a tape, about two or three minutes, that's all they sent me. It sounded terrible to me."[78] An energized Hendrix and Buddy Miles dominated the three jams based on blues riffs, and McLaughlin's guitar static was too distracting to make this a great moment in rock history.

In 1974, Alan Douglas discovered the tape of McLaughlin and Hendrix jamming, and was ecstatic: "The tape we have of them together is not only a historical thing, it's very exciting. It's going to have a very heavy impact on the musical audience. It's Jimi playing in a bag that's never been released before."[79] Douglas quickly drew up a promotion campaign and started feeding the press teasers about the jazz-fusion material he had on tape between McLaughlin and Hendrix. *Oui* magazine reported in February 1975 that Reprise would release one album of this material and that Nemperor Records (McLaughlin's manager's label) would come out with an alternate one. After hearing a sample of these jams, rock music critic Dave Marsh wrote in *Penthouse* magazine: "The McLaughlin/Hendrix tapes are reportedly ten hours long…once they get started, McLaughlin and Hendrix achieve the sort of interplay that producers of supersessions always seek but rarely discover."[80]

Mysteriously, neither record was released and the boasts about hours of recordings full of nonstop jamming were silenced when archivist John McDermott explained in his book *Sessions*: "All that remains of this special summit [March 25, 1969] is one thirty-minute reel of recording tape."[81] No one seems to know what happened to the recordings that inspired Douglas to say, "I felt like I had been to Tibet."[82]

John McLaughlin was happy that this project was aborted. "They were looking to squeeze as much money as possible out of what to me was a scam," he later explained. "Jimi had already been scammed by these people, because most people will want to buy something on the strength of the name. Jimi's name and my name, and who ever else was there—it was just a scam. For me, I would have been delighted to see something good to have resulted from it, but it wasn't a recording session. I didn't play very long. There were other guitar players down there. They were all playing good and Jimi sounded great. Jimi was a revolutionary like Coltrane. He could do things with the guitar that nobody has ever done before. We all owe him a great deal."[83]

STATUS: *When the much-anticipated jazz-influenced* Nine to the Universe *LP was released in 1980, the fabled McLaughlin-Hendrix jams were not included. The thirty minutes of the McLaughlin-Hendrix jam have surfaced in the collectors' network, and apparently this is all that remains of the loosely organized jam that McLaughlin says "lasted from two till eight in the morning." If other reels exist from this six-hour session, they have not surfaced. Since McLaughlin was not too thrilled with the short sample tape that Alan Douglas gave him, it is unlikely he would ever approve a future release. The songs that appear on the thirty-minute tape are "Drivin' South," "Everything's Gonna Be Alright," and some experimental improvisation jams.*

The Last Poets

Long before hip-hop and rap groups like Public Enemy, there were the Last Poets. Abiodun Oyewole, Alafía Pudím, and Umar Bin Hassan released a successful self-titled debut in 1970 on Douglas Records and attracted fans like Miles Davis and Nina Simone. Lawrence Lipton, a reviewer for the *Los Angeles Free Press*, spoke about the group's origins and approach: "Beginning with coffee shop readings in the late Fifties when jazz music was added to poetry, the foundation was laid for rock and roll groups which in ten years have forged poetry and music into the most potent arm of the new lifestyle revolution of youth on a worldwide scale.... Their style and format is based not so much on rock and roll as it is on the rhythmic variations of Beat poetry and jazz, plus percussion.... The three poets ... have captured in their poems the spirit of the ghetto streets along with all that has survived of their ancient African culture."[84]

In 1992, Alan Douglas told *Record Collector* magazine about the November 1969 session at the Record Plant with Alafía Pudím: "That was the first rap record ever, though it wasn't called rap then. They [the Last Poets] were angry kids who'd just got out of jail and had learned the art form of jail toasting. Jail toasts started in Southern prisons where the inmates, or those with some kind of poetic sense, told poems about what was happening on the streets, about hookers and pimps and wives. One guy would start, somebody else would finish, and they'd be accompanied on pots and pans. There were no sophisticated instruments; it was three rappers and a conga player. But they were really into call and response from the original blues hollers."

Douglas recalled that "one day before a Hendrix session, the lead rapper and writer of the Poets came to visit me and I asked him to do 'Doriella Du Fontaine' for Buddy [Miles]. Buddy started to play along, and then Jimi walked in and said, 'What's that?' He wanted to play. We did thirteen minutes non-stop; first take. It was like magic. I sat there with my mouth open. Jimi then overdubbed bass, Buddy overdubbed organ, and that became 'Doriella Du Fontaine.' Jimi was very interested in all that stuff."[85]

"Doriella Du Fontaine" is a song about a talented prostitute who meets a tragic ending. Hendrix keeps an even flow of guitar fills and scratches underneath Pudím's rap. Toward the end of the recording, Hendrix starts to slip into his tune "Villanova Junction" but then returns to the basic riff.

STATUS: *Now out of print, Doriella Du Fontaine, by Hendrix, Lightnin' Rod (a.k.a. both Alafia Pudím and Jalal-Uddin Nurridin), and Miles, was originally released on vinyl as a twelve-inch EP in July 1984, and then later on CD (Metrotone Records 7 72663-2). The CD contains three versions of "Doriella Du Fontaine" — the complete thirteen-minute version, an edited version for radio play, and an instrumental version. A fourth track titled "O.D.," with Buddy Miles on drums and organ, did not involve Hendrix.*

The Hendrix FBI Files and Toronto Court Transcripts

When the Experience played Detroit's Cobo Arena on May 2, someone from their road crew alerted them that there might be problems for the band when they crossed the border into Canada for an upcoming Toronto concert. The next day, Hendrix was busted for heroin possession.

On May 3, the Royal Canadian Mounted Police uncovered several ounces of an unknown chemical substance while searching Hendrix's hand luggage. According to *Rolling Stone*, the Mounties were waiting for Hendrix to step off his plane from Detroit. Hendrix, Mitchell, Redding, and five members of the Experience road crew were going through customs when Officer Marvin Wilson found a metal tube coated with a dark resin and six small packages with white powder inside a small bottle at the top of Hendrix's flight bag. Wilson was unable to positively identify the substances, and the Mounties detained a stunned Hendrix while they called the mobile police laboratory unit to the airport. The lab results identified the drugs as heroin and hashish. After nearly four hours of detainment, the Mounties handcuffed Hendrix and took him downtown to police headquarters. Noel Redding frantically tried to get hold of their manager Michael Jeffery, but he was nowhere to be found. Hendrix was finally released on $10,000 bail and told the press, "I'm innocent and my lawyers will prove it."[86]

After leaving police headquarters, Hendrix checked into his room at the Four Seasons Hotel and then headed straight to the Maple Leaf Gardens for a scheduled performance. He walked on stage to a full house of 12,000 people and, as captured by an audience recording, told the crowd: "I want you to forget about tomorrow and today. Tonight we're going to create a whole new world." This concert recording revealed that Hendrix intentionally altered his song lyrics to suit the serious and sober mood. In "Red House," he told the crowd: "When I get out of jail, I'll come see you." Even a line in "Spanish Castle Magic" was cleaned up to avoid any drug references: "Just float your little mind" became "Just float your little mind—naturally."

There are many speculations about this unfortunate incident. Hendrix said he had no knowledge of the drugs, and took the position that he was simply given a gift by a fan, didn't realize its contents, and forgot about it when traveling. Others, like guitarist Wayne Kramer of the radical rock band MC5, later felt that Hendrix was set up. "I don't have any doubt in my mind that the right-wing government forces were behind all of that," Kramer recalled. "There was an effort, a movement, to stop this threat that rock and roll represented. In bands like certainly the MC5…Jimi Hendrix, anything that was a threat to their power. In those days, rock music really held the potential to turn the entire youth culture against the establishment, which is exactly what we were trying to do. They were right!"[87]

There is some evidence to support Kramer's view of a crackdown on rock musicians. In addition to Hendrix's arrest in Toronto for possession of narcotics, other prominent rock stars were having problems with the law during May 1969. The U.S. Embassy in London revoked John Lennon's standing visa on May 16 based on his November 1968 drug conviction, declaring him an inadmissible immigrant. Also on May 16, 1969, Jefferson Airplane bassist Jack Casady was arrested for possession of marijuana in New Orleans. On May 28, Mick Jagger and his girlfriend Marianne Faithfull were arrested in their London home for possession of marijuana.

In *The Covert War Against Rock*, author Alex Constantine quotes a leaked intelligence memorandum revealed before the U.S. Senate Intelligence Committee and submitted for

Maple Leaf Gardens, Toronto, Canada, May 3, 1969, where Hendrix delivered a spectacular concert despite being arrested and released only a few hours earlier.
Toronto Star

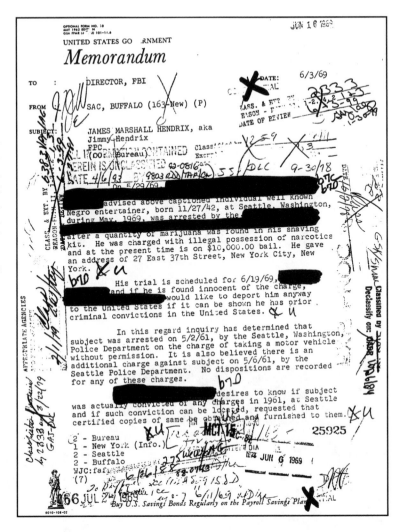

FBI memorandum issued June 3, 1969, one month after Hendrix's arrest in Canada. This document incorrectly states that "a quantity of marijuana was found in his shaving kit."
U.S. Department of Justice, FBI/Steven Roby archives

the record on April 26, 1976. The memorandum explained the tactics of the intelligence sector that were designed to destabilize the lives of politically attuned musicians during the anti–Vietnam War movement in the late 1960s: "Show them as scurrilous and depraved. Call attention to their habits and living conditions, explore every possible embarrassment. Send in women and sex, break up marriages. Have members arrested on marijuana charges. Investigate personal conflicts or animosities between them. Send articles to newspapers showing their depravity. Use narcotics and free sex to entrap. Use misinformation to confuse and disrupt. Get records of their bank accounts. Obtain specimens of handwriting. Provoke target groups into rivalries that may result in death."[88]

The Toronto drug bust caught the attention of the FBI, which immediately opened a file on Hendrix. The seven pages of Hendrix's FBI file, now available through the Freedom of Information Act, include memos from FBI field officers in Buffalo, New York, the

UNITED STATES DEPARTMENT OF JUSTICE . 6-10-69 107 PA?
FEDERAL BUREAU OF INVESTIGATION
WASHINGTON 25, D. C.

J. Edgar Hoover
Director.

The following FBI record, NUMBER 829 158 D , is furnished FOR OFFICIAL USE ONLY.

CONTRIBUTOR OF FINGERPRINTS	NAME AND NUMBER	ARRESTED OR RECEIVED	CHARGE	DISPOSITION
PD Seattle Wash	James Marshall Hendrix #54398	5-2-61	taking car w/o owner's permission	
SO Seattle Wash	James Marshall Hendrix #58067	5-6-61	taking & riding MVWOOP	
Army	James Marshall Hendrix #RA 19 693 532	5-31-61 Seattle Wash		
Metropolitan Toronto Pol Toronto Ontario Canada	James Marshall Hendrix #2199/69	5-3-69	illegal poss narcotics	to appear in court

Since neither fingerprints nor an identifying number which is indexed in our files accompanied your request, FBI cannot guarantee in any manner that this material concerns the individual in whom you are interested

Notations indicated by * ARE NOT BASED ON FINGERPRINTS IN FBI files. The notations are based on data formerly furnished this Bureau concerning individuals of the same or similar names CONFIDENTIAL LISTED ONLY AS INVESTIGATIVE LEADS.

Hendrix's arrest record showing his two prior arrests as a juvenile and the 1969 arrest for illegal possession of narcotics. *U.S. Department of Justice, FBI/Steven Roby archives*

nearest branch to Toronto, and Hendrix's Seattle police record from age nineteen, when he was arrested twice for taking a car without the owner's permission. After his Toronto bust, Hendrix was placed on the Federal "Security Index," a list of "subversives" to be rounded up and placed in detainment camps in the event of a national emergency.[89]

Hendrix returned to Toronto on May 5 for an arraignment. *Rolling Stone* reported on the courtroom situation: "Youthful Hendrix admirers filled the staid old courtroom as Hendrix entered wearing a pink shirt open to the waist, an Apache-style headband, a multi-colored scarf around his neck and beads. His manner was dead serious. When the magistrate called his name, James Marshall Hendrix of New York, he rose and leveled a venomous look at the bench, his lips slightly pursed, which said, without need for words, fuck off. There was no demand for a guilty/not guilty plea. A few words were exchanged, the hearing date was set [June 19], and in three minutes, Hendrix was on his way out the door."[90]

Inside the Toronto courtroom, June 19, 1969. Toronto Star

On May 24, UPI reporter Sharon Lawrence met Hendrix at his hotel room in San Diego. She later wrote about the stressful situation she encountered at the hotel: "Jimi had the drapes drawn against the afternoon sun, and he was standing at an ironing board in his hotel room, wearing jeans and a peach-colored flowered silk kimono. He looked tense and pale. Carefully he pressed the ruffles on a satin shirt he planned to wear for his show at the Sports Arena that night. His voice shook with humiliation and fear. 'Whatever I have done, heroin is not my thing. I'm afraid of needles. Drugs are supposed to be fun. I've seen real junkies. *That's* not fun. I am willing to stand naked in that courtroom. They won't find any needle marks!' He folded up the ironing board and briefly he began to weep."[91]

On June 19, at Toronto's Old City Court House, Judge Robert Taylor announced that Hendrix would stand trial on December 8 for two counts of possession of heroin and hashish. Hendrix was in court less than three minutes.

The final concert for the Jimi Hendrix Experience took place in Denver, Colorado, on June 29. It must have seemed a traumatic time for Hendrix, with the ending of the Experience, the drug arrest, and the suspense of the upcoming trial. Meanwhile, he was receiving stacks of legal papers from his manager, Mike Jeffery, who was trying to get him to sign a longer contract, and Ed Chalpin, with whom Hendrix had signed a one-page agreement back in 1965, was demanding a new album as part of his legal settlement.

Hendrix arrived in Toronto on December 7 to prepare for his court appearance the following day. He dressed much more conservatively than for his May 5 appearance, in his version of a business suit: dark velvet pants and jacket, a silk shirt, and a scarf at his neck.

Reporter Lawrence, who accompanied Hendrix to the courtroom, later recalled: "The prevailing political attitude in Canada seemed to be 'We have to make an example of this fuzzy-haired black weirdo.'"[92] If Hendrix had lost the case, his sentence could have been as long as twenty years. The jury deliberated for eight hours, and returned a verdict of not guilty.

Below are excerpts from the original court proceedings. This includes questions from the attorneys and Hendrix's responses, and some quotations from the transcript. Lawrence's testimony, also excerpted, caused speculation from the crown prosecutor, who found it a little too pat. She explained, however, that her job as a reporter had developed her excellent memory.

THE QUEEN vs. JAMES MARSHALL HENDRIX
Before: His Honour JUDGE KELLY
APPEARANCES: Mr. J. Malone for the Crown
Mr. J. O' Driscoll QC for the Accused
Court Room No. 15, Court House, University Avenue, Toronto
December 8–9, 1969.
EVIDENCE OF JAMES MARSHALL HENDRIX AND SHARON LAWRENCE.

Direct Examination By Mr. O'Driscoll:
Jimi Hendrix's Testimony

Q. Now, can you tell me, Mr. Hendrix, what perhaps some know, perhaps some don't, but what kind of music do you call this; what do you classify it as?
A. I classify it as electronic blues...
Q. These gifts that are handed to you—however they are put to you, either dropped or thrown, you keep them?
A. Yes. Most of them we keep. Well, it is just being gracious, you know. If a fan gives you something it's a very good feeling. They are the ones that support us; they are the ones that buy our records, so there's no harm done to receive a gift from a fan or a friend...
Q. Mr. Hendrix, you have told us you receive gifts. Do you get anything that might be called extraordinary types of gifts?
A. I received a few paintings...teddy bears...pieces of string, yarn...
Q. Yarn?
A. Yes. We get everything...
Q. Now, let's look at Exhibit 3, this tube [hash pipe]. The custom Officers have told this Court that they also found this tube in Exhibit 4 [flight bag], together with Exhibit 1 [Bromo-Seltzer bottle] and its contents, Exhibit 2 [heroin]. We have

heard, and you have been in Court and have heard, that there were traces of hashish found on the inside of this tube.

A. Yes.

Q. Were you aware of that?

A. No, I was not.

Q. Well, can you suggest to me any possible use for that—ordinary use?

A. A pea-shooter. Maybe?

Q. A pea-shooter?

A. Yes . . .

Q. This girl that you say handed you the bottle that you say was later to contain heroin, did you know her?

A. No. I didn't feel very good at all. There were so many people there and I had an upset stomach, plus I was trying to be nice to everybody, you know . . . I wanted to see if I could get rid of everybody in the most polite way possible, so I could be to myself, and Sharon and I was doing an interview together and I made it known that I didn't feel so good . . . the door was open and everybody was coming in and out, the usual scene in hotels . . . somebody said, 'Maybe you might need a Bromo-Seltzer,' and at the same time there was a girl at the door, she stepped in and handed me this bottle and said, 'Maybe this might make you feel better,' and I said, 'Thank you very much, but I must get some rest.' I didn't study the bottle, I didn't look at it too much. I threw it in my bag . . .

Q. How many times have you used [hashish] yourself?

A. I really couldn't tell you how many times.

Q. So many times that you could not remember?

A. No.

Q. You cannot even approximate it?

A. I would say about three times.

Q. Have you ever used LSD?

A. Yes. Five times.

Q. Have you ever used heroin?

A. No.

Q. Have you recently smoked marijuana?

A. Not recently.

Q. What do you burn incense for?

A. For the nice smell.

Q. Would you agree with me that, knowing about marijuana users, that it is sometimes used to cover the marijuana smell?

A. Yes. It is sometimes used for that and for bad kitchen odors.

Q. Am I safe in saying it was not for your bad kitchen odors?

A. No. I don't have a kitchen.

Q. Can you give us any idea how often you would receive drugs from your fans?

A. Most every time that we played at a show, you know.

Q. Would people sign their names to letters they would enclose with these drugs?

A. They might put down Bob or Joe.

Sharon Lawrence's Testimony

Q. Now, as you approached this [Hendrix's] hotel room, Miss Lawrence, can you tell His Honour and the Gentlemen of the jury what you observed?

A. Well, I went up in an elevator, the room was close by the elevator, and there were several young girls in the hallway...

Q. All right. What about the telephone while you were there?

A. People kept coming in and out and the telephone kept ringing. It was hard to conduct an interview...I had been there for about half an hour and Hendrix seemed quite tired...and it was hard to concentrate on talking to him with all the other interruptions, so I said to him perhaps it would be better to do it another time. He didn't feel well and wanted to lie down, so I said I would like to leave.

Q. Yes. What else happened?

A. Well, a few minutes before I could, you know, with some good manners say, 'I think we should do it another time,' he said he didn't feel well, he had a stomach ache, and someone in the room suggested Bromo-Seltzer and at that point the door of the room was open and there were several young girls talking among themselves outside it, and a girl stepped inside the room and handed Mr. Hendrix a bottle and said, 'This will make you feel better.' She appeared to be perhaps 17 to 20, she had long blondish-brown hair and she wore a hippie style long dress...

Q. How, Miss Lawrence, do you know that it was the bottle we are talking about in this trial?

A. When I saw Mr. Hendrix in San Diego [May 24], I asked him what on earth had happened and he said he had a glass bottle in his flight bag and he was stopped at Customs and they took the bottle and I said, 'Is that the bottle you had when I interviewed you?'

Q. The substance in the yellow-topped bottle turned out to be heroin. Other than by using heroin, can you think of any way this would make Mr. Hendrix feel better?

A. I am afraid I don't know too much about heroin.

Q. You must know that they don't have the same properties as Bromo-Seltzer.

A. No, of course not.

Q. Am I misunderstanding your evidence when you connect the statement that some-body suggested that he take a Bromo with this girl giving him heroin; is there some connection there?

A. It is very usual for fans to give pop people gifts.

Q. Heroin?

A. Yes. Drugs, scarves, whatever; anything they think that person might like or any-thing that might get them personal attention.

Q. Including heroin?

A. That's right.

Q. Can you name me one other instance?

A. Some girls that I had addressed at a fan club meeting for the Beatles asked me to deliver a package of things to them. I opened some of the letters and I found some-thing that appeared to be LSD, and I also found some marijuana cigarettes, so I would consider this to be pretty typical of things I have seen a number of times.

After the trial, Hendrix's management told the British press that Hendrix was planning a "farewell tour" with the Experience in the hopes that everything would get back on track. While the press was being fed hype, Hendrix continued to cultivate the Band of Gypsys, with Billy Cox and Buddy Miles.

Written Work in Progress

The following is a list of songs, essays, and other written ideas Hendrix was working on in 1969. Had *Rolling Stone* known about the wealth of material here, surely they would have dropped the "no news" jab in their "No News Is Big News" award to Hendrix in 1970.

"500,000 Halos," "As I Gaze into My Crystal Ball," "Ball and Chain," "Belly Button Window (first draft)," "Black Gold," "Burn Down the Churches," "Calling All the Devil's Children," "Come On Down," "Crying Blue Rain," "Different State of America" (essay), "Don't Expect Me Till You See Me," "The Earth Giveth," "Electric Stagehand" (essay), "Have You Ever Had That Feeling," "Heaven Has No Sorrow," "Hell to Heaven," "Hello Night Bird," "Here Comes the Sun," "I Escaped From the Roman Coliseum" (essay), "If Found Lost...Please Return to Body—West Coast Seattle Boy," "Imagination," "Let It Grow," "Local Commotion," "Love Is Trying Brothers and Sisters," "Meet Me in the Country," "Message to Love," "Mr. and Miss Carriage," "New Drylands" (essay), "Our Lovely Home," *People, Hell and Angels* (possible new LP title), "Please Mr. Lover Man," "Red Velvet Room," "Send My Love to the Universe," "Sippin' Time—Sippin' Wine," "Somewhere,"

"Suddenly November Morning," "Thank You God," "That the Truth Shall Come," "To the Wind," "Trashman," "Valleys of Neptune Arising," and "War Child."

Great Jams, No Tapes

Here are a few recollections about some interesting Hendrix jams in 1969 for which no recordings are known to exist. They illustrate Hendrix's continuous desire to perform with other musicians.

BILLY PRESTON

On March 6, Hendrix jammed with keyboardist Billy Preston, who had just completed sessions with the Beatles and appeared on their single "Get Back" b/w "Don't Let Me Down" (Apple 2490). At the time he jammed with Hendrix, Preston was enjoying his own success with the U.K. single "That's the Way God Planned It" and was working with George Harrison for the upcoming concert to aid Bangladesh. Billy Preston recalled being in England at that time: "I was with George Harrison. It was this club we all used to go to called the Speakeasy. He [Hendrix] came in and asked me, 'Do you want to jam?' and I said, 'Yeah!' We played this one song for about forty-five minutes! He was a very introverted kind of a person, but a very sweet guy, and just a great musician."[93]

STEPHEN STILLS AND BUDDY MILES

Around mid-June 1969, drummer Dallas Taylor attended a jam at Stephen Stills's house in Studio City with Buddy Miles and Hendrix. "As we walked in, I saw Hendrix sitting on one of Stephen's amps, playing his ass off, while Buddy Miles was literally pounding the shit out of my drums. It was very loud and it hurt my ears."[94] Although Taylor claims he still has the tapes from this informal jam, nothing has surfaced.

BLUES IMAGE

Entrepreneur Marshall Brevitz, who helped organize the 1968 Miami Pop Festival, opened a nightclub in Los Angeles called Thee Experience (located at 7551 Sunset Boulevard), similar to the Scene in New York. The first time Hendrix jammed at this club was either June 6 or 7. Nancy Carter, who interviewed Hendrix on June 15, recalled: "I remember the time Hendrix sat in with the Blues Image ["Ride Captain Ride," 1970]. This band had a really hot guitar player [Mike Pinera] who later went on to work with Chicago. Jimi wanted to sit in with the band, but did not bring his own guitar with him. So, a friend of mine went to his car and gave him this $39 guitar to play with. Jimi used it to sit in with the band. He made that $39 guitar hum and sound like a million dollars! This all took place at Thee Experience in Los Angeles."[95]

THE BONZO DOG DOO-DAH BAND

When Hendrix was in L.A. for the Newport Pop Festival (June 20–22), he dropped in at Thee

Experience to jam with the British satirical musical group the Bonzo Dog Doo-Dah Band. On June 21, Bruce Gary, former drummer for the Knack and posthumous Hendrix producer, sat in with the band so that Bonzo drummer "Legs" Larry Smith could go out front and sing the final song, "Rockaliser Baby." As the song ended, Hendrix strapped on a guitar and joined the band for an extended three-chord blues jam. No tape of this jam has ever surfaced.[96] After the jam, Hendrix met Bonzo keyboard player Neil Innes in the men's room and confided his growing dissatisfaction with the Experience. Innes remembered: "It was just the two of us, sort of taking a leak. And he said, 'You know, we're doing the same thing.' I said, 'What, you mean, taking a leak?' He said, 'No—I mean, onstage.' 'Cause he felt part of his act getting almost as daft as the Bonzos, with having to light[en] things [up]."[97]

JOHNNY WINTER

Steppenwolf's John Kay recalled a strange jam that took place between Hendrix and guitarist Johnny Winter in mid-'69: "One of our bass players in later years told me about the time Hendrix played Thee Experience Club in L.A. Apparently one night Jimi showed up dressed practically in all white clothing and sat in with somebody. While he was on stage, in walks Johnny Winter, dressed totally in black! The two of them jammed, and to see both of them play that night, I hear, was like watching positive/negative. He said it was a trip to watch."[98]

How to describe the group? Very funky! Sort of a blues rock type of thing.

JIMI HENDRIX, *MELODY MAKER*, DECEMBER 20, 1969

CHAPTER EIGHT

THE BAND OF GYPSYS: 1969-1970

The Band of Gypsys was formed in mid-October 1969 during a period of jamming at the Record Plant.[1] Hendrix gathered his longtime friends Billy Cox and Buddy Miles and experimented with merging earthy funk rhythms and heavy rock. "We were jamming constantly," Miles explained, "so I said, 'I have an idea…Let's put a band together.' We talked about different things, like having Stevie Winwood, who we both wanted, join the band, but in the end, it came down to just the three of us. The Band of Gypsys was put together in [Alan] Douglas' office."[2] The results proved jawdropping, especially on songs like "Who Knows," "Power of Soul," and "Machine Gun."

In December, two days after the Canadian jury found Hendrix not guilty of all drug-related charges, his intentions for the Band of Gypsys grew more serious. According to percussionist Juma Sultan, Hendrix did not call a formal meeting to break up Gypsy Sun and Rainbows. That group had difficulty with his management, who seemed unable to reconcile their approach with an Experience-type formula. Sultan remembered it this way: "Jimi wanted to get away from that interference. Billy was in and Buddy was available. The Band of Gypsys was just another step to keep rehearsing and playing concerts."[3]

Before the Band of Gypsys could consider long-term plans, Hendrix had to settle his past debt with former producer Ed Chalpin. As part of a 1968 out-of-court settlement, he owed Chalpin an album, and his solution was to provide Chalpin with a live record taken

Hendrix on stage with the Band of Gypsys at Fillmore East, New York City, January 1, 1970.

Joe Sia/Star File

from four upcoming Band of Gypsys shows at the Fillmore East. A live album would be less expensive to produce than a studio recording. Cox and Miles agreed to help him out by performing with him because, as Cox put it, "he couldn't find anybody else to do it."[4] Since the Band of Gypsys was not managed by any one person, Hendrix personally paid Miles and Cox as his employees.

While Hendrix, Cox, and Miles rehearsed, Mitch Mitchell returned to England and joined Jack Bruce's new band, Jack Bruce and Friends. Hendrix and Mitchell were comfortably settling into their separate musical excursions when the British press reported that the Experience would reunite for a "farewell tour." Hendrix was said to have offered Mitchell and Redding a half million pounds for a tour of America, Britain, and Europe. However, in an interview with the *New York Post*, he said he would never even consider playing with Redding again. Some have speculated that Jeffery may have manipulated this entire farewell tour idea with the press.

A Foundation of Funk

On New Year's Eve, the Band of Gypsys premiered at New York's legendary Fillmore East. Hendrix described their first set as tight but scary. Miles, on the other hand, was much more confident about the set: "He [Hendrix] tried to come out and be real modest, but when we jammed for about three or four hours, you could see this whole thing building up, and when we hit 'Wild Thing,' all hell broke loose. Jimi started bending and squatting, and picking his guitar with his teeth, and the audience went nuts."[5] Others felt the performances were not only unforgettable, but also emotional. Ernie Isley, guitarist with the Isley Brothers, said of "Machine Gun": "I've always felt that is about the closest a human being playing guitar can get to the hands of God without being God. When I listen to it, sometimes it puts tears in my eyes."[6]

Billy Cox had a similar reaction: "We felt on stage that the audience was waiting for something new. Something was going to happen. It was going to sound different. That gig was not only fun—it was a different experience. We were all prepared because we had done a lot of rehearsing for it, but a lot of it was impromptu. Sometimes when Jimi would get on stage, we didn't know what song he was going to pick next. I've belonged to some groups where they wrote everything down on a chart or a piece of paper, but we never did that with Hendrix. Whatever Jimi thought of, we supported him one hundred percent. Whatever song he called, we were ready!"[7]

Not all press reaction to the Band of Gypsys was positive. John Woodruff wrote in the rock magazine *Creem* that he had a disappointing musical experience when he attended a Gypsys show: "With each song of the set I found myself starting to compromise—telling myself that next song he will explode...."[8] Woodruff and many others were confused by this new hard funk sound when compared to the three previous psychedelic rock albums by the Experience. The mostly white, stoned-out flower children who had filled Experience concerts, begging for more instrument bashing, were now hearing a blend of

The Band of Gypsys, afternoon sound check, Fillmore East, New York City, December 31, 1969.
Amalie R. Rothschild/Star File

gut-bucket drumming, solid funky bass, and jazz-improvisational guitar played by three obsessed musicians bent on pushing the boundaries.

Part of the confusion in defining Hendrix's new sound came from the way he was marketed by his management and record company. He had become famous as a performer who happened to be black, but his record label never really promoted him to black audiences. Although some copies of Hendrix records were distributed to R&B stations, his psychedelic style of music didn't match radio formats that played Aretha Franklin, the Temptations, and other artists of the time. Frankie Crocker, a deejay at New York's WMCA in 1969, explained: "New York was alive with rock and roll as well as soul and R&B, and everybody went to see everybody else. The only place it was segregated was on the radio."[9]

Hendrix himself may also have been confused about his next musical direction. When he played for a mostly black audience in Harlem in September 1969, a young fan approached him and said he should bring his music back home.[10] He also confronted new social influences like Black Power and the militant Black Panther Party, who asked him to play a benefit concert for the Panther 21, who had been in jail since April 1969 with bail set at $100,000. While he was willing to get involved, his management did not approve.

Hendrix boldly told *Teenset* magazine, "Then get your Black Panthers...not to kill any-body, but to scare them....It's hard to say...I know it sounds like war, but that's what's gonna have to happen, it has to be a war if nobody's going to do it peacefully. Like quite naturally, you say, make love not war, and all these other things, but then you come back to reality and there are some evil folks around and they want you to be passive and weak and peaceful so that they can just overtake you like jelly on bread....You have to fight fire with fire."[11] This strong statement, most likely ignored by much of the *Teenset* magazine audience, shows Hendrix wrestling with important issues.

Guitarist Johnny Winter, Hendrix's friend, remembered that it was a confusing time: "The white guys and managers would say, 'Don't play with these niggers, man—the 14-year-olds can't relate to all that space stuff. Get the cute English guys back.' And the black guys would tell him he was selling out to whitey. Jimi was a pretty sensitive person...and he didn't know what to do."[12]

Four weeks after the Fillmore East shows, the Band of Gypsys played their second and final public appearance at Madison Square Garden for the Winter Festival for Peace. The Festival was organized only one week before the event took place when Vietnam Moratorium Committee organizer Phil Friedman contacted rock entrepreneur Sid Bernstein with the idea of raising fifty thousand dollars for the committee. Alan Douglas was asked to secure the Band of Gypsys for the special benefit concert. This performance marked Hendrix's first public stance against the Vietnam War.

Prior to the concert, Johnny Winter noticed Hendrix's peculiar mood: "He came in [backstage] with his head down, sat on the couch alone, and put his head in his hands. He didn't say a word to anybody, and no one spoke to him. He didn't move until it was time for the show. He really wanted to do that gig, but he never should have. It wasn't that bad, but his whole thing was inspiration, and there wasn't any."[13]

An audience tape recording of this show reveals some of the hysteria that took place in the crowd. As Hendrix tried to get the show started, a young woman in the audience yelled out for him to play "Foxy Lady." He usually had a comedic response to hecklers, but this time it turned nasty. "Foxy lady sittin' over there," he replied, "in the yellow underwear, stained and dirty with blood." Hendrix then attempted "Earth Blues." As the song drew to an abrupt close, he told the crowd, "That's what happens when Earth fucks with space," and sat down in front of his amplifiers.

Alan Douglas, who was in the crowd, saw it from a different perspective: "He [Hendrix] got sick from something and when he came off the stage he actually fell off the apron. At first I thought he was sitting playing the guitar and smiling. I don't know what went through his mind when he was up on stage, but the first thing I noticed, it looked like he was having a big rhythm problem. I think he just got fed up."[14]

Buddy Miles, on the other hand, maintains that Michael Jeffery sabotaged the Band of Gypsys: "We was planning on doing anything we could and Jeffery didn't want that. He wanted Mitch and Noel. He didn't want to have an all-black band, so I got iced. Madison Square Garden was where Michael Jeffery gave him [Hendrix] two tabs of acid. He went on stage and fifteen minutes later he kind of crunched over with a real freaky look on his face and said, 'I can't play anymore.'"[15] Noel Redding was also at the show, and corroborates Miles's account that Hendrix was given acid before the show.[16]

A few days after the Madison Square Garden concert, Hendrix closed the chapter on the Band of Gypsys. He told *Rolling Stone* reporter John Burke: "I figure that Madison Square Garden is like the end of a big long fairy tale. Which is great. I think it is the best ending I could possibly have come up with. The Band of Gypsys was out-a-sight as far as I'm concerned. It was just…going through head changes is what it was."[17] Billy Cox returned home to Nashville and Buddy Miles worked on putting his band, the Buddy Miles Express, back together.

STATUS: *Two weeks after the Fillmore East concerts, Hendrix and Eddie Kramer began mixing for the* Band of Gypsys *album and eventually selected six songs from the four shows. The finished album was passed to Capitol Records, which Ed Chalpin had assigned to release it.* Band of Gypsys *(Capitol STAO-472) was released in America in April 1970, then in the U.K. in June (Track 2406 002). The album contained approximately forty-five minutes of music that was extracted from fifteen hours of tape. The final released tracks were "Who Knows" and "Machine Gun," from the first show on January 1, 1970, and four songs from the second show on the same day: "Them Changes," "Power of Soul," "Message to Love," and "We Gotta Live Together," the last song rather crudely edited.*

A Band of Gypsys *single, "Stepping Stone" b/w "Izabella" (Reprise 0905), was also released in April 1970. It was one of the first stereo singles, but Hendrix commented to* Melody Maker *(May 9, 1970) about its disappointing low-fidelity sound. "Some of the copies out here have no bass on them. I had to go out somewhere and I told the guy to remix it but he didn't. Sure it matters—I'd like a hit single." The single never charted, and the few surviving copies are now collector's items. In 2001, MCA released* Voodoo Child: The Jimi Hendrix Collection *(088 112 603-2), which included these tracks; however, they are still inadequately mixed.*[18]

Future Band of Gypsys *releases were confusing to record buyers. In 1986, Capitol records released* Band of Gypsys 2 *(SJ-12416), which featured three more tracks—"Hear My Train," "Foxy Lady," and an edited version of "Stop"—from the Fillmore East Shows. The sound quality for these extra tracks was inferior because "Foxy Lady" and "Stop" were lifted from a videotape of one of the shows. The rest of the LP contained material from the Berkeley and Atlanta concerts, recorded on May 30 and July 4, 1970. To add to the confusion, Capitol simultaneously released a mispressing that featured several alternate Hendrix concert tracks not listed on the LP jacket. This alternate pressing immediately became highly sought by vinyl collectors.*

In 1991, Polydor released the original Band of Gypsys *album on CD in Germany (847 237-2), tacking on the three extra tracks from* Band of Gypsys 2. *While this release took advantage of the extra time a CD could hold, like the other albums, it did not provide any detailed information about the band's background, the tracks, or the recording dates. Also,*

Buddy Miles was incorrectly given credit for composing the song "Stop." Jerry Ragavoy and Mort Shuman should have been listed.

Band of Gypsys: Lost and Found

In 1971, Michael Jeffery stored twenty master reels of Band of Gypsys Fillmore East concert tapes in his New York office. The following year, when Jeffery moved his office to a different New York location, he left these tapes behind, along with some of Hendrix's clothing, guitars, and amplification equipment. Jeffery also forgot to pay his back rent. In 1972, Jeffery's landlord repossessed the office and its contents.[19]

On March 5, 1973, Jeffery was traveling to a London court appearance related to business affairs regarding Hendrix. He boarded an Iberian Airlines DC-9 during a French civil air traffic control strike. His plane collided with a Spantax Coronado that was inadvertently assigned the same flight route over France. The Iberian Airlines crash killed all sixty-one passengers and seven crew members; Jeffery's body was never found. In the confusion that followed his death, Jeffery's landlord stored all of the repossessed Hendrix items in his barn and forgot about them.

In 1994, the Hendrix belongings that had been in "storage" since 1972 were auctioned in London. The Band of Gypsys' twenty master reels, however, were held for further research, and archivist Tony Brown was brought in to authenticate the material. After he determined that they were the original masters, Paul Allen's Experience Music Project (based in Seattle) purchased the tapes. Peter Blecha, senior curator for Experience Music Project, announced to the press that the Band of Gypsys' tapes contained approximately "50 live recordings . . . [and they are] the aural evidence . . . the missing link . . . proof of his genius comes through loud and clear."[20]

MCA and Experience Hendrix released a double CD in 1999 titled *Band of Gypsys: Live at the Fillmore East* (MCAD2-11931). It is not clear what generation or source tapes were used to produce this CD, but Experience Hendrix did not use the master recordings purchased in 1994 by Experience Music Project. The songs featured on this release were not in any chronological order, and some of them (as well as some of the spoken introductions) were edited.

Most of the CD's sixteen tracks were previously unreleased, but Experience Hendrix took a different approach from the respectful treatment accorded other music legends, such as John Coltrane and Miles Davis. The recorded performances of those artists have been released with strict attention to chronological format, presenting the unedited historicity of the moment. John McDermott explained in his liner notes to *Live at the Fillmore East* that a malfunctioning microphone at the opening of two shows rendered several songs unusable, but that microphone affected only two of the many unreleased tracks documented by audience recordings.

Photographer Amalie R. Rothschild took some excellent still photos of the afternoon rehearsals and concert, and filmed the Band of Gypsys at the New Year's Eve midnight show in 16mm color. Segments of her footage were used in the 2000 Academy Award–winning documentary *Band of Gypsys: Live at the Fillmore East.*

Rothschild described the circumstances of her shoot in detail: "I loaded an Éclair NPR magazine with 400 feet of precious color reversal and filmed the arrival of 1970. After all the fuss at midnight died down, Jimi struck up with 'Auld Lang Syne,' and I became mesmerized. I was sufficiently excited that I felt I absolutely had to shoot something of Jimi playing, but I only had one more roll of 16mm film available now. I filmed all of 'Stepping Stone' from one camera position in the sound booth overlooking the stage, but with the Angenieux 12–120 zoom lens, I felt I couldn't really get good close-ups. So, I went down to the foot of the stage and shot pieces of 'Fire,' 'Ezy Ryder,' and other short bits. Since I only had one seven-inch roll of audiotape, I recorded the soundtrack off the Fillmore East mixing board at 3 3/4 ips on my Nagra. After all was done, I had the film processed with about 200 feet of midnight doings and 600 feet of Jimi [approximately twenty-four minutes]. It was only in 1989, when Bill Nitopi tracked me down, that I got it out, transferred the audio and put the material in sync. I had no idea it would be of such interest to people."[21]

In the early 1980s, Are You Experienced Ltd., headed by Alan Douglas, began organizing and cataloging the various films and videotapes in the official Hendrix archives. One of the items they found was a finished documentary of the 1970 Madison Square Garden Winter Festival for Peace, which Jeffery had assigned film producer Barry Prendergast and director Chuck Wein to capture for a TV special. The unreleased documentary had been part of Jeffery's estate after he died in the plane crash. Throughout the film were performances by Judy Collins; Peter, Paul, and Mary; Harry Belafonte; and Blood, Sweat & Tears, as well as speeches about the Vietnam Moratorium and other narration. The Band of Gypsys segment included only footage for the opening song, "Who Knows," and there was no visual evidence of what actually occurred at the close of "Earth Blues" when Hendrix abruptly ended the show. The entire documentary ran thirty minutes and was in color. It was reported missing shortly after it was cataloged.

STATUS: *The Band of Gypsys recorded a surprising wealth of studio material during the short time they were together. Their unreleased rehearsal tapes reveal multiple studio versions of "Izabella," "Machine Gun," "Mannish Boy," "Who Knows," and "Valleys of Neptune." The complete song list for the Band of Gypsys includes "Astro Man," "Bleeding Heart," "Blue Suede Shoes," "Boomerang," "Burning Desire," "Country Blues," "Earth Blues," "Ezy Ryder," "Honey Bed," "Hootchie Kootchie Man," "Izabella," "Jungle," "Keep on Groovin'," "Look Over Yonder," "Lonely Avenue," "Lover Man," "Machine Gun," "Mannish Boy," "Message to Love," "Night Bird Flying" (with keyboards), "Once I Had a Woman," "Paper Airplanes" (working title for "Power of Soul"), "Room Full of Mirrors," "Seven Dollars in My Pocket," "Sky Blues Today" (working title for "Stepping Stone"), "Strato Strut," "Stop," "Them Changes," "We Gotta Live Together," "Valleys of Neptune," and several lengthy medleys.*

I am not sure I will live to be twenty-eight years old. I mean, the moment I feel have nothing more to give musically, I will not be around on this planet anymore, unless I have a wife and children...otherwise I've got nothing to live for.

JIMI HENDRIX, *ÅRHUS STIFTSTIDENDE*, SEPTEMBER 2, 1970

CHAPTER NINE
GYPSY SUNSET: 1970

As the brief glimmer of the Band of Gypsys faded, Hendrix felt that he had little control over his own life or artistic freedom. His attorney advised him that Warner Bros. was extremely impatient for a new studio album, and if one wasn't delivered in three months, the label had the contractual right to mix one of its own choosing from the numerous tapes Hendrix had accumulated. In addition, he owed $35,000 for damages to the rented house near Woodstock, limousine bills, and reimbursement for several canceled concert dates. Costs for the construction of Electric Lady Studios were also escalating, and in order to put it in full operation, Hendrix needed to come up with $213,000. Touring was his only lucrative option.

Michael Jeffery set up an important interview with *Rolling Stone* to publicize the reformation of the original Experience and three major tours: the U.S., Western Europe and the U.K., and Japan. Both Mitch Mitchell and Noel Redding flew in from London, suspending their current musical projects to attend. Mitchell was still touring with Jack Bruce in a newly formed band called Friends, and Redding was completing his second album with his group Fat Mattress. How Jeffery managed to patch up the hard feelings and offer a solution to keep the band from dissolving again has never been revealed.

During the February 4 interview and photo session with *Rolling Stone*, Hendrix seemed distant, looking up only occasionally to smile politely. Perhaps the thought of

K.B. Hallen, Copenhagen, Denmark, September 3, 1970. *Jørgen Angel*

playing to audiences who only wanted to hear old material and see a routine stage act felt like a giant step backwards. With great hope and contradiction in the same breath, he told *Rolling Stone*, "We're going to go out somewhere into the hills...to get some new songs and arrangements...so we'll have something new to offer, whether it's *different* or not."[1] Hendrix's faithful percussionist Juma Sultan felt that the interview was all hype: "Jimi wanted something else. He wasn't talking the same game about coming back....Jimi didn't want any more tours at the time."[2]

In the previous six months, Hendrix hadn't played with Redding at all and had only briefly played with Mitchell. After the interview, he immediately called Mitchell and announced his intention to drop Redding from the tour. Unfortunately, neither Hendrix nor Mitchell directly confronted Redding, but let management pass on the bad news in late March when Redding showed up for "reunion tour" rehearsals.[3] Suggestions made at the time for alternate bass players included Jack Casady of the Jefferson Airplane, but eventually Billy Cox was asked and agreed to return.

Informal rehearsals began at Hendrix's Greenwich Village apartment with Hendrix on acoustic guitar and Mitchell alternating on brushes and drumsticks. Several interesting demo recordings were made while they worked out new tour and studio material. On a portable tape deck, Hendrix and Mitchell recorded "Power of Soul," "Dance on the Desert," "Stepping Stone," "Sending My Love to Linda," "Freedom," "Here Comes the Sun," "Cherokee Mist," and "Calling All Devil's Children." Mitchell recalled, "We did a lot of recordings at home— me on brushes, phone books etc., Hendrix on his favorite Martin acoustic—which haven't been released, but they weren't supposed to be."[4] While Mitchell correctly stated that these tapes were not "officially" released, these New York apartment demos have been heard by some and reportedly show both a complete break from the psychedelic side of Hendrix and his yearning to explore the depths of funk, jazz, and rock.

In spite of Jeffery's wish that Hendrix would put the past behind him, Hendrix recorded a session with Buddy Miles and Juma Sultan at the Record Plant on February 16. Working without a bass player, the trio recorded two instrumental versions of "Blue Suede Shoes," as well as "Hey Baby (Land of the New Rising Sun)," "Summertime Blues," and several untitled jams. Sultan said that Jeffery continued to discourage Hendrix from playing with him, Miles, Larry Lee, and Jerry Velez: "Management was so busy trying to keep us separate. They were into running such games. They offered me something...trying to buy everybody out so they could control people."[5]

Eric Burdon recalled trying to advise Hendrix around this pivotal time in 1970. "I think he was considering what to do about his life and the future," Burdon said. "My previous managerial situation [with Michael Jeffery] had now become Jimi's situation, and I tried to warn him that it was the Animals' money that was used to get him off the ground. I told him, 'I got fucked and you're going to get fucked the same way if you don't wake up.' And, of course, he just laughed and was too busy conquering the world. I expected this reaction. I didn't think he'd listen to me, but I thought it was worthwhile to tell him."[6]

Sultan has also said that Hendrix hoped to do a session with producer Quincy Jones for

Jones's 1970 album *Gula Matari* (A&M SP3030), but, again, management rejected the idea. Mitchell corroborates this claim, noting that "Quincy first met Jimi when we were living in Benedict Canyon [October 1968] and later on in 1970 he came to see the band at the [L.A.] Forum. I don't think anything was definitely planned, but I know Quincy was up for it and Hendrix always had it in the back of his mind. What a shame it never happened."[7] However, according to Jones, he did plan for Hendrix to record with him on *Gula Matari*. "Jimi always wanted to play jazz," Jones recalls. "He said his dream was to play with Miles. We did 'Hummin'.' 'Hummin'' was arranged to feature him as a soloist on it. He was with a girl at that time named Devon, and she said he was doing everything at the time to avoid that confrontation. I don't know why. He may have gotten nervous and didn't show up that day [for recording]."[8]

Frustrated with the situation in New York, Hendrix contacted Kathy Etchingham, his English ex-girlfriend. Though she had recently married, she was still sympathetic to his cry for help. "It was March 9, 1970, when he arrived," Etchingham remembered. "He phoned me the day before and told me he absolutely couldn't stand it any longer in New York. I picked him up at the airport and he told me he left New York and didn't tell anyone where he was going. I think he was in a general state of depression with all the things he had to do...things were driving him mad....He was just fed up with gigging. He got to the end of his tether. I think he was being made to do more than he wanted to do, like having to produce that album for that prior contract he had signed. It wasn't his management he was blaming—it was the fans. Like having them shout out for songs he had done back in '67. He didn't want to do it, but the fans demanded it."[9]

While in England, Hendrix enjoyed seeing his friends Stephen Stills and Arthur Lee and sitting in on their sessions. Both Stills and Lee have mentioned that there is much more unreleased material that they did with Hendrix, but as of this writing, none of it has surfaced.

The Stephen Stills Solo Album Sessions

Recording for Stephen Stills's first solo album began on March 15 at England's Island Studios. Hendrix played guitar on the song "Old Times, Good Times." Stills said of their collaboration: "Hendrix and I cut a bunch of stuff together. He was a dear friend of mine. We were lonely in London together and hung out a lot. Years later I learned from Mitch [Mitchell] that Jimi had been looking for me everywhere...he wanted me to join the Experience as the bass player, which would have been the greatest dream in my life!"[10] Stills's solo album was released on November 28, 1970, the day after what would have been Hendrix's twenty-eighth birthday. *Stephen Stills* spent thirty-nine weeks in the charts and reached #4.

Over the many years since this session, Stills has only briefly spoken about one other track that he recorded with Hendrix in 1970 besides "Old Times, Good Times," a tune called "White Nigger." He has alluded to many hours of jams that are in storage somewhere, and said they were planning to record a full album together.

STATUS: *Unreleased. The only Stills-Hendrix track that has been made public is "Old Times, Good Times," on the eponymous album* **Stephen Stills** *(Atlantic SD 7202), later released on compact disc (Atlantic 7202-2). Stills dedicated this solo album to James Marshall Hendrix.*

The Arthur Lee and Love *False Start* Session

> *Jimi Hendrix was the greatest guitar player I ever saw in my life. He was just like my brother. I never let him pay for anything! He never bought a cookie around me. I made sure of that.*
>
> Arthur Lee, *Straight Ahead,* October 1992

Arthur Lee and his group Love arrived in London in February 1970 for their first tour of England. On March 17, Hendrix sat in as a guest musician for his old friend Lee during an all-night recording session for Love's album *False Start* at Olympic Studios in London. Lee had met Hendrix at London's Speakeasy club and persuaded him to join him and his band at the session. When I interviewed Lee in 1992, I asked him how he convinced Hendrix to play on *False Start.* He answered, "I told him that neither one of us is going to be around here long, so while we're here together we might as well do something. But who knows how long [long] is?"

Although Hendrix is credited with playing on "Everlasting First," there is still more unreleased material from this session, as Lee revealed in a BBC radio interview on July 4, 1980. "We did a long jam as well as we did 'Everlasting First,'" Lee said. "We did about three versions of that. We did 'Ezy Ryder'...and a couple of other things." *Crawdaddy* magazine (June 1970) reported that "Ezy Ryder" was once planned as a 1970 Love single on the Blue Thumb label, but was canceled.

I asked Lee what had become of these "lost" tapes. "The last I've seen of the audiotapes was when I gave the master reels to Bob Krasnow, who was then president of Blue Thumb Records," Lee responded. "I asked him to hold them for me and I never got them back. He was the one who was all jazzed about Jimi and I being together."[11] Lee added that he had hoped to start a new band with Hendrix at the time.

STATUS: *The 1970 Lee-Hendrix jams remain unreleased.* **False Start** *was released in December 1970 on LP (BTS 22) and later on compact disc (MCAD-22029). At one time, it was rumored that Hendrix played guitar on "Slick Dick" and "Ride That Vibration," two additional tracks from* **False Start,** *but the guitarist is Love band member Gary Rowles.* **Black Beauty,** *a bootleg of Love studio recordings, erroneously identified Hendrix as the lead guitarist.*

The Noel Redding *Nervous Breakdown* Session

Hendrix flew back to New York on March 20. To make up for the embarrassment of dropping

Redding from the 1970 tour, he sat in on a session at Sound Center Studios for Redding's solo album, *Nervous Breakdown*. The rough tracks "My Friend" and "Blues in 3/4" were recorded on March 23. "'My Friend' was a song I had written. Jimi also had a song by that name, but I think he stole the title from me," Redding recalled. "Jimi came over to the studio and offered to play guitar. I think he was trying to make up with me, because he had never spoken to me or even called to say that he was going to be playing with another guy [Billy Cox]."[12] Also helping Redding were Hendrix's friend Paul Caruso on harmonica, vocalist Roger Chapman (Family), Lee Michaels (organ), and fifteen-year-old drummer Steve Angel.

Hendrix later told the press about the session he did with Noel, including a monumental "freak out moment" that featured one of the Irish porters from the Penn Garden Hotel on bagpipes: "This guy insisted on dressing up in his full regimental kilt for the session. He spent a few hilarious minutes trying to keep his cap on over his headphones, but the track ['Highway'] came out very well."[13]

STATUS: *Unreleased. Redding wrote about the status of* **Nervous Breakdown** *in his book* **Are You Experienced?:** *"It went through a lot of hands and is now sitting in Electric Lady Studios pending payment of thousands in storage fees."*[14]

The Cry of Love Tour

> *I called the tour "The Cry Of Love" because that's what it is all about.*
> Jimi Hendrix, *Melody Maker*, May 9, 1970

After much debate, Michael Jeffery agreed to limit the American tour engagements to three-day weekends and allow Hendrix time off to record at his new studio, Electric Lady. Operating under the name "The Cry of Love," the tour featured the newly re-formed Jimi Hendrix Experience, with Mitch Mitchell and Billy Cox, and set out to play thirty-one cities in slightly over three months. To date, twenty-three recordings, official and bootleg, have surfaced from these tour dates.

On the opening night of the new tour, the Experience played an impressive set. From the masterful power chords of "Foxy Lady" through the beautiful yet haunting medley of "Room Full of Mirrors/Hey Baby/Villanova Junction/Freedom," Hendrix had not lost any of his ability to ignite a crowd. Surprisingly, no soundboard recording of this monumental concert is known to exist, even though Hendrix hinted to the press, "We're going to record the first few dates on the tour—get things like 'Rolling Stone' live on an album. The recording is really up to Mitch, but I'd like to do it."[15] While nothing has ever surfaced, Abe Jacob, the Experience's live sound engineer, seemed to feel that Hendrix had a semi-professional recording made that night: "I think he did, but there was no audio feed from the board. Maybe someone walked around with a Nagra [a professional portable audiotape recorder] and a microphone, but that was on their own."[16] Two different members of the L.A. Forum audience did tape the show, unofficially documenting this exciting event.

A California underground record company called Rubber Dubber was one of the first enterprising bootleggers to take advantage of quality audience recordings, such as those of Hendrix's 1970 L.A. Forum concert. It was touted by magazines like *Rolling Stone* and *Esquire* for its fair pricing system and speed at turning out new bootleg titles. *Hendrix Live at the LA Forum 4-25-70* was the first of many titles that Rubber Dubber released. The company's downfall, however, was its open-door policy for illegal items. They sent out review copies to hip youth-oriented magazines and boldly attempted to place ads in *Rolling Stone*, which were quickly refused. In an interview in *Harper's Monthly*, Rubber Dubber's spokesperson explained its radical goals: "We want to put the record companies out of business by simply giving the fans what they want and at the same time not screwing the performer.... We use only the finest materials and only charge six bucks for a two-record set.... We record concerts played into the free air to a paying audience—including us— and for every record we sell, we put 25 cents into an escrow fund payable to the artist himself, not to any of the parasites that surround him. The quarter covers the publisher's fees and the artist's royalties, and any artist can pick up his cash by contacting us through one of our salesmen at any store where Rubber Dubber records are sold."[17] It has never been determined if Hendrix was ever compensated by Rubber Dubber.

The Cry of Love tour continued in California, heading north from Los Angeles to Sacramento (April 26), then moving to the Midwest to play Milwaukee, Wisconsin (May 1); Madison, Wisconsin (May 2); St. Paul, Minnesota (May 3); Norman, Oklahoma (May 8); Fort Worth, Texas (May 9); San Antonio, Texas (May 10); and Philadelphia, Pennsylvania (May 16). The shows scheduled for Cincinnati, Ohio (May 22); St. Louis, Missouri (May 23); and Evansville, Indiana (May 24) were canceled due to Hendrix's illness.

With all of the turmoil and protests in the streets of America at that time, it's no surprise that some of Hendrix's 1970 concerts had a political slant. The two Experience concerts at the University of Oklahoma on May 8 were performed shortly after the Ohio National Guard shot and killed four Kent State University students at an antiwar protest. Six days before the concert, the Nixon Administration ordered offensive attacks in Cambodia and the drafting of 150,000 additional troops. Two days later, on May 4, 1970, the students were shot as Guardsmen, armed with M-1 rifles, submachine guns, and canisters of tear gas, broke up an antiwar rally. Crosby, Stills, Nash & Young addressed the tragic event with their quickly recorded protest song "Ohio," with its memorable line, "Four dead in Ohio." The tension on America's campuses escalated in the days that followed. Norman, Oklahoma's *Transcript* reported that forty state troopers and twenty University of Oklahoma police officers were needed to break up a campus protest resulting from the Kent State shootings. Students pushed and shoved as police attempted to arrest one Oklahoma student who carried a Viet Cong flag. Hendrix arrived to play at the University of Oklahoma in the middle of this confusion and turmoil.

A reel-to-reel audience recording of the second concert at the University of Oklahoma captured Hendrix dedicating "Machine Gun" to the students who were shot at Kent State. "We must get rid of all the hogwash, all the waste, and all the bullshit," Hendrix told the crowd. "Like for instance, this song is dedicated to one of them scenes, and also dedicated to the soldiers fighting in Chicago, Berkeley, Kent State, Oklahoma...completely and always." Instead of the familiar strong opening notes of "Machine Gun," Hendrix improvised a gentle flamenco-flavored introduction similar to the one he used for "Hey Baby (Land of the New Rising Sun)," which contained some unearthly harmonics. Hendrix wore a black armband with the letter "K" in white, symbolizing his alliance with those protesting the Kent State shootings.

STATUS: *The following concerts were recorded by audience members: Los Angeles, California (April 25); Sacramento, California (April 26); Milwaukee, Wisconsin (May 1); Madison, Wisconsin (May 2); St. Paul, Minnesota (May 3); Norman, Oklahoma (May 8); San Antonio, Texas (May 10); and Philadelphia, Pennsylvania (May 16).*

Although there were two concerts performed at the University of Oklahoma, only a sixty-five-minute recording of the second show has surfaced in the collectors' network. This show was documented on a Sony monophonic reel-to-reel deck. Except for a few tape-speed variations, this is a good quality recording. Unlike most Experience concerts, this one featured Hendrix performing a rare encore, treating the crowd to "Voodoo Child (Slight Return)." Recently, a DAT of this concert (transferred from the original reel-to-reel) has made the rounds in the collectors' network.

The Berkeley Concerts

At the end of May, Berkeley, California, was awash in political protests. Three thousand students at the University of California, Berkeley, aggressively attempted to take down a chain-link fence that university officials had erected around a vacant lot known as People's Park, which the students had restored. Ronald Reagan, then governor of California, retaliated and called in two thousand National Guardsmen, who tear-gassed the students from a helicopter and wounded thirty people with shotguns. Yippies and other radical groups demanded to be admitted to the Berkeley premiere of *Woodstock* for free, explaining they were the unpaid true stars of the film.

The Experience rolled into town amid this disturbing environment and encountered angry demands for tickets for their two sold-out concerts at the small 3,400-seat Berkeley Community Theater. Both Berkeley shows were professionally recorded and filmed, including the afternoon rehearsals. Local press reports characterized these performances as evidence of Hendrix's exceptional musicianship, noting that he could vary "his sound from oily to icicle...from blues to steel flamenco" and deliver "shimmering, shattering high notes that shatter the brain like no other musician."[18]

Carlos Santana attended the Berkeley concerts and recalled: "The last time I saw him [Hendrix] was at the Berkeley Community Theater concert in 1970....My band was coming out with a different music than him with congas. People were dancing and going nuts and he knew about it. He told me and Michael Carabello that he was thinking of joining our band. He said this at the Berkeley Community Theater bathroom when we were in there together. I said that would be fantastic, but what am I going to do? He was search-ing for new vistas and new directions. He was in a state of flux. I think my band, with its Afro-eclectic-Cuban sound, really turned him on."[19] Hendrix's search for new musical directions and potential band members continued throughout the summer of 1970.

STATUS: *Although the highly edited fifty-five-minute film entitled* Jimi Plays Berkeley *documents portions of the afternoon rehearsals and both concert performances, an original soundtrack recording was never released. At the time, engineer Eddie Kramer felt that there were not enough worthy tracks from the two concerts to warrant a soundtrack release. After hearing this, Michael Jeffery instructed Kramer to assemble the best tracks from the Berkeley concerts and couple them with other live recordings. The result was an oddly titled album called* Hendrix in the West *(1972, Reprise MS 2049).*

Hendrix in the West featured tracks from Berkeley, but also added songs from San Diego, the Royal Albert Hall, and the Isle of Wight concerts. Over the years, bootleggers have released copies of both Berkeley concerts and of the afternoon rehearsal in excellent sound-board quality. It is a shame that Kramer and others after him who have had the authority to officially release the complete Berkeley concerts have chosen not to do so, as both shows feature some of Hendrix's best live performances for 1970.

A stereo soundboard recording was made of the afternoon sound check. The songs played were "Message to Love," "Blue Suede Shoes," "Hey Baby (Land of the New Rising Sun)," "Ezy Ryder," "Earth Blues," "Room Full of Mirrors," "Villanova Junction/Keep on Groovin'," "Freedom," "Power of Soul" (intro only), and "Machine Gun."

First show recordings: "Fire," "Johnny B. Goode," "Hear My Train a Comin'," "Foxy Lady," "Machine Gun," "Freedom," "Red House," "Message to Love," "Ezy Ryder," "The Star Spangled Banner," "Purple Haze," "Voodoo Child (Slight Return)."

Second show recordings: "Pass It On," "Hey Baby (Land of the New Rising Sun)," "Lover Man," "Stone Free," "Hey Joe," "I Don't Live Today," "Machine Gun," "Foxy Lady," "The Star Spangled Banner," "Purple Haze," "Voodoo Child (Slight Return)," "Keep on Groovin'." All recordings were done by Abe Jacob for Wally Heider.

Summer Concerts and Festivals

On July 17, Hendrix appeared at Downing Stadium on Randall's Island, New York, as part of the three-day New York Pop Festival. Initially, concert promoter Robert Gardiner asked Alan Douglas if Hendrix would be interested in performing. When Hendrix agreed, he was sched-uled as the opening night's main attraction and shared the bill with Steppenwolf, Jethro Tull, Grand Funk Railroad, and John Sebastian. Regrettably, things went downhill from there.

Before the concert, a radical Puerto Rican group called the Young Lords ran a press statement in a local underground newspaper. They declared that the festival took place on the land [El Barrio] of its oppressed people, and since it was an unapproved "outside event," profits should be paid back to the community. Another group known as the RYP/OFF (Revolutionary Youth Party) Collective, which represented other New York radical youth groups, threatened to advertise the concert as a free event in hopes of precipitating a riot if they were not also permitted to share in the proceeds. Under extreme pressure, the promoters acceded to the radicals' strict demands. In a statement to the press, promoter Gardiner agreed that an undisclosed portion of the profits would be contributed to the Young Lords, the Black Panthers, the White Panthers, the Revolutionary Youth Party Collective, the Gay Liberation Front, the Committee to Defend the New York Panther 21, the Youth International Party, and the Underground Press Syndicate. In addition to the

The Second Atlanta
International Pop Festival,
Middle Georgia Raceway,
Byron, Georgia,
July 4, 1970.
Joe Sia/Star File

financial agreement, the promoters agreed to allow various revolutionary youth groups two hours of free stage time for speeches or "community bands" to perform before each day's concert started. The promoters' plans for the New York Pop Festival to be a true rock music celebration, in the tradition of Woodstock, suddenly disappeared.

Despite victory for their demands, radical youth groups still crashed the gates and allowed non–ticket-holders to enter for free. The promoters had hoped to gross $600,000, but sold only $315,000 in tickets.[20] Previously advertised acts, such as Sly and the Family Stone, Richie Havens, and Tony Williams (with special guests Eric Clapton, Miles Davis, John McLaughlin, Larry Young, and Jack Bruce) all canceled. In order to prevent a riot, those who did perform took no payment. Bad acid, lack of security, and crowd violence further fueled disaster.

At one point in the festival, the Experience refused to go on, but when a member of the road crew was threatened at knifepoint, the group quickly changed its mind.[21] Hendrix reluctantly played a short fifty-minute set. His guitar playing was plagued by a local radio station's news broadcast coming through his huge stack of Marshall amps. As he tried to end the performance by dedicating the final song to Devon Wilson, Colette Mimram, and Alan Douglas, the crowd again grew violent. Hendrix fumed and said, "Fuck you, these are my friends." As the angry mob groaned, Hendrix replied, "Yeah, well fuck you and goodnight!" After hurling an explosive version of "Voodoo Child (Slight Return)" at the disruptive crowd, Hendrix left the stage.

STATUS: *There are both audience and soundboard recordings of this restless performance. "Red House," from this concert, was officially released in 2001 on Voodoo Child: The Jimi Hendrix Collection (UTV Records 088 112 603-2). Additionally, a concert film entitled Free (a.k.a. The Day the Music Died) was made in 1973, but like the festival, it was a financial failure. (See Part Two of this book for more details on the film.)*

An audience tape of the Experience's June 7 concert at Assembly Center Arena in Tulsa, Oklahoma, surfaced in 2001. The fifty-four-minute recording is available in the collectors' network. In addition, it is said that after playing two shows at Miami's Jai Alai Fronton on July 5, Hendrix played with jazz bassist Jaco Pastorius, who was performing with the house band at Fort Lauderdale's Bachelors III Club. No photographs or recordings have surfaced of this jam.

The Rainbow Bridge Vibratory Color/Sound Experiment

In spite of Warner Bros.' demand for the overdue studio LP, Michael Jeffery cleverly negotiated a deal with the company to bankroll his film idea in exchange for a potentially successful soundtrack album from Hendrix. Jeffery was given an advance of $450,000 to begin production on *Rainbow Bridge*.

Without a clear premise, plot, or script, Jeffery hired film director Chuck Wein, whom he had known since the "British Invasion" days. Back when Jeffery had managed the Animals, when the band played New York, he and Wein had spent from dinner until dawn going to clubs and talking about films. Jeffery had become interested in the Hawaiian Islands and they decided that the majority of the filming would take place here.

Shortly after completing a concert obligation in Seattle on July 26, the Experience was off to Maui, a tropical dot in the vast Pacific Ocean. They were to play a concert that would appear in the film and Hendrix was to have a brief acting role. Wein selected New York model Pat Hartley—who had previously starred in some of Wein's mid-'60s films for Andy Warhol—as the leading actress, and his friend Melinda Merryweather as art director. Merryweather also appeared as a supporting actress in most of the film.

The cast and film crew descended on Seabury Hall, a section of a private girls' school that was closed for the summer. They were located in an area of Maui known as "Upcountry," not far from Haleakala ("House of the Sun"), a 10,000-foot-high dormant volcano. The Upcountry, worlds away from Maui's beach resorts, was bathed in the surreal muted colors of dawn and the salty ocean air. It's no wonder that Hendrix called Maui "the Cosmic Sandbox."[22]

Wein and Merryweather invited outrageous people to portray themselves in *Rainbow Bridge*. They included dope smugglers, priests and nuns, acidheads, gays, groupies, environmentalists, and a group who claimed to be from Venus. With this volatile combination of people and top-notch film professionals from New York and Hollywood, conflicts could have been expected. "The people [Warner Bros.] brought out couldn't handle the energy and crashed," Wein recalls. "My Hollywood soundman was a sixty-year-old Academy Award nominee who was straight, but took acid with the girl that did yoga. He came to me and said, 'I've been a soundman for forty years, and I've never heard sound like this...like the wind through the trees.'"[23]

One eerie incident happened before Hendrix's non-musical scene in the film. Wein, Hartley, and Hendrix were together in Seabury Hall, and according to Wein, Hendrix suggested a three-way suicide. Wein said, "He was depressed that we were not going to be able to change anything in this world because the world was too fucked up. Hartley was freaking out and wanted to call Devon [Hendrix's girlfriend]...I thought maybe he might, but I wasn't sure, and I wanted to get rid of the suicide talk. So I grabbed Hartley, who was getting really neurotic herself, and I said to Jimi, 'Let's go do this scene, we'll be up there.'"[24]

According to Merryweather, Hendrix may have sensed that his days were numbered: "We were sitting in his room and he said, 'I'm gonna die and leave here.' In my heart, at that second, I knew it was the truth." When he was leaving the island, Merryweather said she would see him in September at Electric Lady Studios. "He looked me right in the eye and said, 'I won't be here,'" she remembered. "Not 'I won't be there,' but 'I won't be *here*.'"[25]

The film crew had waited six hours to film something, and finally Hendrix showed up in the attic. The idea of the scene was for him to talk about reincarnation, and Wein recalled that on some level they were performing, but on another level, they knew these subjects from their own experience. Wein started the scene by asking Hendrix if he had been doing any astral traveling lately. He replied, "I don't know, man, it seems like there's this little center in space that's just rotating...and there's these souls on it, and you're

The Rainbow Bridge Vibratory
Color/Sound Experiment,
Makawao, Maui, Hawaii,
July 30, 1970.
*Daniel Tehaney/Rainbow Bridge
Collection*

sitting there like cattle at a water hole and there's no rap actually going on, there's no emotions. . . . The next thing you know. . . you see yourself looking down at the left paw of the Sphinx . . . next we find ourselves drifting across the desert sands, dry as a bone, but still going towards home. . . . And all of a sudden the Hawaiian mountains open up, rise another 13,000 feet, and we go higher and higher and Cleopatra has this beautiful raven hair. . . . So, I'm laying there playing the part and a grape chokes me almost, but I can't let the choke come out, because, you know, I have to be together, right? So I say, 'groovy grape wine you have there, Cleo.'"[26]

On the following day, July 30, the Experience played two sets in an emerald green meadow near the town of Makawao, an area that was home to cowboys and flower growers. Until recently, the small two-street town consisted of little more than a post office and a **175** feed store. Yet with only a few days notice, a crowd of three hundred people showed up. This was not your typical rock concert—there were guidelines to be followed. "I had zodiac flags and we had everyone sit next to their particular sign," Merryweather explained. "Some people said things like, 'But I'm a Scorpio and I came with a Cancer!' We told them, 'You're going to get to see Jimi on the side of the crater for free, and take part in a concert you'll never forget...just go along with it.'"[27]

Unfortunately, most of the nearly three hours of concert footage shot that day was either lost or destroyed. One of the lost outtakes involved Hendrix's opening segment. Merryweather recalled, "When Jimi got up on stage, he actually played a note for each zodiac sign and then he merged them all together. For example, if you were a Scorpio you could feel the red. People were literally crying when the concert started. It sounded like cellos, then it sounded like violins, and then it sounded like a harp. It rose and fell like a full orchestra. Then out of nowhere comes Billy with this slow funky bass. Jimi then walked up to the mic and started singing 'Hey Baby (Land of the New Rising Sun).' I wish I knew where a lot of that footage is today."[28] The Rainbow Bridge Vibratory Color/Sound Experiment was partly inspired by Emilie Touraine. She also provided Hendrix with the beautiful Hopi shirt and jewelry he wore in the film.

Of the many memorable performances Billy Cox played with Hendrix, he considered the concert on Maui to be the best. "If you've seen the video, Jimi was feeling great. He was smiling, in the best of spirits and we all felt good. We projected that to the crowd and something magical transformed at that particular concert."[29] Perhaps playing to a small audience in this relaxed setting pulled Hendrix out of his depressed state and temporarily allowed him to put his troubles behind him.

When it originally screened, *Rainbow Bridge* received mixed reactions from critics and fans. In Los Angeles, three hundred members of the Laguna Mystic Art Brothers cheered and danced through the movie, but walked out during the scene when a woman in contact with the "Space Brothers" advised the cast to quit using LSD. The next night they picketed the film. Others, such as Hendrix's father, praised the film, saying, "I'm proud of Jimi, comforted he is part of something like this...I know he believed in it."[30]

STATUS: Rainbow Bridge *has undergone several major edits over the years. What started in the fall of 1971 as a 123-minute film was chopped to 70 minutes, with less acting and more music, as it toured the midnight movie circuit. In recent years, Hendrix collectors discovered film cans #4 and #7, which contained unreleased silent footage. Some collectors have been successful in synching a soundtrack with home dubbing equipment.*

When the soundtrack (Reprise MS 2040) was released in 1971, it did not feature any of either of the two concert performances recorded on July 30, in part because technical glitches and high winds prevented Mitchell's drum track from being properly recorded. The other reason was the chaotic atmosphere after Hendrix's death. His dream of a double album called First Ray of the New Rising Sun *was scattered and stretched over three posthumous LPs, including* Rainbow Bridge.

Early in 1971, Eddie Kramer used "Hear My Train a Comin'" from the May 30, 1970, Berkeley concert as a substitute live recording on the Rainbow Bridge soundtrack LP. As of this writing, only "Hey Baby/In from the Storm" from Maui has been officially released, on the Jimi Hendrix Experience box set. However, bootleggers have released pristine soundboard recordings of both concerts. One untitled instrumental studio recording, which plays in the film as Hendrix looks out on a sunset, remains unreleased.

Electric Lady Studios

Electric Lady is different. . . . It has the best equipment in the world . . . it is capable of recording on 32 tracks . . . and I am working on a symphony production to be done there in the near future.

Jimi Hendrix, *New Musical Express*, September 5, 1970

The recording studio became Hendrix's real home, perhaps filling the gap left by his lack of solid family life or permanent residence. He once told his friend Sharon Lawrence about a concept he called "Skychurch": "A home away from everything, with a musical family." According to Lawrence, Hendrix's original idea was to buy a piece of property in the country where he could work on new music, and anyone who truly cared about music could be a part of it. In an article for the *San Francisco Examiner's Image* magazine, Lawrence recalled that he sketched out his idea on hotel stationery for a place to concentrate on music and take it forward.[31] His dream of a country retreat, complete with recording studio, never materialized. He settled for Electric Lady Studios, at 52 West 8th Street in New York City.

Many years before Electric Lady Studios opened its doors, the building housed a big-band nightclub called the Village Barn. In the mid-1960s, new owners transformed it into a rock 'n' roll hangout called the Generation Club. Despite its popularity as a place where you could see Hendrix perform on Tuesday nights, the club went bankrupt. Originally, Hendrix wanted to buy the Generation Club and keep it as a nightclub, but he realized he was spending too much time and money at recording studios. He decided that it would be better to convert the club into his own studio.

After patiently waiting through many months of construction, Hendrix finally had the opportunity to record at Electric Lady Studios on June 15. Over a three-day period, he, Mitchell, and Cox completed master takes for "Straight Ahead" and "Night Bird Flying," and worked on other tunes such as "All God's Children." While jamming and improvising there with friends like Steve Winwood and Chris Wood, Hendrix often generated ideas for new songs. Eddie Kramer recalls, "We would let the tape run . . . a jam would start at one point and end at another. He [Hendrix] would say, 'Wind the tape back' . . . and pull out his reams of paper from various hotels, envelopes, and bits and pieces that were in this huge book. He would pull a line from one page and a line from another, and jumble it around."[32]

In July, Hendrix began work on "Dolly Dagger," a new single and the focal point of the next studio album. It was dedicated to Devon Wilson, who was in the studio when he recorded the basic track. After many overdubs of lead guitar parts, fuzz bass, vocals, and foot stomps, the track was completed. Billy Cox recalled, "I enjoyed the construction that we came up with on 'Dolly Dagger' because it was a joint effort between Jimi, Mitch, and myself. It was almost like putting a symphony together. We were three pieces in a 24-track studio [Electric Lady, Studio A] and I bet we covered every track. When we'd mix it down, it was kind of fun. 'Dolly Dagger' and 'Ezy Ryder' were the most challenging songs we did because there were so many intricate parts we put on them."[33] Hendrix told the British press that he hoped to release "Dolly Dagger" backed with "Night Bird Flying" by October.

One of the side projects Hendrix worked on at Electric Lady during the summer of 1970 was an album called *The Ghetto Fighters*, recorded by his longtime friends Albert and Arthur Allen. Hendrix took time to add a lead guitar solo on several of their tracks, which had been recorded in late 1969 at Fame Recording Studios in Muscle Shoals, Alabama. The album was planned to be a "street opera"—along the lines of a rock opera, but with more contemporary themes intended for the black community. Even though the Allen brothers continued to work on the project for some time after Hendrix's death, it was eventually abandoned in 1972.

Hendrix agreed to tour with Cox and Mitchell, but he still wanted to use Juma Sultan on percussion in the studio. Sultan explains the tense situation that was going on in the background: "I was supposed to have been at the Berkeley concert and at Maui. When he came back from Hawaii, Jimi was concentrating on the completion of Electric Lady Studios. We spent every night from midnight 'til morning at Electric Lady laying down tracks. He had the studio and different people were stopping in that he would try out. He was happy that he had his own studio, but his down was that he had to go out and do things he didn't want to do because he was still committed. What he wanted to do was set up an organization so he could have more control of his life and better utilize his powers. He realized that there were about 50 people living off him through the management which he could eliminate."[34]

When the tension got unbearable in New York, Hendrix occasionally retreated to his old friend Mike Quashie. "Jimi was up here in my apartment and he would talk about all this shit going on with Mike Jeffery," Quashie recalled. "Jimi came over here to sleep and relax. The agreement was that I couldn't tell anybody he was here because he didn't want to be bothered. There were times when he was happy, and there were times when he was depressed, and toward the end, he just wanted to get away from people."[35]

The official opening party at Electric Lady Studios was held on August 26, just a few days before Hendrix left to go to the Isle of Wight Festival in England. Japanese food was catered and invited guests included Johnny Winter, Noel Redding, and other rock stars. Mike Quashie hosted the event and recalled that things got out of hand: "I remember walking in and asking, 'What's going on here?' [Producer] Peter Allen was outside throwing up as I was going in. They had all this Japanese food and were drinking sake wine like it's a groove. I stayed for about an hour and a half and then I was gone. People got mad at me and said I was supposed to host this thing."[36]

Jim Marron oversaw the construction of Electric Lady Studios and remembered that Hendrix was reluctant to attend the grand opening. "He really didn't like social affairs.... He was trying to talk his way out of it and I said, 'Jimi...man to man, what will it take to get you to come?' And that's when he said, 'Get me a police escort to JFK [after the party].' I said, 'Done...but why, Jimi?' He said, 'Those bastards [the cops] been chasing me my whole life, for once I just want to chase them.'"[37]

STATUS: *On June 15, Hendrix jammed at Electric Lady Studios with Chris Wood (saxophone), Steve Winwood (electric piano), and Dave Palmer (drums). A fifty-one minute tape of this session has been bootlegged several times. The trio recorded instrumental versions of "Calling All Devil's Children," "Pearly Queen," and "Hey Baby (Land of the New Rising Sun)," as well as several untitled jams.*

From July 19 through July 21, Hendrix, Cox, and Mitchell continued session work at Electric Lady Studios. Overdubs and rough mixes for "Night Bird Flying," "Straight Ahead," "Astro Man," and "Freedom" were done on July 20, and on the twenty-first, the band worked on "Midnight Lightning." During the session on July 20, Hendrix jokingly performed a falsetto version of Tommy Roe's 1969 hit "Dizzy." When Eddie Kramer suggested that it should be the next single, he replied, "No, that's going to be the B-side. The single is going to be 'Your Evil Underwear.'"[38]

Albert and Arthur Allen, now known as Tunde-Ra and Taharqa Aleem, stored the master tapes for The Ghetto Fighters *in a vault and only began negotiations for its release with the Hendrix family in 1995. Five years later,* Experience Hendrix *magazine (Winter 2000) announced that they would be including an unreleased track with Hendrix and the Aleems titled "Mojo Man" on a CD called* Power of Soul: A Tribute to Jimi Hendrix. *The track was written by both brothers and featured Arthur on lead vocal with Hendrix adding subtle guitar fills. Unfortunately,* Power of Soul *was never released.[39]*

One of the final tracks Hendrix recorded at Electric Lady was a slow improvisation given the title "Slow Blues." The 1:45 track was done on August 20 and was released on the Jimi Hendrix Experience *box set.*

The *Byron and Shelley Project*

During the two-week period Hendrix was recording in New York, he somehow found time to be involved with a film titled *Byron and Shelley Project* (a.k.a. *Byron and Shelley Treatment*). The concept came from "Papa" John Phillips who, while tripping on mescaline, thought it would be fun to make a film about the two Romantic poets Lord Byron and Percy Bysshe Shelley.

In his autobiography, Phillips wrote: "Once we secured a $50,000 commitment from a film producer [Lou Adler], we got to work on our *Byron and Shelley Project*. Mike Sarne was directing us and he put together a small cast that included Jimi Hendrix...and a striking Nicaraguan woman named Bianca [Perez Morena de Macias, later married to Mick Jagger].

Jimi was acid rock's Voodoo Child extraordinaire, and the sultry, mysterious Bianca...had done some modeling, and had been hanging around with Hendrix and his crowd in New York. The movie was to be shot in a cinéma-vérité style, with Mike and I playing Byron and Shelley as modern men....Bianca was to play Teresa, Byron's mistress. We weren't sure exactly where the Voodoo Child fit in but Richard Leacock, who did Monterey Pop with Pennebaker, was the cameraman whose crew followed us everywhere. In the few weeks we worked on the project, we shot scores of hours on sixteen-millimeter film."[40]

STATUS: *Unreleased. Phillips stated in his book that he abandoned the film project shortly after making it. In interviews I conducted in 2001, Mike Sarne and Lou Adler told me that in addition to Hendrix and Bianca, the unfinished United Artists film also featured political activist Abbie Hoffman and artist Andy Warhol. Adler also thought he still had the film somewhere in his archives.*

The Final European Tour

On August 27, Hendrix left New York for the last time to fly to London's Heathrow Airport. When he arrived, a barrage of reporters and cameramen greeted him. It had been eighteen months since he played a British concert and he was apprehensive. On August 29, he told *Melody Maker* reporter Roy Hollingworth: "While I was doing my vanishing act in the States, I got the feeling that I was completely blown out of England. I thought they had forgotten about me over here. I thought maybe they didn't want me anymore, because they had a nice set of bands. Maybe they were saying, 'We had Hendrix, yeah he was okay.' I really thought I was completely through here."[41] In the photos that were taken on his arrival, Hendrix looked a bit slimmer than when he had left England and his hair was neatly trimmed. He seemed in a playful mood and hammed it up for the UPI cameras.

The European tour, however, was a disaster right from the start. When Hendrix arrived in England, he was fighting a cold that grew progressively worse without proper rest and under the stress of traveling across climate zones. His concerts, for the most part, were plagued with constant radio leakage coming through his amps, as had happened at his New York Pop Festival appearance in July. Two past girlfriends showed up to tell him he was now a father. And while he was looking for the security of a solid relationship (but not using good judgment) he asked two new women to marry him. His band began to crumble, and the price of being Jimi Hendrix, world famous rock star, started to take its toll.

A half-million people gathered on the green pastures of the two-hundred-acre East Afton Farm on the Isle of Wight for a five-day festival (August 26–30) billed as "The Last Great Event." The first two days of the festival were devoted to films, records, and multimedia activities. The final three days featured top American and British acts, à la Woodstock.

The festival was poorly organized. Even when the promoter declared the festival free, three angry radical groups ripped down iron fences and smashed lights. Adding further confusion, four advertised acts did not appear. With schedule conflicts and long delays in setting up equipment, many acts, including Hendrix, did not arrive on stage until just before dawn. The festival's crowds exceeded estimates, and a majority stayed to see Hendrix close the festival on Sunday.

Prior to his show, Hendrix confided in his friend and fellow performer Richie Havens about some problems. Havens recalled: "He was terribly unhappy, extremely depressed, and asked for my help. 'I'm having a real bad time with my managers and lawyers,' Jimi said. 'They're killing me; everything is wired against me and it's getting so bad I can't eat or sleep....'"[42] Havens recommended an attorney and invited Hendrix to contact him when he returned to New York.

Hendrix opened his lengthy two-hour, eighteen-song set with a spontaneous medley of "God Save the Queen/Sgt. Pepper's Lonely Hearts Club Band," eagerly hoping to please his British audience. Despite being away from England for so long, and with no new album to promote, he attempted many new and unreleased songs like "Freedom," "Dolly Dagger," "Midnight Lightning," and "In from the Storm." Ian Anderson of Jethro Tull observed that the audience wasn't impressed and demanded more familiar songs: "The air was thick with cries for 'Hey Joe' and 'Purple Haze,' which Jimi Hendrix, at that point in his career, was not particularly enamored of trotting out yet one more time. I left with a sense of foreboding that he was going to have a rough ride that night. It has always lingered in my mind since then, what looked like a bad night for Hendrix might have contributed to his general state of mind that led to the unfortunate events a few days later."[43]

After his set concluded at four in the morning, Hendrix was whisked away by helicopter for a flight from Southampton to Stockholm. During his tour of Europe, he was accompanied for the most part by Kirsten Nefer, a twenty-four-year-old Danish model who was struggling to become an actress. Nefer was introduced to Hendrix by a mutual friend, Karen Davis. Their friendship quickly became intimate.

Hendrix arrived in Sweden exhausted during the afternoon of August 31 with only a few hours before playing yet another concert. Backstage at the Stora Scenen auditorium at the Gröna Lund, he reconnected with Eva Sundquist, whom he hadn't seen since the Experience played in Sweden on January 9, 1969. Over the intervening months, Sundquist had written several letters to Hendrix informing him that she was pregnant and that James Daniel Sundquist (a.k.a. Jimi, Jr.) had been born on October 5, 1969. A backstage photographer asked him to hold up a child for a picture. He agreed and mistakenly thought it was his son, but it turned out to be the daughter of George Clemons, whom he hadn't seen since recording "Mercy, Mercy" for Don Covay.

According to Sundquist, Hendrix asked how his son was and said he was very glad to hear about him. She later reported that they talked of marriage. Hendrix was supposed to go home with Sundquist to see his son, but apparently couldn't get away from the fans and journalists. He never had the opportunity to see his alleged son.[44]

The show at the Stora Scenen was delayed for over an hour. Hendrix had an argument with the concert promoter, who was adamant that his performance last only an hour. Since the Tivoli Gardens Fun Fair had to be closed during the show, the promoter claimed he lost

The Isle of Wight Festival, East Afton Farm, Isle of Wight, England, August 30, 1970.

Laurens van Houten/Star File

revenue from the Fair, and anything over sixty minutes would cut deeply into his profits. Frustrated over the dispute, Hendrix reluctantly took the stage. About halfway into the set, he suddenly walked off to continue arguing with the promoter. Mitchell awkwardly filled in with a drum solo to distract the crowd and kill time. When Hendrix returned, he announced to the crowd, "Sorry for the intermission, but I had to get a load off my mind." Even though the situation backstage was apparently under control, amp interference and the frenzied crowd screaming out for old songs caused Hendrix to lose his temper again. "Fuck you," he angrily told the crowd. "Come up and play the guitar, so I can...." The dramatic concert lasted almost twice the time the promoter had specified.

The next show on the tour was in Liseburg, Gothenburg, Sweden, at the Stora Scenen on September 1. The show opened with the band Cat Mother and the All Night Newsboys, with whom Hendrix had a prior affiliation. The Gothenburg concert tape reveals that his playing was back in true form. However, Chas Chandler attended and felt the show was disastrous: "We sat and talked that night, and I told him exactly what I thought of the show, and he just got angry. I didn't understand what he was trying to do and just left."[45]

After the concert, Billy Cox was tempted into trying LSD at a party.[46] Cox was never into drugs and had a negative and long-lasting reaction, with delusions about someone trying to kill him. His condition grew worse as the tour continued. Cox was later diagnosed by a doctor as suffering from an acute phobic anxiety state with paranoia.

The most disappointing show Hendrix and his band ever performed was on September 2 in Århus, Denmark. He openly admitted to the local press that he was tired and had not slept in three days, and tried to cancel the show. His cold relapsed but he foolishly decided to play.

As he stepped up to the microphone, Hendrix announced, "Welcome to the Electric Circus. Our first song will be called 'Freedom.'" The unfamiliar song was disjointed and out of tune. After a long gap before the next number, Hendrix said, in his confused state, "I actually forgot what I was here for, 'Message to Love,' right?" Finally, he played an eerie but moving instrumental version of "Hey Baby (Land of the New Rising Sun)," before laying his guitar down and walking off stage. Cox's paranoia increased as he watched the incident unfold, while Mitchell played yet another unplanned drum solo.

An announcement was made to the crowd that Hendrix would take a five-minute break before returning. A half-hour later, after insistent handclaps and irritating whistles, the MC confirmed that he was sick and the concert was canceled. As Hendrix went through a back door to a waiting taxi, the stunned audience was told that their money would be refunded and a free make-up concert would be given at a later date. The *Demokraten* newspaper reported the next day that Hendrix was completely "freaked out" on stage and later "collapsed like a wet rag," but they could not confirm if his blackout prior to the show was alcohol- or drug-induced.

Kirsten Nefer remembered the situation after the concert, as well as a strange event that further added to Hendrix's confused state of mind: "We took a cab to the hotel and there was this girl in his room. It was unclear how she got there, but she and Jimi began talking. She told him about the Mafia and how a member of the Vanilla Fudge had a mysterious road accident. Jimi was getting paranoid, no...scared. I was getting mad and told Jimi either she leaves or I do. He got her to leave."[47]

It has been alleged in several biographies that Michael Jeffery had influential underworld connections. The Vanilla Fudge, allegedly controlled by the Mafia, managed to "convince" Jeffery in 1968 to add their group to the Experience's tour as an opening act, stretching it to three support bands (Eire Apparent, Vanilla Fudge, and Soft Machine). In 1969, when Hendrix was reluctant to play the Salvation club in New York City, Jeffery, accompanied by a man with a .38 who demonstrated expert target-shooting skills, "convinced" him otherwise.[48] Jeffery also had a professional relationship with Steve Weiss, an attorney for both the Experience and the Vanilla Fudge.

Earlier on September 2, Hendrix told reporter Anne Bjørndal of Denmark's *Morgenposten*, "I am not sure I will live to be twenty-eight years old...I've been dead for a long time and been resurrected in a new musical body."[49] Nefer said that Hendrix felt like something was going to happen to him. "He'd ask me questions like, 'Do you think I'm going to live to be twenty-eight? What do you think will happen to my music when I die?' And I said, 'You'll be twenty-eight soon. Why talk like that? Stop that talk! When you die, you'll be among Beethoven and all the greats, but you're not going to die.' He said he had left so many tapes around and some that he didn't want people to hear because they weren't very good."[50]

As Hendrix and Cox traveled from Århus to Copenhagen on September 3, Mitchell chartered a plane to England for a brief visit with his wife and newborn daughter Aysha. When he rejoined Hendrix and Cox, the band played their strongest performance on the tour. Prior to the evening's concert, Nefer invited Hendrix to meet her family, who made him feel welcomed and accepted. Seeing how a well-balanced family got along was overwhelming; it was something Hendrix had never had as a child. Nefer recalled: "He hadn't experienced family life, just sitting around the table with a mum! My mother treated him as just a guy, not like *the* Jimi Hendrix...it wasn't a big deal."[51]

Hendrix proposed marriage to Nefer. The Danish magazine *Se og Hor* acquired the exclusive cover story and its headline on September 11 was, "World Star Gets Engaged to Danish Model." The magazine reported that no wedding date had been set, but "the happy newly engaged couple" would make their home in London. This information conflicted with what Hendrix had said in an interview with *Disc and Music Echo* on August 29: "Marriage is a bit risky now...I'd really hate to get hurt." However, in that interview, he went on to say that he seemed to be searching for a secure relationship: "I'd like to meet a quiet little girl—probably one from the country...one can never tell when the time is right." Nefer didn't take the proposal too seriously, remembering, "He did that to a lot of girls. He just wanted a normal life."[52]

Once the press left, Hendrix and Nefer departed for the concert. The Danish paper *Politken* reviewed the concert (September 4, 1970): "Jimi Hendrix at the K.B. Hallen surpassed anything we have heard until now....Jimi was ill and tired in Århus, but

Copenhagen...was true energy...which ran through his fingers, through the guitar and into all of us." Erik Weiderman wrote for the newspaper *Information* (September 5, 1970): "Jimi Hendrix is supposed to have said that he had 'been dead for a long time.' If this is correct, I would suggest that the concert in København [Copenhagen]...was a resurrection from the dead." The evening's performance was highlighted by a rare two-song encore of "Hey Joe" and "Fire," during which he asked the audience to help him out and "have some fun."

Hendrix and Nefer returned to her place after the show. He then asked Nefer to continue on with him for the German leg of the tour, but later changed his mind. Nefer returned to the film she was working on in London, and Hendrix traveled to Berlin.

On September 4, Hendrix was billed as the headliner at Super Concert '70, a six-hour show at the Deutschlandhalle in Berlin, with Procol Harum, Canned Heat, Ten Years After, and others. Jorg Flemming, for *Bravo*, reported that Hendrix appeared unhappy and lonely prior to the show and he could only draw three sentences out of him during their interview (October 5, 1970): "In America I was on the road every day for five months [April to August]. Berlin and Fehmarn are my last concerts. After that I need a break in London."

Hendrix appeared exhausted and uninspired during his performance, and barely spoke to the crowd between songs, giving only "Machine Gun" an introduction. During an interview backstage with American Forces Television, he revealed his dissatisfaction with large, overcrowded festivals: "It's just too big.... You're not getting through to all of them...and the idea to play to them is to try to turn them on." Unfortunately, the large-scale "Open Air Love & Peace Pop Festival" was the final stop on his German tour.

On September 5, Hendrix and his band arrived at the Baltic resort of Fehmarn, but a severe storm forced their concert to be rescheduled to the following day. The festival's "love and peace" vibes were nowhere to be found. *Record Mirror* reported (October 3, 1970) that there were "armed police with dogs, and a genial bunch of Hells Angels with chains, truncheons, and knives were brought in to keep order. But since the crowd was incredibly self-disciplined, the Hells Angels were obliged instead to damage the press tent and all its telephones, set fire to the festival headquarters, destroy a temporary pub after getting rotten drunk, and beat up a few hippies."

After performing six shows in six days in four different countries, the band was worn out. Cox's mood in particular had gone from bad to worse. The night before the Fehmarn concert, Cox witnessed a terrifying barroom brawl. When the hotel hosting the festival's musicians ran out of liquor, chairs were smashed and fights broke out. The next day, Cox worried that the stage would collapse during their show. The disruptive crowd greeted the arriving band with yelling and loud booing. "I don't give a fuck if you boo, as long as you boo in key...you muthas," Hendrix quickly responded, and the crowd yelled back "Go home!" He seemed to ignore them and continued to introduce the band. After playing a standard set, Hendrix, Cox, and Mitchell managed to leave safely before the stage was taken over by the Hells Angels. As the equipment was packed up, a member of the Hendrix road crew was shot in the leg, and not long after that, the stage was burned down by the angry mob.[53]

STATUS: *All seven of Hendrix's last concerts were recorded in their entirety. They document some supremely gifted guitar playing, and yet at other times reveal a lack of concentration and inspiration. The audio quality is very good on most of the audience tapes listed here.*

- ◆ *Isle of Wight (August 31): Although the official CD,* Jimi Hendrix: Isle of Wight *(Polydor 847 236-2; released in 1991), captures most of the set, the complete 110-minute unauthorized soundboard has been in circulation for years in the collectors' network.*
- ◆ *Stockholm, Sweden (August 31): Of three different audience recordings for this concert, the best runs 107 minutes and captures all fifteen songs played.*
- ◆ *Gothenburg, Sweden (September 1): A ninety-two minute audience recording exists, and all thirteen songs are documented.*
- ◆ *Århus, Denmark (September 2): A twenty-five minute tape of this short concert exists in the collectors' network.*
- ◆ *Copenhagen, Denmark (September 3): A ninety-two minute tape (available in the collectors' network) captures this excellent show.*
- ◆ *Berlin, Germany (September 4): The tape for this concert runs sixty minutes and is available in the collectors' network.*
- ◆ *Fehmarn, Germany (September 6): Of three different sources, the best is a seventy-seven minute audience tape. It is available in the collectors' network.*

New Directions

On September 6, Hendrix returned to London and booked into the Cumberland Hotel. Upcoming concerts scheduled in Vienna, Paris, and Rotterdam had to be canceled. Cox, still suffering from the lingering effects of the LSD, refused to take prescribed tranquilizers and on September 9 was sent home to America to recuperate with his parents. Mitchell took advantage of the time off and spent it with his wife and daughter.

Between efforts to line up a new bass player, Hendrix attended a press reception party for Michael Nesmith, who was leaving the Monkees to start a solo career. Nesmith later claimed that Hendrix was interested in returning to his R&B roots: "I heard something [he played] the night before with some horns on it. I said, 'Jimi, you invented a kind of music. You're one of the most important musical powers to have come along in decades, and you're the fulcrum for a major shift in the landscape, not of popular music, but of music in general.' It suddenly dawned on me—it was epiphanous—that this man had no idea who he was or where he fit. He could not see the hurricane because he was sitting in the center of it."[54] In an interview with reporter Keith Altham for Radio One the next day, Hendrix conveyed that he was tired of just being known as a guitar player or a songwriter.

On September 14, Hendrix visited Monika Danneman, a twenty-five-year-old former ice skating teacher from Germany, whom he had first met on January 12, 1969, when the Experience played in Düsseldorf. He spent his final few days with her. Danneman, like others before her, said she and Hendrix were in love and he'd asked her to marry her. Although in her book, *The Inner World of Jimi Hendrix,* she billed herself as his fiancée, she

Cox, Hendrix, and Mitchell before the Isle of Fehmarn concert, September 6, 1970.
Good Times/K&K/Star File

provided no substantial proof. In April 1996, she committed suicide by poisoning herself with carbon monoxide.

STATUS: *Keith Altham's interview with Hendrix from September 11 runs thirty minutes and continues to make the rounds in the collectors' network.*

The Final Jam

Two days before Hendrix died, he sat in with Eric Burdon's new multicultural band War at Ronnie Scott's Jazz Club in London. Although Burdon and Hendrix had become close friends over the years, communication wasn't easy for them during 1970. After disbanding the New Animals, Burdon was enjoying the success of War's Top 10 hit "Spill the Wine" (MGM 14118). Burdon felt that the communication problem between the two men stemmed from Hendrix's reclusive nature. Eric Barrett, Hendrix's stage manager, contacted Burdon during this time and suggested that he and Hendrix get together. Burdon responded, "Hey, I've tried to reach this guy on several occasions. If he's in that kind of mood, ain't nobody can bring him out of it. I ain't going to him. If he wants to come talk to me, I'm playing at Ronnie Scott's Club tonight."[54]

According to Burdon, Hendrix did come to the club on the night of September 16, showing up with a string of ladies on his arm, including Burdon's wife, whom Burdon hadn't seen in a while. War was the first rock band to play Ronnie Scott's Jazz Club, and Burdon felt the gig would be an adventurous experiment, although adding Hendrix to the mix might have been a gamble. "On the night he jammed with us, he came up and played on the last few tunes in the set," Burdon explained. "It was a jazz audience, the 'London jazz brain intellectual circuit.' It's not unknown for them to boo people off the stage, especially if they are rock 'n rollers. We were on cloud nine, but the audience gave him a hard time and booed him off. So, he left and went backstage." Burdon told Hendrix, "'Don't give up— get out there and play, motherfucker!' He went back out but there was a problem between Howard Scott, our guitar player, and Jimi. Howard forced Jimi to the background and Jimi

The final show, Love And Peace Festival, Isle of Fehmarn, Germany, September 6, 1970. *Good Times/K&K/ Star File*

was playing rhythm guitar during 'Tobacco Road.' The fire was building and I heard Howard play solos like I never heard him play before. He really forced Howard to shine that night. Then he came back and did a rip-roaring performance in grand Jimi Hendrix style. Afterwards, Jimi said, 'I'll see you around,' and that was it—I never saw him again."[55]

War's thrilling updated funk arrangement of "Tobacco Road" differed entirely from the Nashville Teens' 1964 pop version. While Burdon is correct in his evaluation of Howard Scott's solo, it was Hendrix who stole the show. His use of sophisticated Wes Montgomery–style chords was outstanding, and Jimi achieved near perfection on the guitar that night.

In addition to "Tobacco Road," Hendrix also played on "Mother Earth." Shortly into the song, Burdon asked him to play the blues. His solo was searing, with hints of his own song "Burning Desire." Hendrix blended and balanced well, with excellent backing from Lonnie Jordan's keyboards and Lee Oskar's harmonica. As his solo ended, War's Charles Miller stepped up for his solo and Hendrix encouraged Miller, shouting "Yeah!" Sadly, this was Hendrix's final performance.

STATUS: *As of this writing, the only known recording of this jam at Ronnie Scott's Jazz Club is a good-quality forty-minute audience tape that includes War's full set. However, it is likely that a soundboard tape was also made.*

When I interviewed researcher Nancy Carter, she said: "In 1970, I went over to England with Eric Burdon and War. They were playing their first U.K. gig in London's Hyde Park and later at Ronnie Scott's Jazz Club. The following night Jimi played with them at Ronnie Scott's . . . this show was recorded by Jerry Goldstein [one of War's managers]. He told me he still has the tape, but I don't think he'll ever release it. This was Jimi's last session; as you know he died shortly after this."[56]

Jerry Goldstein confirmed Nancy Carter's statement and told Goldmine magazine in November 1994, "I built a remote truck with a remote system to record every [War] show, because they were creating every night . . . that would mean there are hundreds of hours from 1970 alone that most fans of the group have never heard, and most never knew existed."

In 1998, the music Web site Launch.com reported that a California firm called Genesis Media Group had acquired the exclusive worldwide rights to Hendrix's last performance. According to the company's statement, "Howard Scott held onto the tapes of the show for nearly 30 years."[57] Genesis Media Group planned to release an album of the recordings in the summer of 1998, but nothing ever came of it.

The Final Hours

Although some of the details concerning Hendrix's final hours have become clearer in recent years, there are still many questions that will never be answered. By many reports, Hendrix was looking ahead in a positive frame of mind during his final days. He had made plans with Eddie Kramer and Chas Chandler to finish the next album, and was considering

K.B. Hallen, Copenhagen, Denmark, September 3, 1970.
Jørgen Angel

starting his own record label. Arrangements had been made with a professor at Juilliard to tutor him in reading and writing music.[58]

Hendrix also called his lawyer and said he wanted to be released from his contract with Michael Jeffery, which was due to expire on December 1, 1970. However, even if that were possible, Jeffery would still be co-owner of Electric Lady Studios, and prior contractual obligations would have kept them associated for at least the next two years.

At approximately 3:00 A.M. on the morning of September 18, Hendrix left a party where he had seen his friends Alan and Stella Douglas, Mike Nesmith, Angie Burdon, and Devon Wilson. From that point on, details of his final hours are sketchy and accounts conflict. In his book *Jimi Hendrix: His Final Days*, the late author Tony Brown assembled the most comprehensive collection of interviews with those who were with Hendrix in his last hours, including the horrific recollections of the ambulance men who arrived at the scene.

Coroner Galvin Thurston's report concluded that "The cause of death was clearly inhalation of vomit due to barbiturate intoxication, but there is no evidence as to intention to commit suicide. He had no worries outside the usual stresses of business and I do not feel it would be safe to regard this as sufficient motive. If the question of intention cannot be answered, then it is proper to find the cause of death and leave an open verdict." Despite this "open verdict," the tabloid newspapers were filled with sensationalistic stories of drugs and sex, which persist over thirty years later.

One final poem titled "The Story of Life" was found by Hendrix's bedside, which concluded with the words "Until we meet again." He was buried in Greenwood Cemetery in Renton, Washington, on October 1, 1970. As he had predicted, he never made it to twenty-eight.

Written Work in Progress

Although Hendrix never had the chance to complete his ideas for songs in 1970, he managed to work on the following: "And Send My Love to Kathy," "As He Passed by the Tree of Personality," "Beam Me up Jupiter," "Come Down Hard on Me Baby," "Give Me Some Room to Breathe," "Heaven Has No Sorrow," "It Wasn't Too Long Ago," "Kiss the Sunshine," "Living in a Graveyard," "Love Bomb," "Love Is Trying," "Midnight Lightning," "Moon Life in Spiral Light," "One Kiss of Your Eyes," "Pass It On," "Send My Love to Joan of Arc," "Through Some Changes," "Red Velvet Room," "She Comes from Iceland," "The Story of Life," "The Warm Hello of the Sun," "The Terra Revolution and Venus" (essay), "War Child," and "With the Wink of an Eye."

In an interview with Hendrix archivist Tony Brown, Monika Danneman revealed that she had Hendrix's demo tapes for the songs "Belly Button Window," "Angel," "Astro Man," "Silver Ships," and "Hey Baby." So far these have not been released.

I'm trying to do too many things at the same time, which is my nature. I just hate to be put as only a guitar player, or only a songwriter, or only a tap dancer! I like to move around.

JIMI HENDRIX, *RECORD MIRROR*, OCTOBER 10, 1970

CHAPTER TEN
LAST NOT LOST

This chapter explores some unusual Hendrix memorabilia and tapes, as well as canceled releases. In some instances these have yet to be released; some may never be. In other cases, like the Chas Chandler tapes, "Scorpio Woman," and *Black Gold*, their complete story has, until now, never been told.

In the early 1990s there was a sort of Hendrixmania at Sotheby's auction house as never-before-released memorabilia became available. In the December 17, 1990, Sotheby's catalog, Ronald Varney described the collection of fifty-six Hendrix items as a "fascinating glimpse of Jimi Hendrix the composer and musician."

When art historian Pepe Karmel stumbled across a sheet of paper with Hendrix's handwritten lyrics and elementary chord patterns at a pre-sale exhibition, he called it "a fundamental discovery." "He [Hendrix] knew in advance *exactly* what he wanted to do in each solo, and could articulate it quite precisely," Karmel said. "All the fog and fuzz of slides and wails and feedback were precisely calibrated in advance, and articulated to the band. *That's* fundamental. I don't think he could read music, and so when he wanted to transcribe his musical ideas he had to do it in this way—as a narrative, a little memo to himself. He got rid of chordal complexity so he could concentrate on tonal complexity. So that sheet is really an attempt to put his search into words. For Hendrix, though, the noise was never noise, and the effects were never effects. It was all simply music."[1]

Sotheby's $324,000 sale of the white Fender Stratocaster Hendrix used to play "The Star Spangled Banner" at Woodstock sent vintage guitar prices skyrocketing into a whole new era. Even though the guitar was not in mint condition, showing both scratch marks and cigarette burns, Tom Wheeler, editor of *Guitar Player* magazine, noted, "It's the magic of the man, not the guitar, that rocketed the dollar amount light-years beyond all previous electric guitar prices."[2]

The Pan Am Flight Bag

One of the more unique items to surface in the Sotheby's Rock 'n' Roll Memorabilia auctions was Hendrix's Pan Am flight bag, an airline "give-away" that he carried with him from 1967–70, which contained a variety of documents and personal items. The Sotheby's catalog noted that the bag and its contents were with Hendrix at the time of his death in London. The bag's contents included a contract dated December 4, 1969, for the Band of Gypsys' New Year's Eve concert at Fillmore East, including a rider to release Hendrix if he was held over or convicted in Toronto, Canada; four keys for his 12th Street, New York City, apartment; a songbook entitled *Bob Dylan: The Original Songs Never Before Published*; twenty-one handwritten pages of poet-philosopher Kahlil Gibran's *The Prophet*, written on parchment paper by a friend on April 25, 1970, and bound together in a wood cover with blue stone centerpiece; Hendrix's TWA airline ticket to New York from London stamped 20 Feb 70; a collection of unusual coins in a suede pouch; two antique glass bottles in a leather case; photocopies of two contracts; and various letters of agreement and letters addressed to Hendrix from his lawyers regarding tours, financial concerns, and a paternity case.

STATUS: *At the December 17, 1991, Rock 'n' Roll Memorabilia auction, Sotheby's offered the flight bag and its contents for an opening bid of $7,000. However, the item was withdrawn and not sold.*

The Record Collection

Hendrix had broad musical tastes, and he collected records in a wide variety of styles, including folk, jazz, blues, and rock 'n' roll. According to Kathy Etchingham, Hendrix's favorite album was comedian Bill Cosby's record *I Started Out as a Child*.[3] Other records in the collection included John Lennon and Yoko Ono's *Two Virgins*, Muddy Waters's *Electric Mud*, John Lee Hooker's *Live At Café Au Go-Go*, Junior Wells's *It's My Life Baby*, Bob Dylan's *Highway 61 Revisited* and *John Wesley Harding*, Richie Havens's *Mixed Bag*, and *Johnny Cash at Folsom Prison*. Hendrix played these records on a Bang & Olufsen turntable, hooked up to a Leak-70 amplifier and two Lowther speakers, which were blown out quite often.[4]

STATUS: *One of the auction acquisitions made by Paul Allen's Experience Music Project was Hendrix's record collection, which is on display at the Experience Music Project museum in Seattle, Washington.*

Hendrix and his diverse record collection, London, England, 1967. *Petra Niemeier/K&K/Star File*

The Personal Diary

While on tour in 1968, Hendrix kept a daily diary that included handwritten entries for March 19 through 23, March 28, March 29, August 1 and 2, and August 7. The entries contained private observations and feelings about friends and activities related to the tour. In his March 19 entry, Hendrix discussed the Experience's arrival in Ottawa, Canada, and his personal conversations with Joni Mitchell: "I talked with Joni Mitchell on the phone. I think I'll record her tonight with my excellent tape recorder (knock on wood) hmm...can't find any wood...everything's plastic." In the August 1 entry Hendrix wrote: "Can you imagine Southern police protecting me?"

STATUS: *Hendrix's diary sold for $4,400 at Sotheby's December 17, 1991, auction. Experience Music Project purchased the item and has it on display.*

The Chas Chandler Tapes

In 1992, Chas Chandler offered Alan Douglas several forgotten master tapes recorded by the Experience that he had discovered at Olympic Sound Studios. These "lost" tapes contained complete sessions from the trio's first two LPs. Chandler said that the sixty-four boxes of original multitrack master tapes included forty-one songs, nine of which had never been heard by the public.

Douglas first took the position that the tapes were stolen—that the Hendrix estate owned them and they should be surrendered. After his failed attempt to buy the material and his angry comments about Chandler, which were published in *Rolling Stone*, Douglas passed on the tapes, stating that they were probably just demos by Noel Redding or more Jimi Hendrix Experience outtakes.[5] Douglas hated outtakes and once threatened to burn all Hendrix tapes that were not commercially releasable.[6]

After the negotiations failed, Hendrix fans were treated to a few of the nine "rare" cuts discovered by Chandler. Some of the material found its way onto bootlegs such as *Studio Haze* and *Out of the Studio*, which had stunning sound quality. A fascinating window had been opened into Hendrix's raw studio work. However, post-production overdubbing by Mitchell and Redding was added between 1988 and 1989 on a few of the previously unreleased tracks. In 1990, Redding explained: "We went to Newcastle and overdubbed everything. I did nine tracks in one day. They're a lot of songs relating to other Hendrix-type songs... we repaired them. I put guitar on as well."[7]

An instrumental from the batch, titled "Little One," was originally recorded at Olympic Studios on January 28, 1968, but twenty years later Redding and Mitchell returned to the studio and added new bass, drums, and a vocal track by Redding, along with new lyrics. The result is titled "There Ain't Nothing Wrong with That." The same type of over-dubbing was applied to a Redding song originally called "Dance." Mitchell added a vocal track and the song was retitled "Cat Talkin' to You."

"Taking Care of No Business" dates back to Hendrix's Curtis Knight period, and was another track from the Chandler cache. The Experience's version, recorded during May 1967, features Hendrix singing and playing rhythm guitar. Tuba and saxophone give the unofficial unreleased version, with overdubs, a Salvation Army Band feel. The version found on the *Jimi Hendrix Experience* box set features the original version with Hendrix accompanied by Mitchell on tambourine.

Other formerly "lost" Chandler tape rarities include "Crying Blue Rain," "Shame, Shame, Shame," and an instrumental version of the French hit "La Poupeé Qui Fait Non," (a.k.a. "No, No, No"). These are all great recordings that document embryonic versions of unreleased songs Hendrix was tinkering with in the studio.

STATUS: *Chas Chandler died on July 17, 1996. Shortly thereafter, Experience Hendrix purchased the "lost" Olympic Studios tapes from his estate, and has begun to parcel out some of the Chandler tapes on releases such as the Jimi Hendrix Experience box set.*

"Room Full of Mirrors" (Spoken Word Version)

Hendrix used the phrase "room full of mirrors" while recording a demo of the song "Voodoo

Child" in early 1968. Over the next few months, he wrote a fully fleshed-out song and debuted "Room Full of Mirrors" at the Royal Albert Hall concert on February 24, 1969, during a loose jam with Kwasi "Rocky" Dzidzournu (percussion), Dave Mason (guitar), Chris Wood (flute), and the Experience.

Like many of Hendrix's songs, "Room Full of Mirrors" is rich in metaphor. He sings about living in a room where all he can see is himself, and through his inner or spiritual strength (depending on the version of the song), he finds the courage to smash the "mirror" and see his real self and the world around him.

Shortly after the February 24 Royal Albert Hall concert, Hendrix recorded an unusual piece on his home tape recorder at his Brook Street flat in London. This spoken-word version of "Room Full of Mirrors" first surfaced in the mid-1980s. The recording begins with Hendrix playing "Love You Lil," a track from Eric Burdon and the Animals' 1968 LP *The Twain Shall Meet* (MGM 4537). For the next thirty-five minutes, apparently without notes or script, Hendrix explored his inner self—his "room full of mirrors." A psychologist would have a field day analyzing this tape. Hendrix talked about a person who enters the room with friends and looks something like him, but whom he doesn't know: "He brings my whole world, my whole day and night…and drives me completely out of my mind."

As the spacey monologue continues, the inner voice tells Hendrix he is in need and that he should "scream hard…and long." Hendrix sounds very emotional at this point, as he says the mirrors are beating the hell out of his mind. "Man, I think you better…call out your loved ones—you better call a little louder because you will be lost very soon, you'll be very lost within yourself, past dimensional stage, you'll be lost in vacuums. I turn to the world. What has the world to offer me except pats on the back?" At one point, he gets so frustrated that he asks for God's help to "tell this idiot to get the hell out of me, and get me out of this damned mirrored room!" Hendrix then moves his microphones to capture the breathing of a "beautiful young girl" sleeping in his bed, while he plays guitar gently through to the end of the tape.

STATUS: *This unusual tape surfaced in the 1980s, and later appeared on the bootleg* **Black Gold.**

Seven Tapes in a Headband

In 1970, when production began on the film *Rainbow Bridge*, Hendrix was the first to arrive on the island of Maui. When Mitch Mitchell arrived, Hendrix took him aside and gave him seven cassette tapes wrapped in a headband, asking Mitchell to take good care of them. Mitchell thought this was rather exceptional; Hendrix often gave him the odd demo tape to listen to for new song ideas, but he had never given such explicit details about what to do with them. Mitchell put the tapes in his suitcase and later brought them home to England, leaving them untouched for twenty-two years.

TAPE ONE: *BLACK GOLD*

Sometime between mid-1969 and the spring of 1970, Hendrix drafted and later recorded a fantasy biography titled *Black Gold,* playing his Martin acoustic guitar in his New York apartment. Like the Who's rock opera *Tommy, Black Gold* included a series of linked songs that formed a story—the tale of a character based on Hendrix himself.

Hendrix alluded to the *Black Gold* character during an interview in 1969: "Three or four different worlds went by within the wink of an eye. Things were happening. Here was this cat came around called 'Black Gold.' And there was this other cat came around called 'Captain Coconut.' Other people came around. I was all these people. And finally, when I went back home, all of a sudden I found myself being a little 'West Coast Seattle Boy' for a second. Then all of a sudden, when you're back on the road again, there he goes, he starts going back. That's my life until something else comes about."[8]

On February 4, 1970, Hendrix hinted to *Rolling Stone* about the material he had been writing after the Experience had broken up: "Mostly cartoon material...there's one cat who's funny, who goes through all these strange scenes. I can't talk about it now. You could put it to music I guess."

Nothing more was said about the *Black Gold* tape until producer Alan Douglas made the following statement to the press in March 1975: "Jimi did a suite of, I think, eight tunes called 'Black Gold,' kind of a phantasmic autobiography about a super stud that goes out on the road, becomes famous and goes up in the sky. One night we sat down and did the entire thing on a cassette set up—it was magnificent! We overdubbed another guitar part, we had the tape, and we were going to do an album from it and a movie and so on. Somebody copped that. I can't even find the lyrics."[9]

Another ten years of silence passed before Douglas said more about the *Black Gold* recordings and told how they disappeared shortly after Hendrix's death: "He wrote the songs and they were beautiful. 'Astro Man' is a takeoff of one of them. Two people who worked in [Michael] Jeffery's office broke into Jimi's apartment and stole legal pads that he used to write lyrics, all his cassettes including *Black Gold* to hold as ransom against money Jeffery owed them."[10]

In 1990, Sotheby's auction house sold both the first (one-page) and the final (ten-page) drafts for *Black Gold.* They appeared in the book *Cherokee Mist: The Lost Writings of Jimi Hendrix* by Bill Nitopi. Oddly, that same year former Experience drummer Mitch Mitchell contacted Douglas and said that he was the owner of the seven Hendrix tapes that included *Black Gold.* In 1992, Hendrix archivist Tony Brown contacted Mitchell about the tapes. At the time, Mitchell believed that the collectors had everything, and consequently that the tapes were of no value. After hearing only a short section, Brown was convinced otherwise.

The information (about all seven tapes) provided here comes from Tony Brown's unpublished notes. According to Brown, Hendrix wrote the letters "B G" for *Black Gold* on the first cassette's box. On side A of the tape itself (an Entronic C90), he wrote "Idea for L.P. Side 1 suite...Black Gold." Side B was simply marked "Cont. from side A."

Brown noted that *Black Gold* featured Hendrix on acoustic guitar playing the following:

SIDE A: "November Morning," "Drifting," "Captain Midnight 1201," "Local Commotion," "Local Commotion 2nd Part," "Here Comes Black Gold," "Black Gold," "Stepping Stone," "Little Red Velvet Room."
SIDE B: "The Jungle Is Waiting," "Send My Love to Joan of Arc," "God Bless the Day," "Black Gold," "Machine Gun," "Here Comes Black Gold," "Trash Man," "Astro Man," "2nd Part of Astro Man," "I've Got a Place to Go."

The notes Brown took while listening to the *Black Gold* tape explain the contents: "The first track on the tape starts with 'Suddenly November Morning.' After a few false starts, Jimi settles nicely into the song. This is immediately followed by possibly one of the first recordings, along with a very much shorter version, of 'Drifting.' Jimi only sings two verses of the song, with very similar lyrics to the track he had recorded in the studio. Changing tempo drastically for the next track was 'Captain Midnight.' At the time I thought this could have been called 'Captain 1201' because that seemed to be the theme that Jimi sang throughout the track. But I had since received more hand-written evidence giving the correct title, and, of course, 12:01 would be a reference to midnight. Next came 'Local Commotion' which seemed to go on for quite some time. And even going into a second version of the song, indicated by Jimi. The next track was 'Here Comes Black Gold,' and was the first appearance on tape pertaining to 'Black Gold' itself. It was performed in almost a fanfare kind of way, as if a special person has just arrived over the horizon. This merges into 'Stepping Stone.' For me personally, the next song was possibly one of the highlights of the tape: 'Little Red Velvet Room.' It's a very emotional song about a girl called Lucy and Jimi is asking her if his child Tami is doing all right.[11] She replies, 'She's doing fine.' Sadly the tape runs out before the song is finished."

"Side Two starts with 'The Jungle Is Waiting,'" Brown continues, "which is a very jazz-flamenco piece with Jimi imitating jungle sounds vocally. The song flows into 'Send My Love to Joan of Arc,' which is the same chord structure as 'Send My Love to Linda.' Again, without any break, Jimi changes the tempo for 'God Bless the Day' and 'Black Gold' playing both in the same style. Next up is 'Machine Gun,' ending the song with 'Thank Hell for Heaven, Thank Heaven for Hell.' Jimi then returns to another version of 'Here Comes Black Gold,' singing 'He comes from the land of the Gypsy Sun.' 'Trash Man' comes next. Although this is a vocal version of the song, and very short, it bears no resemblance to the version released on *Midnight Lightning*. This then runs straight into 'Astro Man.' Obviously a very early version of the song, but fairly close to the recorded version, that is until Jimi announces 'Second part of Astro Man.' After a quick tune up, he launches into a very comic version about a young thirteen-year-old girl flipping out from LSD and falling from a window, being saved at the very last moment by 'Astro Man' of course. Swooping down from the sky announcing, 'I'm coming to save you, you poor little thirteen-year-old girl,' imitating all the voices in Mighty Mouse fashion, even chuckling to himself at one point. The final track starts with Jimi saying 'Damn, I've got this brand new apartment, everything, and now I'm still lonely, no place to go.' Imitating the phone ringing on the dead strings of his guitar, he holds a phone conversation between himself and Rosie, who invites him to her place. In great excitement, Jimi sings 'I've Got a Place to Go,' thus bringing the tape to an end."

TAPE TWO

The second tape was recorded on a Hitachi C60 cassette. The majority of the selections are familiar songs that the Band of Gypsys later recorded; there are also some unfinished demos. Brown noted that this tape features Hendrix on electric guitar. Hendrix labeled side A "[Elect] Laser Blue Rock GPDS No. 1 rough ideas. Here Comes The Sun. Message To Universe." It includes a recording of a conversation between him and an unknown girl (following "Whisper in Your Ear"). The side ends halfway through the last song.

Side B is marked "Rough ideas No II. Message To Universe (yes)." The song "Valleys of Neptune" may have been recorded on June 7, 1969, in Hendrix's suite at the Beverly Rodeo Hotel in Los Angeles.

SIDE A: "Message to Universe," "Whisper in Your Ear," (unknown song), "Message to Love," "Bolero," "Here Comes the Sun" (not the Beatles song of the same name), (unknown song; tape ends halfway through).
SIDE B: "Restless Kiss," "Spanish Riff," "Machine Gun," "Valleys of Neptune," "Machine Gun."

TAPE THREE

On the outside of this Hitachi C90 cassette box Hendrix wrote: "Yes. A side from half way." After "Sunshine of Your Love," the rest of side A is blank. As with the second tape, the material appears to be from 1969. Brown noted that Hendrix wrote "Maria Talking, Universe L.A." on the cassette insert. He also reported that side A contained a conversation about ancient kings between Hendrix, Maria, and other unknown persons in the room. Side B ends with Jimi talking to an unknown girl.

SIDE A: "Universe L.A." (a song with Hendrix and Cox), (unknown song; Hendrix is playing through an Octavia[12]), "Message to Love," (unknown song), "Sunshine of Your Love."
SIDE B: "Spanish Riff," "Cherokee Mist," "Various Rhythms," "Beginnings."

TAPE FOUR

This Ampex C60 tape has nothing written on the box. Side A, labeled "A. This Little Boy practice 1," includes six songs that were never released. Brown noted that Hendrix played acoustic guitar on the songs on this side of the tape. Hendrix labeled side B "Mike—Harp. Buddy—guitar lead. Jimi—guitar rhythm B."

After the blues selection, the tape concludes with a recording of Bill Cosby on television, with Hendrix laughing in the background.

SIDE A: "Please Help Us God," "Meet Me in the Country," "Astro Man," "This Little Boy," "Blues," "Spanish Riff," "Ride Across."
SIDE B: "Astro Man," "Instrumental Solo," "I'm a Man," "Blues."

TAPE FIVE

Tape five (a Sony C90) doesn't include Hendrix. Side A contains a conversation between Noel Redding and Eric Barrett while they are watching television. Side B is blank.

TAPE SIX

The sixth tape (a Sony C60) contains part of a 1969 concert. Judging by the well-behaved audience, Tony Brown felt that the tape was recorded during the January 1969 tour of Germany, possibly on January 15. This tape is unique; it is not one of the tapes presently in circulation. It contains the only known complete performance of "Third Stone from the Sun." The recording captured only a portion of the concert; the first half of each side is blank.

SIDE A: "Fire," "Tax Free," "Third Stone from the Sun," "Getting My Heart Back Together" (incomplete; the tape runs out).
SIDE B: "Spanish Castle Magic," "Purple Haze," "The Star Spangled Banner," "Red House."

TAPE SEVEN

This tape includes the legendary jam that took place between Hendrix and folk/blues singer-guitarist Taj Mahal (born Henry St. Claire Fredericks) at the Beverly Rodeo Hotel in June 1969. Author David Henderson first mentioned its existence in his 1978 book *Jimi Hendrix: Voodoo Child of the Aquarian Age*.

Hendrix labeled side A "Taj + Jimi Jam." It concludes with Taj teaching Jimi the harmonica. Side B was labeled "Jam cont...." Brown noted that Hendrix played electric guitar and Taj Mahal played twelve-string acoustic guitar. This side of the tape includes various people talking at different points.

SIDE A: "Crying Blue Rain," "Long Hot Summer Night," "Sweet Mama," "Hey Gypsy Boy," "African Beat" (actually "Izabella"), a Curtis Mayfield song, "Country Riff," "Flamenco Riff" (as played at Woodstock).
SIDE B: "Slow Blues," "Instrumental Solo" (as played at Woodstock), "Beyond All Flesh" (words spoken by unknown person), "Message to Love," Taj twelve-string blues (Hendrix on bass), "Leroy Vinnegar," Taj banjo riff (with unknown harmonica player), "Light Rain."

As he did with tape one (the *Black Gold* tape) Tony Brown took extensive notes on the contents of this tape: "The tape starts off with the sound of [Topanga Canyon] crickets chirping in the background which was recorded onto a cassette that Taj must have brought along. They both start to play a slow delta blues—Taj on acoustic guitar and Jimi on straight electric guitar with Taj taking lead vocals on a song about a girl called 'Navalene.' Jimi comments while Taj is singing and remarks, 'I'll play the part of the Devil.' Jimi makes some dead string scratches on the guitar and remarks, 'That's a little cricket, that's a little cricket.' Jimi then takes over on lead vocal and sings 'What'd you learn in the big city last time you been there' and continues on with the phrase 'Crying Blue Rain.' The song continues on with a very different version of 'Long Hot Summer Night' and Hendrix remarks 'hear the frogs singing the American anthem in the background' referring to the tape of the chirping crickets. During a guitar solo Jimi makes a mistake and comments, 'Oh shit, that's what happens when space fucks about with earth.'"

In his notes, Brown goes on to say that Taj started singing, "Mama sweet mama, I don't mean to go against your will," while shouting out the chords for Hendrix to follow. At one point during the jam, Hendrix complained that he was having trouble getting his guitar in tune. After a brief tune-up break, he resumed with a very melodic version of "Hey Gypsy Boy." The next song is a twelve-bar riff with Taj joining in. Brown points out that Hendrix continues by "playing wind effects on his guitar through the reverb of the amp and brings the song to a close." Without pause, Hendrix continues with a solo in the vein of "Boléro" still through the reverb of the amp, then stops and remarks, "I can't think properly." The tape of the crickets chirping comes to an end, but Jimi and Taj continue with Hendrix remarking "Do that African beat" while he plays "Beginnings" with Taj trying to work out the chords. They only play the song for a short while and Taj asks about another song, but Hendrix's reply can't be heard.

Brown's notes: "Side Two of the tape starts with Jimi and Taj tuning up, the telephone rings and someone in the room answers, Jimi comments to them, 'Who is that? Oh can you just tell her we're just practicing.' He remarks to Taj, 'I'm sorry I goofed up by taking all these fucking drugs.' Taj comments 'Well nobody's coming down on you really.' The tape is stopped at this point. The tape restarts with Taj playing some slow blues chords on what seems to be a 12-string acoustic. Jimi remarks, 'I can feel myself getting a little more natural now, great.' Jimi continues playing along with Taj on reverb guitar and comments, 'Fucking all in to all these space people now, fuck you, fuck all these god damn space people, fuck me up.' Someone in the room remarks, 'You just gotta learn to say no.' Jimi responds with, 'Definitely, gotta learn to say no.' Jimi continues with a version of the instrumental solo he had played at Woodstock then continues on with various other unknown riffs. Someone in the room produces some paper and reads some lyrics while Jimi and Taj accompany him; Jimi then starts the riff to 'Message To Love'. Taj continues [with] a blues on 12-string guitar about a sign in a drugstore window. Jimi comments, 'I wanna play bass on one of them. Do that one about running.' Taj continues with a song about the prodigal son, but only plays a few lines before stopping. Jimi complains that he has stopped and wants to carry on. Taj picks up the banjo and strums a few chords. Jimi asks what time it is and is told it's five minutes to twelve. Taj continues on the banjo with a song about 'Light Rain' with someone playing harmonica."

According to Brown, at this point in the tape Hendrix asks a young woman in the room where she lives. When she starts to reply, Hendrix interrupts her and says, "Don't say it on the tape recorder, there'll be hard heads might steal this tape. Hard heads a thousand years from now. Fuck you hard heads, a thousand years from now." Someone then mentions to Hendrix that a bass player by the name of Leroy Vinnegar wants to jam with him tonight. Hendrix responds with an impromptu song about Vinnegar. At the end of the tape, Hendrix asks if "Andy Pandy" (Buddy Miles) is sleeping. He's told that he's not there. Hendrix announces that he wants to do a country thing, but unfortunately the tape runs out.

STATUS: *No financial agreement was ever reached between Mitchell and Alan Douglas for the purchase of the Black Gold tape. However, Experience Hendrix and Mitchell reportedly recently concluded a deal for Black Gold and the other recordings.*

The "Scorpio Woman" Tape

On August 1, 1970, Hendrix played the final date on his U.S. Cry of Love tour in Honolulu, Hawaii. Between August 2 and August 13, he took an unauthorized leave of absence on Maui, telling his management he needed time to heal from a cut he had received while surfing. According to Melinda Merryweather, Hendrix had cut his foot, but not as seriously as he implied.

Hendrix spent the time relaxing, composing, and being with his new friend Merryweather, whom he had met a few weeks earlier during the filming of *Rainbow Bridge*. During one of his private moments, he recorded a twenty-three minute homage to Merryweather entitled "Scorpio Woman" (Merryweather's astrological sign being Scorpio). As Merryweather recalls, "He played guitar for hours everyday…experimenting. He just couldn't get enough."[13] "Scorpio Woman" also featured brief segments of new compositions such as "Heaven Has No Sorrow," "Midnight Lightning," and other unreleased tunes in development. Unfortunately the opportunity never came to complete a studio version of "Scorpio Woman."

Hendrix left Maui on August 13 to finish some recording at Electric Lady Studios. Once in New York, Hendrix gave specific instructions to Michael Jeffery that Merryweather be sent the original cassette as a memento of their time together. She was then given the master tape that Hendrix had placed in the cassette case of a promotional copy of Derek and the Dominos' *Layla*. He wrote his initial, "J," and the title "Scorpio Woman" on the tape.

STATUS: *After holding onto the tape for twenty-eight years, Merryweather sold it to Experience Hendrix in 1998. In October 2000, "Scorpio Woman" was released on a CD titled Morning Symphony Ideas (Dagger 088 112 353-2). The CD liner notes state that the track is the centerpiece of the collection, but do not identify Merryweather as the source of Hendrix's inspiration.*

Hendrix and Melinda Merryweather ("Scorpio Woman"), Maui, Hawaii, August 1970.
Bambi Merryweather

Alan Douglas (Slight Return), 1974–1995

A few years after Hendrix's death, sales from his record catalog began to decline. When albums like *War Heroes* (1972) and *Hendrix in the West* (1974) sold only 15,000 to 20,000 units, the idea of producing more Hendrix material for the record stores seemed unimaginable. Even the Hendrix estate couldn't persuade Warner/Reprise or any other major label that Hendrix's music was still of interest and marketable.

In 1973, when Hendrix's manager Michael Jeffery died in a plane crash, full control of Hendrix's musical legacy was turned over to his estate's attorney, Leo Branton. During this confusing time, Don Schmitzerle, Warner/Reprise's executive director of label management, contacted producer Alan Douglas about some Hendrix tapes that had been shipped to a warehouse and apparently forgotten. Douglas, who had believed everyone knew about the warehouse tapes, was eventually hired to evaluate them.

What Douglas found was almost one thousand hours of raw Hendrix studio recordings made during 1969 and 1970. The tapes contained mostly material that Hendrix and Douglas had worked on together. They were originally recorded at either the Record Plant or Electric Lady Studios and had sat untouched in a New Jersey warehouse, where the Hendrix estate had deposited them shortly after Hendrix's death in September 1970. In April 1974, Douglas and engineer Les Kahn sifted through the tapes (nearly 600 hours of sixteen-track, and more than three hundred hours of eight- and four-track recordings) at Shaggy Dog Studios in Massachusetts. Most of the recordings were classified as various types of music suitable for release.

Douglas and Kahn also discovered live recordings in the collection and logged all the promising sections. A tape box marked "H-59" (H for Hendrix) and dated June 15, 1970, contained a session recorded at Electric Lady Studios with Traffic's Chris Wood and Steve Winwood joining Hendrix on various jams, including "Pearly Queen" and a slow version of "Valleys of Neptune." Another tape, marked "H-60," contained more of the same session, but also featured a vocal track by Jennie Dean, a friend of Devon Wilson. Douglas said at the time that Dean sounded a bit like Tracy Nelson (of the band Mother Earth) or Janis Joplin, but her voice "had absolutely no control." He marked the box "NOTHING" in big block letters.[14] Some of the recordings with Wood and Winwood later surfaced on bootlegs and, contrary to Douglas's opinion, are quite interesting.

With the majority of the tapes in order, the Hendrix estate chose Douglas as musical executor. He then established the Hendrix production company Are You Experienced Ltd. and formulated a plan to recall several of the posthumous LPs that were considered to be of lesser quality. Next, Douglas planned a series of new Hendrix albums that would highlight the best tracks from the rediscovered tapes.

In 1974, Warner/Reprise announced in a press release that *Crash Landing* (1975) would be the "pop" album presenting Hendrix's "more radical departures from the familiar Experience formula." A blues album called *Multicolored Blues*[15] was to follow, and then an improvisational jazz album with John McLaughlin and Larry Young. It sounded like a successful marketing plan, but something went wrong. Although *Crash Landing* sold a million and a half records and peaked at #5 on the charts, its contents raised a few eyebrows among critics and fans. Douglas had taken it upon himself to erase the original backing tracks and rerecord the parts with studio musicians, keeping intact Hendrix's solos, rhythm guitar, and finished vocals.[16] Archivist Keith Bollinger and I later revealed that the studio musicians Douglas used on *Crash Landing* were the same players who had appeared on Gloria Gaynor's 1974 Top 10 disco album *Never Can Say Goodbye*.[17]

Eight months after the release of *Crash Landing*, Douglas tried to repeat the successful formula. He ordered overdubbing of the original rhythm players with the same musicians who appeared on *Crash Landing*, but he failed miserably with the album titled *Midnight Lightning*. One review said: "Douglas has assumed the presumptuous roles of producer and artist. He is not Hendrix. Douglas has no right or wit to edit and refine what to Hendrix were formative musical investigations. *Midnight Lightning* shows that in the eyes of Douglas and Warner Bros. Records, Jimi Hendrix still is not an artist. He remains a commodity to be exploited."[18] Engineer Eddie Kramer felt that these new rhythm sections added by Douglas would have not been to Hendrix's liking: "Jimi, never in his right mind would never have wanted any of that stuff…released, at all, period. He wanted everything structured. He was a very structured person."[19]

When Douglas left everything alone and presented compilations such as 1994's magnificent *Jimi Hendrix: Blues* (MCAD-11060), he was right on target. Another one of his interesting projects was the *Hendrix/Dylan* CD/EP, but unfortunately this was canceled and never completed.

In 1988, Douglas wanted to release a mini-CD of Hendrix covering Bob Dylan tunes. The project evolved and won the approval of Bob Dylan, who wrote the liner notes. Dylan acknowledged in his notes that in covering his songs in such an intense manner, Hendrix had made them his songs, too. The *Hendrix/Dylan* CD would have included:

- "Like a Rolling Stone," a live track with Al Kooper on organ, recorded at New York's Generation Club in April 1968.

- "All Along the Watchtower," the classic studio version released on *Electric Ladyland*, but digitally remastered for this rerelease.

- "Drifter's Escape," never released in Hendrix's lifetime. This studio version first appeared on *Loose Ends*, an obscure European LP, in the early 1970s.

- "Can You Please Crawl out Your Window?" This track was recorded on October 17, 1967, for the BBC radio show *Rhythm and Blues*.

- "Like a Rolling Stone," the definitive live version that was performed at the Monterey Pop Festival in 1967.

- "All Along the Watchtower," a fiery version recorded at the Isle of Wight Festival on August 30, 1970.

First Ray of the New Rising Sun

I'm working on my own album called "The Last Rays of the Morning Sun" on which I am having a string section and the Mormon Tabernacle Choir. It's going to give a lot of people the answers to questions they are searching for. It's going to straighten a lot of people out.

Jimi Hendrix, **New Musical Express,** March 15, 1969

In 1995, near the conclusion of Douglas's controversial tenure as producer of Hendrix music and videos, he released one final Hendrix CD. His original hope was to combine the best posthumously released studio tracks, add a little remixing and audio tinkering, and magically create a recipe for *Voodoo Soup* (MCAD-11236). This release, Douglas felt, would be a step closer to Hendrix's vision for his last, unfinished album, *First Ray of the New Rising Sun.*

As he did in 1974, Douglas enhanced the original Hendrix songs by removing backing tracks that he felt weren't up to par and overdubbing new ones. On "Stepping Stone" and "Room Full of Mirrors," Douglas used Bruce Gary, former drummer with the Knack, to replace what he felt was Mitchell's "very uneven" drumming. When *Guitar World* magazine asked why he chose to overdub again, Douglas defensively replied, "I'm the fucking producer, man. I'm not making records for guitar players. I have to make a record for everyone. That's what the business of Jimi Hendrix is all about: deleting what is no longer significant and releasing what is contemporary and significant."[20]

During 1969, Hendrix spoke of several studio projects he had begun that he hoped to complete by the end of 1970. In the January 1970 issue of *Hit Parader*, he told of a late summer release that would be titled either *Shine on Earth, Shine On,* or *Gypsy Sun.* Another album that he looked forward to releasing by Christmas was to be called *First Ray of the New Rising Sun.* "We have about forty songs in the works, about half of them completed," Hendrix said. "A lot comprises jams—all spiritual stuff, all very earthy." Unfortunately the long-awaited follow up to 1968's smash LP *Electric Ladyland* was still far from complete.

Hendrix kept pressing to complete *First Ray.* Billy Cox recalled: "I know that prior to his death, even though as sick as I was at that point in time, he called me on that Monday [September 15] and said, 'Can you get to the studio Friday [September 18], and we'll finish up the album.' We knew we had a couple of more songs to put down. He had to change the words on about five or six songs where he didn't quite have it together...and that never got accomplished."[21]

There is also evidence that Hendrix may have had a cover in mind for the release. On September 17, 1970, he sketched out various faces to form the shape of a cross, with his own face in the middle. The right arm of the cross had faces of white people, including J.F.K. and Hitler and two women and a baby. On the left arm of the cross was Martin Luther King, Jr., a black woman with a crown, an African woman, and a baby. On the bottom shaft, Crazy Horse, Geronimo, Cochise, two women and a baby represented Native Americans. Above Hendrix's head, the top shaft of the cross showed Buddha, Genghis Khan, a Japanese woman, and a Chinese baby, representing the Asian peoples.

Hendrix most likely intended the fourth studio LP to be titled *First Ray of the New Rising Sun,* although the album has also been referred to as *First Rays of the New Rising Sun* (and that title was used when it was finally released). Billy Cox worked on the unfinished album, and recalled the time when Hendrix asked him about the correct wording: "He asked me, 'Is it the first ray, or the rays?' I said, 'I don't know.' He said, 'What do you see when you get up in the morning? When you look over the horizon do you see one ray or rays?' I said, 'I'd have to check that out.' Then we discussed the possibilities of doing a single or double LP, but it really didn't make that much of a difference. You must remember, even though they gave him a lot of freedom in the studio, when the record deal itself came about, he did not have the last say-so."[22]

In 1994, Hendrix's own handwritten track selection for *First Ray* surfaced and was reprinted in the French magazine *Folk & Rock* (November 1994). Surprisingly it was never used when attempts were made to complete the unfinished project in the years that followed. Hendrix only completed a song list for three sides of the double LP, and wasn't sure where to place the track "Night Bird Flying." With a darker-colored pen, he seemed to indicate that it should be the second song on side A. Hendrix's track selection for *First Ray of the New Rising Sun* was:

SIDE A:

- "Dolly Dagger." Hendrix originally mixed this track on August 24, 1970, with several remixes later. He enlisted the help of his buddies from his earlier days in New York, the Allen twins, then professionally known as the Ghetto Fighters. After listening to the song a couple of times, Hendrix joined them in the vocal booth, saying, "Just follow me," as he sang along with them. This track might have been released as the first single with "Night Bird Flying" as the flip side.
- "Night Bird Flying." The final mix for this track was done on August 22, 1970, but Hendrix may have intended to alter the song slightly after returning from Europe. The song is a tribute to deejay Alison Steele, who hosted the midnight to 6:00 A.M. shift on WNEW in New York back in the late '60s and early '70s, and went by the name "The Nightbird." Steele never knew about the tribute behind the song until she got a call from Michael Jeffery during a Hendrix radio tribute in the early '70s: "He said he was Jimi's manager and asked if I knew that Jimi wrote 'Night Bird Flying' for me? I said, 'No,'" Steele recalled, "'I didn't know that.' That was a very poignant moment in my life for me."[23]
- "Room Full of Mirrors." The mix on this track was never completed to Hendrix's specifications. He reportedly said that he did not want the slide guitar to be so loud in the mix.
- "Belly Button Window." Recorded on August 22, 1970, this song was never finished and only various demos exist. The version that appeared on the 1971 *Cry of Love* album is probably the most complete of the four known takes, two of which are incomplete. In the first take, Hendrix tried singing the words to "Belly Button Window" over the slow, haunting melody of "Midnight Lightning." This didn't work, and he told the engineer he'd like to try another version. This second time, Hendrix seemed to put more emphasis on certain passages and ad-libbed other sections. He then added a second guitar part, but abruptly ended the endeavor.
- "Freedom." Hendrix, Cox, and Mitchell recorded and mixed this track several times. One unreleased version includes a piano overdub and fill.

SIDE B:

- "Ezy Ryder." This late 1969 Band of Gypsys track sounds nearly finished. It's hard to know whether Hendrix would have tinkered with it any further.
- "Astro Man." It would be hard to guess whether he ultimately would have used this

fairly polished version from the August 22 session, or whether he would have saved it for the *Black Gold* project.

- "Drifting." This track was recorded and mixed several times with various production touches. Multiple guitar tracks are included, with one played backwards on tape to reproduce Hendrix's imaginary "sea sounds." The vibes played by Buzzy Linhart were added after Hendrix's death.
- "Straight Ahead." Definitely in its embryonic stage, this track sounds as though it was recorded in one pass with a guitar overdub or two. Hendrix began to perform this tune while on tour in 1970, sometimes calling it "Have You Heard."

SIDE C:

- "Drifter's Escape." Hendrix wanted to include another Bob Dylan track on his LP. However, many of the posthumous mixes, with their extensive use of Hendrix's multiple guitar tracks, might not have been to his liking.
- "Comin' Down Hard on Me." Like "Dolly Dagger," this funk-rock track included subtle references to Devon Wilson. Although he and Kramer did a rough mix on August 22, 1970, Hendrix never completed a proper ending to the song, and it remains a work in progress.
- "Beginnings." This song was debuted at Woodstock in the summer of 1969 by Hendrix's newly formed band Gypsy Sun and Rainbows. The studio version of "Beginnings" featured a guitar overdub and was obviously something he saw as a finished cut.
- "Cherokee Mist." Hendrix recorded two unique versions of this song, which pays tribute to his Cherokee Indian heritage. The early 1968 version has more intensity, with tom-tom and wild feedback embellishments. The June 24, 1970, version, cut at Electric Lady, is a lot more polished, but moves into a rhythm pattern that is used for the song "In from the Storm."
- "Angel." This song was never completed. Mitchell rerecorded his drums after Hendrix's death to add a fuller sound. There are also guitar and bass mistakes that Hendrix would never have tolerated in a final version. A mix done on October 19, 1970, was used on the 1971 *Cry of Love* LP.

In addition to the songs previously mentioned, several other tracks, including "Hey Baby (Land of the New Rising Sun)," "Valleys of Neptune," "Lover Man," "Country Blues," "Just Came In" (retitled "In from the Storm" for the *Cry of Love* LP), and "Pali Gap," were recorded around the same time period and might have found their way onto side D.

STATUS: *In 1997, First Rays of the New Rising Sun (MCAD-11599) was, according to the liner notes, "prepared under the direct supervision of the Hendrix family" (stepsister Janie Hendrix with help from engineer Eddie Kramer and archivist John McDermott). John McDermott's liner notes state that Hendrix's final instructions for First Ray of the New Rising Sun were "absent," so the CD's seventeen songs were seemingly randomly selected,*

Hendrix and Cox at the Hit Factory, New York City, 1969.
Jim Cummins/Star File

and "My Friend," a holdover from a March 1968 session, was included with 1970 tracks recorded at Electric Lady Studios.

In August 1997, shortly after First Rays of the New Rising Sun was released, Billy Cox expressed his dismay with this and a wave of other new Hendrix releases in an interview with **Guitar Player** magazine. Cox never received any publishing credits for the songs he helped Hendrix conceive, nor was he paid for the last world tour in 1970: "I'm really not as ecstatic as a lot of people are over what's come out, because the whole world is listening to what me, Buddy, Noel and Mitch have done, but we haven't been paid a penny. Not a dime. People are getting wealthy, building estates, doing everything they can off our backs.... It's just a doggone shame."

Coda

On July 24, 1995, Al Hendrix dropped his fraud dispute with his former attorney Leo Branton and Alan Douglas. As a result of the settlement, Mr. Hendrix regained the rights to his son's legacy, as well as the prerogative to approve two Douglas projects that were in progress and near completion. A film documentary titled *Room Full of Mirrors* and a double CD of previously released concert material called *Hendrix: On the Road* were both shelved by Experience Hendrix once Douglas completed them.

Al Hendrix and his stepdaughter Janie formed Experience Hendrix LLC and began handling Hendrix's business affairs on December 1, 1995. Shortly after Douglas's departure, Experience Hendrix alleged that he had made many serious cataloging and security mistakes over the years. During their first fourteen months in control, Experience Hendrix found more than eighty percent of the original non-EQ'd Hendrix "flat" masters. According to Eddie Kramer and John McDermott, Douglas had been using low-quality high-generation tapes to produce some Hendrix releases, and didn't bother to find the flat masters.[24]

The flat master for *Are You Experienced* somehow disappeared from the vault at Columbia Records and mysteriously made its way into the hands of a collector who then sold it to Experience Hendrix.[25] After further research, the flat master for the 1970 *Band of Gypsys* LP was found in a tape box marked "Do Not Use" in the Capitol Records vaults. Some mistakes were also made after Douglas's 1974 "tape discovery" evaluation project was completed. "What happened was a number of tapes were left behind at Shaggy Dog [studios] because of unpaid studio bills," archivist John McDermott explained. "And the actual flat masters for *Electric Ladyland* were among those tapes. Some of them had been misfiled in wrong boxes."[26]

Amazingly, over thirty years after Hendrix's death, new material is still being found, and undocumented material discovered; we continue to get just a little closer to understanding the phenomenon that was Jimi Hendrix.

I'm thinking of the days when people will be able to have this little room, a total audio-visual environment type of thing. So that you can go in there and lay back, and the whole thing just blossoms with color and sound.

JIMI HENDRIX, *RECORD MIRROR*, OCTOBER 10, 1970

CHAPTER ELEVEN

CAN YOU SEE ME?

Before the 1970s, there were almost no restrictions on concert-goers who brought 8mm movie cameras or bulky audio recording equipment into an auditorium. Consequently, there are a few interesting amateur films of incredible Hendrix concerts. Numerous Hendrix shows were also professionally shot, but after thirty years, the contents and whereabouts of many of them remain a mystery. Some of the original film stock of Hendrix's performances has now been transferred to video.

This chapter contains a chronological catalog of known filmed and videotaped performances of Hendrix, with their availability identified by these codes:

CA: commercially available on video
CN: video available in the collectors' network

It has taken thirty years and a network of fans to track down, sort through, and determine the exact locations and dates of these visual records of Hendrix's all-too-brief career. The growing worldwide network continues to add to this list, and it is hoped that eventually all of the lost footage mentioned here will become available.

1965

DATE: POSSIBLY MAY
EVENT: *NIGHT TRAIN* TELEVISION PROGRAM, WLAC-TV
PERFORMER(S): THE UPSETTERS
SONG(S): "SHOTGUN" (LIVE)
LOCATION: WLAC-TV STUDIOS, NASHVILLE, TENNESSEE

This is the earliest known footage of Hendrix performing. Collector and archivist David Pearcy discovered this gem through sheer luck. It features Hendrix with Little Richard's band, the Upsetters, performing the popular Jr. Walker hit "Shotgun." The lead singers/dancers are Buddy and Stacey, formerly of the King Curtis Band, with the Upsetters behind them. Although the camera is mainly on Buddy and Stacey, Hendrix can be seen fanning the neck of the guitar with his hand and elbowing it. The sound on the video is clean enough to recognize Hendrix's subtle guitar licks.

Several Hendrix biographies have incorrectly identified February 1965 as the date of this appearance. For many years, the only available segment of the show was the "Shotgun" clip, and since this Jr. Walker and the All Stars hit was climbing the charts in February 1965, it was assumed that the *Night Train* show was from that timeframe. However, the complete show recently surfaced, revealing that immediately after "Shotgun" was performed, guest Jimmy Church sang a version of Wilson Pickett's "In the Midnight Hour." This #1 hit wasn't even recorded until May 1965, and didn't hit the charts until July. Consequently, the show could have been taped no earlier than May.

STATUS: *CA and CN. Portions of this black-and-white video turned up in the 1989 South Bank Hendrix documentary and in the 1999 BBC documentary The Man They Made God. The complete three-minute version, along with host Noble Blackwell's introduction, is available in the collectors' network.*

1966

DATE: FILMED OCTOBER 13; ORIGINALLY BROADCAST NOVEMBER 4
EVENT: CONCERT AT NOVELTY
PERFORMER(S): THE JIMI HENDRIX EXPERIENCE
SONG(S): "IN THE MIDNIGHT HOUR," "MERCY, MERCY," "LAND OF 1000 DANCES," AND "HEY JOE"
LOCATION: EVREUX, FRANCE

This was the first official public concert by the Jimi Hendrix Experience. French television filmed it for *Cinq Colonnes à la Une.* The main act was French pop star Johnny Hallyday; others included Long Chris and the Black Birds. The film may contain some footage of the Experience.

STATUS: *Missing.*

DATE: OCTOBER 18
EVENT: RESTAURANT VISIT WITH JOHNNY HALLYDAY
LOCATION: PARIS, FRANCE

Unfortunately, no concert footage has surfaced of the Experience's first tour of France. All that is available is a thirty-second silent black-and-white film showing Hendrix, Chas Chandler, Mitch Mitchell, and French pop star Johnny Hallyday at an unidentified restaurant. Hendrix can be seen blowing smoke rings from a cigarette.

STATUS: *CN. In 1993, this short clip appeared on a French television special (Sacré Soirée) about singer Johnny Hallyday.*

DATE: TAPED DECEMBER 13; ORIGINALLY BROADCAST DECEMBER 16
EVENT: *READY STEADY GO!* TELEVISION PROGRAM, ITV
PERFORMER(S): THE JIMI HENDRIX EXPERIENCE
SONG(S): "HEY JOE" (LIVE)
LOCATION: REDDIFUSION TV STUDIOS, STUDIO 9, KINGSWAY, LONDON, ENGLAND

Dave Clark (of the Dave Clark Five) purchased the *Ready Steady Go!* variety show series in the 1980s and released several episodes, most notably excerpts from the Beatles' show, "Around the Beatles," and an Otis Redding compilation. When contacted, Dave Clark said he does not have a copy of the Hendrix episode. However, Marc Bolan—later of T. Rex—also appeared on the Hendrix episode and has confirmed that the band played "Hey Joe" live.

STATUS: *Missing. Why the Experience's first television appearance hasn't surfaced is still a mystery. It is possible that Clark's purchase did not include this show, which turned out to be one of the last episodes of* **Ready Steady Go!**

DATE: DECEMBER 22
EVENT: GUILDHALL CONCERT
PERFORMER(S): THE JIMI HENDRIX EXPERIENCE
SONG(S): UNKNOWN
LOCATION: SOUTHAMPTON, ENGLAND

This was the first Experience concert to be advertised in a local English newspaper, the *Southern Evening Echo*. However, some major typographical errors in the ad may have diminished a bit of their thunder; they were listed as "The Jimmy Hendricks Experience."

STATUS: *Unreleased. Bill Wyman of the Rolling Stones claims to have color footage from one of the two shows.*[1]

DATE: DECEMBER 29
EVENT: *TOP OF THE POPS* TELEVISION PROGRAM, BBC 1
PERFORMER(S): THE JIMI HENDRIX EXPERIENCE WITH THE BREAKAWAYS ON BACKING VOCALS
SONG(S): "HEY JOE" (LIVE VOCALS OVER A NEW PRERECORDED BACKING TRACK)
LOCATION: LIME GROVE STUDIOS, LONDON, ENGLAND

Since "Hey Joe" was #6 on the British charts, the Experience played it on this popular television show. Hendrix sang live while the band played to a backing track. *Top of the Pops* was never broadcast live; performers went to their studio and taped the show the day before it aired. The BBC has stated that this episode does not exist in their library.

STATUS: *Missing. Fortunately, some later episodes of* **Top of the Pops** *featuring Hendrix have survived. It is possible that this one was lost in one of the BBC's legendary "house cleanings."*

1967

DATE: TAPED JANUARY 18; ORIGINALLY BROADCAST JANUARY 19
EVENT: *TOP OF THE POPS*, BBC 1
PERFORMER(S):THE JIMI HENDRIX EXPERIENCE
SONG(S): "HEY JOE" (LIVE)
LOCATION: LIME GROVE STUDIOS, LONDON, ENGLAND

To introduce Hendrix to the British youth, the *New Musical Express* (January 14, 1967) wrote: "The man for whom the words 'Wild One' were invented has hit us! Jimi Hendrix, 22 [*sic*], from Seattle, Washington, USA, courtesy of ex-Animal Chas Chandler, debuts in the NME Chart at No. 24 with his self-arranged 'Hey Joe.'"
This episode of *Top of the Pops* included an interview with Hendrix.

STATUS: *Missing. The BBC does not have this clip listed in its inventory.*

DATE: JANUARY 29
EVENT: SAVILLE THEATRE CONCERT
PEFORMER(S): THE JIMI HENDRIX EXPERIENCE
SONG(S): "HEY JOE"
LOCATION: LONDON, ENGLAND

The Jimi Hendrix Experience appeared on the bill with the Koobas, Thoughts, and the Who. *Melody Maker* (February 4, 1967) wrote: "Jimi Hendrix vs. The Who! It was a close battle at London's Saville Theatre on Sunday, and fans will still be arguing about the winners. Jimi was hit by PA trouble, but the crowd was so keyed up they laughed sympathetically while Jimi searched for a mike that worked."

STATUS: *CA. The "Hey Joe" promotional film taken from this concert surfaced in the Peter Clifton film* **Superstars in Concert** *(Telstar Video) and the 2001 reissue of* **Experience.** *There are rumors of the existence of footage for the complete concert. Other commercially available non-concert footage includes Hendrix entering the stage door, signing autographs, and leaving in a taxi.*

DATE: JANUARY 31
EVENT: SAVILLE THEATRE CONCERT
PERFORMER(S): THE JIMI HENDRIX EXPERIENCE
SONG(S): "HEY JOE" (LIP-SYNCHED)
LOCATION: LONDON, ENGLAND

STATUS: *CA. This promotional clip now exists on video and can be found on* Superstars in Concert *(Telstar Video), compiled by Peter Clifton, which also includes performances by other artists. The footage was later broadcast on the Swedish television show* **Drop In.**

DATE: FEBRUARY 25
EVENT: CORN EXCHANGE CONCERT
PERFORMER(S): THE JIMI HENDRIX EXPERIENCE
SONG(S): "STONE FREE"
LOCATION: ESSEX, ENGLAND

Roeland Kerbosch filmed some of this concert for Dutch television (KRO) — "Like a Rolling Stone" in addition to "Stone Free." Kerbosch's then-wife, Mady Saks, made an audio recording. The footage was used in the original broadcast on the youth program *Telixer* (July 1967).

STATUS: *CN. Footage of "Stone Free" finally surfaced on the BBC show* Reputations *on June 6, 1999.*

DATE: MARCH 2
EVENT: *BEAT CLUB*, GERMAN TELEVISION PROGRAM
PERFORMER(S): THE JIMI HENDRIX EXPERIENCE
SONG(S): "PURPLE HAZE" AND "HEY JOE" (BOTH LIVE)
LOCATION: MARQUEE CLUB, LONDON, ENGLAND

During this period, the *New Musical Express* (February 18, 1967) wrote: "Jimi Hendrix' second single, the self-penned 'Purple Haze,' will be the first release on the new Track label. It is set for March 24, to coincide with the issue of Jimi's first LP, *Are You Experienced*. The Hendrix Experience plays a string of TV and club dates."

Dave Lee Travis introduces this fourteen-minute black-and-white video. Two takes of each song are known to exist. "Hey Joe" was originally broadcast on March 11, 1967, and "Purple Haze" was first broadcast on May 22, 1967.

STATUS: *CA and CN. This footage has also surfaced on various compilations such as* Rock and Roll Greatest Years: 1967 Vol. 1 *(1988, VC 4058) and occasionally pops up on U.S. cable television's VH1.*

DATE: TAPED MARCH 6; ORIGINALLY BROADCAST MARCH 21
EVENT: *VIBRATO*, BELGIAN TELEVISION PROGRAM, RTB-TV
PERFORMER(S): THE JIMI HENDRIX EXPERIENCE
SONG(S): "HEY JOE" (LIP-SYNCHED)
LOCATION: ZONIEWOUD, ST. PIETERS WOLUWE, BELGIUM

Around this time, the *New Musical Express* (April 8, 1967) wrote: "The Jimi Hendrix Experience are a musical labyrinth—you either find your way into the solid wall of incredible sound, or you sit back and gasp at Hendrix's guitar antics and showmanship, wondering what it's all about."

STATUS: *Lost. RTB-TV was contacted and stated that this footage does not exist in its inventory.*

DATE: MARCH 7
EVENT: *TIENERKLANKEN* TELEVISION PROGRAM, BRT-TV
PERFORMER(S): THE JIMI HENDRIX EXPERIENCE
SONG(S): "HEY JOE" AND "STONE FREE" (BOTH LIP-SYNCHED)
LOCATION: UNIVERSAL STUDIO, WATERLOO, BELGIUM

This black-and-white film runs six minutes. Rebroadcasts on Dutch and Belgian television in the 1980s showed that the footage is still in excellent condition.

STATUS: *CA and CN. The footage appeared in* Rock and Roll Greatest Years: 1967 Vol. 1 *(VC 4058).*

DATE: MARCH 14
EVENT: *FANCLUB* TELEVISION PROGRAM
PERFORMER(S): THE JIMI HENDRIX EXPERIENCE
SONG(S): "HEY JOE" AND "STONE FREE" (BOTH LIP-SYNCHED)
LOCATION: AMSTERDAM, HOLLAND

The live rehearsals were too loud, so the producer of this program decided Hendrix should lip-synch during the live broadcast.

STATUS: *CN.*

DATE: TAPED MARCH 27; ORIGINALLY BROADCAST APRIL 4
EVENT: *DEE TIME* TELEVISION PROGRAM, BBC 1
PERFORMER(S): THE JIMI HENDRIX EXPERIENCE
SONG(S): "PURPLE HAZE" (LIVE VOCALS AGAINST PRERECORDED BACKING TRACK)
LOCATION: MANCHESTER, ENGLAND

This was the debut episode of *Dee Time,* a youth show hosted by Simon Dee. *Mojo* magazine (January 1998) reprinted comments about the show by Michael Wale: "TV is apt to tame the wildness and original-ity out of pop and make it presentable to the hypothetical family audience. And yet it was partly the wildness of the Jimi Hendrix Experience that was responsible for the successful launching of *Dee Time.* The visual collision of Hendrix and a British provincial high-tea audience was an instant success. 'Family audience' equals voyeurism."

STATUS: *Missing. The BBC has stated that it doesn't have this clip in its inventory. However, several other Simon Dee shows from this period are available.*

DATE: TAPED MARCH 30; ORIGINALLY BROADCAST APRIL 6
EVENT: *TOP OF THE POPS,* BBC 1
PERFORMER(S): THE JIMI HENDRIX EXPERIENCE
SONG(S): "PURPLE HAZE" (TWO VERSIONS; LIVE VOCALS AGAINST PRERECORDED BACKING TRACK)
LOCATION: LONDON, ENGLAND

STATUS: *CN. At one time, the BBC claimed it had no listing of this black-and-white clip in its inventory, but a producer discovered the performance while going through the BBC archives.*[2] *He made a copy and brought it to the United States.*

DATE: APRIL 1
EVENT: *GAUMONT,* FRENCH TELEVISION PROGRAM
PERFORMER(S): THE JIMI HENDRIX EXPERIENCE
SONG(S): UNKNOWN
LOCATION: IPSWICH, SUFFOLK, ENGLAND

French television crews filmed part or all of this new ninety-minute pop show, which showed Hendrix and Gary Leeds (drummer for the Walker Brothers) reading American comic strips aloud together.[3]

STATUS: *Missing.*

DATE: TAPED APRIL 17; ORIGINALLY BROADCAST DECEMBER 6
EVENT: *LATE NIGHT LINE UP* TELEVISION PROGRAM, BBC2
PERFORMER(S): THE JIMI HENDRIX EXPERIENCE
SONG(S): "MANIC DEPRESSION" (LIVE)
LOCATION: KINGSWAY, LONDON, ENGLAND

This is the only known live performance of "Manic Depression" available on videotape. It was assumed that the original film suffered water damage, but in fact the show's producers allowed students from the London College of Art to manipulate the black-and-white film with an early version of a visual synthesizer, giving it a psychedelic effect.

STATUS: *CN.*

DATE: MAY (DATE UNKNOWN)
EVENT: CANDID STREET SHOTS
LOCATION: KING'S ROAD, LONDON, ENGLAND

This is a ten-minute black-and-white film of Hendrix and the Experience walking down the street.[4]

STATUS: *CN.*

DATE: MAY 4
EVENT: *TOP OF THE POPS*, BBC 1
PERFORMER(S): THE JIMI HENDRIX EXPERIENCE
SONG(S): "PURPLE HAZE"
LOCATION: LONDON, ENGLAND

"Purple Haze" was at #4 on the charts when it was performed on this show.

STATUS: *Video missing; audio CN. Once again, the BBC states that this clip does not exist. A poor-quality audiotape is the only available documentation. Performances on this show by Tom Jones and Cilla Black have surfaced, but the Experience clips are still missing.*

DATE: TAPED MAY 10; ORIGINALLY BROADCAST MAY 18
EVENT: *TOP OF THE POPS*, BBC 1
PERFORMER(S): THE JIMI HENDRIX EXPERIENCE
SONG(S): "THE WIND CRIES MARY" (LIVE VOCALS AGAINST A PRERECORDED BACKING TRACK)
LOCATION: LONDON, ENGLAND

The third Jimi Hendrix Experience single, "The Wind Cries Mary" b/w "Highway Chile," was released in England on May 5 — perfect timing to debut it on this show.

STATUS: *CN. The version available in the collectors' network only has the prerecorded version dubbed in (no live vocals).*

BLACK GOLD

DATE: MAY 11
EVENT: *MUSIC HALL DE PARIS* TELEVISION PROGRAM
PERFORMER(S): THE JIMI HENDRIX EXPERIENCE
SONG(S): "HEY JOE," "WILD THING," AND THREE OTHER UNKNOWN SONGS (LIVE)
LOCATION: THÉÂTRE D'ISSY-LES-MOULINEAUX, PARIS, FRANCE

Five songs were recorded for this French TV show, but information is available about only two of them. "Hey Joe" was later rebroadcast on May 24 on the French TV show *Tilt*, and "Wild Thing" was rebroadcast on *Music Hall de France d'Ailleurs* on August 13. To date the other three songs from this concert have not surfaced. An incomplete version of "Wild Thing" was rebroadcast on October 19, 1994, for the M6 *Culture Rock* documentary. An incomplete version of "Hey Joe" makes the rounds in the collectors' network.

STATUS: *CA and CN.*

DATE: MAY 18
EVENT: *BEAT, BEAT, BEAT,* GERMAN TELEVISION PROGRAM, SWF
PERFORMER(S): THE JIMI HENDRIX EXPERIENCE
SONG(S): "STONE FREE," "HEY JOE," AND "PURPLE HAZE" (ALL LIVE)
LOCATION: TV STUDIOS, STADTHALLE, GERMANY

This show was originally broadcast on May 29, 1967, and later on July 22, 1986. There is also footage showing Hendrix jamming on bass while Noel Redding plays guitar, "Dave Dee" Harman sings, and John Dymond plays drums.

STATUS: *CN. The video is of excellent quality.*

DATE: MAY 19
EVENT: KONSERTHALLEN AND LISEBURG CONCERTS
PERFORMER(S): THE JIMI HENDRIX EXPERIENCE
SONG(S): "CAN YOU SEE ME," "LIKE A ROLLING STONE," "HEY JOE," "THE WIND CRIES MARY," "PURPLE HAZE," AND "WILD THING"
LOCATION: GOTHENBURG, SWEDEN

The Experience debuted their act in Sweden on this date with two shows—at the Konserthallen and at Liseburg, an amusement park. They played in Karlstad on the following day.

STATUS: *CN. There is a short amateur 8mm silent film taken from both shows on this date.*

DATE: MAY 22
EVENT: *NUORTEN TANSSIKETKI,* FINNISH TELEVISION PROGRAM
PERFORMER(S): THE JIMI HENDRIX EXPERIENCE
SONG(S): UNKNOWN (LIVE)
LOCATION: RATAKATU TELEVISION STUDIO, HELSINKI, FINLAND

"Hey Joe" and three other songs were reportedly performed for this television program.

STATUS: *Missing.*

DATE: TAPED MAY 24; ORIGINALLY BROADCAST JUNE 11
EVENT: *POPSIDE,* SWEDISH TELEVISION PROGRAM
PERFORMER(S): THE JIMI HENDRIX EXPERIENCE
SONG(S): "THE WIND CRIES MARY" AND "PURPLE HAZE" (BOTH LIVE)
LOCATION: STOCKHOLM, SWEDEN

As heard on an audience recording of this concert, here is Hendrix's introduction to "Wild Thing": "Dig, I'd like to say that all this trouble in the world, just forget about it. We'd like to do this last song for everybody here and if you can sing, just join in. And if you don't, just hum. Plug your ears."

STATUS: CA. A new version of Experience (a.k.a. See My Music Talking) was released in 2001 and featured both songs from Popside as bonus footage.

DATE: MAY 24
EVENT: STORA SCENEN CONCERT
PERFORMER(S): THE JIMI HENDRIX EXPERIENCE
SONG(S): UNKNOWN
LOCATION: STOCKHOLM, SWEDEN

After performing in Denmark, the Experience returned to Sweden for the second time in one month.

STATUS: CN. There is an amateur, silent, color 8mm film of this show.

DATE: JUNE 4
EVENT: SAVILLE THEATRE CONCERT
PERFORMER(S): THE JIMI HENDRIX EXPERIENCE
SONG(S): SEE BELOW
LOCATION: LONDON, ENGLAND

The Jimi Hendrix Experience performed two shows that night at the Saville Theatre. Some of the songs played were "Sgt. Pepper's Lonely Hearts Club Band," "Like a Rolling Stone," "Manic Depression," "Hey Joe," "Purple Haze," "The Wind Cries Mary," and "Are You Experienced."

Disc and Music Echo magazine (June 5, 1967) described the show: ". . . then to a smashing, ear-splitting 'Are You Experienced.' Jimi was handed from the wings a guitar he hand-painted in glorious swirling colours and written [*sic*] a poem on the back dedicated to Britain and its audience. Bathed in a flickering strobe light, he crashed the guitar about the stage and hurled what was left of it to eager souvenir hunters in the audience."

Before being destroyed, the poem on the back of the guitar read: "May this be love or just confusion born out of frustration. Wracked feelings—of not being able to make true physical love to the universal gipsie [*sic*] queen true, free expressed music darling guitar—please rest amen." Experience Music Project in Seattle, Washington, now owns the guitar pieces.

STATUS: CN. At least one collector is known to have a copy of film footage from Jimi's early June appearances at the Saville Theatre.[5]

DATE: JUNE 18
EVENT: MONTEREY POP FESTIVAL
PERFORMER(S): THE JIMI HENDRIX EXPERIENCE
SONG(S): "KILLING FLOOR," "FOXY LADY," "LIKE A ROLLING STONE," "ROCK ME BABY," "HEY JOE," "THE WIND CRIES MARY," AND "WILD THING"
LOCATION: MONTEREY, CALIFORNIA

From the *Village Voice* (June 29, 1967): "At Monterey, Hendrix . . . slung a violet maribou over his shoulder and swung into 'Hey Joe,' 'Purple Haze,' and finally 'Wild Thing' — all spasm rock; muddy if stark sound. Like an evil bird of paradise . . . he ended his set by flinging his smashed guitar out over the audience. The real musicians gazed horrified at that plastic mound which once made music. It was a strange moment for the love generation, aroused by all that violent sexuality into a mesmerized ovation."

STATUS: CA. In 1987, Rhino Home Video released Jimi Plays Monterey (R3 2354), a film by D.A. Pennebaker and Chris Hegedus. This film captures almost ninety percent of the concert. However, only the first minute of "Purple Haze" was filmed. This brief segment of "Purple Haze" appears at the close of the video, as the credits run. "Can You See Me" was also omitted from this film.

DATE: JULY 8–9
EVENT: THE MONKEES–JIMI HENDRIX EXPERIENCE TOUR
PERFORMER(S): THE JIMI HENDRIX EXPERIENCE
SONG(S): UNKNOWN
LOCATION: JACKSONVILLE AND MIAMI, FLORIDA

From the *Village Voice* (July 27, 1967): "There were the usual screams, and a constant strobe of flashlights as the Monkees emerged . . . nobody charged the stage. And posters strange to the teen-event — "Peace" and "Love power" — dotted the grandstand. True, a hefty maiden disrupted some whining Jimmy [*sic*] Hendrix electronics with a fervent plea: 'Enough with the psychedelic, already,' but most screamed for the new music, even if what they got was only old noise."

STATUS: Unavailable. Some 8mm footage is said to exist of the ill-fated tour with the Monkees.[6]

DATE: JULY 18
EVENT: COVER SHOOT FOR *WE'RE ONLY IN IT FOR THE MONEY*
LOCATION: NEW YORK, NY

After completing the brief and disastrous tour with the Monkees, the Jimi Hendrix Experience entered New York's Mayfair Studios to record the song "The Stars That Play with Laughing Sam's Dice" (a.k.a. "STP with LSD"). Hendrix invited various friends to create background crowd noises for the song, including Frank Zappa. Zappa returned the favor and invited Hendrix to the photo shoot for the cover of the next Mothers of Invention album, *We're Only in It for the Money* (Verve V6 5045X), which parodied the Beatles' album *Sgt. Pepper's Lonely Heart's Club Band,* released one month earlier. Hendrix, the only one not in drag, stands to the right of Zappa, who is sporting pigtails and a miniskirt.

   Gail Zappa: "The photo shoot was really an unusual situation because we had a fashion photographer [Jerrold Schatzberg] doing it, and we hadn't really done that before. I was obviously very pregnant [Gail is wearing a blue dress, standing between Hendrix and Frank Zappa]. . . . Hendrix showed up with a friend, but the photographer very deftly arranged it, placing Hendrix in at the end of the row so he could cut the friend out of the shot — who knows who that was. He basically came in, very quietly and stood there, and there wasn't any discussion of whose career it was going to help."[7] A photo of producer Herb Cohen's daughter was later inserted in between Hendrix's folded arms.

STATUS: *CA and CN. A 1994 episode of A&E's Biography about Frank Zappa included footage of Hendrix with the Mothers of Invention, preparing for the album cover photo shoot. The brief footage wasn't known to exist before the television show aired.*

DATE: JULY 20
EVENT: CONCERT AT SALVATION
PERFORMER(S): THE JIMI HENDRIX EXPERIENCE
SONG(S): POSSIBLY "LIKE A ROLLING STONE," "RED HOUSE," AND "HEY JOE"
LOCATION: GREENWICH VILLAGE, NEW YORK

There is a silent four-minute 8mm color film with various clips from this performance. In an article for *UniVibes* magazine (August 1996), researcher Thomas Geneser analyzed all the known silent films of Jimi Hendrix. In some instances he was able to identify which songs were played by checking which key or at which fret on the guitar Hendrix was playing chords or soloing. When the film quality was poor he gave an educated guess based on the song's pace or, when available, matching it with a recording of the show. Since there is a recording for this concert, Geneser seemed to feel that "Like a Rolling Stone," "Red House," and "Hey Joe" were filmed.

STATUS: *CN.*

DATE: AUGUST 17
EVENT: PROMOTIONAL FILM
PERFORMER(S): THE JIMI HENDRIX EXPERIENCE
SONG(S): "BURNING OF THE MIDNIGHT LAMP," "ALL ALONG THE WATCHTOWER," AND "FOXY LADY"
LOCATION: RUDOLPH VALENTINO'S MANSION, FORMERLY LOCATED AT 1039 S. ARDMORE, LOS ANGELES, CALIFORNIA

The Experience went on location to the mansion of silent film actor Rudolph Valentino to film a color promotional film (now called a rock video) with Peter Clifton Films. The mansion, built in 1875 and torn down in early 1970, was once a famous spiritualist church were séances were held, and in the 1960s it became known as "The Psychedelic Temple," a hippie gathering place with weekly dances and parties. The 1967 Peter Fonda film *The Trip* was also filmed there.

STATUS: *CN. Portions of this footage have also been used as backdrops in various Hendrix documentaries and for other Hendrix songs.*

DATE: AUGUST 22
EVENT: *DEE TIME,* BBC-TV
PERFORMER(S): THE JIMI HENDRIX EXPERIENCE
SONG(S): "BURNING OF THE MIDNIGHT LAMP"
LOCATION: MANCHESTER, ENGLAND

STATUS: *Missing. This TV show was broadcast live, but no film or recordings have surfaced.*

BLACK GOLD

DATE: AUGUST 24
EVENT: *TOP OF THE POPS*, BBC 1
PERFORMER(S): THE JIMI HENDRIX EXPERIENCE
SONG(S): "BURNING OF THE MIDNIGHT LAMP" (STUDIO TRACK WITH LIVE VOCALS)
LOCATION: LIME GROVE STUDIOS, LONDON, ENGLAND

STATUS: *Missing.*

DATE: SEPTEMBER 2
EVENT: *4-3-2-1* TELEVISION PROGRAM, GERMANY II TV, ZDF
PERFORMER(S): THE JIMI HENDRIX EXPERIENCE
SONG(S): "CAN YOU SEE ME" AND "BURNING OF THE MIDNIGHT LAMP"
LOCATION: BERLIN, GERMANY

STATUS: *Missing. This show was broadcast live and may have been erased.*

DATE: SEPTEMBER 4
EVENT: STORA SCENEN CONCERT
PERFORMER(S): THE JIMI HENDRIX EXPERIENCE
SONG(S): UNKNOWN
LOCATION: STOCKHOLM, SWEDEN

STATUS: *CN. The Experience performed two shows at the Stora Scenen. An amateur 8mm color silent film exists for both shows.*

DATE: TAPED SEPTEMBER 8; ORIGINALLY BROADCAST SEPTEMBER 10
EVENT: *POPSIDE*
PERFORMER(S): THE JIMI HENDRIX EXPERIENCE
SONG(S): "HEY JOE," "FOXY LADY," "PURPLE HAZE," "THE WIND CRIES MARY," AND "I DON'T LIVE TODAY" (ALL LIP-SYNCHED)
LOCATION: HOGO BRUK, SWEDEN

STATUS: *Missing. This Swedish television show is believed to have been erased.*

DATE: SEPTEMBER 11
EVENT: STORA SCENEN CONCERT
SONG(S): UNKNOWN
PERFORMER(S): THE JIMI HENDRIX EXPERIENCE
LOCATION: STOCKHOLM, SWEDEN

STATUS: *CN. There is a four-minute silent 8mm film of this concert.*

DATE: SEPTEMBER 16
EVENT: *MELODY MAKER* AWARDS EVENT
LOCATION: EUROPA HOTEL, LONDON, ENGLAND

This may have been filmed by the BBC. Hendrix received his *Melody Maker* "Top World Musician" award from deejay Jimmy Saville. No songs were performed.

STATUS: *Lost.*

DATE: SEPTEMBER 25
EVENT: GUITAR-IN BENEFIT CONCERT, ROYAL FESTIVAL HALL
PERFORMER(S): THE JIMI HENDRIX EXPERIENCE
SONG(S): UNKNOWN; POSSIBLY "PURPLE HAZE"
LOCATION: LONDON, ENGLAND

The Jimi Hendrix Experience, with guitarists Paco Pena, Bert Jansch, Tim Walker, and Sebastian Jorgenson, performed a benefit concert for International Liberal Year. During some backstage silliness, the Experience was photographed with Liberal leader Jeremy Thorpe.

STATUS: *Missing. According to Noel Redding, TV news crews filmed the event, but it is unknown if the footage still exists.[8]*

DATE: OCTOBER 9
EVENT: L'OLYMPIA THEATRE CONCERT
PERFORMER(S): THE JIMI HENDRIX EXPERIENCE
SONG(S): "WILD THING" (LIVE)
LOCATION: PARIS, FRANCE

STATUS: *CA and CN. "Wild Thing," along with some backstage footage from the concert, was featured in the Peter Clifton films* The Superstars in Concert, Experience *(2001 reissue), and* Sounds of the City. *It is possible that more than one song was filmed, but it is not known if other footage exists.*

DATE: TAPED OCTOBER 10; ORIGINALLY BROADCAST NOVEMBER 12
EVENT: *DIM, DAM, DOM,* FRENCH TELEVISION PROGRAM
PERFORMER(S): THE JIMI HENDRIX EXPERIENCE
SONG(S): "BURNING OF THE MIDNIGHT LAMP" AND "HEY JOE" (BOTH LIP-SYNCHED)
LOCATION: PARIS, FRANCE

The six minutes of existing footage is in black and white. Hendrix looks frustrated during the performance.

STATUS: *CN.*

BLACK GOLD

DATE: TAPED OCTOBER 11; ORIGINALLY BROADCAST OCTOBER 15
EVENT: *AU PETIT DIMANCHE ILLUSTRÉ*, FRENCH TELEVISION PROGRAM
PERFORMER(S): THE JIMI HENDRIX EXPERIENCE
SONG(S): "THE WIND CRIES MARY" AND "BURNING OF THE MIDNIGHT LAMP" (BOTH LIP-SYNCHED)
LOCATION: PARIS, FRANCE

This footage shows the performance of both songs filmed at the ruins of Montparnasse Railway Station during its demolition. There are also scenes of the Experience walking through a market next to Montparnasse. Mitch Mitchell recalled that the show was an early morning filming session on some kind of building site. According to Mitchell, "We did a live version of the 'Marseillaise.' The story I've heard is that the French government were so appalled by this desecration, that the film was seized and, if it survives at all, it is locked in a government vault."[9]

STATUS: *CN.*

DATE: TAPED OCTOBER 12; ORIGINALLY BROADCAST NOVEMBER 12
EVENT: *DISCORAMA*, FRENCH TELEVISION PROGRAM
PERFORMER(S): THE JIMI HENDRIX EXPERIENCE
SONG(S): "BURNING OF THE MIDNIGHT LAMP" AND "THE WIND CRIES MARY" (BOTH LIP-SYNCHED)
LOCATION: PARIS, FRANCE

Hendrix, Mitchell, and Redding appear to be having fun playing during this taping. Hendrix plays a violin during one segment.

STATUS: CA. Segments from this show were used in Jimi Hendrix: Electric Ladyland (1997, Rhino Home Video R3 2386).

DATE: OCTOBER 18
EVENT: FILM PREMIERE, LEICESTER SQUARE PAVILION
LOCATION: LONDON, ENGLAND

This newsreel clip (possibly from BBC-TV) shows Hendrix attending the premiere of the John Lennon film *How I Won the War,* along with his girlfriend Kathy Etchingham and Chas Chandler. It was rebroadcast on GMTV's *Breakfast Show* on December 12, 1993.

STATUS: *CN.*

DATE: TAPED NOVEMBER 10; ORIGINALLY BROADCAST NOVEMBER 11
EVENT: *HOEPLA*, DUTCH TELEVISION PROGRAM, VPRO
PERFORMER(S): THE JIMI HENDRIX EXPERIENCE
SONG(S): "FOXY LADY," "CATFISH BLUES," AND TWO VERSIONS OF "PURPLE HAZE"
LOCATION: VITUS STUDIO, BUSSUM, THE NETHERLANDS

In addition to the television broadcast version of "Purple Haze," there is also a "false start" version and an outtake of this song.

STATUS: CN. Only a silent two-minute 8mm film survives; the synch-sound footage is lost. Film researcher Thomas Geneser feels that "Catfish Blues," segments of Mitch's drum solo, and parts of "Purple Haze" (either version 1 or version 2), were captured on this short 8mm film.[10]

HENDRIX'S LOST SUPER-8 FILMS

As early as 1967, Hendrix made private home movies with an 8mm camera. He captured some moments from the start of the second Experience tour of the U.K., with the Move, Amen Corner, Outer Limits, Eire Apparent, the Nice, and Pink Floyd. Pink Floyd's original guitarist, Roger "Syd" Barrett, recalled: "I toured with him . . . Lindsay [an old girlfriend of Barrett's] and I used to sit on the back of the bus, with him up front; he would film us."[11]

Hendrix was seen using his movie camera at the January 1968 press reception at the Pan Am Copter Club in New York and in photographs taken backstage at San Francisco's Winterland Arena in February, at the start of the 1968 American tour. Photographer Elliot Landy recalled: "He made these super-8 films that no one has ever seen."[12] In addition to informal tour footage, Hendrix also created a series of personal films he titled *The Goodbye Films*. The footage always included a groupie he had slept with the night before waving goodbye on departure from Hendrix's hotel room. According to John McDermott's book *Setting the Record Straight*, Hendrix would ad-lib comic live commentary during private screenings.

STATUS: Hendrix's 8mm camera and films were stolen while he was on tour in America in 1968. The films have never surfaced.

DATE: TAPED NOVEMBER 15; ORIGINALLY BROADCAST DECEMBER 9
EVENT: *GOOD EVENING* TELEVISION PROGRAM, ATV-TV
LOCATION: MAYFAIR HOTEL, LONDON, ENGLAND

The Jimi Hendrix Experience was filmed during an interview with host Jonathan King for the show *Good Evening*.

STATUS: Missing.

DATE: NOVEMBER 25
EVENT: BLACKPOOL OPERA HOUSE CONCERT
PERFORMER(S): THE JIMI HENDRIX EXPERIENCE
SONG(S): "PURPLE HAZE" AND "WILD THING"
LOCATION: LANCASHIRE, ENGLAND

These songs were filmed and recorded by Peter Neal and featured in the movie *See My Music Talking* (a.k.a. *Experience*).

STATUS: CA.

BLACK GOLD

DATE: DECEMBER 4
EVENT: BACKSTAGE AT NEWCASTLE CITY HALL CONCERT
LOCATION: NEWCASTLE-UPON-TYNE, ENGLAND

Musician Andy Fairweather Low recalled that someone was filming in the dressing room.[13]

STATUS: *Missing.*

DATE: TAPED DECEMBER 8; ORIGINALLY BROADCAST DECEMBER 10
EVENT: *GOOD EVENING,* ATV
PERFORMER(S): THE JIMI HENDRIX EXPERIENCE
SONG(S): "SPANISH CASTLE MAGIC" (LIVE)
LOCATION: ELSTREE STUDIOS, BOREHAMWOOD, HERTFORDSHIRE, ENGLAND

The Experience debuted this new song from their second LP, *Axis: Bold As Love.*

STATUS: *Missing.*

DATE: TAPED DECEMBER 16; ORIGINALLY BROADCAST DECEMBER 25
EVENT: *TOP OF THE POPS,* BBC-TV
PERFORMER(S): THE JIMI HENDRIX EXPERIENCE
SONG(S): "PURPLE HAZE"
LOCATION: BBC-TV STUDIOS, LONDON, ENGLAND

The Experience was filmed for the *Top of the Pops* "Survey of 1967" episode.

STATUS: *Missing.*

DATE: DECEMBER 19
EVENT: FILM SESSION AT BRUCE FLEMING'S PHOTO STUDIO
PERFORMER(S): JIMI HENDRIX
SONG(S): "GETTING MY HEART BACK TOGETHER AGAIN"
LOCATION: LONDON, ENGLAND

Filming took place for the movie *See My Music Talking* (a.k.a. *Experience*). Hendrix played solo, performing two takes of "Getting My Heart Back Together Again" on acoustic twelve-string guitar. This segment was released in 1987 as part of Warner Reprise Video's *Jimi Hendrix Experience* (38297-3) and in 2001 on an authorized rerelease by Experience Hendrix. There is also footage of a mock interview conducted by band members Mitchell and Redding, who asked Hendrix, "Did you put a spell on those two white boys?"

Carlos Santana: "Jimi Hendrix was probably the master of impact on the guitar. There is video of him playing acoustic 12-string. Even though he is not playing electric, it's still very electric."[14]

STATUS: *CA.*

DATE: DECEMBER 22
EVENT: CHRISTMAS ON EARTH CONCERT
PERFORMER(S): THE JIMI HENDRIX EXPERIENCE
SONG(S): "SGT. PEPPER'S LONELY HEARTS CLUB BAND," "FOXY LADY," AND "WILD THING"
LOCATION: OLYMPIA, LONDON, ENGLAND

Record Collector (December 1997): "Sadly, the organizers of 1967's last bastion of hippiedom, the ambitious Christmas on Earth, weren't so practical. In a bid to capitalize on the year's 'happenings,' *Image* magazine assembled a remarkable and unique bill comprising the premier league of players of British psychedelia: The Jimi Hendrix Experience, Pink Floyd, the Soft Machine, Eric Burdon & the New Animals. Despite minimal publicity and no promotional experience, however, the organizers lured some ten thousand people on a cold December weekend to witness the most striking assault on the senses ever attempted during the psychedelic era. . . . Hendrix was weird because of the strange sound of the place. It was such a huge space — and Jimi was playing louder than everyone else. . . . The real disaster, long term, was the person who took care of the filming bought outdated film stock, which had it been good, would have made us all millionaires."

STATUS: *CA (incomplete) and CN. Some of the live concert footage of Hendrix was featured in* Jimi Plays Monterey *and* Watch out for Your Ears *(unreleased). There is also some backstage footage that can be seen on the* See My Music Talking *film/video.*

1968

DATE: FEBRUARY 8
EVENT: INTERVIEW WITH KCRA-TV
PERFORMER(S): THE JIMI HENDRIX EXPERIENCE
LOCATION: HOLIDAY INN, SACRAMENTO, CALIFORNIA

In 1998, archivist Matt Taylor discovered that there was a short interview with the Experience stored at the KCRA-TV Film Collection Center. The complete interview was filmed in the courtyard of the Holiday Inn on a 16mm camera with sound, but only about a minute of it remains.

STATUS: *Unavailable.*

DATE: FEBRUARY 1–4
EVENT: NOEL REDDING'S HOME MOVIES
LOCATION: SAN FRANCISCO, CALIFORNIA

At the beginning of the second U.S. tour, Noel Redding decided to document some of the band's personal and fun moments. His footage from the first few days of February includes shots taken from inside a limousine as Hendrix and others head north on Highway 101 to San Francisco; arrival at the hotel; the Experience standing outside the hotel receiving the room keys from roadie Gerry Stickells; Fillmore Auditorium footage; and Hendrix taking Polaroid photographs backstage at the Winterland Arena.

STATUS: *CN. Most of Redding's home movies of the Experience have surfaced in the collectors' network.*

BLACK GOLD

DATE: FEBRUARY 5
EVENT: NOEL REDDING'S HOME MOVIES
LOCATION: TEMPE, ARIZONA

This segment shows Hendrix, holding a movie camera, getting out of a car with a young woman in a motel parking lot; scenes of Hendrix and Mitchell by the motel swimming pool; and Mitchell and Redding with young women in a motel room — possibly filmed by Hendrix.

STATUS: *CN.*

DATE: FEBRUARY 6
EVENT: NOEL REDDING'S HOME MOVIES
LOCATION: ARIZONA

Scenes filmed from a car window going from Tucson to Tempe, Arizona.

STATUS: *CN.*

DATE: FEBRUARY 7
EVENT: NOEL REDDING'S HOME MOVIES
LOCATION: LOS ANGELES INTERNATIONAL AIRPORT

The Experience's arrival by car at the airport was filmed by Redding out of the car window.

STATUS: *CN.*

DATE: FEBRUARY 11
EVENT: NOEL REDDING'S HOME MOVIES
LOCATION: SANTA BARBARA, CALIFORNIA

Redding filmed scenes from the car going from Santa Barbara to Los Angeles.

STATUS: *CN.*

DATE: FEBRUARY 12
EVENT: NOEL REDDING'S HOME MOVIES
LOCATION: SEATTLE AIRPORT, SEATTLE, WASHINGTON

At the Seattle airport Redding filmed scenes of Hendrix greeting his father Al, stepmother June, stepsister Janie, and half-brother Leon.

STATUS: *CN.*

DATE: FEBRUARY 14
EVENT: NOEL REDDING'S HOME MOVIES
LOCATION: DENVER AIRPORT, DENVER, COLORADO

Mitch Mitchell was filmed arriving at the airport. There also may have been an interview with the Experience conducted by Denver TV on this date, but if so, it has not surfaced.

STATUS: *CN.*

DATE: FEBRUARY 19
EVENT: NOEL REDDING'S HOME MOVIES
LOCATION: TRAVEL OFFICE, HOUSTON, TEXAS

Gerry Stickells is seen handing airplane tickets to Hendrix.

STATUS: *CN.*

DATE: MARCH 15
EVENT: CLARK UNIVERSITY CONCERT
PERFORMER(S): THE JIMI HENDRIX EXPERIENCE
SONG(S): "FOXY LADY," "PURPLE HAZE," AND "WILD THING"
LOCATION: ATWOOD HALL, CLARK UNIVERSITY, WORCESTER, MASSACHUSETTS

The Experience was interviewed by Tony Palmer for the BBC. The interview, along with some footage from both March 15 concerts, appeared in the film *All My Loving.*

STATUS: *CA.* **All My Loving** *was broadcast on November 3, 1968.*

DATE: MARCH 19
EVENT: NOEL REDDING'S HOME MOVIES
LOCATION: OTTAWA, CANADA

Noel Redding filmed Mitch Mitchell departing on an Eastern Airlines flight.

STATUS: *CN.*

DATE: MARCH 26
EVENT: PUBLIC MUSIC HALL CONCERT
PERFORMER(S): THE JIMI HENDRIX EXPERIENCE
SONG(S): UNKNOWN
LOCATION: CLEVELAND, OHIO

STATUS: *Unknown. It is rumored that a silent 8mm color amateur film of this performance exists.*

BLACK GOLD

DATE: APRIL 7
EVENT: MARTIN LUTHER KING, JR., TRIBUTE CONCERT
PERFORMER(S): JIMI HENDRIX, BUDDY GUY
SONG(S): UNKNOWN
LOCATION: GENERATION CLUB, 52 WEST 8TH STREET, NEW YORK, NEW YORK

Hendrix was deeply saddened by the assassination of Martin Luther King, Jr. On an episode of the *South Bank Show* from October 1, 1989, Mark Boyle (who designed the light shows for the Soft Machine) recalled the mood at a New Jersey concert two nights prior to the Generation club jam (April 5): "I was terrified that Jimi was going to be killed. At the time everyone thought there was an insane conspiracy to eliminate anyone who was seen as a threat to the extreme right in America, and who was next on the list? Jimi came on very quietly to enormous applause. Then he said softly into the microphone, 'This number is for a friend of mine.' He then began an improvisation that had a beauty. . . . Immediately everyone knew the friend was Martin Luther King [Jr.] and this music seemed to convey all the agony of the black people. The whole audience was weeping . . . when he was finished there was no applause. Jimi just laid his guitar down and walked quietly off stage."

STATUS: *CN. A five-minute color video features clips from the unreleased film by D.A. Pennebaker called A Wake at Generation. The collectors' video shows a jam with Hendrix on guitar and a segment where Hendrix watched Buddy Guy's performance.*

DATE: MAY 10
EVENT: FILLMORE EAST CONCERT
PERFORMER(S): THE JIMI HENDRIX EXPERIENCE
SONG(S): UNKNOWN
LOCATION: NEW YORK, NEW YORK

In a May 17 concert review in the underground newspaper *Rat,* P. Dingle wrote: "Hendrix had something for everybody that night. When a guy called out 'Take off your hat,' Hendrix smiled and said, 'I'll take of my hat if you take off your pants.'. . . The Experience's music — in concert or on record — it makes no difference . . . they're great."

STATUS: *CN. One minute of silent 8mm color concert footage exists.*

DATE: MAY 18
EVENT: MIAMI POP FESTIVAL
PERFORMER(S): THE JIMI HENDRIX EXPERIENCE
SONG(S): UNKNOWN
LOCATION: HALLANDALE, FLORIDA

STATUS: *CN. Approximately two minutes of black-and-white 16mm film, shot by ABC-TV, is all that exists. See Chapter Six for more details of ABC-TV's coverage of this event.*

DATE: MAY 23
EVENT: NOEL REDDING'S HOME MOVIES
LOCATION: LINATE AIRPORT, MILAN, ITALY

Redding filmed Hendrix and possibly roadie Neville Chesters arriving at the airport.

STATUS: *CN.*

DATE: MAY 23
EVENT: PIPER CLUB CONCERT
PERFORMER(S): THE JIMI HENDRIX EXPERIENCE
SONG(S): UNKNOWN
LOCATION: MILAN, ITALY

A cameraman started to film the Experience concert at the Piper Club, but was ordered to stop after several minutes. A Hendrix roadie seized the film, and it is not known if the film still exists.

STATUS: *Lost.*

DATE: MAY 24
EVENT: NOEL REDDING'S HOME MOVIES
LOCATION: MALPENSA AIRPORT, MILAN, ITALY

Someone using Redding's camera captured Hendrix, Redding, Gerry Stickells, and Vicky Redding (Redding's sister) boarding a plane to Rome.

STATUS: *CN.*

DATE: MAY 30
EVENT: NOEL REDDING'S HOME MOVIES
LOCATION: ZURICH AIRPORT, ZURICH, SWITZERLAND

The final Redding footage for May shows Hendrix checking in at the airport.

STATUS: *CN.*

DATE: MAY 30
EVENT: BEAT MONSTER CONCERT
PERFORMER(S): THE JIMI HENDRIX EXPERIENCE
SONG(S): UNKNOWN (SEE BELOW)
LOCATION: HALLENSTADION, ZURICH, SWITZERLAND

STATUS: *CN. A five-minute 8mm amateur color film has surfaced. There is no recording available to cross-reference this film, but it seems that short segments of "Voodoo Child (Slight Return)," "Fire," "Foxy Lady," and "I Don't Live Today" were captured by this photographer.*[15]

BLACK GOLD

DATE: MAY 31
EVENT: BEAT MONSTER CONCERT
PERFORMER(S): THE JIMI HENDRIX EXPERIENCE
SONG(S): UNKNOWN
LOCATION: HALLENSTADION, ZURICH, SWITZERLAND

Swiss television reportedly covered the two-day concert, including a press conference and footage of the Experience in concert. However, two different three-minute 8mm color amateur films have surfaced in the collectors' network. Film researcher Thomas Geneser seems to feel that the first amateur film (3:04 running time) captured parts of "Red House" and "Hey Joe," and the second film (3:30 running time) contains segments of "Hey Joe," "Foxy Lady," "Manic Depression," "Fire," and "Purple Haze."[16]

STATUS: *The Swiss television footage is missing. The two amateur films can be found in the collectors' network.*

DATE: TAPED JUNE 5; ORIGINALLY BROADCAST JUNE 12
EVENT: *IT MUST BE DUSTY!* TELEVISION PROGRAM, ATV
PERFORMER(S): THE JIMI HENDRIX EXPERIENCE AND DUSTY SPRINGFIELD
SONG(S): "STONE FREE," "MOCKINGBIRD" (DUET BY HENDRIX AND SPRINGFIELD), AND "VOODOO CHILD (SLIGHT RETURN)"
LOCATION: STUDIO D, ELSTREE STUDIOS, BOREHAMWOOD, HERTFORDSHIRE, ENGLAND

In addition to the songs, the show included a short interview with Hendrix conducted by Springfield.

STATUS: *Missing. A two-minute silent 8mm black-and-white film, shot off the television screen, is all that has surfaced. An industrious Hendrix fan spent time, money, and energy to cue the home-recorded audio track with this footage, which is available in the collectors' network.*

DATE: JULY 6
EVENT: WOBURN FESTIVAL CONCERT
PERFORMER(S): THE JIMI HENDRIX EXPERIENCE
SONG(S): UNKNOWN
LOCATION: WOBURN ABBEY, BEDFORDSHIRE, ENGLAND

From the July 6 issue of *Melody Maker,* which sponsored the two-day music festival: "Jimi Hendrix — who flew in from New York this week to star in this weekend's MM Woburn Festival — has had to postpone a projected tour of Germany in September. Reason: Jimi has had a massive offer to appear on further dates in September during his new American tour. . . . Jimi is able to command $10,000 a day and 60 per cent of the gate money on his American shows. . . . The date at the Woburn Abbey on Saturday evening is likely to be his only British appearance this year." A *Disc and Music Echo* concert review (July 20, 1968) commented: "Jimi Hendrix proved he is still one of the country's best guitarists at [the] Woburn festival." After the Woburn festival, the Experience didn't perform in the U.K. until the concerts at London's Royal Albert Hall on February 18 and 24,1969.

STATUS: *Lost. An amateur photographer shot about a minute and a half of 16mm black-and-white film before being told to stop. After being developed, the film was given away; its whereabouts are unknown.*

DATE: JULY 16
EVENT: NOEL REDDING'S HOME MOVIES
LOCATION: LAURO VERDE BEACH, PALMA, MAJORCA, SPAIN

Hendrix is seen on the beach in swim trunks and flippers.

STATUS: *CN.*

DATE: JULY 31
EVENT: NOEL REDDING'S HOME MOVIES
LOCATION: BATON ROUGE, LOUISIANA

Noel Redding filmed scenes from a car on the way to Shreveport, Louisiana.

STATUS: *CN.*

DATE: AUGUST 1
EVENT: CONCERT PROMOTION
LOCATION: BEAUREGARDE SQUARE, NEW ORLEANS, LOUISIANA

Hendrix, Mitchell, and Redding went to Beauregarde Square for a local music gathering and invited everyone to come to their concert later that night. One source says that WVUE, Channel 12, New Orleans, may have videotaped the newsworthy event.[17]

STATUS: *Unknown.*

DATE: AUGUST 10
EVENT: AUDITORIUM THEATER CONCERT
PERFORMER(S): THE JIMI HENDRIX EXPERIENCE
SONG(S): POSSIBLY "PURPLE HAZE" AND "WILD THING"
LOCATION: CHICAGO, ILLINOIS

STATUS: *CN. Approximately one minute of silent 8mm color concert footage exists.*

DATE: AUGUST 16
EVENT: BALTIMORE TELEVISION STUDIO INTERVIEW
LOCATION: BALTIMORE, MARYLAND

STATUS: *Unknown. Noel Redding reported that TV reporter Ira Schneida interviewed the Experience on this date.*

BLACK GOLD

DATE: AUGUST 23
EVENT: SINGER BOWL CONCERT
PERFORMER(S): THE JIMI HENDRIX EXPERIENCE
SONG(S): "ARE YOU EXPERIENCED," "FIRE," "PURPLE HAZE," "HEY JOE," AND "WILD THING"
LOCATION: QUEENS, NEW YORK, NEW YORK

STATUS: *CN. A twenty-minute color silent 16mm film of this concert was discovered in the 1990s. The archivist who discovered it later dubbed in sound from an audience recording. This footage was considered for the (canceled) Hendrix documentary* Room Full of Mirrors.

DATE: AUGUST 26
EVENT: KENNEDY STADIUM CONCERT
PERFORMER(S): THE JIMI HENDRIX EXPERIENCE
SONG(S): UNKNOWN
LOCATION: BRIDGEPORT, CONNECTICUT

The entire concert was reportedly filmed by a member of the audience.

STATUS: *Unknown.*

DATE: SEPTEMBER 2
EVENT: TELEVISION INTERVIEW
PERFORMER(S): THE JIMI HENDRIX EXPERIENCE
SONG(S): UNKNOWN
LOCATION: DENVER, COLORADO

A Denver disc jockey was said to have filmed Hendrix for the local PBS affiliate.[18]

STATUS: *Unknown.*

DATE: SEPTEMBER 7
EVENT: PACIFIC COLISEUM CONCERT
LOCATION: VANCOUVER, BRITISH COLUMBIA, CANADA

This six-minute black-and-white footage captured a backstage interview with the Experience by Terry David Mulligan for CBC-TV. No songs were filmed.

STATUS: *CN.*

DATE: SEPTEMBER 9
EVENT: PRESS CONFERENCE
LOCATION: PORTLAND, OREGON

A television interview with Hendrix and Redding was probably taped during this press conference.

STATUS: *Unknown.*

DATE: SEPTEMBER 14
EVENT: HOLLYWOOD BOWL CONCERT
PERFORMER(S): THE JIMI HENDRIX EXPERIENCE
SONG(S): "ARE YOU EXPERIENCED," "VOODOO CHILD (SLIGHT RETURN)," "FIRE," "HEY JOE," AND "I DON'T LIVE TODAY"
LOCATION: LOS ANGELES, CALIFORNIA

Noel Redding has fifteen minutes of silent footage from the Hollywood Bowl concert in his private archives. There is also a two-minute silent color 16mm film of this show. The songs listed above were synched with an audience recording.

STATUS: *Unreleased.*

DATE: SEPTEMBER 18
EVENT: JAM AT WHISKY A GO-GO
PERFORMER(S): THE JIMI HENDRIX EXPERIENCE, BUDDY MILES, ERIC BURDON
SONG(S): UNKNOWN
LOCATION: LOS ANGELES, CALIFORNIA

STATUS: *Lost. A 16mm color film was made of the jam session but no footage has surfaced.*

DATE: OCTOBER 22–29
EVENT: STUDIO SESSIONS
PERFORMER(S): THE JIMI HENDRIX EXPERIENCE, JACK CASADY, GRAHAM BOND, LOWELL GEORGE
SONG(S): "GLORIA" AND "LOVER MAN"
LOCATION: TTG STUDIOS, HOLLYWOOD, CALIFORNIA

Fifteen minutes of 16mm color silent footage has surfaced from these sessions. Hendrix is seen jamming with Lowell George (flute), Jack Casady (bass), and Mitch Mitchell. The footage with Noel Redding is from the beginning of the session, when they recorded "Lover Man" and "Gloria." A promo film for "All Along the Watchtower" that used some of this silent studio footage was made in the 1980s.

On Rombox.com (http://membrane.com/rombox/andy/hendrix.html) Andy Cahan (ex-Turtles) recalled: "I started working for a subsidiary of Mercury Records called Pulsar Records. . . . I was assigned 'personal assistant' to Graham Bond, originator of the "Graham Bond Organization" with Ginger Baker and Jack Bruce (pre-'Cream'). He was the first one to bring the Mellotron over from Europe to the States. . . . One morning he told me to pick him up in my VW bus and to bring my Baldwin electric harpsichord, (that I had hooked up through a Hammond Leslie), pretty cool for that time! There I was at 'TTG' studios on Highland Ave. and Sunset Blvd. in Hollywood California November 1968, setting up my Baldwin, while Jack Casady of the Jefferson Airplane was setting up his bass, Lowell George of Little Feet [*sic*] was warming up on flute, Graham, turning on the Hammond B3 and Mitch Mitchell setting up the drums. Noel Redding was in the control room with the engineer. My back was to the studio door. Then I felt something behind me . . . I looked over my shoulder . . . there was Jimi Hendrix, accompanied by two gorgeous blonds, one carrying his amp and the other his guitar. He sat down, plugged in and proceeded to play the blues in the key of A. His veins were popping out of his neck as he squealed the high notes out of his Fender's Fender. It was totally awesome! The jam lasted two hours.

"As we all finished gloating, list[en]ing to the playback, Hendrix, myself and some guy, I think he was a studio tech., stood in the corner, smoking a joint and pretend[ing] we were instruments. I was the drums, making "ka doom doom bop" noises with my mouth, Hendrix was . . . you guessed it, lead guitar with his mouth, and the guy was bass. I still don't know what happened to that tape. It's out there somewhere . . . anyone know where it is?"

The film footage from October 29 captured random selections from the Experience's renditions of "Gloria" and "Lover Man." The "Gloria" footage, coupled with clips from the August 17, 1967, filming, was expertly synched with the recording of the song.

STATUS: *CN.*

DATE: OCTOBER 30
LOCATION: LAUREL CANYON, CALIFORNIA

Four minutes of silent color footage of the Experience was shot around a house in Laurel Canyon. There are also scenes of the Experience driving cars up and down the road.

STATUS: *CN.*

DATE: NOVEMBER 10
EVENT: *ED SULLIVAN SHOW,* CBS
LOCATION: NEW YORK, NEW YORK

One week before the show, *Disc and Music Echo* reported: "American TV audiences are in for something very radical, during the next few weeks Jimi Hendrix and Country Joe and the Fish have been scheduled to appear on the *Ed Sullivan Show.*" Unfortunately, the U.S. television debut for the Jimi Hendrix Experience was canceled, allegedly because of a camera crew strike.

STATUS: *According to Bob Levine (of Hendrix's management staff), Ed Sullivan really wanted to have Hendrix on the show. Sullivan's idea was to have the Vienna Ballet dance while Hendrix played in front of an orchestra, but Michael Jeffery never got back to him or told Hendrix about Sullivan's concept.* [19]

DATE: NOVEMBER 28
EVENT: AN ELECTRONIC THANKSGIVING CONCERT
PERFORMER(S): THE JIMI HENDRIX EXPERIENCE
SONG(S): UNKNOWN
LOCATION: PHILHARMONIC HALL, NEW YORK

Mitch Mitchell: "Philharmonic, lovely hall, no rock band had ever played there. It was a great gig, the whole thing was filmed, and I'd love to see it." [20]

STATUS: *Unknown. This film has never surfaced.*

1969

DATE: JANUARY 4
EVENT: *HAPPENING FOR LULU* TELEVISION PROGRAM, BBC
PERFORMER(S): THE JIMI HENDRIX EXPERIENCE
SONG(S): "VOODOO CHILD (SLIGHT RETURN)," "HEY JOE," AND "SUNSHINE OF YOUR LOVE" (DEDICATED TO CREAM)
LOCATION: STUDIO 4, LONDON, ENGLAND

Jimi Hendrix: "It was the same old thing, with people telling us what to do. They wanted to make us play

'Hey Joe.' I was so uptight about it, so I caught Noel and Mitch's attention and we went into the other thing. I dream about having our own show where we would have all contemporary artists as guest stars. Everybody seems to be busy showing what polished performers they are and that means nothing these days — it's how you feel about what you are doing that matters."[21]

STATUS: CA and CN. This video has been included in several Hendrix television documentaries, such as The Old Grey Whistle Test and Sounds of the Sixties.

DATE: JANUARY 7
EVENT: *THROUGH THE EYES OF TOMORROW* TELEVISION PROGRAM, CBC-TV
LOCATION: HENDRIX'S FLAT, 25 BROOK STREET, LONDON, ENGLAND

Hugh Curry, a former Canadian disc jockey, interviewed Hendrix for Canadian television.

STATUS: CN. The eight-minute interview was filmed in black and white. Short segments of it were used in A Film About Jimi Hendrix.

DATE: JANUARY 8
EVENT: LORENSBERGS CIRKUS CONCERT
PERFORMER(S): THE JIMI HENDRIX EXPERIENCE
SONG(S): UNKNOWN
LOCATION: LORENSBERGSPARKEN, GOTHENBURG, SWEDEN

STATUS: CN. This is an amateur silent two-minute color film of the second concert.

DATE: TAPED JANUARY 9; ORIGINALLY BROADCAST JANUARY 20
EVENT: KONSERTHUSET CONCERT (FIRST SHOW)
PERFORMER(S): THE JIMI HENDRIX EXPERIENCE
SONG(S): "KILLIN' FLOOR," "SPANISH CASTLE MAGIC," "FIRE," "HEY JOE," "VOODOO CHILD (SLIGHT RETURN)," "RED HOUSE," AND "SUNSHINE OF YOUR LOVE"
LOCATION: STOCKHOLM, SWEDEN

The first show of the night was videotaped by Johan Segerstedt of Swedish 1 TV in black and white and runs fifty-six minutes. The 2001 reissue of *Experience* features "Red House" and "Sunshine of Your Love" from this concert as bonus footage.

STATUS: CA and CN.

DATE: TAPED JANUARY 13; ORIGINALLY BROADCAST JULY 4, 1987
EVENT: *BEAT CLUB*, GERMAN TELEVISION PROGRAM, RADIO BREMEN
SONG(S): NONE
LOCATION: STUDIO DU MONDE, COLOGNE, GERMANY

In circulation is a two-minute interview, filmed in black and white for the German television show *Beat Club*. This footage includes an autograph session at a book shop or record store, with German narration, and was originally broadcast years later on another television show, *Abgestaupt*. Several concerts during this tour of

BLACK GOLD

West Germany were documented on film for the movie *The Last Experience,* which was produced by Joe Levine.

STATUS: *CN.*

DATE: JANUARY 23
EVENT: EVENTS RELATED TO SPORTPALAST CONCERT
LOCATION: BERLIN, GERMANY

Some of the scenes that were captured by Oets Kempe for the film *The Last Experience* included: the Experience arriving at the Tegel airport; driving through the city and arriving at the Hotel Kempinski; back-stage conversation between the Experience and road manager Gerry Stickells, who reports excitedly that riots are going on in the concert hall; Eric Barrett; several girls; scenes before the concert; Hendrix's spoken introduction to "Fire" plus the first few bars of the song.

STATUS: *CN.*

DATE: FEBRUARY 13
EVENT: MARY HOPKIN'S RECORD RELEASE PARTY
LOCATION: POST OFFICE TOWER, LONDON ENGLAND

Five minutes of black-and-white newsreel footage exists of Hendrix attending singer (and Beatles protégée) Mary Hopkin's record release party for her debut album, *Postcard.* Others in attendance included Maurice Gibb.

STATUS: *CN.*

DATE: FEBRUARY 14
EVENT: *DISC AND MUSIC ECHO* AWARD SHOW
LOCATION: SEYMOUR HALL, LONDON, ENGLAND

This short clip shows Hendrix receiving the *Disc and Music Echo* award for "World Top Musician" from Maurice Gibb (the Bee Gees). The event was filmed in black and white for *Movietone News* and runs fifteen seconds. It was rebroadcast in 1991 on the British TV show *Those Were the Days.*

STATUS: *CN.*

DATE: FEBRUARY 18
EVENT: FILMING FOR *THE LAST EXPERIENCE*
PERFORMER(S): JIMI HENDRIX
SONG(S): "HOUND DOG/TWO OLD MAIDS"
LOCATION: HENDRIX'S FLAT, 25 BROOK STREET, LONDON, ENGLAND

This five-minute segment from *The Last Experience* includes an interview and Hendrix performing a medley of two unrehearsed songs on acoustic guitar in a party atmosphere.

Kathy Etchingham remembered: "There was a knock on the door and I went downstairs to open it and this bloody great big microphone just came shoving through and the spot lights came on and I thought, 'What the hell's going on?' Jimi hadn't mentioned it to us at all. We were just hanging around having a joint. It wasn't very late when they turned up. 'That's Jimi's [acoustic] guitar,' I think they said, 'Well, let's play something.' I can't remember the exact sequence leading up to it, but I know that [Steve] Gold tried to get me to get Jimi to come downstairs because they wanted to catch him in the street, but he wouldn't go. He said, 'No, what for?'" [22]

STATUS: *CN.*

DATE: FEBRUARY 24
EVENT: ROYAL ALBERT HALL CONCERT
PERFORMER(S): THE JIMI HENDRIX EXPERIENCE
SONG(S): "LOVER MAN," "I DON'T LIVE TODAY," "FOXY LADY," "BLEEDING HEART," "FIRE," "LITTLE WING," "VOODOO CHILD (SLIGHT RETURN)," "ROOM FULL OF MIRRORS," "PURPLE HAZE," AND "WILD THING"
LOCATION: LONDON, ENGLAND

The Experience's magnificent concert at the Royal Albert Hall represented the band at their creative peak. *The Last Experience,* a film commissioned for the event and produced by Steve Gold and Jerry Goldstein, also captured the spirited pre-concert sound check.

Legal difficulties over the years have unfortunately prevented the release of either the film or an authorized soundtrack album. In 1969, Hendrix signed away his rights to this movie in a contract between Michael Jeffery, Gold and Goldstein, and their partner, Bernie Solomon. Eric Burdon recalls, "I just started with War and Gold and Goldstein. . . . The company we had just shot a movie of him [Hendrix] at the Royal Albert Hall in 1969. . . . This is where the pain for me comes in because my deal with Jerry Goldstein was, 'you find us several acts to build a company, and that movie will be yours.' . . . we were just about ready to the deal and then Jimi died. . . . Six months later . . . I went over to Gold and Goldstein and the story unfolded that they never intended to turn it over in the first place." [23] In spite of the legalities, poor-quality and highly edited LPs and CDs of this concert recording have been around for years.

STATUS: CN. In his book Don't Let Me Be Misunderstood, Eric Burdon explained why the film has never been released: "Steve Gold is dead and Hendrix's estate is handcuffed, unable to do anything with the material since [Bernie] Solomon's widow, Donna, now owns the negative." [24]

Hendrix collectors have had an unauthorized 105-minute version of this unreleased movie in their collections since the early 1990s, but according to Kathy Etchingham, "There's much more to that film than the bit we have. They filmed for a long, long time, but apparently, a lot of it was wasted on the cutting room floor." [25]

The original producers superimposed special effects of burning sparklers and shots of waves crashing on a beach, essentially vandalizing significant portions of the Experience's concert footage. We all hope a future release would not include these unnecessary enhancements.

DATE: MARCH 17–18
EVENT: TELEVISION SPECIAL
PERFORMER(S): JACK BRUCE, ROLAND KIRK, ERIC CLAPTON, AND SPECIAL GUESTS (SEE BELOW)
SONG(S): JAM PERFORMED WITH ARTISTS LISTED BELOW, EXCEPT HENDRIX
LOCATION: STAINES STUDIOS, ENGLAND

The March 22, 1969, issue of the *New Musical Express* jumped the gun when they reported the following: "Jimi Hendrix and Jack Bruce jammed with jazz saxist Roland Kirk at Staines Studios this week, when several noted musicians spent two days filming a colour special for U.S. TV. Also taking part were Stephen Stills (ex–Buffalo Springfield), Buddy Guy, Buddy Miles, Chris Mercer and Dick Heckstall-Smith (Colosseum)."

STATUS: *No Hendrix involvement. The televised special was organized by producer Tom Parkinson and director John Crome for a company called Colour-Tel, the company responsible for filming the Rolling Stones' Rock 'n Roll Circus and Hendrix's February 24 Royal Albert Hall concert. The jam session was filmed over two days (March 17–18) at a television studio in Staines, Middlesex, but did not include Hendrix. He had jammed with Roland Kirk at Ronnie Scott's Club sometime between March 7 and March 9 and left for New York on March 13. Hendrix was supposed to take part in the filming, but missed a plane in New York. In addition to the musicians mentioned above, Eric Clapton also performed.*

DATE: APRIL 26
EVENT: LOS ANGELES FORUM CONCERT
PERFORMER(S): THE JIMI HENDRIX EXPERIENCE
SONG(S): "TAX FREE," "FOXY LADY," "RED HOUSE," "SPANISH CASTLE MAGIC," "THE STAR SPANGLED BANNER," AND "PURPLE HAZE"
LOCATION: LOS ANGELES, CALIFORNIA

The *Los Angeles Times* (April 29, 1969) reviewed the concert unfavorably: "The National Anthem has become part of his repertoire (he also played it at the Hollywood Bowl last summer) and its performance provided the low point of the evening. 'Here's a song that we was all brainwashed with,' Hendrix said. 'Remember this oldies but goodies?' In this context, his National Anthem remark is meaningless and constitutes the cheapest kind of sensationalism."

STATUS: *CN. There is a four-minute silent 8mm black-and-white film of concert footage from this performance. The songs listed above have been matched with the professionally recorded audiotape.*

DATE: MAY 3
EVENT: MAPLE LEAF GARDENS CONCERT
PERFORMER(S): THE JIMI HENDRIX EXPERIENCE
SONG(S): POSSIBLY "FIRE," "RED HOUSE," "FOXY LADY," AND "ROOM FULL OF MIRRORS"
LOCATION: TORONTO, ONTARIO, CANADA

STATUS: *CN. Two short, silent amateur films of this concert have surfaced. The first is a poorly shot 16mm that runs 3:07. The second was filmed slightly better, but still is shaky at times. This 8mm color film runs 3:30.*

DATE: MAY 5
EVENT: ARRAIGNMENT FOR NARCOTICS POSSESSION
LOCATION: TORONTO COURT HOUSE, TORONTO, ONTARIO, CANADA

Three minutes of silent 16mm footage of Hendrix was shot at the Toronto Court House.

STATUS: *CN.*

DATE: MAY 11
EVENT: STATE FAIRGROUNDS COLISEUM CONCERT
PERFORMER(S): THE JIMI HENDRIX EXPERIENCE
SONG(S): UNKNOWN
LOCATION: INDIANAPOLIS, INDIANA

There is a silent color 8mm film of a few minutes of this concert.

STATUS: *CN.*

DATE: MAY 16
EVENT: CIVIC CENTER CONCERT
PERFORMER(S): THE JIMI HENDRIX EXPERIENCE
SONG(S): "LOVER MAN," "HEAR MY TRAIN A' COMIN,'" "FIRE," "RED HOUSE," "I DON'T LIVE TODAY," AND "VOODOO CHILD (SLIGHT RETURN)"
LOCATION: BALTIMORE, MARYLAND

There is a four-minute silent color 8mm of this concert. The songs listed have been identified based on the audience tape that was made at this concert.

STATUS: *CN.*

DATE: MAY 18
EVENT: MADISON SQUARE GARDEN CONCERT
PERFORMER(S): THE JIMI HENDRIX EXPERIENCE
SONG(S): "LOVER MAN," "COME ON (PART 1)," "RED HOUSE," "FIRE," "I DON'T LIVE TODAY," "VOODOO CHILD (SLIGHT RETURN)," AND
  "PURPLE HAZE"
LOCATION: NEW YORK, NEW YORK

Billboard (May 31, 1969) reported on the concert: "Hendrix, of course, was loose and leering, bucking and flinching to the groans of his guitar, which is his specialty. His fierce, almost sadistic manipulation of the guitar's personality, is arrogantly featured in his act as he humiliates the instrument by raking it across the microphone stand, playing it disinterestedly behind his back, pushing the volume till it whines out in pain and, finally, popping a string and discarding it altogether."

There is a silent, professionally shot 16 mm film that runs nine minutes. The songs listed above have been matched with the audience recording.

STATUS: *CN.*

DATE: MAY 25
EVENT: SAN JOSE POP FESTIVAL CONCERT
PERFORMER(S): THE JIMI HENDRIX EXPERIENCE
SONG(S): "HEAR MY TRAIN A COMIN'," "I DON'T LIVE TODAY," "FOXY LADY," "PURPLE HAZE," AND "VOODOO CHILD (SLIGHT RETURN)"
LOCATION: SANTA CLARA, CALIFORNIA

Carlos Santana remembered this concert: "The first time I saw Jimi was at the Santa Clara Fairgrounds. It was probably the most incredible concert I ever heard in my life. I have never heard him play better after that. Jimi Hendrix was at the peak of his art. He would make you, as a listener, be aware of all the galaxies — from the infinitesimal to the infinite, like that! I've never been exposed to that drastic form of expression. The closest was

John Coltrane. You know, when they just go out, and it's more than notes, it's more than just a Fender guitar or a Marshall amplifier. They are painting with a different kind of palette, if you will."[26]

Nancy Carter, who also interviewed Hendrix in 1969, shot three minutes of silent 16 mm color film of the Experience's performance. The songs listed above have been matched with the audience recording.

STATUS: CN.

DATE: MAY 30
EVENT: WAIKIKI SHELL CONCERT
PERFORMER(S): THE JIMI HENDRIX EXPERIENCE
SONG(S): UNKNOWN
LOCATION: HONOLULU, HAWAII

Three minutes of silent 8mm color concert footage exists.

STATUS: Unavailable.

DATE: JUNE 19
EVENT: COURT HEARING
LOCATION: CITY HALL COURT HOUSE, TORONTO, ONTARIO, CANADA

A three-minute silent color 8mm film shows several shots inside and outside the courtroom. On this date, Judge Robert Taylor set Hendrix's trial — for two counts of possession of heroin and hashish — for December 8, 1969.

Rolling Stone (May 31, 1969) reported: "There is the added possibility that by the time of Hendrix's June 19th hearing, the Canadian feds will have tacked charges of trafficking and transporting onto the possession rap. And if he is convicted on all three of these charges, the penalties could be much stiffer. The best guess is that conviction would put Hendrix behind bars for from two to seven years."

STATUS: CN.

DATE: JUNE 20
EVENT: NEWPORT '69 POP FESTIVAL CONCERT
PERFORMER(S): THE JIMI HENDRIX EXPERIENCE
SONG(S): UNKNOWN
LOCATION: SAN FERNANDO VALLEY STATE COLLEGE, DEVONSHIRE DOWNS, NORTHRIDGE, CALIFORNIA

According to a review in the *Los Angeles Free Press* (June 27, 1969): "Jimi Hendrix . . . then began what must have been one of the professional bummers of his career. Behind him was constant movement and shuffling of equipment, in front there were teeny-boppers screaming out for favorites. Ultimately, he told one group they were teeny-boppers, told another to fuck off, and played one of the most up-tight sets I've ever seen. He left the stage angry and to light applause. It was almost two o'clock and everyone had [had] enough for the day."

STATUS: CA and CN. Brief footage from this show was used in Peter Clifton's 1989 film Superstars in Concert (Telstar Video Entertainment) and Jimi Hendrix: Electric Ladyland (Rhino Home Video R3 2386).

DATE: JUNE 22
EVENT: NEWPORT '69 POP FESTIVAL CONCERT
PERFORMER(S): JIMI HENDRIX, BUDDY MILES, ERIC BURDON, TRACY NELSON, AND MORE (SEE BELOW)
SONG(S): "EARTH VS. SPACE MEDLEY," "THE THINGS I USED TO DO," "RED HOUSE," "VOODOO CHILD (SLIGHT RETURN)," AND "WE GOTTA LIVE TOGETHER"
LOCATION: SAN FERNANDO VALLEY STATE COLLEGE, DEVONSHIRE DOWNS, NORTHRIDGE, CALIFORNIA

The *Los Angeles Image* (June 27, 1969) covered the event and gave it glowing marks: "Sunday's program, when Hendrix was at his zenith, was the best of three days' shows and got the best audience response. Included was an unprecedented two-hour jam session which may artistically have been the greatest achievement in live rock music history. Among the participants were Eric Burdon's Review [*sic*], the Janis Joplin Review [*sic*] (without Janis), Tracy Nelson and some members of Mother Earth and Hendrix. Hendrix came across with perhaps the greatest playing in all of rock's brief existence, and maybe even the greatest accomplishment with the electric guitar."

This professionally shot 16mm color film runs twenty minutes. In addition to the songs listed above, there is also footage of Hendrix on stage with Buddy Miles, Tracy Nelson, and Eric Burdon. There's also some excellent 8mm footage, running nine minutes, that has been effectively synched with the audio recording.

STATUS: *CN.*

DATE: JUNE 29
EVENT: DENVER POP FESTIVAL CONCERT
PERFORMER(S): THE JIMI HENDRIX EXPERIENCE
SONG(S): "TAX FREE" AND "HEAR MY TRAIN A COMIN'"
LOCATION: MILE HIGH STADIUM, DENVER, COLORADO

The *Ann Arbor Argus* (July 29, 1969) reported on the concert, which erupted into a riot: "'Hendrix: We saw some tear gas. That's the sign of the third world war. Just make sure you pick your side now,' he said wryly. Then he announced the impending break-up of the Experience."

All of the performances of the festival were reportedly filmed. Scenes of the tear-gassed riot were broadcast on British television, but all that has surfaced is a two-minute silent color 8mm film.

STATUS: *CN.*

DATE: JULY 7
EVENT: *THE DICK CAVETT SHOW,* ABC-TV
PERFORMER(S): JIMI HENDRIX WITH THE BOB ROSENGARDEN ORCHESTRA
SONG(S): "HEAR MY TRAIN A COMIN'" (LIVE)
LOCATION: ABC-TV STUDIOS, NEW YORK, NY

Hendrix, responding to a question from Dick Cavett: "We plan for our sound to go inside the soul of the person, and see if it can awaken some kind of thing in their minds, because there are so many sleeping people out there."

The total running time for the Hendrix segment is fifteen minutes. A section of this show was used in the documentary *A Film About Jimi Hendrix* (Warner Home Video) and later broadcast on VH1.

STATUS: *CN.*

BLACK GOLD

DATE: JULY 10
EVENT: *TONIGHT SHOW*, NBC
PERFORMER(S): JIMI HENDRIX WITH BILLY COX AND THE *TONIGHT SHOW*'S DRUMMER, ED SHAUGHNESSY
SONG(S): "LOVER MAN" (TWO LIVE TAKES)
LOCATION: NBC-TV STUDIOS, NEW YORK, NEW YORK

Flip Wilson: "So many people have been asking — because they've heard you regard your performances as a spiritual experience — if there's some comments you'd like to make about that. We'd all be very interested."

Jimi Hendrix: ". . . After going to church so few times and getting thrown out because you had tennis shoes on with a blue and black suit, brown shirt, and after politics tells you this hogwash about this and that, you decide and say, 'Well, let me get my own thing together. . . .' Music is my scene, and my whole life is based around it, so quite naturally it becomes more than a religion . . . if they dig the sounds, it's like church actually, like going into a gospel church, and we're trying to get the same thing through modern music."

Hendrix then dedicated "Lover Man" to Brian Jones of the Rolling Stones, who had drowned a week earlier.

STATUS: Missing. Apparently all the tapes of the Tonight Show made before the program's move to Los Angeles in 1972 have long since been lost or destroyed. All that remains is an amateur audiotape recording.

DATE: AUGUST 10
EVENT: TINKER STREET CINEMA CONCERT
PERFORMER(S): JIMI HENDRIX, JUMA SULTAN (BASS), EARL CROSS (TRUMPET), ALI KABOI (DRUMS), MICHAEL CARABELLO (CONGAS), AND
  JOSÉ "CHEPITO" AREAS (PERCUSSION)
SONG(S): "THE DANCE," "SUNDANCE," "EARTH BLUES," AND "THE STAR SPANGLED BANNER"
LOCATION: WOODSTOCK, NEW YORK

Amateur filmmaker Linda Chan filmed the entire jam, but all that has surfaced is an audience recording of the music.

STATUS: Lost.

DATE: AUGUST 18
EVENT: WOODSTOCK MUSIC AND ART FAIR
PERFORMER(S): GYPSY SUN AND RAINBOWS
SONG(S): "FIRE," "IZABELLA," "RED HOUSE," "BEGINNINGS," "VOODOO CHILD (SLIGHT RETURN)/STEPPING STONE," "THE STAR SPANGLED BANNER,"
  "PURPLE HAZE," "GUITAR IMPROVISATION," AND "VILLANOVA JUNCTION"
LOCATION: BETHEL, NEW YORK

Director Michael Wadleigh recalled the film crew's technical difficulties: "We were down to two cameras . . . we'd had these electrical shorts as a result of the storm, and it had knocked out the motors on the cameras. We were almost out of film, and, on the camera I had, the motor was malfunctioning so badly that it was red hot. I had to wrap it in a towel to keep it from burning my chest. So, with these conditions, on comes the great Jimi Hendrix." Wadleigh began to film, but was not impressed, "Well, in my opinion, the set sucked. I mean the band just wasn't together. It wasn't exciting. It was jazz, it wasn't kick-ass rock and roll. Hendrix noticed, of course, that we'd stopped filming, but finally he sort of made eye contact with me and nodded, like 'roll it.' At the same time, he shut down the whole band and then you heard those famous notes, as he launched into this incredible version of 'Star-Spangled Banner.' The hair came up on the back of my neck, and the back of everybody's neck. We thought, 'Holy s---!' We didn't know what he was going to do next, but we knew it was going to be mean. And, of course, he had cranked his amps up as far as they could go. The experience of standing in front of Hendrix — no more than six feet farther than he was from his amps — was awesome. You did not hear the sound through your ears; you heard it through your diaphragm. It vibrated. It kicked your body, it was so loud. And to watch his fingers, if you look at my coverage of it, the camera zooms in and you see just those little flesh fingers pluck that string, but when that subtle little action happened there, you'd get hit in the f---ing gut with the sound that came out of just one pluck. He's doing no overdubs. He's doing it live, with these amazing sound effects—bombs going off, people screaming and dying in the streets. This was his challenge to American foreign policy."[27] These comments explain why some footage may be missing.

The fifty-seven-minute video *Jimi Hendrix at Woodstock* (MCAV-11989) was released in 1999 and is identical to the version produced by Alan Douglas that was released in 1992. Douglas rearranged the original song order and edited the length of several songs for the '92 release. There is also an amateur 8mm color film of this performance. It runs 1:22 and features segments of "Purple Haze," "Villanova Junction," and "Hey Joe."

STATUS: *CA and CN.*

DATE: AUGUST 18
EVENT: *MUSIC-SOUND AND SYMPOSIUM* TELEVISION SPECIAL, ABC
PERFORMER(S): JONI MITCHELL, JEFFERSON AIRPLANE, DAVID CROSBY, STEPHEN STILLS
LOCATION: ABC-TV STUDIOS, NEW YORK, NEW YORK

Hendrix, Joni Mitchell, Jefferson Airplane, David Crosby, and Stephen Stills were lined up to tape a television special with Dick Cavett on August 18 that would be aired the following night. Had Hendrix not performed an exhausting two-hour concert at 8:00 A.M. at the Woodstock festival, he might have made the show.

In his introduction, Cavett apologized for Hendrix's absence and joked that he might appear later and sing "Don't Get Around Much Anymore." Later in the show, Cavett conducted a "hip" round-table-type discussion session with all the musicians present, asking for their opinions on the Vietnam War and the Woodstock festival. Cavett also posed the question, "Where do you think Hendrix is?" David Crosby replied, "Asleep! Asleep!" Cavett then suggested Hendrix was probably "zonked-out," as Cavett's people had called him and knocked on his door that day with no response.

This show was aired in its entirety on VH1 in the late 1990s.

STATUS: *CN.*

DATE: SEPTEMBER 3
EVENT: UNITED BLOCK ASSOCIATION BENEFIT PRESS CONFERENCE
LOCATION: FRANK'S RESTAURANT, HARLEM, NEW YORK, NEW YORK

WTN-TV New York conducted an interview with Hendrix during a press conference announcing the "United Block Association Benefit." The total running time for the color video is seven minutes.

Hendrix at the press conference: "Sometimes when I come up here, people say, 'He plays white rock for white people — what's he doing up here?' Well, I want to show them that music is universal — that there is no white rock or black rock. Some of these kids haven't got the six dollars to go to Madison Square Garden; besides, I used to play here myself at Small's over at 135th and Seventh."

STATUS: *CN.*

BLACK GOLD

DATE: SEPTEMBER 5
EVENT: UNITED BLOCK ASSOCIATION CONCERT
PERFORMER(S): GYPSY SUN AND RAINBOWS
SONG(S): UNKNOWN
LOCATION: 139TH STREET AND LENOX AVENUE, HARLEM, NEW YORK, NEW YORK

Juma Sultan remembered the event: "We had a good time playing, but the band itself hadn't played for a black audience. I remember after the show this one little kid came up to Jimi and said, 'Why don't you guys come back home?' In other words, why don't you come back to the neighborhood? Jimi replied, with something like, 'you gotta do what you gotta do.'"[28]

STATUS: *Unreleased. The show was reportedly videotaped, but no tape has ever surfaced.*

DATE: SEPTEMBER 8
EVENT: *THE DICK CAVETT SHOW,* ABC
PERFORMER(S): JIMI HENDRIX, BILLY COX, MITCH MITCHELL, AND JUMA SULTAN
SONG(S): "IZABELLA/MACHINE GUN"
LOCATION: ABC-TV STUDIOS, NEW YORK, NEW YORK

The Hendrix interview and performance run thirteen minutes and were rebroadcast on VH1.
Cavett: "Have you ever had a nervous breakdown?"
Hendrix: "Yeah, about three since I've been in this group—since I've been in this business."
Juma Sultan: "A few weeks after the festival [Woodstock] we went down to the Cavett show. They [Hendrix's management] took all the equipment and left my drums because they didn't want me to be on the show with him—they wanted it back to a trio. I saw that they didn't have any of my instruments, so I went and got other drums."[29]
This was the television debut of Hendrix's new band, minus Larry Lee and Jerry Velez.

STATUS: *CN.*

DATE: SEPTEMBER 10
EVENT: CONCERT AT SALVATION
PERFORMER(S): GYPSY SUN AND RAINBOWS
SONG(S): UNKNOWN
LOCATION: GREENWICH VILLAGE, NEW YORK

In *Distant Drummer*'s November 8, 1969, issue, Bill Boehlke wrote: "The appearance of Jimi at Salvation, a small club in New York, was the best kept secret in the city. Only a handful of press showed up despite invitations sent by the club. After keeping the audience waiting for two hours, Hendrix hit the stage. . . . The set began with an untitled instrumental jam. There were no gymnastics, he stood calmly, making himself part of an excellent entity rather than an entire show. As the set continued with improvised jams the audience grew restive waiting for 'Foxy Lady.' In the midst of a superb improvisation, a good portion of the audience walked out. . . . Hendrix fans who paid more attention to his pelvis than his music are going to be lost—the cycle of Jimi Hendrix Superstar is nearing its end."

STATUS: *Unreleased. One collector claims to have found footage of this concert.*

DATE: NOVEMBER 27
EVENT: FILMING OF *GIMME SHELTER*
LOCATION: MADISON SQUARE GARDEN, NEW YORK, NEW YORK

On November 27, 1969, Hendrix's twenty-seventh birthday, his close friends the Rolling Stones played Madison Square Garden. Hendrix and Mick Jagger hung out together before the show. Fortunately, the Stones had hired the Maysles Brothers to film their entire tour. The cameras were rolling the night of the twenty-seventh as the Stones arrived with Hendrix at the Garden several hours before the concert.

As this rare footage begins, the entourage is seen getting out of the limousine. Hendrix steps out carrying his red TWA flight bag over his shoulder. In the next scene, he is sitting backstage with Keith Richards and drummer Charlie Watts. Hendrix strums Keith's clear plastic guitar, and occasionally drinks some Schaffer beer.

STATUS: *CN. This footage runs seven minutes and some segments are without sound.*

DATE: DECEMBER 31
EVENT: FILLMORE EAST CONCERT
PERFORMER(S): BAND OF GYPSYS
SONG(S): "STEPPING STONE," "FIRE," AND "EZY RYDER"
LOCATION: NEW YORK, NEW YORK

Photographer Amalie R. Rothschild shot this silent, color, 16mm footage (from the second show) that runs fifteen minutes. It was later synched with sound from the soundboard tapes. Some of this footage appeared in the Academy Award–winning video *Band of Gypsys: Live at the Fillmore East* (MCAV-11931), released in 1999.

Record Mirror (January 1, 1970) reported: "Jimi really went into training for his New Year's Eve, New Year's Day concerts (four in all) at the Fillmore. He rehearsed 12 hours a day for a whole week previous and even then took the group into a small club and tested it on a live audience. Jimi also arranged to have both evenings videotaped and recorded — certainly a new Jimi."

STATUS: *CA and CN.*

1970

DATE: JANUARY 1
EVENT: FILLMORE EAST CONCERT
SONG(S): "WHO KNOWS," "MACHINE GUN," "THEM CHANGES," "POWER OF SOUL," "STEPPING STONE," "FOXY LADY," AND "STOP"
PERFORMER(S): BAND OF GYPSYS
LOCATION: NEW YORK, NEW YORK

Filmmaker Jan Blom obtained permission from Michael Jeffery to videotape the Band of Gypsys. The following day Blom was invited to Jeffery's flat to screen the Band of Gypsys video for Hendrix. Blom's black-and-white video (of the first show of the evening) was shot from the balcony and runs fifty-three minutes.

Blom's friend Woody Vasulka also videotaped the show, but from the hall. His tape runs twenty-nine minutes and includes the songs "Who Knows," "Them Changes," "Power of Soul," "Foxy Lady," "Stepping Stone," and "Earth Blues." A Hendrix archivist has skillfully edited and synchronized the two collections of footage. A copy of this exists in the collectors' network.

STATUS: *CN.*

DATE: JANUARY 28
EVENT: WINTER FESTIVAL FOR PEACE CONCERT
PERFORMER(S): BAND OF GYPSYS
SONG(S): "EARTH BLUES"
LOCATION: MADISON SQUARE GARDEN, NEW YORK, NEW YORK

David Crosby described the situation at the Winter Festival for Peace: "In 1967, Hendrix made a few public comments in support of the war, primarily because he believed it was an important place to take a strong stand against the threat of Communist world domination. His view changed after somebody pointed out to him that although only 10 percent of the U.S. population was black, somehow blacks accounted for almost twice that percentage of our troops in Vietnam. . . . Although the symbolism of Hendrix's appearing at the Winter Festival for Peace was very important to the antiwar movement, his performance there was one of the saddest public displays of his career. . . . It was left to poor Peter Yarrow to placate a monumentally disappointed crowd of Hendrix fans who had waited seven hours for almost nothing. Peter says he told them how committed to the cause Jimi obviously was for trying to play even though he had the 'flu."[30]

STATUS: *CN. All that has surfaced so far is one minute of footage of "Earth Blues," shot on color 16 mm film.*

DATE: MARCH 17
EVENT: *FALSE START* RECORDING SESSIONS
PERFORMER(S): JIMI HENDRIX, LOVE
SONG(S): UNKNOWN
LOCATION: OLYMPIC STUDIOS, LONDON, ENGLAND

In 1970, Arthur Lee asked Hendrix to be guest artist on the Love album *False Start*. During my interview with Lee in 1992, he stated that the recording session was videotaped: "Someone just told me that the session was videotaped, and they have seen the tape."

STATUS: *Missing. So far, no videotape of this recording session has surfaced.*

DATE: APRIL 25
EVENT: LOS ANGELES FORUM CONCERT
PERFORMER(S): THE JIMI HENDRIX EXPERIENCE
SONG(S): UNKNOWN
LOCATION: LOS ANGELES, CALIFORNIA

In his introduction, Hendrix said to the audience: "Yours truly on video." Concertgoers attest that there was a large-screen projection of Hendrix throughout the show and the video camera remained mainly on Hendrix.

STATUS: *Missing. So far, no videotape of this performance has surfaced. While doing research, archivist John McDermott discovered a 16mm film of this concert that photographer Chuck Boyd independently shot.[31] It has not surfaced as of this writing.*

DATE: APRIL 26
EVENT: CAL EXPO '70 CONCERT
PERFORMER(S): THE JIMI HENDRIX EXPERIENCE
SONG(S): UNKNOWN
LOCATION: STATE FAIRGROUNDS, SACRAMENTO, CALIFORNIA

According to a review in the *Sacramento Bee* (April 27, 1970): "Hendrix, bright band around his natural, wielding his guitar, left-handed, like an extra, loose-footed limb, sang and played his way through some sensual music. It mourned, it shouted, it bragged, it belted. And it ranged, in style and tempo, from turgid to hectic."

STATUS: *Unreleased. Archivist John McDermott discovered a professionally shot 16mm black-and-white film of this concert.*

DATE: MAY 4
EVENT: HOLDING TOGETHER: A BENEFIT FOR TIMOTHY LEARY
PERFORMER(S): THE JIMI HENDRIX EXPERIENCE, JOHNNY WINTER WITH NOEL REDDING
SONG(S): "GETTING MY HEART BACK TOGETHER AGAIN," "FREEDOM," AND "RED HOUSE"
LOCATION: THE VILLAGE GATE, NEW YORK, NEW YORK

Johnny Winter confirmed this gig with Hendrix: "Jimi and I use[d] to play together whenever we had the chance. . . . We even did a benefit for Tim Leary at the Village Gate. . . ."[32]

STATUS: *CN (incomplete). Experience Hendrix purchased an unreleased and uncirculated twenty-minute black-and-white video of this show. The video was shot with one camera positioned directly in front of Hendrix. A short excerpt from this video appears in the film* Blue Wild Angel: Jimi Hendrix Live at the Isle of Wight *(see August 30, 1970 entry).*

DATE: MAY 16
EVENT: TEMPLE UNIVERSITY STADIUM CONCERT
PERFORMER(S): THE JIMI HENDRIX EXPERIENCE
SONG(S): UNKNOWN
LOCATION: PHILADELPHIA, PENNSYLVANIA

STATUS: *CN. A silent, color 8mm film that runs three minutes has surfaced.*

DATE: MAY 30
EVENT: BERKELEY COMMUNITY THEATER CONCERT
PERFORMER(S): THE JIMI HENDRIX EXPERIENCE
SONGS: FIRST SHOW: "JOHNNY B. GOODE," "HEAR MY TRAIN A COMIN'," "THE STAR SPANGLED BANNER," AND "PURPLE HAZE." SECOND SHOW: "I DON'T LIVE TODAY," "HEY BABY (LAND OF THE NEW RISING SUN)," "LOVER MAN," "MACHINE GUN," AND "VOODOO CHILD (SLIGHT RETURN)."
LOCATION: BERKELEY, CALIFORNIA

Mitch Mitchell remembered: "We did do Berkeley on this tour during the riots. It was weird not being a political band, that we were in the right — or perhaps the wrong — place at the right time. We'd been through Chicago, looking out through the hotel window and seeing kids being beaten up really badly . . . at Berkeley we arrived in the middle of mass confusion and demonstrations. How this affected Hendrix, I'm not sure . . . Jimi did look a bit rough around that time, you can see it in the Berkeley film."[33]

In his concert review (*San Francisco Chronicle*, June 1, 1970), John L. Wasserman wrote: "Hendrix really is an exceptional musician. His playing appears effortless, even to the point of locking his right hand into a fixed position on the guitar's neck (he is, of course, left-handed), and then playing for what seemed 30 seconds or a minute varying only his finger-work, not his hand position."

STATUS: CA and CN. The afternoon rehearsals and both shows were filmed in their entirety; however, only a fraction of the footage made it to the fifty-five-minute movie Jimi Plays Berkeley (Warner Home Video). An amateur, silent, color 8mm film from the second show has also surfaced, and runs three minutes.

DATE: JUNE 5
EVENT: MEMORIAL AUDITORIUM CONCERT
PERFORMER(S): THE JIMI HENDRIX EXPERIENCE
SONG(S): UNKNOWN
LOCATION: DALLAS, TEXAS

According to Mitch Mitchell: "After Berkeley it was a case of more stadium gigs. . . . By contrast the majority of the last gigs on the tour, in their own way, were memorable. . . ."[34]

STATUS: Missing. While going through files at Warner Bros., Hendrix archivist John McDermott turned up evidence that this 1970 performance was videotaped. According to McDermott, the paperwork was very detailed, indicating that a company from Texas shot the show on open-end Ampex video and was offering it for sale to Warner Bros. shortly after Hendrix died. Warner Bros. turned it down at the time and the paperwork was never seen again until McDermott discovered it.[35]

DATE: JUNE 13
EVENT: CIVIC CENTER CONCERT
PERFORMER(S): THE JIMI HENDRIX EXPERIENCE
SONG(S): UNKNOWN
LOCATION: BALTIMORE, MARYLAND

STATUS: CN. A silent, color 8mm film has surfaced. The total running time is four minutes.

DATE: JULY 4
EVENT: SECOND ATLANTA INTERNATIONAL POP FESTIVAL CONCERT
PERFORMER(S): THE JIMI HENDRIX EXPERIENCE
SONG(S): FEATURED IN *JIMI HENDRIX AT THE ATLANTA POP FESTIVAL* (WARNER HOME VIDEO): "FIRE," "SPANISH CASTLE MAGIC," "ALL ALONG THE WATCHTOWER," "FOXY LADY," "PURPLE HAZE," "HEY JOE," "RED HOUSE," "STONE FREE," "THE STAR SPANGLED BANNER," "STRAIGHT AHEAD," AND "VOODOO CHILD (SLIGHT RETURN)." FEATURED IN *JOHNNY B. GOODE* (SONY HOME VIDEO): "STONE FREE," "PURPLE HAZE," "FOXY LADY," "ALL ALONG THE WATCHTOWER," "THE STAR SPANGLED BANNER," AND "VOODOO CHILD (SLIGHT RETURN)."
LOCATION: BYRON, GEORGIA

According to *Rolling Stone* (August 8, 1970): "The biggest pop festival of the summer happened here over the Fourth of July weekend, drawing about a quarter of a million people into Lester Maddox' state. . . . Highlights were Jimi Hendrix doing "The Star Spangled Banner" on the Fourth as fireworks exploded behind the stage. . . . "

STATUS: *CA and CN. In addition to these commercial releases, a few uncut versions from different camera angles exist: one with seven minutes of "Foxy Lady," another with "Purple Haze," and a third with a single camera angle that captures four minutes of "Purple Haze."*

DATE: JULY 17
EVENT: NEW YORK POP CONCERT
PERFORMER(S): THE JIMI HENDRIX EXPERIENCE
SONG(S): "FOXY LADY" AND "THE STAR SPANGLED BANNER"
LOCATION: DOWNING STADIUM, RANDALL'S ISLAND, NEW YORK, NEW YORK

Billy Cox: "I don't remember all the occasions the shows were recorded, but I do remember the times we were filmed. The cameras would sometimes be in the way—a guy moving behind me while I'm in the middle of 'Purple Haze.' The Randall's Island concert is one I would like to see as a video."[36]

STATUS: *CN. Seven minutes of edited footage of these two songs were included in a 1977 film called* The Day the Music Died. *This film was produced and directed by Bert Tenzer, and the total running time is 85 minutes. Additionally, a silent, color 8mm film from this concert has surfaced in the collectors' network. The two-minute film features clips of "Stone Free," "Fire," and "Red House."*

DATE: JULY 25
EVENT: SPORTS ARENA CONCERT
PERFORMER(S): THE JIMI HENDRIX EXPERIENCE
SONG(S): UNKNOWN
LOCATION: SAN DIEGO, CALIFORNIA

The *San Diego Union* reported on the concert (July 27, 1970): "Appearing in red velvet bell-bottoms and a poncho with exaggerated sleeves, Hendrix oscillated the pulse of most every teenybopper in the near sold-out house as well as most older ones too."

STATUS: *CN. A silent color 8mm film running four minutes has surfaced. Unfortunately, it is too dark in several parts to determine which songs were filmed.*

DATE: JULY 26
EVENT: SICKS STADIUM CONCERT
PERFORMER(S): THE JIMI HENDRIX EXPERIENCE
SONG(S): "FIRE," "SUNSHINE OF YOUR LOVE," "MESSAGE TO LOVE," "LOVER MAN," AND "MACHINE GUN"
LOCATION: SEATTLE, WASHINGTON

STATUS: *CN. A silent two-minute 8mm color film, shot from the audience, has surfaced. The songs listed above have been identified from the audience recording. Some eyewitnesses noticed Al Hendrix filming segments of the concert from the stage on what appeared to be an 8mm home movie camera.*[37]

DATE: JULY 30
EVENT: A VIBRATORY COLOR SOUND EXPERIMENT CONCERT
PERFORMER(S): THE JIMI HENDRIX EXPERIENCE
SONG(S): FIRST SHOW: "HEY BABY (LAND OF THE NEW RISING SUN)," "IN FROM THE STORM," "FOXY LADY," "HEAR MY TRAIN A COMIN'," "PURPLE

HAZE," AND "VOODOO CHILD (SLIGHT RETURN)" SILENT OUTTAKES FROM THE FIRST SHOW: "HEAR MY TRAIN A COMIN'" (ENDING), "VOODOO CHILD (SLIGHT RETURN)," AND "FIRE" (BEGINNING). SECOND SHOW: "HEY BABY (LAND OF THE NEW RISING SUN)." SILENT OUTTAKES FROM THE SECOND SHOW: "DOLLY DAGGER," "INSTRUMENTAL SOLO," "EZY RYDER"

LOCATION: NEAR THE TOWN OF MAKAWAO, MAUI, HAWAII

From the *Maui News* (August 1, 1970): "The scene on the slopes of Haleakala above Seabury Hall Thursday afternoon looked as though preparations were underway for a jousting tournament in King Arthur's day. The brilliant green of the grassy slopes, the blue and white of the tent, and the colorful zodiacal banners lent an air of festivity to the scene.... More than 800 of the long-haired set walked about a mile up the mountain slope to enjoy the music of Jimi Hendrix, who is doing the score for the film [*Rainbow Bridge*]. One witness said that 'actually it sounded better from about a mile away.' All in all, it made for an enjoyable afternoon for almost everyone except for a few who complained about the 'noise' from the batteries of loudspeakers amplifying the Hendrix sound."

STATUS: CA and CN. In addition to the professional film and recording, an amateur silent sixteen-minute color 16mm film (from a different angle) has surfaced. It features clips of "Hear My Train A Comin'," "Ezy Ryder," "Hey Baby (Land of the New Rising Sun)," "In from the Storm," "Dolly Dagger," "Spanish Castle Magic," and "Lover Man."

DATE: AUGUST 1
EVENT: HONOLULU INTERNATIONAL CENTER ARENA CONCERT
PERFORMER(S): THE JIMI HENDRIX EXPERIENCE
SONG(S): POSSIBLY "FREEDOM," "EZY RYDER," "THE STAR SPANGLED BANNER," "PURPLE HAZE," "FOXY LADY," "MESSAGE TO LOVE," "VOODOO CHILD (SLIGHT RETURN)," AND "ALL ALONG THE WATCHTOWER"
LOCATION: HONOLULU, HAWAII

Billboard (August 29, 1970) reported: "It was a trip to decibel city: a cacophony of electrical storms, coupled with a blizzard of frenzied artistry. It was loud and lethal for the senses, but the wizard of the whining guitar had warned his audience early in the program: 'It's going to be loud. It will get louder. It will get loudest.' He wasn't kidding."

The following month, Hendrix spoke about this period: "When the last American tour finished, I just wanted to go away for a while, and forget everything. Then I started thinking about the future. Thinking that this era of music — sparked off by the Beatles — had come to an end. Something new has got to come, and Jimi Hendrix will be there."[38]

STATUS: CN. A silent 16mm color film of this concert has surfaced. The total running time is five minutes. The songs listed above were identified by researcher Thomas Geneser in an article that appeared in UniVibes magazine (December 1996). This was the final U.S. concert performance for Hendrix.

DATE: AUGUST 30
EVENT: ISLE OF WIGHT FESTIVAL CONCERT
PERFORMER(S): THE JIMI HENDRIX EXPERIENCE
SONG(S): "GOD SAVE THE QUEEN," "SGT. PEPPER'S LONELY HEARTS CLUB BAND," "SPANISH CASTLE MAGIC," "ALL ALONG THE WATCHTOWER," "MACHINE GUN," "FREEDOM," "RED HOUSE," "DOLLY DAGGER," "FOXY LADY," "PURPLE HAZE," "VOODOO CHILD (SLIGHT RETURN)," AND "IN FROM THE STORM"
LOCATION: EAST AFTON FARM, ISLE OF WIGHT, ENGLAND

The entire concert was filmed by at least two independent film crews, and film crews from the BBC, Peter

Clifton Films, and Swiss television were also present. *Jimi Hendrix at The Isle of Wight* (BMG Video) was released in 1990 by MLF Productions/Are You Experienced Ltd. In addition to the concert footage, the film includes an interview with Hendrix and French radio, as well as backstage conversations between Eric Barrett and Hendrix. The total running time is fifty-seven minutes.

The Murray Lerner film *Blue Wild Angel* (2000) drew on all of Lerner's footage of Hendrix from the Isle of Wight Festival. Unfortunately, no footage exists of either "Midnight Lightning" or "Land of the New Rising Sun."

A four-minute silent 8mm color film was also made; it captured segments of "God Save the Queen," "Sgt. Pepper," "Spanish Castle Magic," "All Along the Watchtower," and "Machine Gun."

STATUS: *CA and CN.*

DATE: AUGUST 31
EVENT: STORA SCENEN CONCERT
PERFORMER(S): THE JIMI HENDRIX EXPERIENCE
SONG(S): "COME ON (PART 1)," "ROOM FULL OF MIRRORS/LAND OF THE NEW RISING SUN," AND "IN FROM THE STORM"
LOCATION: GRÖNA LUND, STOCKHOLM, SWEDEN

From Ludvig Rasmusson's review, "Jimi Hendrix Plays on Old Memories," in *Vi tonären* (September 6–12, 1970): "It was a strange concert. Jimi started one hour too late. Some thought it was unpleasant to keep standing and started yelling to people to sit down. At the end almost everyone sat except for a few disco-snobs. Apparently they were afraid for their expensive trousers. 'Its only cloth,' people yelled. 'Sit down.' Jimi had with him his old drummer Mitch Mitchell and new bass player Billy Cox. . . . The electronic gimmicks were there as before, but they did not work out. . . . At the end Jimi played some bars of 'The Star Spangled Banner' for a few seconds, and then it was all over; he threw flowers into the audience."

STATUS: *CN. Eric Seagal and Dave van Dijk videotaped this concert in black and white. The running time is fifteen minutes.*

DATE: SEPTEMBER 2
EVENT: VEJLBY-RISSKOV HALLEN CONCERT
PERFORMER(S): THE JIMI HENDRIX EXPERIENCE
SONG(S): UNKNOWN
LOCATION: ÅRHUS, DENMARK

In a concert review (September 3, 1970) for *Århus Stifstidende*, Poul Blak wrote: "Even world famous people can be sick. Maybe this is a reminder that the beat gods are not Gods. Jimi Hendrix, who claims to be a traveler in electric religion, was forced to his knees at [Golgotha] yesterday evening. 'Do you feel all right?' Hendrix asked, when he finally walked on stage. It was clear to everyone who had eyes to see with, that Hendrix did not."

STATUS: *CN. Three minutes of silent 8mm color film have surfaced. Since the lighting at this concert was poor, it is hard to identify the songs that were filmed.*

BLACK GOLD

DATE: SEPTEMBER 3
EVENT: K.B. HALLEN CONCERT
PERFORMER(S): THE JIMI HENDRIX EXPERIENCE
SONG(S): "EZY RYDER," "RED HOUSE," "PURPLE HAZE," "VOODOO CHILD (SLIGHT RETURN)," "HEY JOE," AND "FIRE"
LOCATION: COPENHAGEN, DENMARK

The *Politiken* (September 4, 1970) noted in its concert review: "The label 'Concert of the year' has been used many times, but this time it is justified. Jimi Hendrix at K.B. Hallen last night surpassed anything we have until now. . . . As a warrior of love he stood, dressed in many colours, and was the best guitarist rock 'n' roll music can offer. What Hendrix, Cox, and Mitchell gave those who were at the K.B. Hallen, no one can take away."

STATUS: CN. A silent color 8mm film of this concert that runs three minutes has surfaced. The songs listed above were identified from the audience recording.

DATE: SEPTEMBER 4
EVENT: BACKSTAGE INTERVIEW
LOCATION: DEUTSCHLANDHALLE, BERLIN

Chris Bromberg and Keith Roberts filmed and interviewed Hendrix backstage for the Armed Forces Network during this concert.

STATUS: Unreleased. The ten-minute 16mm film is believed to be owned by Experience Hendrix.

DATE: FILMED SEPTEMBER 6; ORIGINALLY BROADCAST NOVEMBER 13
EVENT: LOVE AND PEACE FESTIVAL CONCERT
PERFORMER(S): THE JIMI HENDRIX EXPERIENCE
SONG(S): "VOODOO CHILD (SLIGHT RETURN)"
LOCATION: FEHMARN, GERMANY

In an October 5 concert review for *Bravo*, Jörg Flemming wrote: "A dozen audacious figures in black leather, with truncheons and knives, build a cordon around the stage. They push reporters, who are sitting in front, a couple of meters back, but no one dares to argue. The top star comes on stage, wearing lilac trousers, a white crochet shirt, open at the front, a jacket made of parrot-coloured patchwork, and a turquoise-coloured headband. The first guitar is white and badly tuned. The show lasts one hour and forty minutes."

STATUS: CN. Two minutes of color footage of Jimi arriving by car and climbing up the stairs to the festival stage were filmed for the documentary Pop-Grusical, directed by Roman Brodmann. The footage was first broadcast on November 13, 1970, and was rebroadcast in 1986. Additionally, three minutes of footage of Jimi on- and off-stage were broadcast on Jimi Hendrix auf Fehmarn: das letzte Konzert, on August 20, 1994.

Finally, a silent four-minute 8mm color film has surfaced of this final official concert performance. This film captures clips of "Killin' Floor," "Spanish Castle Magic," "All Along the Watchtower," "Hey Joe," "Hey Baby (Land of the New Rising Sun)," "Message to Love," and "Foxy Lady."

EYES AND IMAGINATION

On August 28, Jimi Hendrix was in a positive mood as he gave several interviews in his suite at the Londonderry Hotel. He spoke about the future and developing a bigger band "full of competent musicians." He told *New Musical Express* reporter Gillian Saich, "It's going to be something that will open up a new sense in people's minds...with the music we will paint pictures...so that the listener can be taken somewhere....I'm going to develop the sound, and then put a film out with it. It's so exciting, it's going to be an audio/visual thing that you sit down and plug into, and really take in through your ears and eyes. I'm happy, it's gonna be good."[39] Hendrix's dreams of melding a true audiovisual experience for an audience have finally developed with today's improved technology—including digital videos and surround sound—some thirty years after his death. In some respects he achieved that goal during his lifetime—using only guitar, bass, drums, and his imagination.

Notes

Chapter 1: Broomsticks and Guitar Picks: 1942–1961

1 On page 15 of *Electric Gypsy* (New York: St. Martin's Press, 1990), Hendrix biographers Shapiro and Glebbeek report that "Lucille was a hard drinker" and Minnie Gautier "wouldn't hand over Johnny to Lucille unless she was sober."

2 Paul de Barros, *Jackson Street After Hours: The Roots of Jazz in Seattle* (Seattle: Sasquatch Books, 1993), 76.

3 Freddie Mae Gautier, unpublished interview with the author, 1994.

4 On page 119 of *San Francisco: The Musical History Tour* (San Francisco: Chronicle, 1996), Joel Selvin reports that while in Berkeley, Johnny Allen Hendrix lived in a low-rent housing project for Navy famiies called Savo Island Village. Although the exact address is not listed in the book, Selvin notes that Savo Island Village was located where Martin Luther King Way and Derby Street now meet.

5 James A. Hendrix, as told to Jas Obrecht, *My Son Jimi* (Seattle: AlJas Enterprises, 1999), 44.

6 This house was located at 2603 S. Washington in Seattle's Central Diestrict. According to the *Seattle Times* (20 November 2001), two Seattle developers have recently stepped in to save the house from destruction. After relocating in, they plan to fill it with Hendrix artifacts and multimedia presentations, and to build a recording studio and youth hostel around it.

7 Kathy Etchingham, unpublished interview with the author, 2000.

8 Johnny Black, *Jimi Hendrix: The Ultimate Experience* (New York: Thunder's Mouth Press, 1999), 11.

9 *A Film About Jimi Hendrix*, Warner Bros., 1973.

10 Tony Brown, *Jimi Hendrix: A Visual Documentary* (London: Omnibus Press, 1992), 19.

11 Ibid., 10.

12 Steven Roby, "Seattle Speaks," *Straight Ahead*, February/March 1994.

13 James A. Hendrix, *My Son Jimi*, 126.

14 Robert Palmer, *Deep Blues* (New York: Viking Press, 1982), 154.

15 *House of Blues Radio Hour*, air dates 17 and 18 September 1994, show # 94-54.

16 Steven Roby, "Seattle Speaks."

17 Paul de Barros, *Jackson Street After Hours*, 172.

18 Pat O'Day, "Pat O'Day Interview," interview by Darrell Clingman, *Straight Ahead*, March 1990.

19 Tony Brown, *Jimi Hendrix in His Own Words* (London: Omnibus Press, 1994), 11.

20 Steven Roby, "Seattle Speaks."

21 Paul de Barros, *Jackson Street After Hours*, 148.

22 Ibid.

23 Alfred G. Aronowitz, "Brash Buccaneer with a Wa-Wa," *Life*, 15 March 1968.

Chapter 2: No Direction Home: 1961–1963

1 *Melody Maker*, 9 October 1967.

2 Billy Cox, "Billy Cox," interview by Jas Obrecht, *Guitar Player*, September 1995.

3 *A Film About Jimi Hendrix*, Warner Bros., 1973.

4 *Guitar Player*, September 1987.

5 Ibid.

6 *A Film About Jimi Hendrix*.

7 This information was obtained under the Freedom of Information Act.

8 *Rave*, June 1967.

9 Ibid.

10 *Beat Instrumental*, March 1967.

11 *Rave*, June 1967.

12 *Guitar Player*, September 1987.

13 Ibid.

14 Tommy Chong, "Up from the Skies," interview by David Pearcy, *Straight Ahead*, August/September 1994.

15 Brian Ward, *Just My Soul Responding: Rhythm and Blues, Black Consciousness, and Race Relations* (Berkeley: University of California Press, 1998), 139.

16 Michael Willmore's book, *The History of Vancouver Rock 'n' Roll*, further explained the origins of Bobby Taylor and the Vancouvers: "One of the most popular club bands [in Vancouver in the early 1960s] was Little Daddy and the Bachelors. Their funky blues sound and dynamic stage presentation incorporated comedy routines. On their only single, the b-side "Junior's Jerk"

[1964] was an original instrumental featuring the lead guitar work of Tommy Chong. Besides Tommy Chong on guitar, the band consisted of Wes Henderson on bass, Floyd Sneed on drums and Bernie Sneed on keyboards. They later changed their name to Four Niggers and a Chink and bombed completely. No one would book a band with a name like that, so a few weeks later they changed it to Four Colored Fellows and an Oriental Lad. By this time the local branch of the NAACP got after them, and the whole affair was written up in Jack Wasserman's column in the *Vancouver Sun*. They relented, finally, and shortened it to just Four N's and a C. Now everyone was happy, except for the group that broke up shortly thereafter. But all's well that ends well. Tommy Chong and Wes Henderson got together with other musicians and formed Bobby Taylor & the Vancouvers, who eventually left town to join the Tamla Motown roster in Detroit. Floyd Sneed, after moving to Los Angeles, became the drummer for Three Dog Night."
17 Tommy Chong, "Up from the Skies."

Chapter 3: The Chitlin' Circuit: 1963–1965

1 Craig Werner, *A Change Is Gonna Come* (New York: Penguin Putnam, 1999), 73.

2 Nix is quoted on page 74 of Craig Werner's *A Change Is Gonna Come*. Werner also notes that the black audiences of the Chitlin' Circuit were shocked to find that the Mar-Keys were white.

3 To get a feel for the difference in these sounds, compare Spector's production of "Be My Baby" by the Ronettes (1963, Phillies 116) to the Southern Soul sound in "Green Onions" by Booker T. and the MG's (1962, Stax 127).

4 Michael Thomas, "The Persecution & Assassination of Rock and Roll...," *Eye*, July 1968.

5 Hendrix wrote to his father, Al, from Nashville, and sent a photo of the band at the Del Morocco club on 19 May 1963.

6 Charles White, *The Life and Times of Little Richard: The Quasar of Rock* (New York: Harmony Books, 1984), 127.

7 Curtis Mayfield, "Curtis Mayfield Interviewed," interview by Narada Michael Walden, *Straight Ahead*, June/July 1996.

8 Tony Brown, *Jimi Hendrix: A Visual Documentary* (London: Omnibus Press, 1992), 28.

9 Fairmont Records released its first title in March 1963 and closed in January 1965.

10 Brothers Richard and Robert Poindexter (known as the group the Icemen) also wrote and produced "It's Gonna Take a Lot" performed by Linda Jones, another recording from this time frame that is believed to have Hendrix on guitar. The Poindexters went on to compose "Thin Line Between Love and Hate," a #1 R&B hit in 1971 for the vocal group the Persuaders. Linda Jones had a minor hit with "Hypnotized" in 1967 for Loma Records.

11 Jimmy Norman was an R&B singer. In 1962, his song "I Don't Love You No More" reached #21 on the R&B charts and #47 on the pop charts.

12 Steve Newton, "First Experiences," *Experience Hendrix*, Spring 2000.

13 Ibid.

14 There are known to be over five hundred different worldwide releases containing altered Youngblood-Hendrix recordings, according to *Experience Hendrix*, Spring 2000.

15 "Hi-Tech Illusion," *CBS Evening News*, CBS-TV, 1986.

16 Ibid.

17 This was confirmed in a personal e-mail from Youngblood to the author on 24 August 2000. Still active on the music scene, Youngblood often performs at New York supper clubs, parties, and a regular Saturday gig at Sylvia's, a well-known soul-food establishment located at 126th Street and Lenox Avenue in Harlem. He has released twelve albums.

18 Fayne Pridgon [sic], "I Remember Jimi," *Gallery*, September 1982.

19 Ralph Cooper with Steve Dougherty, *Amateur Night at the Apollo* (New York: HarperCollins, 1990), 178.

20 Fayne Pridgon [sic], "I Remember Jimi."

21 *A Film About Jimi Hendrix*, Warner Bros., 1973. Hendrix further explained feeling out of place in Harlem: "When I was staying in Harlem, I used to go to clubs and my hair was really long then. Sometimes I might tie it up, or I might do something with it, you know. The cats said, 'Look at that! Black Jesus or something? What is this supposed to be?' So, oh man, even in your own section...like I have friends with me in Harlem, 125th Street, you know. We were walking down the street. And the cats, girls, old ladies, anybody, they're just peeping out, saying, 'What is this? A circus or something?'" Johnny Black, *Jimi Hendrix: The Ultimate Experience* (New York: Thunder's Mouth Press, 1999), 73.

22 Billy Mitchell, unpublished interview with the author, September 2000.

23 Hendrix talked about his Apollo Theater prize in a Swedish radio interview, "Pop 67 Special," conducted by Klas Burling on 28 May 1967.

24 In fact, Cooper said a Cleveland deejay took tapes of *The Ralph Cooper Show* and went wild over them, later adopting Cooper's original concept, format, and playlist. The deejay, Alan Freed, was also known as the Father of Rock and Roll for his role in the early careers of performers such as Chuck Berry and his efforts to break down racial barriers on radio stations by playing black artists' music.

25 Ernie Isley, from a speech given on 21 November 1991 at the Hollywood Walk of Fame ceremony for Jimi Hendrix.

26 Hendrix's influence on the Isleys has been noticed in their post–Motown era hit, "That Lady" (1973, T-Neck 2251).

27 This version would later inspire guitarist Stevie Ray Vaughan to cover it on his debut album.

28 Tony Brown, *Jimi Hendrix...In His Own Words* (New York: Omnibus Press, 1994), 18.

29 In 1994, singer Michael Bolton was accused of lifting portions of the melody from the 1964 Isley Brothers hit "Love Is a Wonderful Thing" for his song with the same title. In a 1994 television interview for *Entertainment Tonight*, Ronald Isley commented: "We wrote the song years ago, and it was one of the early songs we did when Jimi Hendrix was in the band." Bolton lost the case and was ordered to pay millions of dollars.

30 George Clemons, unpublished interview with the author, July 2000.

31 Don Covay, unpublished interview with the author, September 2000.

32 Steve Cropper, liner notes for *Drivin' South* (Freud CD 065).

33 Johnny Black, *The Ultimate Experience*, 33.

34 Charles White, *The Life and Times of Little Richard: The Quasar of Rock* (New York: Harmony Books, 1984), 127.

35 *Guitar Player*, September 1987.

36 Charles Sharr Murray, *Crosstown Traffic* (New York: St. Martin's Press, 1991), 162.

37 *Rolling Stone*, 28 May 1970.

38 Dewey Terry, unpublished interview with the author, October 2000.

39 Rosa Lee Brooks, "Rosa Lee Brooks Speaks," interview by Steven Roby, *Straight Ahead*, June 1992.

40 Arthur Lee, "Arthur Lee's Rebuttal," interview by Steven Roby, *Straight Ahead*, October 1992.

41 Rosa Lee Brooks, "Rosa Lee Brooks Speaks."

42 Rosa Lee Brooks continues to honor Hendrix by occasionally performing in the Los Angeles area. She recently appeared in the BBC Hendrix documentary *The Man They Made God* (1999).

43 Curtis Knight, *Jimi: An Intimate Biography of Jimi Hendrix* (New York: Praeger Publishers, 1974), 25.

44 Ibid.

45 Carol Shiroky, "Carol Shiroky: The *Straight Ahead* Interview," interview by Steven Roby, *Straight Ahead*, December/January 1995.

46 Mike Quashie, "Interview with Mike Quashie," interview by Steven Roby, *Straight Ahead*, February/March 1995.

47 *UniVibes*, April 2000.

48 Doug Bell, notes to the author, August 2000.

49 Ed Chalpin,"An Interview with Ed Chalpin: The Jayne and Jimi Session," interview by Steven Roby, *Straight Ahead*, June/July 1994.

50 According to Noel Redding, Mansfield was hanging out to see Engelbert Humperdinck's set, and eventually left with him after the concert was over.

Chapter 4: My Own Scene, My Own Music: 1966

1 Tony Brown, *Jimi Hendrix: A Visual Documentary* (London: Omnibus Press, 1992), 38.

2 "The Black Elvis?" *New York Times*, 25 February 1968.

3 Ibid.

4 Letters to the Editor, *Village Voice*, 25 August 1966.

5 Valerie Wilmer, "Jimi Hendrix: An Experience," *Down Beat*, 4 April 1968.

6 Keith Altham, "Wild Jimi Hendrix," *New Musical Express*, 14 January 1967.

7 *Guitar World*, May 1994.

8 Ray Simonds, notes to the author, July 1994.

9 Ibid.

10 Harry Shapiro and Caesar Glebbeek, *Jimi Hendrix: Electric Gypsy* (London: Heinemann, 1990), 576.

11 Ray Simonds, notes to the author.

12 Charles Sharr Murray, *Crosstown Traffic: Jimi Hendrix and the Rock 'n Roll Revolution* (New York: St. Martin's Press, 1989), 162.

13 Tamika Laurice James was born on 11 February 1967 and neither Hendrix nor Carpenter's real name appear on the birth certificate (Carpenter was using the name Regina Jackson and Hendrix was going by Jimi James). Hendrix's attorney Henry Steingarten made him aware of Carpenter's paternity suit on 15 September 1970. In 1972, Carpenter lost a court case to have her daughter Tamika recognized as Jimi Hendrix's heir when a judge ruled that she had taken too much time to bring the case to trial and lacked a blood test to identify the father. In an article for *UniVibes* magazine (April 2001), Diana Carpenter said that she "would like to see Tamika and her children have some portion of Jimi's inheritance . . . and a trust fund set up for Tamika and all three of her children."

14 Nan Ickeringill, "And Here's . . . Cheetah," *New York Times*, 28 April 1966.

15 Bob Kulick, "Will I Live Tomorrow?" interview by Mike Mettler, *Guitar Player*, September 1995.

16 Richie Havens, unpublished interview with Keith Bollinger, 1994.

17 Ibid.

18 Bob Kulick, "Will I Live Tomorrow?" Kulick remembered that when Hendrix "watched other bands, he would even take notes. I remember him sitting there with a pad and pen . . . we were totally intimidated, wondering what he was doing."

19 Michael Hicks, *Sixties Rock: Garage, Psychedelic & Other Satisfactions* (Illinois: University of Illinois Press, 1999), 50. William ("Billy") Moses Roberts, Jr., is credited as the composer of "Hey Joe." Hicks notes that Rose "changes the key of the song to E and begins it not with the "Needles and Pins" riff, but with a distinctive blues-based guitar lick."

20 Carol Shiroky, "Carol Shiroky: The *Straight Ahead* Interview," interview by Steven Roby, *Straight Ahead*, December/January 1995. Shiroky also recalled that Hendrix corrected her on the spelling of Jimi when she gave him a card around this time.

21 Ibid.

22 Steven Roby, "Reflections on Jimi," *Straight Ahead*, November 1994.

23 Ibid.

24 Steven Roby, "Playin' Hooky with Hendrix," *Straight Ahead*, November 1994.

25 *Musician*, May 1981.

26 Bob Kulick, "Will I Live Tomorrow?" Kulick recalled that Hendrix played a primitive version of "Third Stone from the Sun." In my 1994 interview with Frank Von Elmo, he said they played an early version of "Foxy Lady."

27 "Experience," *Great Speckled Bird*, 30 August 1968.

28 *UniVibes*, May 1993. Paul Caruso: "I saw him at a club called Ondine's ... it was sort of a jet-setters type of watering hole ... that's when I heard him really sound determined and polished."

29 Carol Shiroky, "Carol Shiroky."

30 Ibid.

31 Steven Roby, "Reflections on Jimi."

32 John Hammond, Jr., "Hendrix Remembered," *Guitar Player*, September 1975.

33 Stuart Nicholson, *Jazz-Rock: A History* (New York: Schirmer, 1998), 102.

34 Michael Bloomfield, "Jimi Hendrix Remembered," *Guitar Heroes*, Spring 1992.

35 Australian radio, Jimi Hendrix special, September 1982.

36 Keith Bollinger's research on this meeting was published in "Countdown to Experience," *Straight Ahead*, December/January 1995. He found press reports showing that the Animals played in New York at Fordham University on 15 April 1966, and their tour ended on 3 August at New York's Rheingold Central Park Music Festival. Chandler himself was quoted in John McDermott's book *Hendrix: Setting the Record Straight*, saying he met Hendrix on the afternoon of their Central Park concert, which would place the meeting on 3 August 1966.

37 John McDermott with Eddie Kramer, *Hendrix: Setting the Record Straight* (New York: Warner Books, 1992), 11.

38 Bob Kulick, "Will I Live Tomorrow?"

39 Geoffrey Giuliano, *Jimi Hendrix: If Six Were Nine* (audio book, Laserlight 12 824), Durkin Hayes Publishing, 1997.

40 *Setting the Record Straight* radio special, 1992.

41 Kathy Etchingham, unpublished interview with the author, 2000.

42 Ibid.

43 Ibid.

44 Jim Capaldi, "Winwood and Capaldi Interviewed," interview by David Pearcy, *Straight Ahead*, February/March 1996.

45 Eric Burdon, "Yes I Am Experienced: A Conversation with Eric Burdon," interview by Steven Roby, *Straight Ahead*, October/November 1995.

46 Geoffrey Giuliano, *Jimi Hendrix: If Six Were Nine*.

47 Ibid.

48 Paul Trynka and Harry Shapiro, "Eric Clapton," *Mojo*, April 1998.

49 Alan Di Perna, "Wild Thing," *Guitar World*, November 2000.

50 Geoffrey Giuliano, *Jimi Hendrix: If Six Were Nine*.

51 Caesar Glebbeek, Douglas Noele, Paul Trynka, and Harry Shapiro, "The Day the World Turned Day-Glo," *Mojo*, January 1998.

52 Michael Hicks, *Sixties Rock*, 51.

53 Alan Walsh, "Three Working Mums Who Earn a Lot of Loot," *Melody Maker*, 18 May 1968.

54 Caesar Glebbeek, Douglas Noele, Paul Trynka, and Harry Shapiro, "The Day the World Turned Day-Glo."

55 Arthur Brown, unpublished interview with Keith Bollinger, 1994.

56 Keith Bollinger, unpublished liner notes for *Best of the Bootlegs*, 1994. This album was never released.

57 Noel Redding and Carol Appleby, *Are You Experienced?: The Inside Story of the Jimi Hendrix Experience*, (New York: Da Capo Press, 1996), 34. Redding additionally notes, "Chas Chandler's name was not on Hendrix's December 1 contract. Michael Jeffery amended it on June 5, 1967 and gave Chandler half of the forty percent. Another contract that the Experience signed allowed Jeffery and Chandler the right to proceed on behalf of the Jimi Hendrix Experience without consultation."

58 Bonhams Rock, Pop and Guitars catalog, 22 August 1996, 80.

Chapter 5: The Experience Begins: 1967

1 *Lifelines: The Jimi Hendrix Story* (Reprise 9 26435-2).

2 Keith Altham, "Wild Jimi Hendrix," *New Musical Express*, 14 January 1967.

3 Keith Bollinger, unpublished liner notes for *Best of the Bootlegs*, 1994. This album was never released.

4 Geoffrey Giuliano, *Jimi Hendrix: If Six Were Nine* (audio book, Durkin Hayes Publishing, Laserlight 12 824), 1997.

5 *Hit Parader*, June 1969.

6 *Melody Maker*, 22 April 1967.

7 Keith Altham, "Question Time with Jimi Hendrix," *New Musical Express*, 13 May 1967.

8 Noel Redding and Carol Appleby, *Are You Experienced?: The Inside Story of the Jimi Hendrix Experience* (New York: Da Capo Press, 1996), 71.

9 Caesar Glebbeek, "Purple Haze Scoop!" *UniVibes*, November 1992. According to *UniVibes*, the story in the novel concerns the planet Dante Joy where, because of sunspot activity, the nighttime sky sometimes turns violet. Berkley Medallion Books first published the complete novel in paperback in June 1966.

10 *Hendrix Speaks* (Rhino Records RS70771), 1990. The cited interview with Meatball Fulton is from December 1967.

11 Paul McCartney, "Paul McCartney Reviews the New Pop Singles," *Melody Maker*, 23 February 1967.

12 Associated Press, "'Purple Haze' Sells for $17,600," *Buffalo (New York) News*, 21 December 1990.

13 Michael King, *Wrong Movements: A Robert Wyatt History* (England: SAF Publishing Ltd., 1994), 3.

14 Geoffrey Giuliano, *Jimi Hendrix: If Six Were Nine*.

15 Irish radio interview, September 1992.

16 Arthur Brown, unpublished interview with Keith Bollinger, 1994.

17 Bill Wyman with Ray Coleman, *Stone Alone: The Story of a Rock 'n' Roll Band* (New York: Viking, 1990), 395.

18 French pop singer Michael Polnareff released his debut EP, *La Poupée Qui Fait Non* (France, AZ EP 1024) in April 1966. The mid-tempo folk-rocker was an enormous hit in continental Europe and featured Jimmy Page playing acoustic guitar.

19 Kathy Etchingham, *Through Gypsy Eyes* (London: Orion Books Ltd., 1999), 94.

20 On the inside jacket of the U.S. *Electric Ladyland* LP, Hendrix included the dedication: "to…Bil of some English town in England."

21 Michael Hicks, *Sixties Rock: Garage, Psychedelic & Other Satisfactions* (Illinois: University of Illinois Press, 1999), 73.

22 Paul Trynka and Harry Shapiro, "Eric Clapton," *Mojo*, April 1998.

23 "2 Billion Worth of Noise," *Forbes*, 15 July 1968.

24 Paul McCartney, "Paul McCartney," interview, *Guitar Player*, July 1990.

25 *Monterey Peninsula Herald*, 13 June 1967.

26 Eric Burdon, "Yes I Am Experienced: A Conversation with Eric Burdon," interview by Steven Roby, *Straight Ahead*, October/November 1995.

27 Ibid.

28 Andy Wickham, "KPPC's Tom Donahue: King of Underground Radio," *Los Angeles Free Press*, 22 December 1967.

29 Claude Hall, "Rock Stations Giving Albums Air Play," *Billboard*, 22 July 1967.

30 A statement made by legendary San Francisco deejay Tom Donahue regarding the repetitious sound heard on Top 40 AM radio in the late 1960s. David P. Szatmary, *Rockin' in Time: A Social History of Rock and Roll* (New Jersey: Prentice-Hall, 2000), 154.

31 "Chain Broadcaster McLendon Warns U.S. Mothers of Evils in Disk Leerics," *Variety*, 17 May 1967. McLendon was probably referring to the Beatles' song "A Day in the Life" (actual lyric: "4,000 holes in Blackburn, Lancashire").

32 Mickey Dolenz with Mark Bego, *I'm a Believer: My Life of Monkees, Music and Madness* (New York: Hyperion, 1993), 131–132.

33 Noel Redding, interview for Irish radio, September 1992.

34 John McDermott with Eddie Kramer, *Hendrix: Setting the Record Straight* (New York: Warner Books, 1992), 81.

35 "Hendrix—Did He Quit, or Was He Pushed?" *New Musical Express*, 29 July 1967.

36 Hendrix performing on the Monkees tour may have been as humiliating for him as James Brown's experience lip-synching "I Got You (I Feel Good)" for the 1964 teen movie *Ski Party* was for the "Godfather of Soul." For those who haven't seen this outrageous cinematic moment, Brown tore it up with his dancers before a bunch of pearly-white kids who couldn't clap in time if their life depended on it, let alone try to keep the rhythm. The same was true about the audiences Hendrix played for on the Monkees tour.

37 Mickey Dolenz with Mark Bego, *I'm a Believer*, 135–136.

38 Jim Miller, "Album Reviews," *Rolling Stone*, 6 April 1968.

39 Leon Hendrix, unpublished interview with the author, 1992.

40 Eddie Kramer, "My Hendrix Experience," *EQ*, November 1992.

41 Ibid.

42 Michael Hicks, *Sixties Rock*, 72.

43 Eddie Kramer, "My Hendrix Experience."

44 "Integrated Rock," *Jazz & Pop*, July 1968.

45 *Setting the Record Straight* radio special, 1992.

46 John McDermott, "Back to Mono," *Experience Hendrix*, Summer 2000.

47 *Record Collector*, September 1997.

48 Anders Lind interview conducted by Gene Kraut, http://www.spectra.net/`craig/h_k_interview.html.

49 John Rocco, *Dead Reckonings: The Life and Times of the Grateful Dead* (New York: Schirmer Books, 1999), 92. Rocco adds that this jam led to another a few days later in San Francisco's Golden Gate Park, when on June 25, the Experience gave a free concert from the back of a flatbed truck. Rocco: "We set up the borrowed [Fender] equipment in a city park and bootleg the electricity. We park the Hell's [sic] Angels on top of the amps. Everyone gets to play a set." (page 93).

50 *Setting the Record Straight* radio special.

51 Seth Affoumado, "The Mickey Hendrix Experience," *Straight Ahead*, April/May 1994.

52 William Ruhlman, "The John Cipollina Story," *Relix* #28.

53 John Kay, "John Kay Interview," interview by David Pearcy, *Straight Ahead*, April/May 1994.

54 *Billboard*, 14 November 1979.

55 *Setting the Record Straight* radio special.

56 John Hammond, Jr., "Hendrix Remembered," *Guitar Player*, September 1975.

Chapter 6: Music in 3-D: 1968

1 "It Happened in 1968," *Rolling Stone*, 1 February 1969.

2 Frank Zappa, "The Jimi Hendrix Phenomenon," *Life*, 28 June 1968.

3 Pat O'Day, "Pat O'Day Interview," interview by Darrell Clingman, *Straight Ahead*, March 1990.

4 Abe Jacob, "The Abe Jacob Interview," interview by Darrell Clingman, *Straight Ahead*, January 1992.

5 Andy Ellis, "Regal Bluesman," *Guitar Player*, October 2000.

6 Mike McCartney, *The Macs: Mike McCartney's Family Album* (New York: Delilah Books, 1981), 85.

7 Albert Goldman, *Sound Bites* (New York: Random House, 1992), 88.

8 The CD that accompanies *Voodoo Child: The Illustrated Legend of Jimi Hendrix* is twenty-eight minutes long and was edited from the thirty-six-minute master. The book with CD is rather hard to find these days, but is still in print from the original publisher, Berkshire Studio Productions, West Stockbridge, Massachusetts.

9 The rare Miami Pop footage first surfaced during ABC-TV news report of Hendrix's death on September 18, 1970.

10 Sly Stone's agent, Al DeMarino: "Sly drove that audience insane. He was working the Hammond B-3 organ . . . stage center. Of course, much of that crowd was there to see Hendrix . . . but Sly literally marched a good part of that audience into the streets. There had to be a lengthy intermission to bring that crowd down." Joel Selvin, *Sly and the Family Stone: An Oral History* (New York: Avon Books, 1998), 64.

11 In 1998, BBC/VH1 produced a special on the making of the *Electric Ladyland* LP that was later released on Rhino Home Video. This documentary features 1968 footage of Hendrix working in the studio. The video implies that the footage was shot during the making of the album, when, in fact, it was shot at TTG, a Los Angeles studio, months after the LP was finished.

12 Mike Mettler, "A Pro's-Eye View of the Impact of *Electric Ladyland*," *Straight Ahead*, February/March 1994.

13 *The Mix* Vol. 6, August 1982.

14 Eric Burdon, "Yes I Am Experienced: A Conversation with Eric Burdon," interview by Steven Roby, *Straight Ahead*, October/November 1995.

15 Michael Finnigan, "Cats From Kansas," interview by Michael Fairchild, *Straight Ahead*, April/May 1994.

16 Liner notes to *Electric Ladyland* (MCAD-10895).

17 Ibid.

18 "Jimi Hendrix Album Banned in Provinces," *Record Mirror*, 9 November 1968.

19 In 1992, Alan Douglas conducted market research for Polygram Records in Europe, and discovered that sixty percent of Hendrix's audience was under twenty years old.

20 Liner notes to *Electric Ladyland* (MCAD-10895).

21 Tony Glover, "A Jimi Hendrix Doubleheader," *Hullabaloo*, February 1969.

22 Carlos Santana, "Carlos Santana Interviewed," interview by Cheryl Roby, *Straight Ahead*, June/July 1994.

23 Wayne Robins, *Behind the Music: 1968* (New York: Pocket Books, 2000), 21.

24 By the end of 1967, record companies equalized the price of mono and stereo discs—by raising the price of mono records by one dollar—in an effort to phase out the format. Since the discrete mono mix of *Axis: Bold As Love* differs immensely from its stereo counterpart, Hendrix collectors for years have hoped to find an alternate mono mix of *Electric Ladyland*.

25 Mitch Mitchell with John Platt, *Jimi Hendrix: Inside the Experience* (New York: Harmony Books, 1990), 104.

26 Steven C. Pesant, "The Marriage of Jazz and Jimi," *Experience Hendrix*, November/December 1997.

27 Paul Verna, "From Auto Sound to Infra Sound . . . ," *Billboard*, 1 July 1995. The Record Plant eventually increased their equipment to sixteen tracks in February 1969 and twenty-four tracks in June of that year.

28 Ibid.

29 Eric Burdon, "Yes I Am Experienced."

30 *UniVibes*, December 1999.

31 Verna, "From Auto Sound to Infra Sound. . . ."

32 Robert Wyatt, "Robert Wyatt Interview," interview by David Stubs, *Uncut*, July 2000.

33 Alan Welsh, "Hendrix Shock—Experience to Split," *Melody Maker*, 9 November 1968.

34 Sharon Lawrence, "Castles Made of Sand . . . ," *Image*, 25 November 1990.

35 Mitch Mitchell with John Platt, *Jimi Hendrix: Inside the Experience*, 116. On 19 July 2001 I interviewed bassist Carol Kaye about her TTG session with Hendrix and Mitchell: "It was a record date, but I don't think we recorded anything. At that time, I was just

thinking of it purely as a work call. Not being a rocker—I'm a jazz musician…he was a fine rocker…and I was duly impressed."
36 Eddie Kramer, "My Hendrix Experience," *EQ*, November 1992.
37 "Hendrix—What Next?" *Melody Maker*, 18 March 1969.
38 John McDermott, *Jimi Hendrix: Sessions* (New York: Little, Brown and Company, 1995), 120.
39 "Our Experience with Jimi," *Open City*, 24 August 1967.
40 Sotheby's catalog, Sale #6258, Lot #479, auction dates 14 and 17 December 1991.
41 Robert Shelton, "2 Hendrix Shows Attract Throngs," *New York Times*, 29 November 1968.
42 Ed Ochs, "Hendrix Knocks the Stuffings out of Hall," *Billboard*, 14 December 1968.
43 Pat O'Day, "Pat O'Day Interview."
44 "The Black Elvis," *Melody Maker*, 16 March 1968.
45 Jancee Dunn, *Rolling Stone*, 15 December 1994.
46 *House of Blues Radio Hour*, air dates 17 and 18 September 1994, show # 94-54.
47 "Ted Nugent: The Cuts," *Guitar Player*, June 1988.
48 *UniVibes*, December 1997.
49 "Jimi Hendrix: The *Guitar World* Tribute," *Guitar World*, November 2000.
50 Ron Wood, "Faces to Stones," *Guitar Player*, December 1975.
51 Ibid.
52 Mitch Mitchell with John Platt, *Jimi Hendrix: Inside the Experience*, 67.
53 Tony Wilson, "Ten Years After—Learning and Jamming in the U.S.," *Melody Maker*, 24 August 1968.
54 Larry Coryell, "Hendrix Remembered," *Guitar Player: Collector's Edition—Legends of Guitar*, 1984.
55 Michael Finnigan, "Cats from Kansas."
56 Ibid.

Chapter 7: The End of the Beginning: 1969

1 "The Year in Rock," *Rolling Stone*, 7 February 1970.
2 Terry Quinn, "It's All Happening for Lulu," *New Musical Express*, 28 December 1968.
3 "Terry Quinn's TV," *New Musical Express*, 6 January 1969. BBC tape librarian Nick Maingay miraculously uncovered the Jimi Hendrix Experience footage from Lulu's show while sifting through hours of steam train footage that was about to be thrown out.
4 Noel Redding and Carol Appleby, *Are You Experienced?: The Inside Story of the Jimi Hendrix Experience* (New York, Da Capo Press, 1996), 199.
5 Wolfgang Vogel, "Sounds from Utopia," *Frankfurter Rundschau*, 20 January 1969.
6 Ben Valkhoff, *Eyewitness: The Illustrated Jimi Hendrix Concerts 1969–1970* (The Netherlands: Up From The Skies Unlimited, 1997), 26, which cites the original source as the *Stuttgarter Zeitung*, 21 January 1969.
7 Noel Redding and Carol Appleby, *Are You Experienced?*, 114.
8 Peter Bauman, "Porridge," *Der Tagesspiegel*, 25 January 1969.
9 This note was supplied to the author from the Tony Brown archives.
10 Ian Carr, Digby Fairweather, and Brian Priestley, *Jazz: The Rough Guide* (London: Penguin Books, 1995), 712. Young died of pneumonia in 1978.
11 Abe Jacob, "Abe Jacob Interview," interview by Darrell Clingman, *Straight Ahead*, January 1992. Abe Jacob mixed the sound at nearly all of Hendrix's concerts from 9 August 1967, Ambassador Theatre, Washington, D.C. through 30 August 1970, Isle of Wight, with the exception of Woodstock, the Fillmore East 1969/1970 shows, and some of the July 1970 festival dates.
12 Jim Capaldi, "Steve Winwood and Jim Capaldi Interviewed," interview by David Pearcy, *Straight Ahead*, March 1996.
13 Bill Milkowski, "Jimi Hendrix: The Jazz Connection," *Down Beat*, October 1982.
14 "Integrated Rock," *Jazz & Pop*, July 1968.
15 John Kruth, *Bright Moments: The Life and Legacy of Rahsaan Roland Kirk* (New York: Welcome Rain Publishers, 2000), 223. Rahsaan Roland died of a heart attack in 1977.
16 Kathy Etchingham, unpublished interview with the author, 2000.
17 Steph Paynes, "Producing," *Music and Sound Output*, October 1988.
18 Noel Redding and Carol Appleby, *Are You Experienced?*, 119.
19 Ben Valkhoff, *Eyewitness*, 38.
20 Ibid.
21 Side two of the album contained part of Otis Redding's performance.
22 The author's eyewitness account was recounted in the article "Experience + One," *Straight Ahead*, April 1996.
23 Noel Redding and Carol Appleby, *Are You Experienced?*, 124.
24 Pat O'Day, "Pat O'Day Interview," interview by Darrell Clingman, *Straight Ahead*, March 1990.
25 "Jimi Hendrix," *The Inquisition #3*, June 1969.
26 *Charleston Gazette*, 17 May 1969. The songs Hendrix spoke about were probably "Belly Button Window" and "Machine Gun."

27 Johnny Winter, "Hendrix Remembered," *Guitar Player*, special edition, 1984.

28 Steven Roby, "Soul Bending," *Straight Ahead*, June/July 1996.

29 *UniVibes*, special "Best of" issue, November 1994.

30 Ibid.

31 Abe Jacob, "Abe Jacob Interview."

32 Rick Carroll, "Deafening Spell Woven by 'The King of Rock'," *San Jose Mercury News*, 26 May 1969.

33 Carlos Santana, "Carlos Santana Interviewed," interview by Cheryl Roby, *Straight Ahead*, June/July 1994.

34 Jerry Applebaum and Paul Cabbell, "Devonshire Downer," *Los Angeles Free Press*, 27 June 1969.

35 As heard on the unreleased soundboard recording from 20 June 1969.

36 John McDermott, "Jimi Hendrix Sessions: The John McDermott Outtakes," *Straight Ahead*, February/March 1996.

37 "Jimi Hendrix Has a Brand New Bass," *Rolling Stone*, 12 July 1969. The 23 May 1969 edition of the *San Jose Mercury News* also mentioned that the Experience would be breaking up soon and that the show on 25 May 1969 would be "Jimi's farewell appearance" as a member of the group.

38 "Redding on Jimi: 'I Said Stuff It,'" *Rolling Stone*, 15 November 1969.

39 Nancy Carter, "Carter Speaks," interview by Steven Roby, *Straight Ahead*, February/March 1995.

40 Ibid.

41 Chuck Wein, unpublished interview with the author, 2000.

42 Ibid.

43 *Disc and Music Echo*, 22 April 1967.

44 Random Notes, *Rolling Stone*, 23 August 1969.

45 Ben Valkhoff, *Eyewitness*, 9.

46 Billy Cox, "Billy Cox Interviewed," interview by Gary Serkin, *Straight Ahead*, July 1992.

47 In an article for the February/March 1996 issue of *Straight Ahead*, John McDermott noted: "Incredibly, the [tape] contents were later erased in favor of three mediocre folk-rock takes by an artist identified as Dorothy. Neither Jimi, Billy, or Juma took part in the new recording."

48 Juma Sultan, "Juma Sultan Interviewed: Part One," interview by Steven Roby, *Straight Ahead*, February 1992.

49 Ibid.

50 Ibid. This is the poorly recorded tape that was incorrectly touted as the Kirk-Hendrix jam.

51 Ibid.

52 Mitch Mitchell with John Platt, *Jimi Hendrix: Inside the Experience* (New York: Harmony Books, 1990), 142.

53 Liner notes to *Jimi Hendrix: Woodstock* (MCAD-11063).

54 Ibid.

55 Juma Sultan, "Juma Sultan Interviewed: Part One."

56 Juma Sultan, "Juma Sultan Interviewed: Part Two," interview by Steven Roby, *Straight Ahead*, March 1992.

57 Billy Cox, "Billy Cox Interviewed."

58 Hendrix's press conference in New York for the United Block Association benefit, 5 September 1969.

59 Sheila Weller, "Jimi Hendrix: I Don't Want to Be a Clown Anymore," *Rolling Stone*, 15 November 1969.

60 Juma Sultan, "Juma Sultan Interviewed: Part One."

61 *Music Now*, 12 September 1970.

62 Juma Sultan, "Juma Sultan Interviewed: Part One." Author Charles Sharr Murray also backs up this claim: "Albums have surfaced derived from his [Hendrix's] New Thing jams with Juma Sutan [*sic*] and pianist Mike Ephron; the latter sold the tapes to various budget-album houses under the title *Jimi Hendrix '64*." *Crosstown Traffic* (New York: St. Martin's Press, 1989), 201.

63 Mary Paytress, "The Jimi Hendrix Legacy," *Record Collector*, May 1992.

64 Tommy Erdelyi, unpublished interview with Keith Bollinger, 1995.

65 Alan Douglas, "Jimi Hendrix Remembered," *Guitar Heroes*, Spring 1992.

66 Eric Burdon, "Yes I Am Experienced: A Conversation with Eric Burdon," interview by Steven Roby, *Straight Ahead*, October/November 1995.

67 Miles Davis with Quincy Troupe, *Miles: The Autobiography* (New York: Simon and Schuster, 1989), 293.

68 *Rolling Stone*, 15 November 1969.

69 Miles Davis with Quincy Troupe, *Miles*, 292.

70 Bob Belden, a noted Miles Davis scholar, pointed out in the August 2001 issue of *Jazz Times* that Hendrix's music also influenced Miles Davis: "If you listen to 'Inamorata' from *Live/Evil*, that's the bass line to 'Fire.' 'Mademomoiselle Mabry' from *Filles de Kilimanjaro* is derived from Jimi's 'The Wind Cries Mary'; 'What I Say' from *Live/Evil* is basically 'Message To Love' from *Band of Gypsys*, and so on."

71 Carlos Santana, "Carlos Santana Interviewed," interview by Cheryl Roby, *Straight Ahead*, June/July 1994. The Miles Davis album *A Tribute to Jack Johnson* (CK 47036) was released after Hendrix's death.

72 Michael Carabello, "Michael Carabello Interviewed," interview by Steven Roby, *Straight Ahead*, August/September 1994.

73 Ibid.

74 Roy Carr, "The Last Days of Jimi Hendrix," *Uncut*, July 2000. While this Carr interview was conducted on 16 September 1970, it did not appear in print until the July 2000 issue of *Uncut* magazine.

75 Liner notes from *The Gil Evans Orchestra Plays the Music of Jimi Hendrix* (RCA 8409-2-RB).

76 Raymond Horricks, *Gil Evans* (New York: Hippocrene Books, 1984), 59.

77 Alan Douglas, "Jimi Hendrix Remembered."

78 John McLaughlin, "John McLaughlin Interviewed," interview by Steven Roby, *Straight Ahead*, June/July 1996.

79 Frank Roe, "Hendrix: Setting the Record Straight," *Zoo World*, 29 August 1974.

80 Dave Marsh, "The Hendrix Tapes," *Penthouse*, February 1975.

81 John McDermott, *Jimi Hendrix: Sessions* (New York: Little, Brown and Company, 1995), 97.

82 Frank Roe, "Hendrix: Setting the Record Straight."

83 Ibid.

84 Lawrence Lipton, "New Black Poets Find a Voice," *L.A. Free Press*, 8 May 1970. The Last Poets' debut album sold over three hundred thousand copies and spent one week at #40 on the *Billboard* album charts in 1970.

85 Mary Paytress, "The Jimi Hendrix Legacy," *Record Collector*, May 1992.

86 Ritchie Yorke and Ben Fong-Torres, "Hendrix Busted in Toronto," *Rolling Stone*, 31 May 1969.

87 Wayne Kramer, unpublished interview with Keith Bollinger, 1994.

88 "Intelligence Activities and Rights of Americans," Book. II [sic], 26 April 1976 Senate Committee with Respect to Intelligence Report.

89 Alex Constantine, *The Covert War Against Rock* (California: Feral House, 2000), 61.

90 Ritchie Yorke and Ben Fong-Torres, "Hendrix Busted in Toronto."

91 Sharon Lawrence, "Castles Made of Sand," *San Francisco Examiner, Image* magazine, 25 May 1990.

92 Ibid.

93 *The Skin I'm In*, cable television special, New York Times/Showtime Productions, 2000.

94 Johnny Black, *Jimi Hendrix: The Ultimate Experience* (New York: Thunder's Mouth Press, 1999), 193.

95 Nancy Carter, "Carter Speaks," interview by Steven Roby, *Straight Ahead*, February/March 1995.

96 Bruce Gary, interview by Steven Roby, *Straight Ahead*, August/September 1994. In this interview, Gary said that the Bonzo Dog Doo-Dah Band was in Los Angeles as the opening act for the Who at the Hollywood Palladium. Gary was invited to join them later at Thee Experience.

97 Richie Unterberger, *Urban Spacemen and Wayfaring Strangers* (San Francisco: Miller Freeman Books, 2000), 114.

98 John Kay, "John Kay Interviewed," interview by David Pearcy, *Straight Ahead*, April/May 1994.

Chapter 8: The Band of Gypsys:1969–1970

1 Seth Affoumado, "Little Wing Meets Nightbird," *Straight Ahead*, October/November 1994. One of the Band of Gypsys' first sessions included an attempt at the song "Night Bird Flying," a tribute to Alison Steele, an all-night deejay at New York's WNEW.

2 John McDermott, *Jimi Hendrix: Sessions* (New York: Little, Brown and Company, 1995), 125.

3 Juma Sultan, "Juma Sultan Interview: Part One,"interview by Steven Roby, *Straight Ahead*, February 1992.

4 Steven Roby, "Gypsy Quotes," *Straight Ahead*, September 1992.

5 Ibid.

6 Ibid.

7 Ibid.

8 John Woodruff, "Hendrix & Miles Dead at the Fillmore," *Creem*, February 1970.

9 Ben Fong-Torres, *The Hits Just Keep on Coming* (San Francisco: Miller Freeman Books, 1998), 143.

10 In a 1992 interview, Sultan commented on the 5 September 1969 concert in Harlem: "We had a good time playing there, but the band itself hadn't really played for a black audience. I remember after the show this one little kid came up to Jimi and said, 'Why don't you guys come back home?' Jimi replied with something like, 'You gotta do what you gotta do.'" "Juma Sultan Interview: Part Two," interview by Steven Roby, *Straight Ahead*, March 1992.

11 "Jimi Hendrix, Black Power and Money," *Teenset*, January 1969.

12 Charles Sharr Murray, "How Jimi Got His Groove Back," *Mojo*, November 1999.

13 Steven Roby, "Gypsy Quotes."

14 Ibid.

15 Buddy Miles, "Interview with Buddy Miles," interview by Adam Keane Stern, *20 Seconds*, 1994.

16 In his book *Are You Experienced?* (page 142), Noel Redding wrote, "Before Jimi went on I saw [Michael] Jeffery give him a tab [of LSD]. Perhaps he thought it would pep him and liven up the act. But Jimi freaked instead...."

17 John Burks, "Hendrix: The End of a Beginning, Maybe," *Rolling Stone*, 19 March 1970.

18 In a 1995 interview, Bruce Gary explained why the "Stepping Stone" single could not be remixed: "It seems something happened when the 1972 LP *War Hereos* was being produced. Eddie Kramer and Mitch Mitchell were not satisfied with Buddy's drum

track and overdubbed it with Mitch playing it. In the process Buddy's drum part was wiped. It simply doesn't exist anymore. They didn't even run a safety master." "Bruce Gary Interview," interview by Steven Roby, *Straight Ahead*, June/July 1995.

19 This information was supplied to the author in 2000 by Tony Brown via e-mail.

20 Press statement found on emplive.com in 2000. In an e-mail to author (8 November 2000), Peter Blecha of Experience Music Project noted, "Experience Hendrix did not use these master tapes for the CD. Not sure what generation or source they used, but, I have seen more than one CD review that has noted less-than-pristine audio quality on various tracks."

21 Letters to the Editor, *Straight Ahead*, February 1993.

Chapter 9: Gypsy Sunset: 1970

1 John Burks, "Hendrix: The End of a Beginning, Maybe," *Rolling Stone*, 19 March 1970.

2 Juma Sultan, "Juma Sultan Interview: Part Two," interview by Steven Roby, *Straight Ahead*, March 1992.

3 On page 146 of *Jimi Hendrix: Inside the Experience* (New York: Harmony Books, 1990), Mitch Mitchell noted, "Jimi and I had a great affection for Noel as a player…but something didn't feel right. Anyway the unfortunate thing about Noel was that he wasn't told until he came back to America, expecting to rehearse for the tour. Basically no one had the balls to do it."

4 Ibid., 168.

5 Juma Sultan, "Juma Sultan Interview: Part Two."

6 Eric Burdon, "Yes I Am Experienced: A Conversation with Eric Burdon," interview by Steven Roby, *Straight Ahead*, October/November 1995.

7 Mitch Mitchell with John Platt, *Jimi Hendrix: Inside the Experience* (New York: Harmony Books, 1990), 168.

8 Quincy Jones disclosed this information to the author on 15 November 2001. "Hummin'" was a song written by coronet player Nat Adderley. The album *Gula Matari* was recorded on 25–26 March and 12 May 1970, in Los Angeles, California. On those days in March, Hendrix was in New York finishing up sessions at the Record Plant. He was on tour in May.

9 Kathy Etchingham, unpublished interview with the author, 2000.

10 Liner notes to *Crosby, Stills & Nash* (Atlantic 82319-2), 1991.

11 Arthur Lee, "Arthur Lee's Rebuttal," interview by Steven Roby, *Straight Ahead*, October 1992.

12 John McDermott, *Jimi Hendrix: Sessions* (New York: Little, Brown, 1995), 139.

13 "Hendrix: I'd Like a Hit Single…," *Melody Maker*, 9 May 1970.

14 Noel Redding and Carol Appleby, *Are You Experienced?: The Inside Story of the Jimi Hendrix Experience* (New York: Da Capo, 1996), 140.

15 "Hendrix: I'd Like a Hit Single…."

16 Abe Jacob, "Abe Jacob Interview," interview by Darrell Clingman, *Straight Ahead*, January 1992.

17 *Harper's Monthly*, January 1974.

18 John L. Wasserman, *San Francisco Chronicle*, 1 June 1970.

19 Carlos Santana, "Carlos Santana Interview," interview by Cheryl Roby, *Straight Ahead*, June/July 1994.

20 "Rock Festival Admits All Free After Randall's Gate-Crashing," *New York Times*, 17 July 1970.

21 On page 270 of John McDermott's *Hendrix: Setting the Record Straight*, road manager Gerry Stickells commented: "We weren't going to go on, but the Young Lords held us at knife point and wouldn't allow us to leave."

22 In my interview with Melinda Merryweather for *Straight Ahead*, she said that Hendrix loved Maui and referred to it as "the Cosmic Sandbox." "Melinda Merryweather Interview," *Straight Ahead*, October/November 1995.

23 Chuck Wein, unpublished interview with author, 2000.

24 Ibid.

25 Melinda Merryweather, "Melinda Merryweather Interview."

26 Liner notes to *Rainbow Bridge* (Reprise MS 2040). Many have commented that Hendrix seemed incoherent or stoned in this film, but Wein refuted those claims in my 2000 interview: "The bottle of rosé you see there was about 60 percent full and there were no other drugs involved."

27 Melinda Merryweather, "Melinda Merryweather Interview."

28 Ibid.

29 Billy Cox, "Billy Cox Interview," interview by Gary Serkin, *Straight Ahead*, July 1992.

30 1971 Aquarius Theatre handbill, provided to author by Melinda Merryweather.

31 Sharon Lawrence, "Castles Made of Sand: Remembering Jimi Hendrix," *San Francisco Examiner, Image* magazine, 25 November 1990.

32 *Rolling Stone Radio Magazine*, September 1982.

33 Billy Cox, "Billy Cox Interview."

34 Juma Sultan, "Juma Sultan Interview: Part Two."

35 Mike Quashie, "Mike Quashie Interview," interview by Steven Roby, *Straight Ahead*, February/March 1995.

36 Ibid.

37 Jym Fahey and Elizabeth Heeden, "Birth of an Electric Lady," *Experience Hendrix*, Summer 2000.

38 John McDermott, "Jimi Hendrix Sessions: The John McDermott Outtakes," *Straight Ahead*, February/March 1996.

39 During June 2001, "Mojo Man" by the Ghetto Fighters, with Jimi Hendrix on lead guitar, was offered for sale on the auction Web site eBay at a starting bid of $10,000 (item #1438040147). It did not sell, and the item was withdrawn.

40 John Phillips with Jim Jerome, *Papa John: An Autobiography* (New York: Dolphin, 1986), 242.

41 *Melody Maker*, 5 September 1970.

42 Richie Havens with Steve Davidowitz, *They Can't Hide Us Anymore* (New York: Avon, 1999), 105.

43 *The Last Days of Jimi Hendrix*, BBC Radio One, September 1995.

44 From 1972 through 1975, Eva Sundquist presented evidence to the Swedish courts, who finally ruled that James Henrik Daniel Sundquist was the offspring of Jimi Hendrix. This Swedish judgment was then contested by Hendrix's father Al, on the grounds that a blood test could not be carried out to establish paternity. Under those circumstances, the U.S. courts did not recognize James Sundquist as Jimi Hendrix's son.

45 *The Last Days of Jimi Hendrix*.

46 Harry Shapiro and Caesar Glebbeek, *Jimi Hendrix: Electric Gypsy* (London: Heinemann, 1990), 454.

47 Kirsten Nefer, unpublished interview with Francine Szymanoski, January 2001.

48 In my interview with Juma Sultan, I asked him about Hendrix's reluctance to play the show at the Salvation in New York on September 10, 1969. "The Salvation was a Mafia-owned club and he [Hendrix] was forced to do that show. He said no, so they came to the house and took him upstairs by himself and changed his mind—read him his rights. We were ready to battle, but we didn't have the guns, so they won." "Juma Sultan Interview: Part Two," interview by Steven Roby, *Straight Ahead*, March 1992.

49 Anne Bjørndal, "I Am Not Sure I Will Live to Be 28 Years Old," *Morgenposten*, 6 September 1970.

50 Kirsten Nefer, unpublished interview with Francine Szymanoski.

51 Ibid.

52 John McDermott with Eddie Kramer, *Hendrix: Setting the Record Straight* (New York: Warner, 1992), 279.

53 *The Last Days of Jimi Hendrix*.

54 Eric Burdon, "Yes I Am Experienced"

55 Ibid.

56 Nancy Carter, "Carter Speaks," interviewed by Steven Roby, *Straight Ahead*, February/March 1995.

57 "Final Hendrix Performance Coming Soon?," Launch.com Web site, http://www.launch.com/music/content/, 1 July 1998.

58 Andy Aledort, "Electric Landlord," *Guitar World*, July 1995.

Chapter 10: Last Not Lost

1 "Dreamer," *New Yorker*, 31 December 1990.

2 Tom Wheeler, From the Editor, *Guitar Player*, August 1990.

3 Kathy Etchingham, unpublished interview with the author, 2000.

4 *Guitar Player*, April 1996.

5 The war of words began when Douglas said "Fuck Chas Chandler," in the 6 February 1992 issue of *Rolling Stone* in response to Chandler's declining Douglas's offer to buy the tapes. In an October 1991 interview with the author, Douglas said: "I don't know what he [Chandler] has either. We keep hearing rumors. All I know is that he has lots of outtakes...like home tapes."

6 Letters to the Editor, *Straight Ahead*, September 1992. Alan Douglas: "Just because we have outtakes in the can doesn't mean I have to release them. As far as I'm concerned, I'd burn them all up. He [Hendrix] was not God. He made mistakes."

7 Noel Redding, "Noel Redding on Jimi Hendrix," interview by Michael Fairchild, *Music Revue*, December 1990.

8 Tony Brown, *Jimi Hendrix: In His Own Words* (New York: Omnibus Press, 1994), 59. The original interview with Hendrix was conducted in December 1969.

9 Alan Douglas, "Jimi Hendrix Remembered," *Guitar Player*, March 1975. Douglas might have been referring to another tape of *Black Gold* since he mentions an overdubbed guitar part.

10 Alan Douglas, "Interview with Alan Douglas," *Guitar World*, September 1985.

11 Perhaps the child whom Hendrix sang about in this song was Tamika (Tami) Laurice James Carpenter. Hendrix may have had a child with Diane Carpenter while living in New York during May 1966. "Tami" was born on February 11, 1967.

12 The Octavia is an effect device for the guitar made by Roger Mayer in early 1967. The device doubles the frequency and produces the sound an octave higher. Hendrix first used the device while recording "Purple Haze," and later used a more perfected one in the Band of Gypsys.

13 Melinda Merryweather, "Melinda Merryweather Interview," interview by Steven Roby, *Straight Ahead*, October/November 1995.

14 Frank Roe, "Hendrix: Setting the Record Straight," *Zoo World*, 29 August 1974.

15 *Multicolored Blues* was never released; however, according to John McDermott's book *Setting The Record Straight*, the following tracks were selected for the album: "Seven Dollars in My Pocket/Hootchie Cootchie Man," "Midnight Lightning/Lee Blues," "Izabella Blues," "Blue Suede Shoes," "Farther on Down the Road," "Winter Blues," "Slow Time Blues," "Blues for Me and You," "Last Thursday Morning," and "Comin' Down Hard."

16 McDermott also states that prior to Douglas's decision to add new instrumentation, a version of *Crash Landing* with Hendrix's

original accompaniment was prepared: "Crash Landing," "Somewhere," "Anything Is Possible (With the Power)," "New Rising Sun," "Message to Love," "Scat Vocal-Lead 1-Scat Vocal 2-Lead Vocal 2," "Stone Free," "Peace in Mississippi," and "Here Comes Your Lover Man."

17 Steven Roby and Keith Bollinger, "Jimi's Disco Connection," *Straight Ahead*, April/May 1995.

18 *Cincinnati Enquirer*, 7 December 1975.

19 Jeffrey Ressner, "Hendrix's Legacy," *Rolling Stone*, 6 February 1992.

20 Andy Aledort, "Electric Landlord," *Guitar World*, July 1995.

21 Billy Cox, "Billy Cox Interviewed," interview by Gary Serkin, *Straight Ahead*, August 1992.

22 Ibid.

23 Alison Steele, "Alison Steele Interviewed," interview by Seth Affoumado, *Straight Ahead*, October/November 1994.

24 Alan di Perna, "A Not So Slight Return," *Guitar World*, March 1997.

25 Ibid. According to John McDermott, up until 1969, Warner/Reprise used Columbia Records's mastering facility, since they didn't have their own. In his opinion, "The people there had no sympathy for the music."

26 Ibid.

Chapter 11: Can You See Me? Hendrix on Film and Video

1 "Missing Hendrix," compiled from the archives of Tony Brown and Kees de Lange, supplied to author June 2000.

2 Darrell Clingman, "Can You See Me?" *Straight Ahead*, July 1992.

3 Ibid.

4 Ibid.

5 Ibid.

6 Ibid.

7 Gail Zappa, unpublished interview with the author, 2001.

8 "Missing Hendrix."

9 Mitch Mitchell with John Platt, *Jimi Hendrix: Inside the Experience* (New York: Harmony Books, 1990), 75.

10 Thomas Geneser, "Yours Truly on Silent Film," *UniVibes*, August 1996.

11 Earl Kirsmer, "The Madcap Who Named Pink Floyd," *Rolling Stone*, 23 December 1968.

12 Elliot Landy, unpublished interview with Keith Bollinger, 1994.

13 "Missing Hendrix."

14 Carlos Santana, "Carlos Santana Interview," interview by Cheryl Roby, *Straight Ahead*, June/July 1994.

15 Thomas Geneser, "Yours Truly on Silent Film."

16 Ibid.

17 "Missing Hendrix."

18 Ibid.

19 Johnny Black, *Jimi Hendrix: The Ultimate Experience* (New York: Thunder's Mouth Press, 1999), 169.

20 Mitch Mitchell with John Platt, *Jimi Hendrix: Inside the Experience*, 118.

21 *Melody Maker*, 1 March 1969.

22 Kathy Etchingham,. "Kathy Etchingham Interview," interview by Michael Fairchild, *Straight Ahead*, January/February 1993.

23 Eric Burdon, "Yes I Am Experienced: A Conversation with Eric Burdon," interview with Steven Roby, *Straight Ahead*, October/November 1995.

24 Eric Burdon with J. Marshall Craig, *Don't Let Me Be Misunderstood* (New York: Thunder's Mouth Press, 2001), 117–119.

25 Kathy Etchingham, "Kathy Etchingham Interview."

26 Carlos Santana, "Carlos Santana Interview."

27 *Newsweek*, 28 June 1999.

28 Ibid.

29 Ibid.

30 David Crosby and David Bender, *Stand and Be Counted* (San Francisco: HarperSanFrancisco, 2000), 50–51.

31 Steven Roby, "Communication Comin' on Strong!" *Straight Ahead*, April/May 1996. This information was found on the Jimi Hendrix Official Home Page—which was maintained by the Jimi Hendrix Foundation, an Alan Douglas operation—in 1996.

32 *New Musical Express*, 6 February 1971.

33 Hendrix archivist Bill Nitopi shared this information with me in an e-mail dated 22 May 2000.

34 Mitchell and Platt, 149.

35 Ibid.

36 Billy Cox, "Billy Cox Interview: Part One," interview by Gary Serkin, *Straight Ahead*, July 1992.

37 As mentioned in the Hey Joe newsgroup, 2000.

38 Gillian Saich, "Hendrix Today," *Melody Maker*, 5 September 1970.

39 Ibid.

Appendix I: Selected Bibliography

Listed here are the materials that have been cited in this book. It is by no means a complete record of all the works and sources I have consulted over the years on topics related to Jimi Hendrix. In addition to the interviews conducted specifically for this book, I have also used an extensive archive of 1960s newspapers and magazines (mainstream and underground) which include the following: *Beat Instrumental, Berkeley Barb, Billboard, Crawdaddy, Creem, Disc and Music Echo, Down Beat, East Village Other, Ebony, Eye, Great Speckled Bird, Hit Parader, Hullabaloo, The Inquisition, Jazz & Pop, L.A. Free Press, Look, Los Angeles Times, Life, Melody Maker, New Musical Express, Newsweek, New York Times, Rat, Rave, Record Mirror, Rolling Stone, San Diego Door, Time, Teenset, Variety, Village Voice,* and *Zoo World.* Keith Bollinger's unpublished liner notes for *Best of the Bootlegs* were helpful as well.

The following books were also useful:

Bisbort, Alan, and Parke Puterbaugh. *Rhino's Psychedelic Trip.* San Francisco: Miller Freeman Books, 2000.

Black, Johnny. *Jimi Hendrix: The Ultimate Experience.* New York: Thunder's Mouth Press, 1999.

Brown, Tony. *Jimi Hendrix: A Visual Documentary—His Life, Loves and Music.* London: Omnibus Press, 1992.

———. *Jimi Hendrix: In His Own Words.* London: Omnibus Press, 1994.

Buskin, Richard. *Inside Tracks.* New York: Avon Books, 1999.

Carr, Ian, Digby Fairweather, and Brian Priestley. *Jazz: The Rough Guide.* London: Penguin Books, 1995.

Constantine, Alex. *The Covert War Against Rock.* California: Feral House, 2000.

Cooper, Ralph. *Amateur Night at the Apollo.* New York: HarperCollins, 1990.

de Barros, Paul. *Jackson Street After Hours: The Roots of Jazz in Seattle.* Seattle: Sasquatch Books, 1993.

de Lange, Kees, and Ben Valkhoff. *Plug Your Ears.* The Netherlands: Up From The Skies Unlimited, 1993.

Etchingham, Kathy, with Andrew Crofts. *Through Gypsy Eyes.* London: Orion Books, 1998.

Geldeart, Gary. *Look Over Yonder.* Cheshire: Jimpress, 1997.

Graff, Gary, Josh Freedom du lac, and Jim McFarlin. *Music Hound R&B: The Essential Album Guide.* Detroit: Visible Ink Press, 1998.

Guralnick, Peter. *Sweet Soul Music: Rhythm and Blues and the Southern Dream of Freedom*. New York: Harper & Row, 1986.

Henderson, David. *'Scuse Me While I Kiss the Sky: The Life of Jimi Hendrix*. New York: Bantam, 1981.

Hendrix, James A., as told to Jas Obrecht. *My Son Jimi*. Seattle: AlJas Enterprises, L.P., 1999.

Horricks, Raymond. *Gil Evans*. New York: Hippocrene Books Inc., 1984.

Heylin, Clinton. *Bootleg: The Secret History of the Recording Industry*. New York: St. Martin's Griffin, 1994.

Knight, Curtis. *Jimi: An Intimate Biography of Jimi Hendrix*. New York: Praeger Publishers, 1974.

McDermott, John, with Eddie Kramer. *Hendrix: Setting the Record Straight*. New York: Warner Books, 1992.

McDermott, John, with Billy Cox and Eddie Kramer. *Jimi Hendrix: Sessions*. New York: Little, Brown and Company, 1995.

Mitchell, Mitch, with John Platt. *Jimi Hendrix: Inside the Experience*. New York: Harmony Books, 1990.

Murray, Charles Sharr. *Crosstown Traffic: Jimi Hendrix and the Post-war Rock 'n' Roll Revolution*. New York: St. Martin's Press, 1991.

Nitopi, Bill, ed. *Cherokee Mist: The Lost Writings of Jimi Hendrix*. New York: HarperCollins, 1993.

Potash, Chris, ed. *The Jimi Hendrix Companion: Three Decades of Commentary*. New York: Schirmer Books, 1996.

Redding, Noel, and Carol Appleby. *Are You Experienced?: The Inside Story of the Jimi Hendrix Experience*. New York: Da Capo Press, 1996.

Selvin, Joel. *Sly and The Family Stone: An Oral History*. New York: Avon Books, 1998.

Shapiro, Harry, and Caesar Glebbeek. *Jimi Hendrix: Electric Gypsy*. London: Heinemann, 1990.

Szatmary, David P. *Rockin' in Time: A Social History of Rock and Roll*. New Jersey: Prentice-Hall, 2000.

Valkhoff, Ben. *Eyewitness: The Illustrated Jimi Hendrix Concerts 1969–1970*. The Netherlands: Up From the Skies Unlimited, 1997.

Welch, Chris. *Hendrix: A Biography*. New York: Flash Books, 1973.

Werner, Craig Hansen. *A Change is Gonna Come: Music, Race, and the Soul of America*. New York: Plume, 1999.

Whitburn, Joel. *The Billboard Book of Top 40 Hits*, 6th ed. New York: Billboard Books, 1996.

White, Charles. *The Life and Times of Little Richard: The Quasar of Rock*. New York: Harmony Books, 1985.

Appendix II: Selected Discography

These Hendrix recordings proved to be especially inspirational while writing this book:

The Essentials
- *Are You Experienced*, released May 12, 1967 (MCA)
- *Axis: Bold As Love*, released December 1, 1967 (MCA)
- *Electric Ladyland*, released October 19, 1968 (MCA)
- *Band of Gypsys*, released April 1970 (Capitol)

Posthumous Releases
- *Jimi Hendrix: Blues* (MCA)
- *Jimi Hendrix Live at Woodstock* (MCA)
- *Jimi Hendrix/Isle of Wight* (Polydor; out of print)
- *Jimi Hendrix: Morning Symphony Ideas* (Dagger Records)
- *BBC Sessions* (MCA)
- *Cry of Love* (Reprise; out of print)
- *Rainbow Bridge* (Reprise; out of print)
- *War Heroes* (Reprise; out of print)
- *Loose Ends* (Polydor; out of print)
- *The Jimi Hendrix Experience* (MCA)

Selected Studio Bootlegs
- *Studio Haze*
- *Out of the Studio: Demos from 1967*
- *Olympic Gold Volumes 1 & 2*
- *Jimi Hendrix & Traffic—A Session*
- *Unsurpassed Studio Takes*
- *Band of Gypsys Volume 3*
- *The Sotheby Auction Tapes*

Selected Live Recordings
- *Paris 10/9/67*
- *Ottawa 3/19/68* (second show)
- *Stockholm 1/9/69* (second show)
- *San Jose 5/25/69*
- *L.A. Forum 4/25/70*
- *Berkeley 5/30/70* (both shows)
- *Copenhagen 9/3/70*

Index